ARE ITALIANS WHITE?

ARE ITALIANS WHITE?

HOW RACE IS MADE IN AMERICA

EDITED BY JENNIFER GUGLIELMO & SALVATORE SALERNO

ROUTLEDGE
NEW YORK & LONDON

Published in 2003 by
Routledge
29 West 35th Street
New York, NY 10001
www.routledge-ny.com

Published in Great Britain by
Routledge
11 New Fetter Lane
London EC4P 4EE
www.routledge.co.uk

Routledge is an imprint of the Taylor & Francis Group.
Printed in the United States of America on acid-free paper.

10 9 8 7 6 5 4 3 2 1

Library of Congress Cataloging-in-Publication Data

Are Italians white? how race is made in America / edited by Jennifer Guglielmo and Salvatore Salerno.
p. cm.
Includes bibliographical references and index.
ISBN 0-415-93450-8 (acid-free paper) — ISBN 0-415-93451-6 (pbk. : acid-free paper)
1. Italian American—Social conditions. 2. Italian American—Race identity. 3. United States—Race relations. I. Guglielmo, Jennifer, 1967– II. Salerno, Salvatore, 1949–

E184.I8A74 2003
305.85'1073—dc21 2003046531

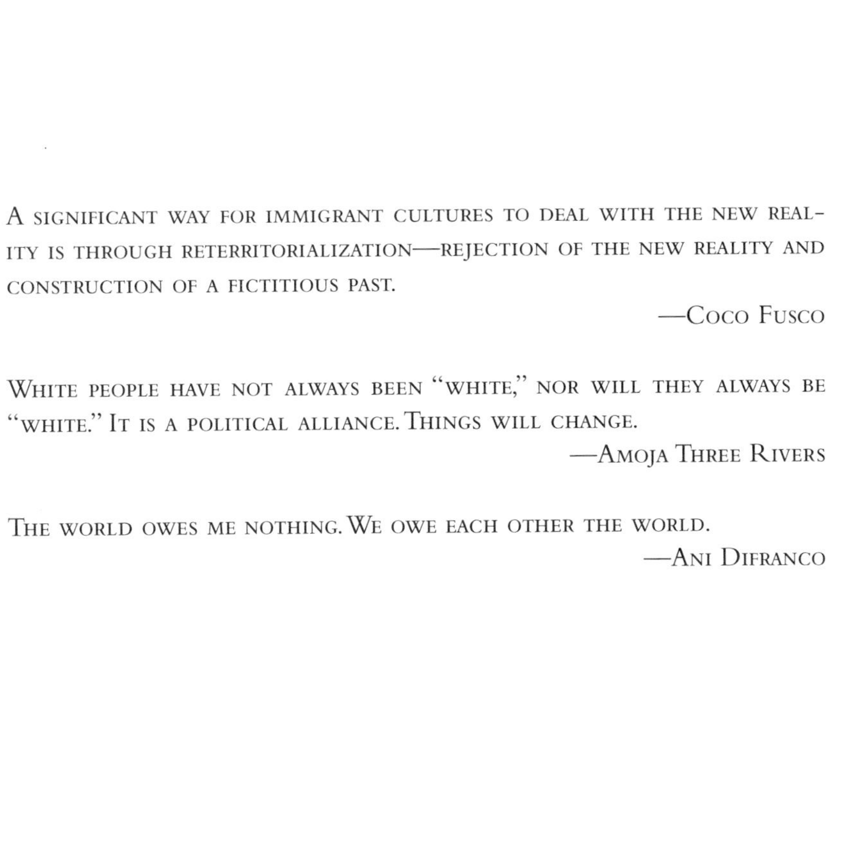

A significant way for immigrant cultures to deal with the new reality is through reterritorialization—rejection of the new reality and construction of a fictitious past.

—Coco Fusco

White people have not always been "white," nor will they always be "white." It is a political alliance. Things will change.

—Amoja Three Rivers

The world owes me nothing. We owe each other the world.

—Ani Difranco

WE DEDICATE OUR WORK TO RACE REBELS EVERYWHERE

Contents

II. RADICALISM AND RACE

III. WHITENESS, VIOLENCE, AND THE URBAN CRISIS

IV. TOWARD A BLACK ITALIAN IMAGINARY

Acknowledgments

This book is a labor of love that required many years of work and the assistance of a community. Along the way we received a great deal of help, guidance, and support from many folks who understood what we were trying to do and believed in the importance of creating this kind of forum. David Roediger and Peter Rachleff helped us from the very beginning. We are grateful for the energy, support, and guidance they continually provided this project, and for helping us to believe that this anthology was possible.

We would also like to thank all of the contributors for writing such beautiful essays and enriching our thinking on this subject. In particular, Tom and Mark Guglielmo, Kym Ragusa, Donna Gabaccia, Edvige Giunta, and Joseph Sciorra deserve special thanks. They each read many of the essays in this collection and provided their wise insight, which helped the editorial process immeasurably.

In addition, conversations and friendships with the following individuals deepened our analyses and understandings of race in America in profound ways, which we hope is somehow reflected here: Majdi Abu-Sharar, Louis Alemayehu, Ciccio and Andrea Belvedere, Giorgio Bertellini, Marjorie Bryer, Philip V. Cannistraro, Ron Chisom, Catherine Ceniza Choy, Teresa Cordova, Melchia Crowne, Lawrence DiStasi, Kevin Dotson, Dana Frank, May Fu, Coco Fusco, Carl Galmon, Adrian Gaskins, Amelia Gavin, Victoria C. González, Deena J. González, Alicia Gaspar de Alba, Jim Hayes, Antonio Lauria-Perricelli, Franca Iacovetta, Ingrid Johnson, Nadia Kim, Kiarina Kordela, Rachel Maxine Koch, Dorothea Hrossowyc, Erika Lee, Alina Martino Marazzi, Denise Mayotte, Michal McCall, Todd Michney, Franco Montalto, Adele Negro, Jean O'Brien-Kehoe, Gaye T. M. Okoh, Yuichiro Onishi, Robert Orsi, Adam Pagán, John Nieto Phillips, James Robinson, Caterina Romeo, Danilo Romeo, Karen Starr, Mateo L. Sánchez, Arlene Holpp Scala, Diane Wiley, Nadia Venturini, Stephanie Romeo, and the entire Guglielmo and Salerno famiglie.

Introduction

WHITE LIES, DARK TRUTHS

JENNIFER GUGLIELMO

Italians are niggaz with short memories. In late June 2002, Chuck Nice, an African American deejay at WAXQ-FM in New York City casually made this remark on-air while hosting an early morning talk show. Within days, a response came back. The Order of the Sons of Italy in America, the oldest and largest organization of Italian Americans in the United States, announced that it was "puzzled by such a statement and the station's refusal to do an on-air apology. We understand that Mr. Nice is African American, but we don't understand why it is wrong for a white person to call an African American that name, but okay for an African American to use it to describe white people."[1] What the organization's spokesperson saw as so offensive was not the entire phrase, just the epithet, which made no sense since it was used by an African American to describe whites. What they seem to have missed, however, was how this radio host was calling Italians out on their particular whiteness: Italians were not always white, and the loss of this memory is one of the tragedies of racism in America.

Chuck Nice has not been alone in his observations. Throughout the twentieth century, many people of color have critiqued the ways Italian Americans have asserted and claimed a white identity. W.E.B. Du Bois, Bernardo Vega, James Baldwin, Malcolm X, Ann Petry, Ana Castillo, Piri Thomas, and other influential writers and activists have also commented on the complicated and contradictory ways Italians have adopted and challenged the practices of white supremacy.[2] In fact, Chuck Nice's words echo those of Malcolm X, who thirty years earlier reminded Italian Americans of Hannibal's conquest of Rome: "No Italian will ever jump up in my face and start putting bad mouth on me, because I know his history. I tell him when you talk about me, you're talking about your pappy, your father. He knows his history, he knows how he got that color."[3] James Baldwin developed his insight into the peculiar ways Italian Americans dealt with the color line in his Greenwich Village neighborhood in the 1940s and 1950s. For example, he noted how the Italian owners of the San Remo, a local restaurant, threw him out every time he entered, but let him stay when he arrived with the president of the publishing firm Harper & Row. Indeed, from that point on, they and most of the Italians in the neighborhood never bothered him again. He remembered that one night, when a mob of menacing whites threatened him, the owners of the San Remo closed the place, turned out the lights, and sat with him in the back room before judging it safe to drive him home. "Once I was in the San Remo," he wrote,

> I was *in*, and anybody who messed with me was *out*—that was all there was to it, and it happened more than once. And no one seemed to remember a time when I had not been there. I could not quite get it together, but it seemed to me that I was no longer black for them and they had ceased to be white for me, for they sometimes introduced me to their families with every appearance of affection and pride and exhibited not the remotest interest in whatever my sexual proclivities chanced to be. They had fought me very hard to prevent this moment, but perhaps we were all much relieved to have got beyond the obscenity of color.[4]

Baldwin's story of the complex way Italians in his neighborhood treated him as a gay African American writer conveys how they revered the color line to some degree, but also applied their own cultural value system in crossing and challenging it. The "price of the ticket" for full admission into U.S. society, Baldwin recognized, was "to become 'white,'" and European immigrants faced this "moral choice" immediately upon arrival.[5]

The United States that Italian immigrants encountered was a nation founded upon processes of colonization, dispossession, and slavery, and therefore deeply fractured by race-based hierarchies of inequality. To this day, the persistence of disfranchisement, segregation, ghettoization, profiling, and other forms of structural racism continues to enforce the material rewards of whiteness.[6] Democracy, freedom, and other ideals that Americans hold sacred have not been a given, but rather struggled for from the bottom up, often by those most excluded.[7] Virtually all Italian immigrants arrived in the United States without a consciousness about its color line. But they quickly learned that to be white meant having the ability to avoid many forms of violence and humiliation, and assured preferential access to citizenship, property, satisfying work, livable wages, decent housing, political power, social status, and a good education, among other privileges. "White" was both a category into which they were most often placed, and also a consciousness they both adopted and rejected.

Historian David Roediger notes that Baldwin was one of many African American writers who expertly critiqued how participation in the lie of white supremacy "helped to steal the vitality from immigrant communities of the Irish, Italians, Jews, Poles, and others," since it required the desperate hope that all the fear, exclusion, hatred, violence, and terror upon which whiteness is consolidated would be worth it.[8] As Chuck Nice pointed out, it required that Italians distort their histories to condemn and disown those parts of themselves which most resembled the dark "other." "America became white," Baldwin asserted, "because of the necessity of denying the Black presence, and justifying the Black subjugation. No community can be based on such a principle—or, in other words, no community can be established on so genocidal a lie."[9] The cost of admission was learning to demonize and reject, "And in the debasement and defamation of Black people, they debased and defamed themselves."[10]

The rich and incisive analysis of whiteness by people of color has much to teach us about the costs of this destructive system for all of humanity. Yet, as poet and activist Audre Lorde has written, it is not the responsibility of people of color to teach whites their mistakes. Rather, it is the responsibility of everyone to create a society in which we can all flourish. Revolutionary change, as Lorde pointed out so eloquently, "is never merely the oppressive situations which we seek to escape, but that piece of the oppressor which is planted deep within each of us." It is imperative that each of us reach down and "touch that terror and loathing of any difference that lives there. See whose face it wears."[11]

This book was brought together to do this—to excavate our lives and histories in order to critically examine how Italian Americans have made race in America. In this effort, we seek to answer a question posed by cultural critic bell hooks, among others: How is race linked to cultural and material practices that reinforce and perpetuate racism?[12] The essays here answer this question by exposing the way this one group of European immigrants and their descendents have learned, reproduced, and at times challenged white supremacy in ways that are rooted in a particular history of migration, settlement, and incorporation into the United States.

Since many Italians remained poor and working-class longer than most other European immigrants, they have often lived in the nation's blue-collar neighborhoods, amid people of color. As historian Robert Orsi has powerfully documented, this proximity—in terms of class, color, and geography—has given Italians a particular anxiety to assert a white identity in order to effectively distance themselves from their Brown and Black neighbors, and receive the ample rewards that come with being white.[13] Sociologist Jonathan Rieder's research on 1970s and 1980s Canarsie, Brooklyn, demonstrated that Italians often distance themselves through a narrative of self-righteousness about their own struggles in the United States. The result is the blaming of poverty, joblessness, homicide, and other socioeconomic problems on the supposedly deficient character of African Americans, Puerto Ricans, and other people of color, rather than on the political institutions and methods of economic production that preserve white upper-class power. This position of blaming and demonizing those with relatively little political and economic status, Rieder found, "hurt the larger social order, dividing citizens who were dependent on each other without forging a conception of the public good."[14] Anthropologist Micaela di Leonardo's ethnography of Italian Americans in San Francisco during the 1970s confirmed many of Rieder's findings.[15] Moreover, scholars such as Alexander Saxton, Robin D. G. Kelley, Tera Hunter, Dana Frank, George Lipsitz, Dolores Janiewski, and others, have also demonstrated that while whiteness has acted as a huge subsidy to working-class whites, it has also severely limited their ability to effectively dismantle the systems of inequality that threaten their own lives.[16]

Have Italian Americans always acted this way? The essays in this collection suggest a very complicated history of collaboration, intimacy, hostility, and distancing between Italian Americans and people of color, and the significance of both choice and coercion, as Baldwin argued, in their developing a "white consciousness." Today, Italian Americans stand in for the very image of white ethnic working-class right-wing conservativism. These essays explain how and why this identity gained the power to mobilize so many, and its deep roots in the desperate desire of Italians to escape their own class and race oppression in the United States. They also demonstrate that this identity was by no means inevitable. Throughout the twentieth century, Italian Americans crafted a vocal, visionary, and creative oppositional culture to protest whiteness and build alliances with people of color. In mapping this history, this collection teaches us about the power we have as individuals to take action against oppression in all its forms.

This book developed over many years, during weekly conversations between Salvatore Salerno and myself. We began meeting seven years ago in Minneapolis. I was there working on a doctorate in history, while Sal was teaching sociology at a local college, and our paths crossed often. As some of the few Italian Americans studying the histories of Italian radicalism, labor activism, and other forms of immigrant political culture, in a place that felt so far removed from these worlds, we easily gravitated toward one another. Race was always at the center of our conversations, and we quickly realized our mutual interest in interrogating Italian American whiteness. We came from very different places, however. Sal had grown up in one of the few Sicilian immigrant families in working-class East Los Angeles during the 1950s and 1960s, and often passed for Latino with his dark complexion. I, on the other hand, was raised just north of The Bronx in a predominantly middle-class Italian, Irish, and Jewish suburban community during the 1970s and 1980s, the light-skinned child of working-class Irish and southern Italian immigrant families.

We shared a history of progressive grassroots activism, and our humbling and inspiring experiences as participants in different movements—whether fighting racism in local businesses and schools, opposing police brutality, defending immigrant rights, or working toward greater reproductive rights for women—had taught us that political solidarity grows out of a common commitment to ending all systems of oppression. This required confronting our own assumptions about race, gender, sexuality, class, and other divisive systems. We had both grown up hearing things like "we were nothing but a bunch of guineas to the '*mericani*" and "why can't these immigrants assimilate like we did?" Self-righteousness and blame were a way the Italians around us continually distinguished themselves from people of color. The collective memory of oppression, it seemed, was rarely used to fight racism and challenge systemic inequality. It was clear to us that we desperately needed to remember that we *are* white, that our whiteness has guaranteed us access to an exclusive system of unearned, unacknowledged, and often invisible advantages that have not been available to African Americans, Latinos, Asians, and other people of color. Our conversations revealed to us the many ways color, class, gender, region, generation, and many other factors are critical in determining how Italians experience and live race in America, and led us to devote ourselves to creating a larger forum for collective discussion and action.

We became committed to the project of editing this anthology after hearing of the near-death beating of Leonard Clark, a thirteen-year-old African American child in the white working-class Chicago neighborhood of Bridgeport in 1997. The attackers had Italian, Spanish, and Polish last names. Outraged and deeply saddened, we decided to post a message to the American Italian Historical Association's discussion board to express our desire for some kind of action. After alerting members to the attack, we asked, "What are we going to do to fight racism within our communities?"[17] For months it seemed as if the board had been dominated by discussions of the media defamation of Italians with portrayals of *mafiosi* and traditional Italian Christmas celebrations. We wanted to intervene and generate conversation about the role Italian Americans must play in ending racist violence. We were troubled by what was posted. In a list with close to five hundred subscribers, there were only three responses. It was clear to us that as a community we did not have the language or space with which to fully address these issues, and that this was urgently needed.

Every few years it seemed there was another story of some Italian Americans beating up and/or murdering a person of color. I was just one year out of high school in 1986 when Michael Griffith, a twenty-three-year-old African American man, was beaten and chased by a group of white male teenagers (including two Italian Americans), and then killed by a car on the Belt Parkway, in the predominantly Italian American neighborhood of Howard Beach in Queens, New York. Three years later, in the Brooklyn Italian American neighborhood of Bensonhurst, thirty young, predominantly Italian American, men brutally attacked and killed Yusuf Hawkins, a young African American man who had ventured into the area with some friends to check out a used car. In both cases, Italian American community members justified the violence with a chorus of "What were they doing here in the first place?" In Howard Beach, for example, Michelle Napolitano told reporters, "We're a strictly white neighborhood. They [the victims] had to be starting trouble."[18] In objectifying all African Americans and projecting onto *them* the stigma of criminality, local Italian Americans not only legitimated racist violence, they distanced themselves from the crime by focusing on their own fear.[19]

After Hawkins and Griffith were murdered, some individual Italian Americans expressed outrage, but almost no one organized to protest the violence. Joseph Sciorra's essay in this collection documents the two-person march he and Bensonhurst native Stephanie Romeo conducted alongside African American protesters in 1989. Their action, as he writes, was met with venomous hatred by Italian American bystanders who gathered in large crowds to shout racial slurs at African American protesters and denounce the race traitors. This spectacle was picked up by the media, who positioned working-class Italian Americans as the most racist of whites. Some Italian American organizations responded, but they did so in defensive journalistic essays that refocused the debate from Italian American racism to media defamation of Italians with portrayals of criminality.[20] This concern over defamation did not expose how media focus on the "uncivilized" racism of working-class whites made invisible the larger structures of racism and white supremacy that give rise to and support such violent acts. Rather, it enforced a collective public silence about the role of Italians in the U.S. racial hierarchy, and a narrative of Italian American victimization took the place of critical antiracist dialogue and action.

The tragedies in Chicago, Bensonhurst, and Howard Beach, and more recently Justin Volpe's torture of Abner Louima in 1997, as well as many other horrific events, including the innumerable polarizing actions of New York City's former mayor, Rudolph Giuliani, the role of Philadelphia's former mayor Frank Rizzo in terrorizing civil rights activists (as Stefano Luconi documents in his essay here), and the 1997 Ku Klux Klan cross burnings on Long Island under the leadership of the self-described Grand Dragon of the American Knights, Frank DeStefano,[21] force us to come to terms with the power Italian Americans have to enact whiteness, despite our own history of being the object of racial vilification.

In our weekly conversations, Sal and I turned to the rich critiques of whiteness produced by writers/activists of color, such as Frederick Douglass, Harriet Jacobs, Black Elk, Ida B. Wells, Américo Paredes, Haile Selassie, Langston Hughes, Jesús Colón, Assata Shakur, Angela Davis, Mary Brave Bird, Bob Marley, Public Enemy, and many others, to help us unravel the social practices, material privileges, and moral decisions that have led to white violence and terror. We also looked to the rich body of critical work that has grown out of this literature, by Toni Morrison, Cherríe Moraga, Cheryl Harris, Patricia Williams, George Lipsitz, David Roediger, Ronald Takaki, Noel Ignatiev, Ian Haney Lopez, Matthew Jacobson, Tomás Almaguer, Grace Elizabeth Hale, Arnoldo De León, Michael Rogin, Karen Brodkin, and many others, to help us understand how white identity has been learned, enacted, and perpetuated over time.[22] It is our hope that this collection contributes to this body of creative work, and helps us to better understand the role that immigrants and their descendents play in making race—that is, confronting and implicating themselves in U.S. racial systems.

It was not hard to identify people writing on this subject. During our many years of discussion and debate, we located and developed friendships with a wide range of people doing powerful critical work on Italian Americans and race. Most of the authors here "had the pieces inside them" and just needed the encouragement to put them on the page. Others had material they had been tinkering with for years, and just needed the right venue. We knew we wanted this book to be interdisciplinary, and thus we invited a wide range of writers—historians, sociologists, folklorists, filmmakers, musicians, activists, cultural and literary critics—to participate in this project. Many of the essays also combine poetry, memoir, and critical analysis, to break down the subject–object opposition and connect the personal to the political. Most of the authors are Italian American themselves, but differ in their regions of origin, class, generation/age, sexual identity, and ethnicity (half of the Italian Americans here are of mixed ancestry and trace their roots also to Native America, Africa, China, Germany, Ireland, and Russia). By putting into print these critical voices, our goal has been to make visible the many, often difficult, conversations that take place around dinner tables, and in neighborhoods, classrooms, and workplaces, about Italian Americans and race. From the very beginning, our goal has been to create space for collaborative antiracist cultural work. What has resulted is a rich public dialogue and the first anthology ever published that addresses the particular and distinct relationship Italians have had to race in America.

We have chosen the title *Are Italians White?* to represent the book because it interrogates the practice of racism by Italian Americans and asks: Will we continue to choose whiteness? This title also marks the complex and contradictory experiences that Italians have had with race in the United States, having lived through both harsh racial discrimination and the many privileges of whiteness.[23] The authors here argue that Italians were positioned as white in the most critical of ways immediately upon their arrival in the United States, even while they endured racial prejudice. Yet, their own sense of identity as whites took much longer to form. The essays, then, examine not only how Italians were racially categorized, but also how Italians developed an awareness of the color line, and the many ways they acted on this consciousness.

The vast majority of Italian immigrants were peasants and manual laborers who came from the poor, economically underdeveloped, southern agricultural provinces of Basilicata, Calabria, Campania, Puglia, and Sicily. These were regions with histories of colonial subjugation and subaltern politics (to use Antonio Gramsci's terms), in which the people of the South were considered racially "other" by the northern Italian ruling classes.[24] Italy's history of African, Arab, Greek, Norman, and Spanish settlements defied all theories of racial purity, but southerners' dark complexions and "primitive" cultural practices were, to many northerners, evidence of their racial inferiority. Southern Italy was more than a geographical space with flexible boundaries (it includes or excludes Rome, Abruzzo, and Sardinia, for example), it was a metaphor for anarchy, rebellion, poverty, and the lack of "civilization." Indeed, the saying "Europe ends at Naples. Calabria, Sicily, and all the rest belong to Africa" can still be heard throughout Europe, and these ideologies of southerners as backward continue to inform national political movements.[25]

The racialization of the South became pronounced during the late nineteenth century when the northern bourgeoisie sought to unify the disparate regions of the peninsula and surrounding islands into a single nation. Crafting a national identity from the history of medieval city-states, the Renaissance, and the "glory" of the Roman Empire, they attempted to discipline the "barbarous" South through a process of military occupation and mass arrests of anyone who opposed the new taxes, private land-owning practices, and other impoverishing policies brought about by the government.[26] Northern political leaders confronted southern resistance movements against the state not only with martial law but also by stigmatizing peasants "as criminal members of a racially inferior people who preferred the superstitions of religion to *civiltà italiana*."[27] To justify such beliefs, they relied on the "evidence" provided by Italy's leading positivist anthropologists, who argued that the darker "Mediterranean" southerners were racially distinct from the lighter "Aryan" northerners because they possessed "inferior African blood" and demonstrated "a moral and social structure reminiscent of primitive and even quasibarbarian times, a civilization quite inferior." Southern Italy's location as a crossroads joining Africa, Europe, and the East, they believed, had given birth to a people with an "inherent racial inferiority."[28]

These popular ideologies were also mediated by modern bourgeois notions of gender and sexuality. As cultural critic Anne McClintock has argued, the project of imperialism and the invention of race were "fundamental aspects of Western, industrial modernity." Because of this, gender, race, and class were and are not distinct areas of experience; they "come into existence in and through relation to each other—if in contradictory and conflictual ways."[29] Italy's politicians, novelists, scientists, and other popularizers of race discourse routinely made use of a sexual idiom by feminizing the South and sexualizing southern Italian women.[30] In this way, the Italian elite built their national identities and crafted policies of expansion upon the premise that their economic and political supremacy was not only providential, but necessary for the spread of "civilization." They did so by developing identities in opposition to Africans, who became the quintessential racial "other."

These ideologies traveled across the Atlantic and informed the thinking of native-born white Americans who also denigrated southern Italians as prone to violence, whether of a revolutionary or a criminal nature. As a result of alarm at what was seen as hordes of dark, dirty, ignorant, lazy, subversive, superstitious criminals, the movement to limit Italians' civic participation and restrict their ability to immigrate gathered a great deal of momentum in the early twentieth century. This occurred in part because Italians were the largest group to participate in the mass immigration to the United States from 1880 to 1920. The vast majority were young male peasants and workers who came in search of jobs in the mass-production industries of emergent global capitalism. They often worked as manual laborers, rarely became U.S. citizens, and over half returned to Italy. After 1913, women began to migrate, often in larger numbers than men, leading to a process of more permanent settlement and community formation. Few migrants saw themselves as "Italians" since Italy formally became a nation only in 1861. Few spoke Italian and most despised the Italian national state. Rather, they spoke their own regional dialects and loyalties were formed at the local level, to kin and *paesani* (townspeople). When they developed political affiliations, it was most often to socialist and anarchist leaders. Even those who were not radicals, though, witnessed the popular antinationalist, antimilitarist, and anticlerical movements that erupted throughout Italy in this period. And the experiences Italians faced in the United States as workers in sweatshops, mines, construction, and other low-paid, dangerous, and dirty work convinced many that revolution was not only desirable but also of urgent necessity. For this reason, Italians formed a significant component of the U.S. industrial union movement, where they struggled not only to obtain more humane working conditions but also to overthrow all systems of exploitation, including capitalism, imperialism, nationalism, and racism. The U.S. government's execution of Italian immigrants and anarchists Nicola Sacco and Bartolomeo Vanzetti in 1927, after a highly prejudicial and inconclusive trial for the shooting of two men during a 1920 robbery, demonstrated to many Italians the costs of revolutionary culture and racialized criminalization in the United States. Moreover, the court proceedings (occurring in the wake of the Red Scare) and contemporary debates concerning the fitness of southern Italians for American citizenship included intense public debate over Italian racial status.

As historian Matthew Jacobson has written, "It was not just that Italians did not look white to certain social arbiters, but that they did not *act* white."[31] In many cities, Italian immigrants not only were stigmatized as outlaws and political subversives, they also accepted work coded as "black" by local customs, mobilized alongside people of color, and incited the wrath of white supremacists by their transgressions across the color line. David Roediger and James Barrett's work elsewhere has shown that the racial oppression of Italians had its roots in the racialization of Africans. The epithet *guinea*, for example, was used by whites to mark African slaves and their descendents as inferior before it was applied to Italians at the turn of the twentieth century.[32] Italians also learned that they were racially "other" in the United States in ways that went beyond language: lynchings; the refusal of some native-born Americans to ride streetcars with or live alongside "lousy dagoes"; the exclusion of Italian children from certain schools and movie theaters, and their parents from social groups and labor unions; segregated seating in some churches; and the barrage of popular magazines, books, movies, and newspapers that bombarded Americans with images of Italians as racially suspect.[33] These conventions received approval from the federal government in the 1920s when entry of immigrants from Italy was restricted on racial grounds. Yet, paradoxically, as far as the state was concerned, Italians were quite unequivocally "white"—they had access to citizenship; could vote, own land, and serve on juries; and were not barred from marrying other Europeans.

The essays in section I, "Learning the U.S. Color Line," examine the complex ways Italians were positioned in the U.S. racial hierarchy at the end of the nineteenth and early twentieth centuries. The demonstrate, as Louise DeSalvo writes, how "agents of the government were using their power to *create* rather than *record* difference in physical appearance" in their marking of Italians as "dark white." Thomas A. Guglielmo documents how naturalization officials recorded Italian immigrants' "color" as "white," their "complexion" as "dark," and their "race" as "Italian." Moreover, he argues, the color status of Italians as "white on arrival" guaranteed them access to material resources which were consistently and systematically denied to people of color, even though they were stigmatized as "dark" and were remarkably slow to claim a "white" identity for themselves. Moreover, Donna R. Gabaccia argues that such a conceptualization meant that the hyphenated identities of Italian American would "reflect the impact of Social Darwinist ideas about race on efforts—common in the British Empire—to define nations as groups of consenting citizens." Vincenza Scarpaci's essay takes us to a place where the color line was particularly fierce and where Italians' whiteness was perhaps most challenged—Louisiana. In their attention to international, national, and the local realms, as well as collective and personal experiences, the authors in this section are able to examine the deep significance of region, nation, class, political economy, and gender to early Italian American racial formation.

The essays in section II, "Radicalism and Race," examine how Italian immigrants and their descendents have confronted this complex racial positioning in radical political arenas—in anarchist, socialist, surrealist, and other revolutionary cultural movements of the twentieth century, including hip-hop. Caroline Waldron Merithew, Michael Miller Topp, and Salvatore Salerno document three very different case stories of Italian radicals coming to terms with racism in the United States in the first decades of the twentieth century. Their essays dramatically challenge a progressive, linear narrative that situates European immigrants on a trajectory of assimilation from nonwhite to white. Rather, taken together, they demonstrate how the combination of white privilege and racial discrimination led to a history of racemaking in which Italian Americans themselves have alternately asserted, challenged, reified, and subverted whiteness. In addition, both this section and section III collectively demonstrate the significance of coercion, in the context of rising industrial capitalism, imperialism, and state-sanctioned white supremacy, in the decision of Italians to assert a white identity. The last two essays in section II, by Franklin Rosemont and Manifest, examine the Italian American radical imagination from a more personal perspective, to explore how collaboration with artist–activists in the African diaspora have inspired individual commitments to revolutionary struggle through poetry and music in the second half of the twentieth century.

The essays in section III, "Whiteness, Violence, and the Urban Crisis," examine the post–World War II era, when white privilege and power became deeply institutionalized in the United States, and Italian Americans began to organize more self-consciously as whites. During this period, New Deal programs such as the Wagner Act, the Social Security Act, and the Federal Housing Act legislated job protections and benefits for white industrial workers, thus giving groups like Italians, eastern European Jews, and other southern and eastern Europeans, who may not have identified as white, a powerful reason to assert such an identity. Whiteness guaranteed access to federally subsidized loans that they used to abandon the inner-city for segregated suburbs, and allowed them to attain positions of authority in the newly empowered trade unions. At the same time, people of color were routinely denied access to citizenship and property, and excluded from many New Deal reforms because of overtly racist practices in government agencies.

Additionally, two areas in which people of color were overrepresented—agricultural and domestic labor—were exempt from New Deal reforms. As cultural critic George Lipsitz has observed, the policies of this era "widened the gap between the resources available to whites and those available to aggrieved racial communities."[34] Thomas A. Guglielmo's research findings elsewhere have identified the 1940s were a powerful turning point for Italian Americans, since it was the first time they began to identify and mobilize as whites en masse.[35]

The essays by Gerald Meyer, Stefano Luconi, and Joseph Sciorra each examine how Italian Americans chose to cope with the crises brought on by Cold War economic restructuring—including the loss of jobs to deindustrialization and the government's massive disinvestment in the inner city—by turning to organized resistance against neighborhood integration, direct violence against people of color, and white flight. They powerfully demonstrate the conditions under which Italian American identities of class and race oppression could be mobilized in defense of social justice, in coalition with people of color, *or* organized in the service of reactionary and racist measures. Together, they chart the development of a "white ethnic" identity—that is, a panethnic ideology that emphasizes the shared values and grievances of the descendents of white immigrants in opposition to the civil rights and Black Power movements. From such an identity, the fallacious idea that the rights of people of color have come at the expense of "white ethnic" working classes gained powerful currency. In addition, these essays, and those which come before, demonstrate how whiteness is consolidated through terror and violence, in such practices as racial profiling, mass incarceration, mob lynching, and the attempt to silence those who denounce white supremacy. In doing so, they show us that democracy and freedom have never been brought about through repression and violence.

These authors and others in the collection also detail the continued significance of radical politics and oppositional culture for the children and grandchildren of immigrants who sought to challenge the homogenization of mainstream, white middle-class, conformist capitalist and imperialist culture, which so infused "white ethnic" movements. They faced, as Rosemont writes of the 1950s, 1960s, and 1970s, "the myth of an all-pervasive national (as well as national*ist*) self-satisfaction underscored by a paranoid antiradicalism that upheld white supremacy, union-busting, Christian fundamentalism, misogyny, and all the other staples of an exploitative social system." Many of the authors here illustrate how people survived the despair, isolation, and trauma brought about by this "culture of miserablism" with their spirits intact by turning to poetry, music, collective action, and other arts, often by following the lead of the liberatory cultural and political movements of African Americans, Puerto Ricans, and other people of color. Such activity has been deeply informed by a return to the pre-U.S., pre-Empire connection between Italy and Africa, and by the conscious attempt to heal the subject–object split within the psyche, within families, and within communities that is at the heart of racism. As Edvige Giunta writes, "I learned to take pride in the cultural identity that I was supposed to shed."

This book ends at the crossroads between Africa and Italy in America. The essays in the final section, "Toward a Black Italian Imaginary," explore the clash of cultures, races, and worlds in the lives of those who are Italian American and African American. Kym Ragusa, Giunta, John Gennari, and the dialogue between Ronnie Mae Painter and Rosette Capotorto take inventory of lives lived at the borders, of working-class and transnational lives, of migratory lives, and examine the personal effects of racist denial and rejection. These are stories of what it means to reside is a space that is simultaneously not recognized by the dominant culture and deemed illegitimate by one's own people. They reveal what it means to keep one's identity and dignity intact amid attempted annihilation, and the power of creative cultural work in envisioning alternative practices. The leading critic and analyst of whiteness, historian David Roediger, concludes our collection with a meditation on the many ways W. E. B. Du Bois's writing helps us to understand under what conditions antiracist coalitions are possible.

PART I

LEARNING THE U.S. COLOR LINE

Chapter One

COLOR: WHITE/ COMPLEXION: DARK

Louise DeSalvo

Journalist to construction boss, 1890s:
"Is an Italian a white man?"
Construction boss:
"No sir, an Italian is a Dago."[1]

My father calls to tell me he has been cleaning out his files. He has found some documents, he says, that I might want, since I have recently shown such interest in my immigrant Italian grandparents. I ask him what they are.

"Oh, naturalization papers, visas, some birth records, death certificates," he says. "Nothing really important."

I tell him to bring them over right away, for to me they *are* important. I know that if I do not claim them immediately, they might wind up in the trash like other family mementos did after my father remarried, for my father likes to jettison what he considers to be the detritus of his former life.

My father, more than anyone I know, lives in the present, considers his past a burden, an obstacle that he overcame that is unconnected to who he has chosen to become: an American. That he once lived in Italy in a small village near Sorrento, that his heritage is southern Italian, that he grew up poor in Hudson County, New Jersey, that he was taunted as a boy for being Italian and short and scrawny, that he was savaged by a superior in the Navy during World War II for the same reasons, he shrugs off as insignificant. So that, in the 1940s and 1950s, I did not grow up with stories of "life in the old country," with a sense that I was from a family newly arrived in the United States, as others did.

The way my father (and mother, too) dealt with their Italian heritage was to not discuss it. Nor did they discuss *anyone's* race, *anyone's* ethnicity. They did not use ethnic or racial labels when talking about world or national affairs or about anyone we knew. And anytime I mentioned that a friend was this or that (for I began, in high school, to think in terms of ethnic and racial categories, as I listened to my friends' conversations about who could or could not date whom), my parents would shrug and say, "So what? Underneath, everyone's the same"[2] or "You can't tell a book by its cover"—their way of saying that when you know someone's ethnicity or race, you know nothing at all about them. So anyone's ancestry seemed unimportant to my parents, even though they were both extremely interested in history. But this was so that they could understand that which was puzzling to them: why, for example, prejudice existed; why people were persecuted; why wars happened.

My father is eighty-six, and I am afraid that everything he knows about my grandparents will die with him. As I edge toward my sixtieth year, I want to urge from my father all the stories he knows about my grandparents that can nourish and sustain me in this phase of my life. I want them, too, so I can tell my grandchildren; so that our forebears, these people, their lives, our past, will not be forgotten. So that they can learn, earlier in their lives than I did, who these people were.

My father's ancestry as a *southern* Italian is something I learned about only recently. Still, he has always been interested in Italian culture—the works of Michaelangelo and Da Vinci, and Italian opera, and this was what he told me about, not the poverty stricken Italy that his parents and his wife's parents left under desperate circumstances. An Italy that I myself did not learn about until I was in my fifties. And not from my father.

My interest in my grandparents, and in how they, and other Italian immigrants, were regarded and treated when they came to this country is recent, and it is urgent. In the 1940s and 1950s in the United States, some Italian Americans, like my parents, buried the past, tried to assimilate. It was, in part, because of the war; but it was also the ethos of the times: racial and ethnic differences were not valued but, instead, condemned and ridiculed. And there was (and still is) always a peculiar silence in the United States about the Italian diaspora and the injustice inflicted here upon Italian Americans.[3]

I knew nothing about my grandparents' lives in Italy. I certainly did not know about the horrific mistreatment, exploitation, and enforced starvation of *contadini* (peasants) and farm laborers in the Mezzogiorno that appears, now, to have been a form of "ethnic cleansing."[4] And what I learned in my fifties about that history, and about their lives in the United States upon arrival, about how they were treated because they were Italian (how policemen invaded the Italian neighborhood in Hoboken, New Jersey; that Sacco and Vanzetti were assumed to be guilty despite evidence to the contrary; that Italian Americans were lynched in the South; that they were incarcerated during World War II), by reading works such as Richard Gambino's *Blood of My Blood: The Dilemma of the Italian-Americans,* was painful.

What I knew as a child was very little: that none of them spoke English; that they (and we) lived in a working-class Italian neighborhood until we moved to the suburbs when I was seven; that they cooked foods that I didn't like until I was older; that my grandfather worked on the railroad; that my grandmother was our tenement's superintendent. Which is to say I knew almost nothing at all.

I later learned that Italian men who worked on the railroad earned less money for their work than "whites"; that they slept in filthy, vermin-infested boxcars; that they were denied water, though they were given wine to drink (for it made them tractable)—which, I am sure, shortened my grandfather's life.[5] And that my paternal grandmother worked for meager wages as a garment worker, and that she took my father to work into the factory when he was a small child, and hid him under her sewing machine because she had no one to care for him, and that when the boss discovered him, my father was put to work—he was four or five years old.

My father, like his parents before him, is disinclined to talk about how he was treated because his family was Italian. I think this is because he is, and they were, products of *contadina* culture: proud, accepting, and fatalistic. Because they were proud, they got on with what had to be done, considered talk a waste of time and energy, and didn't like to admit they were mistreated even though they were: they called what happened to them, when they talked about it, *la miseria,* as if their plight were something that had happened to them rather than something that was done to them. Because they were accepting of whatever circumstances they encountered, they didn't regard exploitation or abuse as abnormal. And because they were fatalistic, they believed that prejudice against them was in the scheme of things.

So, they didn't complain. And because lamentation is essential for an oral history to exist, and because they did not recount their grievances, but instead buried them, I have almost no stories to share about these grandparents; nothing that has come down to me about how my grandparents and their parents lived in Italy or when they came to the United States; nothing about how they were treated or about the difficulties they encountered. And because, unlike other migrations, these people were often illiterate, they left very few documents with which we can write their history. And their grandchildren are just beginning to write their stories.

But this silence is cultural, too: To recount that you were mistreated and to see this as significant, demands that you can imagine a world in which people are treated (or should be treated) humanely. My grandparents, it seems, could not imagine such a world. Though my parents (especially my mother) could.

So now it has come to me to eke out what I can from the very little I have. And the documents my father gives me help me immeasurably.

The next time we meet, my father presents me with a manila envelope. On the front, in my mother's hand, the words *FAMILY PAPERS* are printed. The letters waver, so I know she gathered them together near the end of her life to make sure (I surmise) that they wouldn't be lost or destroyed after her death. That my father saved these records seems a small miracle: he threw or gave away almost everything else before starting a new marriage and a new life after my mother's death.

When he gives me the envelope, my father tells me a few things: that my maternal grandparents came from a small village near Bari, he didn't remember the name, and that my grandfather had come to work on the railroad.

"Only he really didn't know what he was getting himself into," my father says. "It took him a long time to pay back his passage.

"The grandmother you knew, he sent for to care for your mother after her mother died. Really, there was no love between your grandfather and her. She was a 'mail order bride.' And although she had a hard life there, she had a hard life here, and she managed to find work as a super in the tenement where we all lived.

"Your grandfather, though, was never sorry he came. He had wanted an education in Italy, which was out of the question. The happiest day of his life was the first day your mother went to school."

I wait until my father leaves to read these papers. Any show of emotion makes my father uncomfortable, and as I approach my sixtieth birthday, any relic from my family's past provokes tears. For I am aware of the press of time and my own eventual death. Preserving and recording whatever I can of our family's past has become urgent, yet I sense that I will discover something disquieting and unnerving here: official documents often reveal truths one has never known.

I unfold the first paper carefully. It is my maternal stepgrandmother's certificate of naturalization. Affixed to the document is her "official" photograph, which brings back memories—how she protected me from my father's rages; helped me endure my mother's depression; taught me to knit; gave me money from her small pension; called me *figlia mia;* sang me Italian songs (one, that scared me, about a wolf devouring children); made me pizza for supper and *zeppoli* for Sunday breakfast.

But the picture also reminds me how her appearance (black dress, black sweater, black cotton stockings, black headscarf knotted on her chin when she went to church) marked me as different, as not quite American.

A friend: "Where does your grandmother come from? She looks like a witch. How did she get here? On a broomstick? Ha. Ha." A boyfriend: "My mother says I could never marry you, should stop seeing you. Your grandmother. Can you imagine her at the wedding?"

My grandmother was a God-sent protector in my house of anger and sorrow. But she also was someone I was ashamed of, that I made fun of to my friends so my friends wouldn't make fun of me because of her. As if in repudiating her I could leach out the Italian in me and become what I then thought was important. Being American, whatever that was.

But in the 1950s when I was growing up in suburban New Jersey (where we moved after my grandfather's death), being American didn't include having such a grandmother. And so, in public, I mocked her, scorned her. In private, I ran to her, buried my head in her lap, and secretly begged her forgiveness.

In her photograph, my grandmother is dressed in black (as she always was, her life, one of perpetual mourning, even before my grandfather died). Double-chinned (not a fat woman, but well nourished). Light-skinned (that burned unless she was careful during summers she farmed with relatives in the country; but that, by autumn, tanned because of her outdoor work). Dark-haired, though graying at the temples, hair pulled back from her face, though not austerely, so that one wave dipped over each temple (its lustrous length braided and fashioned into a neat circlet at the nape of the neck, though this does not show in the picture). Smile playing at the corners of her mouth (and she could be wickedly insightful in describing people's foibles, this grandmother, and merciless in mocking my father's bravura, my mother's rigidity, the incomprehensible ways of her adopted land, but never of me).

On the document, my grandmother has inscribed her signature carefully—*Libera Maria Calabrese*—because she does not often write her name, never her full name, and because she understands the importance of this moment of becoming a United States citizen. It is wartime and being Italian is dangerous. When the United States declares war on Italy, four thousand Italian Americans are arrested.[6] This news sends shock waves through the country's Little Italys. Though relatives here (including my father) are fighting the war against Fascism, against family and *paisani* in Italy, demonstrating loyalty to the new land, still Italians and Italian Americans are suspect.

But because she is Italian, my grandmother is eligible for naturalization because she is legally considered Caucasian, though in the 1890s Italians weren't popularly considered white.[7] (Until 1952, people not considered white were not eligible for naturalization.[8])

Not pledging allegiance to the United States, not becoming a United States citizen at this time, would have been dangerous for my grandparents. Italians were warily regarded, risked being prosecuted as "enemy aliens"—and my grandfather worked on the piers in New York City where warships docked. Until the United States declared war on Italy, they had sent nonperishable food, money, and clothing to relatives "back home" in Italy. And until Mussolini's abuses became known, they had supported him and followed the progress of the war because of his support for the South. After the United States joined the war, they desperately wanted to know the fate of their people—parents, brothers, sisters, uncles, aunts, cousins—but this concern was suspect.

Renouncing their Italian citizenship was fraught with difficulty. For although they knew they had opportunities here that would have been foreclosed to them in Italy (such as working for a wage that could sustain them, albeit modestly), still it meant disavowing allegiance to their homeland, and though they were deeply suspicious of government, this constituted a betrayal of what they valued most highly: loyalty to their families.[9] To become a United States citizen was the single most difficult, significant act of their lives in this country.

Becoming a naturalized citizen granted my grandmother (some) rights and privileges of a native-born American but neither the privilege of being completely accepted nor absorbed into the mainstream of North American life. Still, my grandmother's naturalization papers remained precious to her always, I know, for she kept the document in a locked box that held her visa, her transport ticket for coming to the United States (listing every meal, like *Riso o pasta asciutta al sugo—Carne e ragu con piselli,* that would be served in transit), her birth certificate, a lock of my grandfather's hair (after his death), and a set of crystal rosary beads. She showed her papers to me on one occasion: when I brought home a certificate of my own: my grammar school diploma. Now each of us had important papers.

I am a toddler when my grandmother becomes naturalized and my father is fighting somewhere in the Pacific. My mother and I live next door to my grandparents in a tenement on Fourth and Adams Street in an Italian American neighborhood in Hoboken, New Jersey. And although I do not remember the event, I know that I attended this ceremony, for there is a picture in our family album of my grandparents and me commemorating the occasion.

I am in my good tweed winter coat, leggings, and hat, and I stand next to my grandparents, who are soberly attired in their black winter coats. We stand on the steps of the courthouse; my grandfather holds my hand. Though I am not then aware of it, this is a defining moment in my life. For who I am (not quite Italian, not quite American) and who I will become (aware of inequities faced by Italian Americans in a country that has not yet fully equated the Italian American experience with the human experience) in one important sense, begins here.

NATURALIZATION[10]

1. *The act of admitting an alien to the position and privileges of a native-born subject or citizen.* (Well, not always and not really.)

2. *The act of introducing plants or animals or humans to places where they are not indigenous, but where they can thrive freely under ordinary conditions.* (This, says the *Oxford English Dictionary*, is Charles Darwin's meaning of the term, he who coined the term "favored races"; he who, in *The Descent of Man*, said "I would as soon be descended from that heroic little monkey . . . ; or from that old baboon. . .—as from a savage who . . . who knows no decency."[11]

But what, we may ask, are "ordinary conditions"? And what does it mean to "thrive freely"? And it can't have escaped you that according to this definition, everyone in the United States except Native Americans is not native but naturalized. But that nonindigenous peoples should decide what other nonindigenous peoples should have a legal right to be "naturalized" is, of course, preposterous.)

3. *The action of making natural.* (Which, of course, means that what you were—Italian, in this case—was unnatural.)

4. *The act of becoming settled or established in a new place.* (All those Italian Americans who feel settled, established, accepted, and completely at home in this place, kindly raise your hands. Or have you ever, like me, been told that you were "an embarrassment," "irrational," "too emotional," "too noisy," or "too shiny"—these last words were those of a former employer of mine, and

on that day, I wasn't even wearing my plaid taffeta blouse, pink stockings, and patent leather shoes.)

5. The act of becoming naturalized, of settling down in a natural manner. (If settling down in a "natural manner" means doing things the way things are supposed to be done in the United States, then neither I nor my parents nor my grandparents ever became fully naturalized. I remember reading "Self-Reliance" in high school, and not understanding how anyone could consider that a virtue. I remember arguing in college that not wanting to move away from your family, that calling your parents daily, was not necessarily neurotic. I remember arguing against a twenty-three-minute lunch period when I taught high school. Recently, in Liguria, my husband and I saw the student body of a rural school having a leisurely three-course lunch in a celebrated local restaurant. We learned they dined there three times a week at the government's expense. I am certain this does not occur anywhere in the United States. Now *that,* I thought, looking at those children eating their pasta, is civilized.)

Libera Maria Calabrese. My grandmother has signed her name beneath her picture and on the line of the document that calls for the *complete and true signature of the holder*, and she has signed slowly, for this writing of her name, I know, took much effort and much concentration.

(Years later, I remember her watching *Sesame Street* with my children, still trying to learn how to read and write English. And I remember her signing the back of the Social Security check that she received after my grandfather's death; remember, too, that it was the only time I saw her write her name. And I wonder, now, what it was/is like to live a life where you almost never had an occasion to sign your name; wonder what it meant/means not to be able to use the act of writing to tell people about yourself and who you were and where you came from; wonder what it meant/means not to be able to participate in the creation of your identity, for you did/do not have the language to do so.)

And I can imagine the clerks waiting impatiently for this small and soberly dressed foreign woman to finish signing, before they scrawled their names (illegibly, of course) at the bottom. (Who were these people? And why did they write their names in a way that makes it impossible to read what they have written? But I have noticed this: that people with authority rarely sign their names so we can read their signatures; but poor people, foreign people, people without power, usually sign their names carefully so that we will know who they are.)

No matter how much my grandmother cherished it, this is a strange and terrible document.

After the clerk recorded the petition number (84413) s/he typed a *personal description of holder as of date of naturalization.* A verbal portrait of my grandmother by a paid functionary who took my grandmother's testimony (about, for example, how much she weighed), filled in information from documents provided, but who also wrote down what s/he observed. Much like the secretary who worked in the mental hospital where my husband was an intern: after listening to discussions among the doctors about a diagnosis, she preempted their decision by writing the words *Paranoid schizophrenic* on the form before her. Those, who have the power to fill in forms have the power to define us, to tell us, to tell the world, who and what we are. And so it was with my grandmother.

I make my living analyzing texts, mulling over the nuances of words, wondering why something is phrased one way and not another, teasing out innuendos. And when I study this document, I realize that there is something very fishy here. There is what Virginia Woolf would call "an aroma" about the page.

The physical description of my grandmother, which she must swear to as true for naturalization to occur, reads: *Age 57 years; sex Female; color White; complexion Dark; color of eyes Brown; color of hair Gr. Black; height 5 feet 0 inches* (she was short, my grandmother), *weight 120 pounds; visible distinctive marks Mole on forehead; Marital status Married; former nationality Italian.*

I can understand that some of what is recorded is significant—age, color of eyes, color of hair, height, weight, distinctive marks—so that no one else could use this document. And I know that stating that my grandmother's "color" was "White" at this time in the history of the United States was significant, for it meant that at this time (although not always), Italians were deemed Caucasian, hence White, hence eligible for naturalization. And so I can understand why that was recorded, though I do not agree with what that signified (that race exists; that it can be determined; that those deemed members of certain races should be permitted privileges, others not; etc.; etc.; etc.)

But why was it important to record my grandmother's complexion as dark? What was so significant about complexion? There was, after all, a picture of my grandmother appended to the document that clearly showed what she looked like. And, as anyone could see, her complexion was fair though the document insists that it was *dark.*

The description above given. Now, what does this mean, exactly? Does it mean *The description given above?* But if that was the meaning, then the *description above* was *given* by someone, and it would be important to know by whom it was *given.*

So which is it? *The description that the person named above* (my grandmother) *has given to the clerk?* Or *The description that has been given to the above-named person by the clerk?* Or *The description that in part the person named above* (my grandmother) *has given to the clerk and in part has been given by the clerk to the person named above?*

Well. I have learned that when things are unclear, they are unclear for a reason. Especially on government documents. (There is, you see, an advantage to being almost sixty years old.)

That my grandmother testified that she was fifty-seven years old, and a female, and that she was exactly five feet tall, and that she weighed 120 pounds and that she said she had a mole on her forehead, I can imagine (although I can also hear her mocking voice later telling my grandfather that this clerk, surely he was a *cretino* to make her say she had a mole on her forehead or that she was a woman when anyone with an eye to see could look at her and learn these things for themselves).

But that my grandmother told the clerk that her complexion was *Dark* I am absolutely certain never happened. For there is no way that in March, in the dead of winter, my grandmother would have described herself as dark or could been considered dark by anyone who looked at her, who witnessed her face on that day. In March, my grandmother was not dark. In March, as in her photograph, my grandmother was most certainly fair.

Whatever else my grandmother was—a peasant, poor, irreverent, an Italian from a small town near Bari, she was not stupid and she was no liar. My grandmother either spoke the truth or, when the truth could not be told because telling the truth was dangerous, she remained silent and shrugged her shoulders. And although she disrespected and distrusted all authority, nonetheless, when it came to this official form, my grandmother would have been scrupulously honest about the answer to any question put to her, for she was wary of the consequences of misrepresenting herself on official sheets of paper that were stamped and that had official seals. This was wartime, after all.

And so my grandmother did not answer the question "What is your complexion?" with the answer "My complexion is dark." Because, had she been asked, my grandmother would have said "Sometimes fair; sometimes dark," and then she would have told a story. She would have told the clerk (if she imagined he would listen) how she had to tie her scarf in a special way to protect her face from the sun; how she had to cover her arms when she worked in the vegetable garden so that her skin wouldn't burn; then she would have digressed and talked about the beauty of vegetables at harvest, but also, the wrenching pain in the back at day's end; she would have described how, by autumn, if she was careful, she would be a nice shade of *bruno,* like the color of a toasted pignoli.

But my grandmother could not be fair, not to the clerk who inscribed this document, and therefore not in the United States, because my grandmother was not only Italian, she was from the South of Italy, a peasant, a *terrone*—a creature of the earth,[12] and so the color of the earth, and because of this, she *had to be dark*, not fair.

Here, then, on a document that my grandmother kept until she died, and that my mother kept until she died, and that I will keep until I die, is evidence that my people's whiteness was provisional, that agents of the government were using their power to *create* rather than *record* difference in physical appearance.[13]

One of the clerks decided, perhaps without looking too closely (for who would want to look closely at a poor Italian peasant woman?), that my grandmother's complexion was *Dark,* and if my grandmother wanted citizenship, she had no choice but to sign her name on the line. She had to attest that though she was *White,* she was not completely *White,* for she was also *Dark*. There was not one white race; there were several, and some were not as good as others.[14]

Because my grandmother was not quite white,[15] she was also thought to be not quite (or not very) smart, not quite (or not very) reliable, not quite capable of self-government,[16] not quite (or not very) capable of self-control, not quite capable of manifesting the traits of duty and obligation, not quite adaptable to organized and civilized society, not quite clean enough, not quite (or not at all) law-abiding (remember the Mafia). But, at this time, her (my) people were believed able to build the nation's railroads, its subways, its buildings; fight its war; mill its fabric; sew its clothing; mine its coal; stow its cargo; farm its fruits and vegetables; vendor its foods; organize its crime; play its baseball; and, of course, make its pizza, its ravioli, and its spaghetti and meatballs.[17]

Notice, please, that the clerk did not write *wretched refuse, human flotsam.* The words *WOP, Dago, greaser, guinea, Mafioso* do not appear anywhere on the form, and for this, I should, perhaps, be grateful, even though this is what the clerk might have thought as the word *Dark* was written and this is what my people were then called (and often are still called). But the law had provided a category—complexion—whereby clerks of the United States government (thank God) could insinuate what they thought about the person standing before their gaze. (Notice, please: there was no space on the form for my grandmother to describe what the clerk looked like to her.) *Dark* made its implied meaning clear: my grandmother had become "racialized."[18]

To become a citizen, my grandmother had to perjure herself. She had to admit that she manifested an attribute that was not true, but that someone else insisted was true. She had to sign her name, *Libera Maria Calabrese,* verifying that, yes, she was dark, not fair. She had to *certify that the description above given is true.*

And there is the picture of a man's hand pointing to the line where my grandmother was to sign her name. Upon which my grandmother signed her name (as I have told you) and thereby testified that what had been written was true. That her complexion was dark although her complexion was fair.

The picture of the hand, you must understand, is completely unnecessary. For the blank line would have been sufficient to tell petitioners where they must sign their names. But the hand is there. And it is not there for the purposes of decorating this document, you see, for it is the hand of authority, and it has dressed itself very formally for this occasion, in white shirt and dark suit, and there can be no mistaking that it is a white hand, and that the white hand is a man's hand, and that the complexion of the white man's hand is not dark, like my grandmother's is supposed to be, but fair. It is the fairest hand of all.

Libera Maria Calabrese
(Complete and true signature of holder)

My grandmother had to be made to understand that though she was privileged, she was not that privileged. She had to learn that just as there are several grades of hamburger meat, there were (are) several shades of whiteness. She was chuck, with lots of fat and gristle; she was not sirloin; she was not even ground round. And signing this document where the light white man's hand pointed meant that she agreed that she was offered a citizenship which was contingent, that certainly did not confer upon her all the rights and privileges of someone whose color was white and whose complexion was fair, very, very fair.

My grandmother, then, became a "Dark White" citizen of the United States of America.[19] A "white nigger."[20] Someone not truly white. Someone Italian American.

CHAPTER TWO

"NO COLOR BARRIER"

Italians, Race, and Power in the United States

THOMAS A. GUGLIELMO

Looking back on their and their ancestors' early immigrant experiences in America, many Italian Americans, especially since the 1970s, have prided themselves on making it in America by working hard and shunning government assistance. Examining interviews of Chicago's Italian Americans conducted in the early 1980s, I came across these views over and over again. Leonard Giuliano stated: "With determination and perseverance . . . the Italian was able to . . . pull himself up by his own bootstraps. . . . His greatest desire, of course, was for his children and his family to have a better life than he had left in Italy, but he did not expect this for nothing. He had to work." Constance Muzzacavallo agreed: "I think we've updated ourselves. I'll give the Italian 100 percent credit for that. You didn't have the government helping you." Joseph Loguidice added: "The immigrants in those days didn't have . . . the things today . . . or the help that they have today. Today is a cake walk. Everybody gets help. They didn't have no aid . . . like you have today. . . . Those people were too proud."[1]

These views—coming to life most forcefully during the post-1960s "backlash" years—address far more than simply the value of hard work and the proper role of the federal government; they are also deeply about race. As one Al Riccardi told an interviewer in the early 1990s, "My people had a rough time, too. But nobody gave us something, so why do we owe them [African Americans] something? Let them pull their share like the rest of us had to do."[2]

This essay was written, in part, as a response to Giuliano, Muzzacavallo, Loguidice, Riccardi, and the countless others who share their views. Focusing on the early years of migration and settlement—approximately 1890–1918—I am interested in Italian immigrants' hardships, hard work, and perseverance, but also in something too often overlooked in romantic retrospectives on the European "immigrant experience"—white power and privilege. Most broadly, this essay examines where Italians were located within America's developing racial order and what consequences this had on their everyday lives and opportunities. This essay is written as an invitation to other scholars to further explore Italians' (and other immigrants') encounters with race in the United States. If it demonstrates anything, it is that we still have much to learn about these critical issues.

Beginning in earnest with the onset of mass migration from Italy (particularly southern Italy) in the late nineteenth century and continuing well into the twentieth century, racial discrimination and prejudice aimed at Italians, southern Italians, Latins, Mediterraneans, and "new" immigrants were fierce, powerful, and pervasive. And some of this anti-Italian sentiment and behavior questioned Italians' whiteness on occasion. In the end, however, Italians' many perceived racial inadequacies aside, they were still largely accepted as whites by the widest variety of people and institutions—the U.S. census, race science, newspapers, unions, employers, neighbors, real estate agents, settlement houses, politicians, political parties, and countless federal and state laws regarding naturalization, segregation, voting rights, and "miscegenation." This widespread acceptance was reflected most concretely in Italians' ability to immigrate to the United States and become citizens, work certain jobs, live in certain neighborhoods, join certain unions, marry certain partners, patronize certain movie theaters, restaurants, saloons, hospitals, summer camps, parks, beaches, and settlement houses. In so many of these situations, one color line existed separating "whites" from the "colored races"—groups such as "Negroes," "Orientals," and "Mexicans." And from the moment they arrived in the United States—and forever after—Italians were consistently and unambiguously placed on the side of the former. If Italians were racially undesirable in the eyes of many Americans, they were white just the same.

They were so securely white, in fact, that Italians themselves rarely had to aggressively assert the point. Indeed, according to my work on Chicago, not until World War II did many Italians identify openly and mobilize politically as white. After the early years of migration and settlement, when Italy remained merely an abstraction to many newcomers, their strongest allegiance was to the Italian race, not the white one. In the end, however, how Italians chose to identify proved to be of little consequence when it came to the "wages of whiteness." As it turned out, Italians did not need to be openly and assertively white to benefit from the considerable rewards and resources of whiteness. For a good part of the late nineteenth and early twentieth centuries, then, Italians were white on arrival, not so much because of the way they viewed themselves but because of the way others viewed and treated them. For this reason, and because of space constraints, I will not focus on Italians' race/color self-identification here.

Two conceptual tools are critical to my analysis. First is the simple point that we take the structure of race seriously. Race is still too often talked about as simply an idea, an attitude, a consciousness, an identity, or an ideology. It is, to be sure, all of these things—but also much more. It is also rooted in various political, economic, social, and cultural institutions, and thus very much about power and resources (or lack thereof). Particularly helpful on this point is sociologist Eduardo Bonilla-Silva, who argues that we use "racialized social system" as an analytical tool. In all such systems, he argues,

> The placement of people in racial categories involves some form of hierarchy that produces definite social relations between the races. The race placed in the superior position tends to receive greater economic remuneration and access to better occupations and/or prospects in the labor market, occupies a primary position in the political system, is granted higher social estimation . . . often has a license to draw physical (segregation) as well as social (racial etiquette) boundaries between itself and other races, and receives what Du Bois calls a "psychological wage." The totality of these racialized social relations and practices constitutes [a racialized social system].[3]

Such a system existed throughout the nineteenth- and twentieth-century United States. Whether one was white, black, red, yellow, or brown—and to some extent Anglo-Saxon, Alpine, South Italian, or North Italian—powerfully influenced (along with other systems of difference, such as class and gender) where one lived and worked, the kind of person one married, and the kinds of life chances one had. Thus, race was not (and is not) completely about ideas, ideologies, and identity. It is also about location in a social system and its consequences.

To fully understand these consequences, one more conceptual tool is critical: the distinction between race and color. Several years back, when I began research on Italians and race, I envisioned a "wop to white" story, an

Italian version of Noel Ignatiev's *How the Irish Became White*. I quickly realized, however, that this approach had serious shortcomings. For one, Italians did not need to become white; they always were, in numerous, critical ways. For another, race was more than black and white. Though Italians' status as whites was relatively secure, they still suffered, as noted above, from extensive *racial* discrimination and prejudice as Italians, South Italians, Latins, and so on.

Nor was this simply "ethnic" discrimination. To be sure, few scholars agree on how best to conceptually differentiate between "race" and "ethnicity." Some have argued that whereas race is based primarily on physical characteristics subjectively chosen, ethnicity is based on cultural ones (e.g., language, religion, etc.). Others have maintained that "membership in an ethnic group is usually voluntary; membership in a racial group is not." Still others have argued that "while 'ethnic' social relations are not *necessarily* hierarchical, exploitative and conflictual, 'race relations'" almost always are.[4] None of these distinctions, though all are valid in certain ways, is very helpful for our purposes. None of them, that is, helps us to better understand Italians' social experiences and their particular social location in the United States. After all, a group like the "South Italian race" was purported to have particular "cultural" *and* "physical" characteristics; included both voluntary *and* involuntary members; and was created in Italy and used extensively in the United States to explicitly rank and exploit certain human beings.

How, then, to navigate between Italians' relatively secure whiteness *and* their highly problematical racial status, without resorting to unhelpful conceptual distinctions between race and ethnicity? The answer, I contend, is race and color. I argue that between the mid-nineteenth and mid-twentieth centuries there were primarily two ways of categorizing human beings based on supposedly inborn physical, mental, moral, emotional, and cultural traits. The first is color (or what might be called "color race," since this is what many Americans think of as race today): the black race, brown race, red race, white race, and yellow race. Color, as I use it, is a social category and not a physical description. "White" Italians, for instance, could be darker than "black" Americans. Second is race, which could mean many things: large groups like Nordics and Mediterraneans; medium-sized ones like the Celts and Hebrews; or smaller ones like the North and South Italians.

This race/color distinction was, of course, never absolute during this time period, and it certainly changed over time. But some people and institutions were very clear on the distinction. The federal government's naturalization applications throughout this time period, for instance, asked applicants to provide their race and color. For Italians, the only acceptable answers were North or South Italian for the former and white for the latter. Most important, for all of its discursive messiness, the race/color distinction was crystal clear throughout the United States when it came to resources and rewards. In other words, while Italians suffered for their supposed *racial* undesirability as Italians, South Italians, and so forth, they still benefited in countless ways from their privileged *color* status as whites.

Italians are a particularly good group on which to test this argument, because they faced such severe racial discrimination and prejudice in the United States, which all started prior to migration in Italy. In the late nineteenth century, an influential group of positivist anthropologists, including Cesare Lombroso, Giuseppe Sergi, and Alfredo Niceforo, emerged on the scene with scientific "proof" that southern Italians were racially distinct from and hopelessly inferior to their northern compatriots. Sergi, for instance, using skull measurements to trace the various origins and desirability of the Italian people, argued that while northern Italians descended from superior Aryan stock, southerners were primarily of inferior African blood. Similarly, Niceforo argued in his widely read study, *L'Italia barbara contemporanea*, that two Italies existed, whose fundamental racial differences made unification impossible. After all, "One of the two Italies, the northern one, shows a civilization greatly diffused, more fresh, and more modern. The Italy of the South [however] shows a moral and social structure reminiscent of primitive and even quasibarbarian times, a civilization quite inferior."[5]

Such ideas were by no means restricted to the academy; a great deal of Italian mass culture and many public officials absorbed and disseminated them as well. For instance, Italy's leading illustrated magazine of the time, *Illustrazione italiana*, repeatedly and "patronizingly celebrate[d] the South's anomalous position between Italy and the Orient, between the world of civilized progress and the spheres of either rusticity or barbarism." As one of the magazine's reporters noted after a trip through Sicily in 1893, "In the fields where I interviewed many peasants I found only types with the most unmistakable African origin. My how much strange intelligence is in those muddled brains." Similarly, Filippo Turati, a Socialist Party leader at the turn of the twentieth century, no doubt spoke for many of his compatriots when he referred to the "Southern Question" as a battle between "an incipient civilization and that putrid barbarity."[6]

Just at this moment—at the height of the scientific and popular racialist assault on the Mezzogiorno (southern Italy) and its people—the origins of Italian immigration to the United States shifted dramatically from the North to the South. As hundreds of thousands of these much-maligned *meridionali* (southern Italians) arrived in America each year, a wide variety of American institutions and individuals, alarmed by this massive influx, made great use of Italian positivist race arguments. In 1899, the U.S. Bureau of Immigration, for instance, began recording the racial backgrounds of immigrants and distinguishing between "Keltic" northern Italians and "Iberic" southern Italians. In 1911, the U.S. Immigration Commission, throughout its highly influential forty-two-volume report, made a similar distinction. Citing the works of Niceforo and Sergi, it argued that northern and southern Italians "differ from each other materially in language, physique, and character, as well as in geographical distribution." While the former was "cool, deliberate, patient, practical, as well as capable of great progress in the political and social organization of modern civilization," the latter was "excitable, impulsive, highly imaginative, impracticable," and had "little adaptability to highly organized society."[7]

Social scientists like Edward Ross, also citing the work of Italian positivists, made a similar set of arguments. In popular magazine articles and books, Ross warned that while northern Italians were well-fitted for citizenship, their southern counterparts certainly were not because of their horrifying "propensity for personal violence," "inaptness" for teamwork, strong dose of African blood, and "lack of mental ability." Deeply anxious about many of these characteristics, in 1914 the popular magazine *World's Work* urged the federal government to pass an exclusion law "aimed specifically at the southern Italians, similar to our immigration laws against Asiatics," since southern Italians "are a direct menace to our Government because they are not fit to take part in it."[8]

A wide range of local institutions shared these anti-*meridionali* racialist ideas. Newspapers from New York to Florida, and Chicago to Louisiana, regularly lambasted southern Italians as being "injurious," "undesirable," and of the "lowest order."[9] Typical for the time was the *Chicago Tribune*, which in 1910 sent anthropologist George A. Dorsey to the Mezzogiorno to study immigrants in their homeland. Traveling from one small hill town to the next and writing daily columns on his impressions, Dorsey offered, in the end, the most damning view of southern Italians. These people, he claimed, were unmanly and primitive barbarians who had clear "Negroid" ancestry, who shared much more in common with the East than the West, and who were "poor in health, stature, strength, initiative, education, and money." "They are," concluded Dorsey after five months, "of questionable value from a mental, moral, or physical standpoint."[10] And throughout the United States many local governments, local politicians, labor unions, and employers could not help but agree with Dorsey and the *Tribune*.[11]

These ideas had a popular appeal as well, which was reflected in Italians' rocky relations with their neighbors in a wide range of communities nationwide. In northern cities like New York, Chicago, Milwaukee, Rochester, New Haven, Buffalo, and Philadelphia, various immigrant groups vigorously resisted the influx of Italians (particularly those from the South of Italy). In Rochester, one character in Jerre Mangione's *Monte Allegro* recalled that neighborhood animosity was so intense against Italians that "the storekeepers would not sell them food and the landlords would not rent them homes."[12] Likewise, on Chicago's Near North Side, bloody battles involving sticks, guns, knives, and blackjacks occurred regularly between Swedes and Sicilians. The former also held homeowner meetings to devise more genteel ways of ridding the neighborhood of the dreaded "dark people." The problem, in the words of one local Swedish pastor, was that Sicilians "do not keep their places clean; they tear up the cedar blocks of the sidewalk; and they also bring the district into disrepute in many other ways." Meanwhile, children engaged in similar battles on the playgrounds and streets of the neighborhood as Swedish girls kept Sicilians girls off the swings and out of the sandboxes at Seward Park by exclaiming: "Get out! Dagoes! Dagoes! You can't play here!" And Irish and Swedish boys regularly engaged in street battles with their Sicilian counterparts. On one occasion an Italian youngster led a charge of his compatriots against their neighborhood aggressors on horseback.[13]

Relations were often no friendlier in other parts of the country. Most dramatically, lynchings were none too rare an occurrence for Italians throughout the South, West, and Midwest at this time. Certainly the most infamous and shocking of these took place in New Orleans in 1891 when an angry mob, bent on avenging the murder of Police Chief David Hennessy, lynched eleven Sicilian suspects in one night. Other lynchings took place in locations as diverse as Denver, Tampa, Tallulah, Mississippi, and southern Illinois. Indeed, as late as 1915, an armed posse in Johnston, Illinois, a mining town some one hundred miles east of St. Louis, lynched Sicilian Joseph Strando for his alleged murder of a prominent town resident.[14]

Taken together, many Italians, particularly those from the Mezzogiorno, encountered powerful, pervasive, and often racialized discrimination and prejudice upon arrival in the United States. Thus, if *meridionali* emigrated from Italy in part to escape a racialized social system that relegated them to the bottom tier, they entered another social system in the United States fairly close to the bottom again. But the social systems of turn-of-the-century Italy and the United States were very different. Most important, in contrast to the

Old World, southern Italians never occupied the lowest of social positions in the United States. This was because the United States had both racial *and* color hierarchies, and if Italians were denigrated and exploited in the former, they were greatly privileged in the latter. That is, for all of the racial prejudice and discrimination that Italians faced in these early years, they were still generally accepted as white and reaped the many rewards that came with this status.

To be sure, this statement needs serious qualification, for certainly at no other time in Italian American history was the color status of *meridionali* more hotly contested. We have already seen that prominent social scientists publicly ruminated on southern Italians' "Negroid" roots, and that lynching—a punishment often reserved for African Americans—occurred with some frequency against Italians in these years. Color questions came in other forms. In 1911, the U.S. House Committee on Immigration openly debated and seriously questioned whether one should regard "the south Italian as a full-blooded Caucasian"; many representatives did not seem to think so. From the docks of New York to railroads in the West, some native-born American workers carefully drew distinctions between themselves—"white men"—and "new immigrant" foreigners like Italians.[15] Meanwhile, in the South, where color questioning may have been most severe, one Mississippi Delta town attempted to bar Italians from white schools, and Louisiana state legislators in 1898 fought to disenfranchise Italians, along with African Americans, at the state constitutional convention. As one local newspaper at the time wrote, "When we speak of white man's government, they [Italians] are as black as the blackest Negro in existence." In the sugarcane fields of Louisiana, one Sicilian American recalled, "The boss used to call us niggers" and "told us that we weren't white men."[16]

This important evidence notwithstanding, we should not exaggerate the precariousness of Italians' color status. Color questioning never led to any sustained or systematic positioning of Italians as nonwhite.[17] That is, if U.S. congressmen openly debated whether southern Italians were full-blooded Caucasians, they never went so far as to deny *meridionali* naturalization rights based on their doubts; if magazines like *World's Work* called for the exclusion of southern Italian immigration, Congress never enacted such measures; and if some Louisianans tried to disenfranchise Italians, their efforts, in direct contrast to those regarding African Americans, failed miserably.

Italians' whiteness, however, was most visible in communities all across the country. In Chicago, for example, when famous African American boxing champion Jack Johnson attempted to marry a "white" woman in 1912, a rowdy and menacing crowd of a thousand "whites" protested on the Near North Side by hanging Johnson in effigy. Italians, by contrast, could marry "white" women without anywhere near this level of resistance.[18] Regarding housing, battles took place to prevent Italian infiltration in places like the Near North Side and the Grand Avenue area. These efforts, however, were never as violent as those in areas just west of the Black Belt, where bombings, rioting, and gang attacks against African Americans occurred regularly as the Great Migration got under way during World War I. As a result, while the few wealthy Italians could move to any Chicago neighborhood that they could afford, African Americans (and many Asians) were forced to live in the most blighted of Chicago's neighborhoods, regardless of their wealth or education.[19]

In the workplace, Italians faced discrimination from both unions and employers. However, they always enjoyed far more employment options and opportunities than did the "colored races."[20] Finally, Italians were refused admission to a movie theater or restaurant on occasion. But such instances were rare indeed, and certainly paled in comparison to what many African Americans and some Asians had to endure: systematic exclusion from or segregation in countless Chicago restaurants, theaters, hotels, bars, prisons, hospitals, settlement houses, orphanages, schools, and cemeteries.[21] Thus, even in this early period when the "colored races" remained a small fraction of the city's population, a distinct and pervasive color line separated them from "whites." And for all their alleged racial inadequacies, Italians were placed firmly among the latter.[22]

A very similar story applies to Baltimore. Here, according to historian Gordon Shufelt, from the earliest days of Italian immigration, the "white citizens of Baltimore . . . invited Italian immigrants to join the white community." As in Chicago, this color position made all the difference in the world. In 1904, when a massive fire swept through the city, destroying almost everything in its path, the city distributed relief and relief jobs strictly according to color criteria—"whites" (Italians among them) got jobs and relief, "blacks" did not. Similarly, in the following decade, when local Democratic politicians repeatedly tried to pass anti-African American disfranchisement legislation and segregation housing ordinances, they never intentionally targeted Italians and instead welcomed them into the white fold as key constituents. By the early 1900s, one local politician for Italians campaigned openly as the "white man's ward leader," and began speeches with the boast: "There's no man in the state who hates the darky more than I do."[23]

Out West, Italians suffered from indignities on account of their race. They faced some workplace and neighborhood discrimination in cities like

San Francisco, and severe violence throughout the West. Italians were lynched in Gunnison, Colorado, in 1890 and in Denver three years later. This mistreatment extended to explicit color questioning on occasion. One Italian from rural Washington recalled: "Many of the natives were kind and generous; but others spared no effort to let us know that we were intruders and undesirables." In fact, one classmate called him "a goddamn wop" and insisted that he did not "belong to the white race." Similarly, in Arizona, some copper companies categorized their workers into three main groups—whites, Mexicans, and Italians/Spaniards.[24]

As in other parts of the country, however, this color questioning seems to have been sporadic at best (probably more sporadic in the West, where far fewer Italian immigrants settled and where, of these, fewer came from the Mezzogiorno) and rarely institutionalized. Indeed, as scholars like Tomás Almaguer and Yvette Huginnie have shown, whiteness mattered monumentally in the West, and all people of European descent belonged to this most privileged color category. In a region of "white man's towns"—where pervasive color lines prevented many African Americans, Asians, Latinos, and Native Americans from owning land, marrying anyone they chose, serving on juries, joining particular unions, claiming land to mine, swimming in the local pool, or attending the best schools—Italians were white and, as usual, benefited greatly from this arrangement.[25]

But what about the Deep South, where Italians' whiteness may have been most seriously challenged? Though far more research needs to be done, it appears that Italians' whiteness was more evident on a daily basis here than perhaps anywhere else. After all, the Deep South had, by the turn of the twentieth century, the most visible colorized social system in the form of disfranchisement, antimiscegenation laws, and Jim Crow segregation. And while evidence certainly exists that Southerners ("black" and "white") and some of their organizations occasionally categorized Italians as nonwhite, I have found no evidence that Italians were ever subjected in any systematic way to Jim Crow segregation or disfranchisement, or legally barred from marrying "white" men and women.[26]

Indeed, it was Italians' very whiteness that largely explains their arrival in the South in the first place. Many southern planters recruited Italians explicitly as "white" laborers who, in direct contrast to African Americans and Asians, could address their two major turn-of-the-century concerns: the "colored problem" and the declining pool of cheap labor. As historian J. Vincenza Scarpaci has pointed out, "The growing interest of the planters for Italians paralleled the post-war concern for an increased white population."

As one southern newspaper joyfully announced in 1906, "The influx of the Italians between 1890–1900 made Louisiana a white state."[27]

To be sure, many Southerners, even planters among them, came to deeply regret recruiting Italians and other southern and eastern Europeans. Indeed, during the first few decades of the twentieth century growing anti-immigrant fervor swept through the region. Still, anti-Italian feelings and actions—while intense for a time—seldom lasted long. Having completed an extensive survey of southern towns in the early 1900s, the U.S. Immigration Commission found that in many locations Italians had "fought their way inch by inch through unreasoning hostility and prejudice to almost unqualified respect, or even admiration." Equally prevalent, reported the commission, was that if in some cases parents held fast to their anti-Italian prejudice, similar feelings were breaking down among the "American" children with whom Italians played and mingled freely in "white" schools.[28]

Furthermore, even at their height, anti-Italian feelings had their limits. Even the most virulent attacks on Italians often took their whiteness for granted. During Louisiana's debates about disfranchisement in 1898, for instance, New Orleans's main paper, the *Daily Picayune*, suggested under the headline "White Foreigners Should Not Have Privileges over White Natives"—that Italians might be too ignorant and illiterate to be trusted with the ballot. In 1906, the *Memphis Commercial Appeal* asked: "Does the South want white labor to piece out or to compete with its Negro labor? . . . . What class of settlers are they bringing here? Are they of that character that they would help maintain a white man's Dixie; or are they so ignorant or careless as to become in effect allies of those *across* the color line? We want immigration to a certain extent, but we do not want 'just anybody'" (emphasis added). One journal article from 1903, titled "Italian Immigration into the South," put it best by asking: "Is the immigrant of today the kind of white man whom the South stands ready to welcome?" That Italians were white was assumed; that they were desirable was another question entirely.[29]

This point becomes even clearer, perhaps, when we compare Italians' experiences with those of another marginalized immigrant group in the South—the Chinese. As James Loewen has shown convincingly in his book *The Mississippi Chinese*, the Chinese were initially grouped along with African Americans and systematically excluded from white schools, organizations, and social institutions. By the 1930s and 1940s, when their reputations and status improved considerably, the Chinese were, generally speaking, still not accepted as white. Instead, many towns in the South developed triply segregated school systems. Nothing in Italians' experiences in the Deep South ever approached this sort of treatment.[30]

In sum, whether in the North, South, or West; whether by the government, newspapers, employers, social scientists, or neighbors; Italians faced their share of racial discrimination and prejudice. During these early years of migration and settlement, however, their whiteness was rarely challenged in any sustained or systematic way. Italians were white on arrival in America, then, regardless of where they happened to arrive.

Why was this the case? Given the widespread doubts about (chiefly) southern Italian *racial* fitness and desirability, why was their *color* status as whites not more seriously contested? First, scientists, for as long as they had attempted to construct racial/color taxonomies, placed Italians firmly within the white category. The weight of scientific opinion in the United States supported some variation of Johann Friedrich Blumenbach's classification scheme from the late eighteenth century, which divided humankind into "five principal varieties": the American ("red"), Caucasian ("white"), Ethiopian ("black"), Malay ("brown"), and Mongolian ("yellow"). As the U.S. Immigration Commission's *Dictionary of Races and Peoples* noted in 1911, "in preparing this dictionary . . . the author deemed it reasonable to follow the classification employed by Blumenbach. . . . The use of this classification as the basis for this present work is perhaps entirely justified by the general prevailing custom in the United States [to follow Blumenbach], but there is equal justification in the fact that recent writers, such as Keane and the American authority Brinton, have returned to practically the earlier [Blumenbach] classifications." Significantly, Blumenbach placed Italians (both southern and northern) within the Caucasian "variety." To question Italian whiteness, then, required one to challenge widely accepted theories in race science as well.[31]

Second, the history of the Italian peninsula—particularly that of the Roman Empire and the Renaissance—also supported the classification of Italians as white. As Eliot Lord argued in the early twentieth century, "The far-reaching ancestry of the natives of South and Central Italy runs back to the dawn of the earliest Greek civilization in the peninsula and to the Etruscan, driving bronze chariots and glittering in artful gold when the Angles, Saxons and Jutes, and all the wild men of Northern Europe were muffling their nakedness in the skins of wild beasts." As a result, asked Lord in conclusion: "Upon what examination worthy of the name has the Southern Latin stock, as exhibited in Italy, been stamped as 'undesirable'? Is it undesirable to perpetuate the blood, the memorials and traditions of the greatest empire of antiquity, which spread the light of its civilization from the Mediterranean to the North Sea and the Baltic?"[32] Given these points, anti-immigrant racialists had to exercise caution in their color-questioning of Italians, for if Italians were not white, a good deal of Western civilization might not have been either.

Finally, if various branches of the American state deeply institutionalized the *racial* differences between northern and southern Italians in their immigration statistics, studies, and applications, they just as surely secured the two groups' *color* commonalities. For one, American naturalization laws during this time allowed only "free white male persons" or "aliens of African nativity or persons of African descent" to become U.S. citizens; and American courts repeatedly denied Asian and Middle Eastern immigrants access to American citizenship because of the color stipulation in the law. Italians never once encountered any problems.[33]

Just as important as naturalization laws was the U.S. census. The color/race category and the kinds of answers the census requested changed many times between 1880 and 1920; the census, for instance, alternated frequently between asking for people's "color," "race," and "color or race." At some points it also asked enumerators to distinguish between "whites" and "Mexicans," between "mulattos," "octoroons," "quadroons," and so forth. Throughout all of these variations, however, Italians were always listed as foreign-born or native-born "whites." Because the census represented the federal government's final word on color categories, this classification was no small thing. Indeed, census categorization schemes must have had an immense influence on everyday Americans and their color conceptions. With the largest collection of social data on Americans anywhere, the U.S. census offered invaluable information to countless people—from social scientists and politicians to government bureaucrats and journalists. When using this information, one often unwittingly reproduced the various ways the census organized it—and, in the process, reproduced Italian whiteness.[34]

In the end, Italians' firm hold on whiteness never loosened over time. They were, at different points, criminalized mercilessly, ostracized in various neighborhoods, denied jobs on occasion, and alternately ridiculed and demonized by American popular culture. Yet, through it all, their whiteness remained intact. The rise of immigration restriction in the early 1920s demonstrates this point well. Anti-immigrant racialists—from Madison Grant to Kenneth Roberts, from mass circulation magazines like *Collier's* to mass movements like the Klan—roundly condemned Italians (particularly, though not exclusively, those from the South) for mongrelizing and menacing the nation. Interestingly, however, they stopped well short of questioning Italians' whiteness. If all racialists agreed that Italians were a hopelessly inferior lot, they also agreed that they were "white" or "Caucasian" just the same. They were, in the fitting words of former Seattle Mayor Ole Hanson, "the White Peril of Europe."[35]

Lothrop Stoddard's popular book, *The Rising Tide of Color* (1920), typified this point. Stoddard, an ardent Nordic supremacist, sounded the alarm against the unrestricted immigration of the Alpine and Mediterranean races, who as "lower human types" "upset standards, sterilize better stocks, increase low types, and compromise national futures more than war, revolutions, or native deterioration." And yet for all this doom and gloom, Stoddard was much more concerned about "colored" immigrants from Asia, Africa, and Central/South America. "If the white immigrants can gravely disorder the national life," declared Stoddard passionately, "it is not too much to say that the colored immigrant would doom it to certain death." The Immigration Act of 1924 made eminently clear the practical implications of this distinction between "whites" and "coloreds": while "new" European immigrants, branded as racial inferiors, were severely reduced in numbers, the Japanese, branded as racial *and* color inferiors, were excluded altogether.[36]

Whiteness continued to deeply shape Italian Americans' lives and opportunities in the interwar and postwar years. The Federal Housing Administration redlined every major city in the country; local institutions distributed GI Bill benefits, ensuring that people of "color" would not receive their fair share; and Congress excluded farmers and domestic workers—the vast majority of whom were African Americans and Latinos—from receiving Social Security and labor union protections.[37] If whiteness, as historian Matthew Jacobson aptly put it, "opened the Golden Door" for so many European immigrants, it also kept it wide open for years to come.[38]

Many Italian Americans (among other people), as noted, have had a hard time appreciating this point. Often contrasting themselves explicitly with African Americans, they have spoken (and continue to speak) proudly of the ways in which they pulled themselves up by their bootstraps by working hard and shunning government assistance. And, of course, these narratives have some truth to them. Many Italian Americans did work hard and their success in the United States is, in part, a testament to this fact. However, the idea that they, unlike groups such as African Americans, did it all by themselves without government assistance could not be more inaccurate. Indeed, the opposite was often the case. Italian Americans' whiteness—conferred more powerfully by the federal government than by any other institution—was their single most powerful asset in the "New World"; it gave them countless advantages over "nonwhites" in housing, jobs, schools, politics, and virtually every other meaningful area of life. Without appreciating this fact, one has no hope of fully understanding Italian American history.

Chapter Three

RACE, NATION, HYPHEN

Italian-Americans and American Multiculturalism in Comparative Perspective

Donna R. Gabaccia

An astute observer once noted, "It is possible to be an Italian in France, but it is not possible to be an Italian-Frenchman in the same way it is possible to be an Italian-American."[1] Latin Americans, counting no Italo-Argentines among them, claim "Argentines are Italians who speak Spanish who think they are British."[2] Descendants of Italians in Argentina maintain ties to relatives in Italy and support Italian cultural institutions, but their national identities are unitary, unmarked by ethnic modifiers. They thus offer a sharp contrast to the plural identities of Italian-Americans in the United States, where hyphens unite rather than divide ethnic and national identifications.[3] So does Italy where regional identities flourish without hyphens but regionalism still sparks concern about national collapse. Still, Italo-Australians and Italo-Canadians also sport hyphens, pointing to shared themes in the histories of the English-speaking settler colonies of the British Empire.

As the foundation for national celebrations of multiculturalism, the origins of ethnic identities and hyphens are thus worth pondering. According to David Hollinger, they originated in Americans' sense of belonging to communities of descent.[4] Historically, theories of descent have loomed large in the construction of race, nation, and ethnicity.[5] But concepts of race and of nation, like understandings of their relationship, have varied from place to place and have not always generated ethnic identities. In this essay, I argue that the hyphenated identities of Italian-Americans reflect the impact of social Darwinist ideas about race on efforts—common in the British Empire—to define nations as groups of consenting citizens.

To explore the influence of theories of race on the formation of national self-concepts, I compare three sites—the United States, Argentina, and Italy—in one of the largest migratory systems of the modern world.[6] Between 1870 and 1970, over twenty-six million persons—roughly the population of Italy in 1861—left home to work or live abroad, many of them temporarily. Between 1876 and 1914 a third of Italy's fourteen million migrants went to North America (mainly the United States) and a quarter to South America, mainly to Argentina and Brazil. (The rest migrated within Europe and, in far smaller numbers, to Africa and Australia).[7] Today, about sixty million persons of Italian descent live outside Italy, about equaling the number of Italy's modern inhabitants. Two-thirds of this Italian diaspora live in the Americas. Roughly half of modern Argentines and 10 percent of Americans in the United States have Italian forebears.[8]

Migration was only one important connection among these three countries. Modern definitions of race and of nation emerged from an international history of empire building that connected Europe and the Americas from the fifteenth until the twentieth century. The importance of the seventeenth- and eighteenth-century slave trade in consolidating Europe's American empires sparked a transatlantic discussion of physical and cultural difference among humans. European colonizers were puzzling over biological explanations for the inferiority they ascribed to the natives they conquered and the Africans they enslaved even before François Bernier (1620–1688), Georges Louis Leclerc Buffon (1707–1788) and Johann Friedrich Blumenbach (1752–1840) wrote their influential treatises on race and biological difference between 1684 and 1775.[9] By the late eighteenth century, nationalists on both sides of the Atlantic drew on these treatises, along with theological and environmental explanations of human variation, to define nations and to draw boundaries around them.

Analyses of race and of nation became even more entwined in the hundred years between the Napoleonic Wars and World War I when scientific racism informed the thinking of empire builders and nationalist anti-imperialists alike.[10] In an era of massive international migration, mobile men and women with their local, regional, and religious identities posed significant challenges to the ambitions of both.[11] To foster loyalty to one national state became the practical goal of state-initiated public policies for citizenship, migration, and education on both sides of the Atlantic, especially in the years bridging World War I. By examining three sites in Italy's migration system, we can develop an international interpretation of the construction of national self-concepts during two important eras of cross-cultural confrontation. This should help readers see some of the distinctively American assumptions that inform interpretations of whiteness and of American multiculturalism.

RACE AND NATION-BUILDING BEFORE DARWIN

At least since the eighteenth century, nationalists like Johann Gottfried von Herder (1744–1803) have defined nations as descent groups that—like lineages or families—reproduce culture as they reproduce themselves. Nations were often imagined as descended from common ancestors, sharing common blood.[12] European nationalist movements often defined nations through descent from common ancestors and shared blood.[13] Others claimed, more ambiguously, that national civilizations (or cultures) had emerged organically from soil, environment, or territory only to be reproduced biologically—following the evolutionary thinking of Jean Baptiste Lamarck (1744–1829)—as acquired traits.[14] By linking the nation to biology, nationalists helped to make *race* and *nation* loosely interchangeable terms in many European languages.

Even in the eighteenth century, however, a different stream of thought challenged this linkage of race and nation through biological descent. French and American revolutionaries insisted that citizens voluntarily adopted republican civic ideology to create nation-states. Representing their collective will, national states were the highest achievements, or centerpieces, of national culture or civilization. This association of nation-building with political liberty also had deep roots in European history, as Maurizio Viroli has argued.[15]

It was in this context, between 1776 (the start of the American Revolution) and 1862 (the end of Argentina's Civil Wars), that modern nation-states formed in the United States, Argentina, and Italy. Armed struggle against European empires produced new states, and the most important eras of nation-building followed independence in all three. Despite these similarities, however, environment, culture, and race—understood variously as shared descent or inherited physical characteristics—assumed differing roles in each new country's early understanding of its new nation.

The United States—like the other settler colonies of the British Empire—built its understandings of race and nation on imperial precedent. In the seventeenth century, English settlers distinguished themselves culturally as civilized Christians from the "savage heathen" Africans they enslaved and the American natives they conquered.[16] With few contacts to the cultures of Africa or Asia prior to the slave trade, the English came to associate dark skin with savagery, slavery, and subordination, and they viewed the extermination of natives in the New World as proof that God intended the Americas for the newcomers.[17] While colonial law discouraged or prohibited sexual relations between Africans and Europeans and slavery became an inherited status in North America, Protestants from Europe could by the eighteenth century acquire British citizenship through royal consent to a process called naturalization.[18] Whether whiteness, the Protestant faith, language, or citizenship defined a British nation was scarcely clear in the 1700s.[19]

Between 1776 and 1865, the United States wrestled with but never resolved a fundamental tension between a nation formed through citizens' consent to republican ideology and an American people understood to be culturally plural. The revolution was itself a withdrawal of consent to British rule. At the time of their independence, British North Americans were busily measuring the physical traits that defined racial difference while still hoping that life in the American environment might lighten the dark-skinned descendants of Africans.[20] Already, however, the greatest of the physical and moral traits separating slaves from civilized Americans, was in the words of Thomas Jefferson, that "of colour."[21]

Color, class, age, and gender limited access to consensual citizenship to those individuals—white adult men and property owners—already possessing the autonomy on which republican governance was predicated. Slaves, women, and children had no such autonomy, and Native Americans were dismissed as savages who were deemed members of foreign nations or tribes with their own governments and rulers.[22] That dark-skinned people could not consent to citizenship was clearest in the new country's procedures for naturalization, which from 1790 until the Civil War was open exclusively to whites.[23] At the same time, even nativists who feared new arrivals (especially from Catholic Ireland) as bearers of corrupt European civilization, assumed that exposure to the American environment transformed them into trustworthy citizens.[24] Like white boys born on American soil (the principle of *jus soli*), they could, with time and naturalization, vote and hold most political offices. New arrivals from Europe became symbols of the consensual foundations of a civic nation that linked liberty and citizenship.

In these discussions, American nationalists generally avoided acknowledging any link at all between descent and citizenship. They called themselves Americans (a term wrested with considerable effort from the "savage" natives) in order to emphasize their separation even from their colonial parent, Great Britain.[25] The new American constitution avoided even a single reference to slavery as an inherited status, as it did also to the civic privileges of whiteness. When in the 1850s Congress granted citizenship through blood descent (*jus sanguinis*) to children born abroad to American fathers, it carefully limited that right to boys born abroad who returned to live on American soil.[26]

Americans thus invented their own terminology for belonging, attempting to sever the term *nation* from its European associations with common descent and common culture. Of course European observers, like the Frenchman Hector St. John Crèvecoeur in the 1780s, wrote in the language of romantic nationalism about "that strange mixture of blood" resulting from intermarriage so that "all nations [of Europe] melted into a new race" of Americans.[27] But Benjamin Franklin in the previous decade had already referred to Americans instead as the "happiest People," completely sidestepping the term *nation*.[28]

Ultimately, white Americans followed Franklin, not Crèvecoeur, in imagining themselves as a culturally (and especially religiously) diverse people rather than as a single nation or descent group. The American nation was the nation-state and its citizens; the American people was a broader concept. Race—meaning color—excluded Africans and Native Americans from the civic nation of citizens. But even African slaves and women (along with Jews, Catholics, Virginians, and Vermonters) had small claims to being part of the American people. For example, they—unlike Native Americans—counted (in the former case as three-fifths of a person) when fixing representation in Congress.

Spain's legacy for the Argentine nation would be quite different. Spanish discussions of empire-building also contrasted European conquerors to African and native subordinates, and they used similar language to distinguish civilized Christians from savage and heathen Africans and natives. Unlike the American South, however, South American grasslands supported no extensive plantation economy and slavery was of limited importance.[29] As Catholics, furthermore, Spaniards were early committed to converting heathens. Informed by centuries of cross-Mediterranean intercourse with more advanced Arab and African civilizations, furthermore, Spanish and Portuguese empire builders were also more familiar with variations in human skin tones and less likely to associate them with subordination. In the New World, they intermarried extensively with natives and Africans alike.[30]

Compared to the United States, the creation of Argentina involved no sharp break with Europe.[31] The areas around the Plata River gained independence almost accidentally during the Napoleonic Wars when England invaded Buenos Aires in 1806 and Napoleon toppled the Spanish monarchy in 1808. With no revolution against Spain, nationalists in the region celebrated neither the superiority of America nor consensual citizenship. On the contrary, decades of civil wars and uncertainty about the contours of the nation preceded Argentina's final consolidation under Bartolomé Mitre and the liberals of Buenos Aires in 1862.

Writing in the middle of civil war, nationalist Domingo Sarmiento captured well his contemporaries' ambivalence about their nation and its origins. "Are we European?," he wondered, only to answer, "So many copper-colored faces prove us wrong! Are we indigenous?—The disdainful smiles of our blond ladies may give us our only answer. Of mixed race?—No one wants to be that . . ." before concluding, ". . . there are millions who would not wish to be called either American or Argentine."[32]

Like their counterparts in North America, Argentina's early nationalists were scarcely color-blind promoters of racial mixing or equality. Yet in his influential *Facundo* or, *Civilization and Barbarism*, Sarmiento portrayed Argentine nation-building not as a struggle for domination between races of differing colors but between the so-called barbarians of the pampas and the purportedly civilized who lived in the country's river valleys and coastal cities, notably Buenos Aires.[33] More important, he described both factions as racially mixed. For Sarmiento urban Africans, mulattoes and *zambos* (racially mixed peoples) all exhibited a tendency "to become civilized, and [. . .] talent and the finest instincts of progress."[34] Men of mixed descent (mestizo) were prominent military leaders on all sides of the Argentine civil wars.[35] When writing of mestizo pampas dwellers, Sarmiento attributed their barbarism to their environment (which he compared repeatedly to the deserts of Asia and Africa, calling them American bedouins), rather than to their color or descent.[36]

For early nationalists like Sarmiento, then, acquisition of a superior European civilization, more than descent from European blood, defined the Argentine nation. Argentina, like the United States, would be a nation of immigrants but Mitre, Sarmiento, and others looked to Europe, and to European immigrants, with great hope precisely because they expected them to intermarry with those of mixed blood, thus continuing biological amalgamation and uplifting the nation culturally.[37] Color was not the key concern, as it was in the United States. Sarmiento's political rival and fellow liberal, Juan Bautista Alberdi, noted mainly immigration's civilizing influence: "Who comes to our shores brings more civilization in his habits, which will be passed on to our inhabitants, than many books of philosophy . . . A hardworking man is the most edifying catechism."[38]

In the Argentine nation of immigrants, quite unlike the United States, consent to European civilization—not to republican citizenship—was the key to membership in the nation. Like the United States, Argentina opened citizenship to newcomers through male naturalization (and to all children born on Argentine soil), but it imposed onerous obligations (notably military service) without offering many rights, notably male suffrage.[39] As a result, relatively few immigrants bothered to become Argentine citizens.

On the other side of the Atlantic, Italy's nation-building had scarcely begun in 1862; the country had become independent and unified only in 1861.[40] For the previous generation, however, conflicting concepts of an Italian nation had sharply divided Italy's nationalists. Itself a colony of Spain and Austria, Italy was, as Count Metternich noted, little more than a geographic expression until the nineteenth century. From the years of the French Revolution, its earliest nationalists were romantics who imagined the Italian nation as the descendants and reproducers of a distinctive Italian culture or civilization (*civiltà*) that included medieval and Renaissance art, literature, urbanity, technology, and philosophy. (Influenced by the ideas of the secular Enlightenment, most dismissed the contributions of Catholicism to *civiltà italiana*.) Believing a national Italian government could foster a *risorgimento* or resurgence of Italian civilization, romantic nationalists viewed Italy's vast population of peasants as firmly outside the nation. "There is no case for discussing the plebes," romantic poet and nationalist Ugo Foscolo concluded "since in any form of government all they need is a plough or some other means to earn their bread, a priest and an executioner." Foscolo especially feared popular participation in the civic realm, where it "always finished in theft, blood and crime."[41] Most ethnic nationalists in Italy favored a national monarchy, perhaps guided by a constitution.

By the 1830s, republicans like Giuseppe Mazzini, the founder of both Young Italy and the international Young Europe, offered a more consensual vision of the Italian nation. Mazzini believed that political liberty was itself a central tenet of Italy's civilization.[42] He imagined a nation in which the poor could eventually find a place. In the struggles that preceded Italy's unification, and as a political exile, Mazzini advocated education for poor, usually urban, workers. He argued that plebeian volunteer soldiers under the tutelage of republicans consented to joining the nation—an idea perfected by Giuseppe Garibaldi, whose soldiers often came from humble backgrounds.[43]

The moderates who actually created Italy's state in 1861, under Piedmont's monarchy, had little patience with Mazzini's enthusiasm for peasant volunteers or worker education. In prophetic—and by now, familiar—language, an envoy sent in 1861 to the newly conquered Naples by King Vittorio Emanuele reported back, "What barbarism! Some Italy! This is Africa: the Bedouin are the flower of civil virtue compared to these peasants."[44]

Even before Darwin, then, nationalists on both sides of the Atlantic used human differences rooted in biological descent to define their new nations. All three countries understood themselves as civilized while also recognizing barbarians within their boundaries. In the Americas, nation builders were particularly conscious of color as a marker of descent, excluding Africans and natives from citizenship. But they also differentiated between a nation of citizens and the majority of the American people, representing a variety of descents and cultures. For Argentines, by contrast, the nation itself was a descent group—an amalgam through intermarriage of European immigrants and New World mestizos—inheriting its civilization from Europe. Italy's earliest nationalists, like Americans, wanted to exclude the less civilized from their nation, but viewed that nation, as Argentines did, as a descent group. Republicans in Italy resembled North Americans in making liberty an element of national civilization, an issue of less concern in Argentina. Well before Darwin, Italy had also begun to stigmatize its future emigrants while in the New World, Argentines and Americans positioned themselves to offer Italian immigrants vastly different receptions.

SCIENTIFIC RACISM AND NATION-BUILDING DURING THE MASS MIGRATIONS

Just as Italy became a nation-state and as Argentina and the United States ended their civil wars, the 1859 publication of Charles Darwin's *Origin of Species* sparked international debates among the scientific racists we now usually call social Darwinists in the English-speaking world and positivists elsewhere. Albeit in somewhat different ways, both linked a wide variety of measurable and presumed inherited physical traits (brain size, hair type, cranial shape, skin color) to the human history (which Darwin called evolution) of cultural, linguistic, and religious groups, thus consolidating the equation of race with nation. But while social Darwinists sought the engine of cultural evolution in racial competition and domination by the fittest races, positivists more often invoked Lamarckian notions of racial improvement by means of characteristics acquired through education, social intercourse, and biological amalgamation.[45]

In all three countries, scientific racism had significantly altered national self-understandings by the late nineteenth century. Creating a nation of

Italians after the country's unification in 1861 proved to be a violent and long undertaking, for as Cesare Lombroso presciently observed, "Italy is one but it is not unified."[46] Today, historians describe southern Italians' opposition to national unification as a civil war but at the time Italy's rulers dismissed attacks on state property and policemen, along with riots against draft and milling taxes, as either crime (brigandage) or criminal anarchy and rebellion, not as a rational hostility to its governance.[47] By the 1870s, Italy's ruling elite claimed to have located the problem of nation-building in the peculiarities of the Mezzogiorno (the South).[48] In the face of internal conflict and a fragile unification, republicans' demands for consensual citizenship seem downright dangerous.

Two streams of Italian positivism sought to explain the new nation's problems.[49] The first came from Italian criminology and the work of Cesare Lombroso, supported in the latter years of the century by his student and son-in-law Enrico Ferri. For forty years, Lombroso collected crime statistics, measured crania, and developed his theory that "born criminals" were biological throwbacks or atavisms to savagery. His main agenda as a public activist was to identify and isolate the born criminals present in all races.[50] No orthodox racist, Lombroso rejected anti-Semitism as unscientific, and viewed northerners and southerners as equally white.[51] Solving the problem of regional difference was never central for Lombroso, although as a young nationalist he had served as a soldier in Calabria, and he often noted the differing forms of criminality in North and South.[52] Impressed by Italians' international prominence as political assassins, Lombroso gave anarchism, as a form of criminality, as much attention as regional difference.[53]

More important in identifying racial differences between northern and southern Italians were Italy's positivist anthropologists.[54] Working from analysis of human crania, the southerner Giuseppe Sergi claimed to discover evidence of a long-headed Mediterranean race that had originated in Africa and in prehistoric times had conquered Europe as far north as Scandinavia. From northern Italy to Great Britain, Mediterraneans had then been displaced by the Aryans. Sergi dismissed them as "savages when they invaded Europe." Sergi on occasion referred to Mediterraneans as brown, to distinguish them from sub-Saharan black Africans and from white Aryans.[55]

Building on Sergi's work in an 1898 publication, Sicilian anthropologist and positivist Alfredo Niceforo caused a national furor with his own thoughts on regional variation. Unlike Sergi, Niceforo seemed ambivalent about the biological origins of southern barbarism, alternately blaming feudalism, Spanish rule, cranial anomalies, and miscegenation (with Semitic and Arab conquerors). Rather than conflate race and nation, Niceforo argued that two races had emerged "from the womb of the Italian nation," and he argued that southerners, while fine individualists, lacked the genius for cooperation typical of more highly evolved northerners.[56] Southerners were "un popolo donna" (a womanly people) in contrast to the more masculine northerners. Rather like Argentine's early nationalists, Niceforo argued that in the South "modern Italy has a high mission to fulfill and a great colony to be civilized."[57] The nation, in short, could civilize its racial barbarians, and turn them into modern men.

In the early twentieth century, a new generation of Italian nationalists took up Niceforo's plea for civilizing and masculinizing the racially backward parts of the nation. But unlike Niceforo they insisted that the Italian nation itself was a single race (*razza* or *stirpe*). Nationalist Enrico Corradini admitted that mass migration from Italy had already proved that Italians were, if not "an inferior people, at least . . . a people at an inferior stage of existence."[58] At the same time, he insisted that Italy was an imperial nation that could civilize not just its barbarian south, but also the Africa from which Sergi believed it had first emerged. In the eyes of Italian nationalists of this generation, emigration was demographic imperialism—a fertile race seeking living space.[59] Just before World War I, Italy's legislature confirmed the new nationalists' conflation of race with nation. Even as it extended suffrage to adult male peasants and workers, it granted citizenship through descent (*jus sanguinus*) to the many children born abroad of Italian men.[60]

In the Americas, where millions of Italians were working and settling by 1900, scientific racism also significantly revised Argentine and American understandings of their nations.[61] In Argentina, nationalists transformed the older expectation that European immigrants could civilize Argentina into a popular theory (later proclaimed scientific by Latin American eugenicists) that immigrants whitened the mestizo population through a process of "constructive miscegenation."[62] In sharp contrast to North Americans and to Domingo Sarmiento, but rather like Italy's youngest nationalists, Argentines like Jose Ingenieros began to speak explicitly of an amalgamated Argentine race.[63]

At the same time, however, glorification of Argentina's descent from European civilization came into question, especially as immigration from southern Europe, including Italy, rose. Social Darwinist and positivist thought alike pointed to the racial degeneration of all Latin civilizations.[64] Even a strong proponent of immigration like Alberdi had second thoughts later in the century, arguing that

> To govern is to populate . . . but with hard-working, honest, intelligent and civilized immigrants; in other words, educated. But to populate is to plague, to corrupt, to brutalize, to impoverish the richest and most salubrious nation when it is populated with immigrants from the most corrupt and backward parts of Europe.[65]

Argentines feared Italian immigration less as biological pollution than as a potential source of social disorder. Perhaps that is why the Italian positivists' division of northern from southern Italian races found little place in Argentine debates over immigration policies. Instead, scientific racists like Augusto Bunge read Niceforo to argue that "the rich race" and "the poor race" could diverge physically.[66] With the onset of industrialization in Argentina, the so-called social question—exacerbated by immigration—endangered national unity.[67]

Like Italy's leaders in the 1870s, Argentine nation builders equated social conflict and crime. Positivist criminologists soon reported that foreigners dominated among criminals.[68] Unsurprisingly, Lombroso and his theories of criminality were more influential than Niceforo's or Sergi's in shaping Argentine policy toward immigrants. Enrico Ferri toured Argentina several times, promoting his and Lombroso's ideas.[69] Italians' supposed predilection for mafia and camorra or vendettas, and—even more important—their association with political violence and anarchism ultimately drove Argentina's limited restriction of immigration.[70] In Buenos Aires, Italian immigrants were prominent as leaders and activists among anarchists and in the anarcho-syndicalist labor movement. They promoted the first general strikes and were prominent in demonstrations that often became violent street battles with urban police.[71] Argentine criminologists claimed that strikes generated criminality generally, since they appealed to the "base passions and appetites of criminals."[72]

At the same time, and in an interesting reversal, the mestizo gauchos whom Sarmiento had castigated for their purportedly bedouin life on the rural pampas became a symbol to nativist nationalists of the social harmony lost in Argentina's industrializing immigrant cities.[73] In a law of social defense, and a law of residence, passed in the twentieth century's first decade, Argentina provided for the deportation and exclusion of anarchists, and Italians dominated among those deported.[74] Nativist critics of the Buenos Aires leaders who dominated Argentine government after 1862 began to argue that the country needed protection not just from anarchists but from rapacious European capitalists as well. After World War I, populist nationalists—many of them in the Argentine military—would reject liberalism itself as inappropriate for the Argentine nation.[75] Argentina never closed its door to Italians as racially undesirable and its immigration policy remained freer than that of the supposedly more liberal United States. There, recent arrivals from Italy had to prove not their racial capacity for citizenship but their commitment to social order.

In the United States, the simultaneous end of the Civil War and the popularization of Darwin's ideas about human evolution created an explosive new version of the tension between a nation of consenting citizens and a plural American people. In the aftermath of the Civil War, the United States abolished slavery and opened citizenship first to former slaves and then more gradually to Native Americans. At the same time social Darwinism encouraged white Americans (now often calling themselves old stock) to embrace their descent from British forebears. Anglo-Saxonists emphasized that consensual citizenship itself had originated in the forests or blood of Nordic, Aryan Europe, raising new questions about which American people could join the nation.[76] The result was many dutch doors–partially open, partially closed—to citizenship.[77]

Despite the fact that constitutional amendments abolished slavery as an inherited status; opened citizenship to all children born on American soil, regardless of race, color, parentage, or previous condition of servitude; and allowed foreigners of African descent to naturalize, American understandings of the nation remained narrow after the Civil War. Granting full citizenship rights to emancipated slaves proved too revolutionary for white citizens, especially as they sought to re-incorporate the white rebels of the South.[78] From the 1880s until 1965, local, state, and even federal laws based on the racial assumptions of social Darwinism limited access to citizenship and the full rights of citizenship for former slaves, Native Americans, and new immigrants arriving from Asia, Mexico, and Europe. Color was no longer the only basis for exclusion from the nation. "One drop" rules—replete with genealogical tables in cases of judicial contestation—sought to prevent light-skinned persons from passing as full citizens. The American turn toward immigration restriction between 1870 and 1924 has also been studied exhaustively.[79]

Beginning in 1899, the United States categorized all newcomers, even Europeans, as members of thirty-six different races, including northern or southern Italians. The authors of the Dillingham Commission's *Dictionary of Races or Peoples*, published in 1911, offered a somewhat belated published explanation for these racial distinctions.[80] It distinguished between very broad-headed Alpine northern Italians and a "long-headed, dark

'Mediterranean' race of short stature" in the South, and drew the line separating the two so far north that even those from Genoa were deemed southerners.[81] Its authors drew explicitly on the work of Giuseppe Sergi, labeling southern Italians, Iberians of Spain, and the Berbers of North Africa as a single descent group originating in the so-called Hamitic stock of North Africa.[82] Following Sergi, it noted that Hamites were "not Negritic or true African, although there may be some traces of an infusion of African blood in this stock in certain communities of Sicily and Sardinia."[83] The *Dictionary of Races* raised the specter of white Europeans introducing an invisible single drop of black blood into the American nation.

Perhaps more important, the *Dictionary of Races* introduced a new term for the cultural differences–elsewhere deemed national—between races, calling them ethnical. It followed Niceforo in describing Southern Italians ethnical character, focusing on southerners' predilection for criminality (but not anarchy).[84] Brigandage, mafia and vendetta were, however, all noted by its authors as dangers to democratic citizenship. In the years during and after World War I these ethnical traits, along with the possibility of mixed blood, assumed increasing importance in nativist arguments for the restriction of Italians and other southern and eastern European immigration. The racially restrictive immigration quotas imposed on Italians in 1921 and 1924 did not exclude them from citizenship once they had entered the Unites States, but made it increasing difficult for large numbers of immigrants to enter the country in order to claim citizenship.

Scientific racism thus redefined Americans' understandings of their nation during these years. In a country already obsessed with color, the physical darkness of many Jews, Italians, and Chinese immigrants would in any case have made them seem in-between additions to the biracial American people.[85] But it was social Darwinism, not color, that made them questionable citizens of the nation. Southern Italians were especially dangerous because they might carry African blood. More generally, the fertility of white Alpine, Slavic, and Mediterranean immigrants reproduced ethnical traits that seemed dangerous to a political system now viewed as a product of evolution and of the superiority of Nordic, or Aryan, blood. Thus, while Argentine and Latin American eugenicists celebrated constructive miscegenation, the United States saw miscegenation only as mongrelization, threatening degeneracy.[86] Theorists predicted the racial suicide of the great race that had produced Anglo-Saxon civilization and consensual citizenship. Here, in immigrants' dutch door to citizenship, lay the origins of hyphenated ethnical identities within, rather than outside, the American nation.

HYPHENS, WHITENESS, AND AMERICAN MULTICULTURALISM

Scientific racism transformed the national self-understandings of all three of the most important nodes of Italy's transatlantic migration system. Argentines and Italians moved away from earlier definitions of their nations as distinctive European civilizations, and away from more consensual understandings of national belonging, to define their nations as unified races. In neither country was race understood as a color difference, but rather as a product of inheritance, descent, and biological amalgamation as positivists viewed them. In the United States, social Darwinism rooted consensual citizenship not just in whiteness (as it had been since 1790), but in the Anglo-Saxon race, thus segmenting the nation into those racially more and less fit for citizenship. As social Darwinists might have wished, access to citizenship rights was open to the races of Europe but limited opportunities to enter the United States as immigrants blocked access to citizenship even for many Europeans.

This essay suggests that the hyphenated ethnic identities of the United States are the legacy of racial exclusion from the nation as Americans defined it, not whiteness, and that they originated in state policies to enforce their exclusion.[87] The use of the term *ethnical* in the United States emerged as part of social Darwinist racial discourse, and was used for Italians in a context that justified limiting their right to enter the country, which was also their first step to claiming citizenship and membership in the civic nation.

Of course, the purportedly scientific foundations for scientific racism subsequently dissolved rather quickly in the twentieth century. By 1950 race had ceased to command respect as a scientific category, although popular notions of racial difference remained widespread after the Holocaust, even in the face of anti-imperial movements abroad and demands for civil rights by African-Americans at home.[88] The United States finally abandoned scientific racism as state policy only when it repudiated Jim Crow laws and racially discriminatory immigration policies, almost simultaneously, in 1964 and 1965.

My comparison of the racialized meanings of nation and ethnicity in three countries in a single migration system should be helpful in two ways. First, it should remind readers of this collection of essays on Italian-Americans in the United States of the long, and complex history that lurks behind American notions of communities of descent and Americans' hyphenated identities. Second, it should introduce them to the fact that discussions of race have long been international, allowing them better to grasp the particular meanings of race, nation, and ethnicity developing in the English-speaking world.

While once studies of Italian-Americans described how they became American (and acquired national identities), now most analyze instead how they became white, usually in the interwar years of the twentieth century.[89] These were years when Italian-Americans were seen as fascist as a result of their enthusiasm for Mussolini, when they began their own sometimes violent competition for housing and recreational spaces with African-Americans whose migrations were themselves sparked by immigration restriction, and when their complete assimilation into the American nation was often proclaimed.[90] From the longer historical perspective offered in this essay, it would appear that older understandings of race (as defined by color) and of nation, limited to white citizens regardless of ethnicity, reasserted themselves during these years as social Darwinism waned.

Studies of whiteness, however, still leave us with the puzzle of hyphens. Scholars have offered surprisingly diverse interpretations of white ethnicity. For some, the hyphen among whites is symbolic—a casual choice, signifying little.[91] Italians, Richard Alba once claimed, were even abandoning, rather than embracing, the hyphen after 1965.[92] Others disagree, however, arguing that ethnic Americanization or ethnicization marks national identities in the United States, even across color lines, down to the present.[93] In rather sharp contrast, legal scholar David Richards has recently argued that demands for Americanization required Italians to reject ethnicity in order to be considered white. Does the hyphen then mark Italian-American resistance to this demand, marking Italian-Americans, as Richards argues, as "nonvisible blacks?"[94]

Although I do not find Richards's concept particularly helpful (implying as it does too much commonality in Italian-American and African-American history), my comparison does suggest how scientific racism in the United States linked ethnicity to communities of biological descent. Outsiders commenting on the hyphenated identities so common in the English-speaking world are often explicit in labeling them racial expressions. That Americans do not usually see them that way is a consequence of their distinctive understandings of both race and nation, which differed from those in Italy and in Argentina before, and especially after, Darwin. Scientific racism made *ethnic*, *ethnical*, and *ethnicity* terms for discussing difference mainly where nationalists insisted that their nations were groups of consenting citizens, not the product of social and biological reproduction. In languages like Spanish, Italian, and French, *ethnicity* did not become a term for a community of descent; for Italians and Argentines nations, as races, were themselves communities of descent. Even today when Americans argue over the meaning of terms like *ethnic* or *ethnic racial*, *people*, and American *nation*, they seem unaware that for speakers of other languages, nations themselves *are* ethnic groups (and sometimes are still called races) that reproduce culture across generations, or that nationalism itself can be suspect as a form of racism.

Not surprisingly, when North American scholars write the history of Latin countries like Argentina and Brazil, they see the impact of race (that is, of color) everywhere. They discover Afro-Argentines whom Argentines claim not to see. They note the predominance of dark faces among laborers and white faces among the wealthy. And they remain puzzled when Argentines dismiss their observations and probably, in private, find them typical of American color consciousness. Latin Americans believe that by marrying across color lines, they—unlike racist North Americans—ignore descent, and thus race, *within* their nations.[95]

Because descent has historically been a more important way of defining nations outside the United States, multiculturalism is also not celebrated widely as a liberal nation-building strategy outside the English-speaking world. Argentines are not the most critical of U.S. multiculturalism, however, perhaps because citizenship has never been central to their understanding of their nation. Instead, it is French scholars who have been particularly skeptical and sharp critics of American multiculturalism, which they view as a violation of a voluntary, open, and consensual nation of citizens–a concept of the nation that they, as republicans, supposedly share with the United States. The hyphen, they suggest, continues the legacy of race and descent which they have tried to erase from the civic realm within their own nation of citizens.[96] While Americans continue to have good reason to ponder the consequences of color in their national history, this essay asks readers also to reflect on what it is they memorialize with their ethnic identities and celebrate with their visions of a multicultural nation.

CHAPTER FOUR

WALKING THE COLOR LINE

Italian Immigrants in Rural Louisiana, 1880–1910

VINCENZA SCARPACI

In his *Autobiography of Miss Jane Pittman,* Ernest J. Gaines describes the relationship of Louisiana's rural Italians and African Americans during the 1960s. Miss Jane leads plantation workers to protest segregation in Bayonne, a small town near Baton Rouge, whose courthouse until only a year before had neither a drinking fountain nor an inside bathroom for "colored." Blacks had to go down to the basement and use a toilet so filthy you "couldn't get inside the door." Miss Jane remarked how most women avoided that bathroom and instead used bathrooms in "back of town" cafés.

> Other times they would go to Madame Orsini and ask her could they use her bathroom. Madame Orsini and her husband owned a little grocery store there in Bayonne. They was very nice people, and I think they called themselves Sicilians. Everyday dagoes far as I'm concerned, but they said Sicilians, and they was very nice to colored.[1]

Why did these "everyday dagoes" display attitudes toward African Americans that differed from the general mainstream norm of racial inequity and segregation? To trace the origins of this behavior, we need to explore the experience of Sicilian immigrants in rural Louisiana between 1880 and 1910, as they worked alongside African Americans, mostly on sugar plantations but also on strawberry farms and in lumber regions.

This history of interaction has been only partially explored by scholars interested in documenting relations between immigrants and native-born black Americans. Initially, Sicilian immigrants and African Americans in rural Louisiana shared the same low socioeconomic status as wage laborers in rural industries. Regarded by the native white society as racially different and socially inferior, Sicilians interacted freely with their black coworkers while retaining their separate ethnic identity apart from both white Americans and African Americans.[2] Also, as another racialized minority in Louisiana, Sicilians occasionally suffered from forms of white violence, terror, and exclusion. Coming from a nation whose government regarded Sicilians as retarded and inferior, the immigrants arrived in the United States somewhat preconditioned to official discrimination.[3] Elsewhere, native-born white American workers often resented Italian immigrants as unwelcome competitors for jobs. However, in Louisiana, Sicilian immigrants did not threaten to replace their black coworkers on the plantations, who in turn appear to have considered Sicilians to be white, though different from native-born whites.[4] Over time, most Sicilian immigrants moved out of the wage-earner class and became agricultural and commercial entrepreneurs, an opportunity not equally accorded to African Americans. Yet, even at their new socioeconomic level, many Italians continued to interact with their former coworkers as providers of goods and services and, in some instances, as employers. During this period of transition, Sicilian immigrants and African Americans developed a relationship that allowed some interaction and cooperation which modified, to some extent, the rigid boundaries of segregation and the blatant injustices of the Jim Crow system.[5]

This essay argues that while Sicilian immigrants complied with the outward signs of Louisiana's racist practices, their behavior fell short of strict adherence. Instead, they followed their own traditions of economic individualism and chose self-sufficiency. Especially telling are the "gray areas"—those spaces where the immigrants' enlightened self-interest and self-identity served to modify the full extent of discrimination in their personal, everyday interaction with African Americans.

The period 1880–1910 constitutes the time frame from the first organized recruitment of Sicilian immigrants to the highest level of Sicilian settlement in rural Louisiana. From the 1880s into the first decade of the twentieth century, thousands of Italians (the vast majority of whom were Sicilian) came to Louisiana to labor in the sugar fields during the *zuccarata* (cane harvest season). Many followed the trade routes that brought citrus fruit and immigrants from Palermo to New Orleans. From 1890 to 1907, most ship arrivals in New Orleans from Italy occurred between September and December, to coincide with cane harvesting. Moreover, reporters noted that many of these steerage passengers already had been in America.[6] Immigrants came to the sugar fields not only from far-off central and north-central Sicily, but also from New York, St. Louis, Kansas City, Chicago, and nearby New Orleans. Although most of this migration remained seasonal, with various estimates placing the annual floating population from thirty thousand to eighty thousand,[7] some Italians settled permanently in rural Louisiana, either in the sugar parishes or in the truck-farming and berry-producing areas along transportation corridors connected to New Orleans. Fewer immigrants settled in the lumber mill and cotton-growing areas of the state.[8]

Some Sicilian workers followed a step migration—first to New York or Chicago and then, on a seasonal basis, to Louisiana's cane harvest. Vincent Lamantia, a labor agent in New Orleans who had served as American consul in Catania, illustrated this steady stream of workers in his 1891 letter to Father Bandini of the St. Raphael Society. Lamantia directed Bandini to send fifty Italians for whom he had secured jobs for the sugar-making season with an option to remain year round. He continued, "I have already orders for 1000 more, having filled others for 700 and I could employ 5000 had I the place to procure them from."[9]

State officials and sugar planters encouraged Sicilians to settle in southeastern Louisiana parishes already characterized by a mixture of ethnic groups and a heritage of Roman Catholicism. They regarded immigrant labor as a remedy to their reliance upon native African American plantation workers, whom they characterized as less productive, unreliable, and undependable. In the February 1889 issue of the *Louisiana Planter and Sugar Manufacturer*, sugar planter Gleason of McManor plantation, Ascension Parish, lamented the shortage of field hands, which, he argued, necessitated his search for "Dagoes" on the lower coast. It appeared that planters desired eventually to replace native black workers with foreign workers.[10]

In a variety of ways, the arrangements available for agricultural labor in Louisiana—both sharecropping and wage labor—paralleled that of Sicily. While the majority of Sicilians who came to Louisiana originated in the grain producing areas of western and central Sicily, they were familiar with the system of large landholdings where laborers operated as day laborers, salaried workers, and sharecroppers. Peasants borrowed from the middlemen (the *gabellotti*) who leased the land from the landowners and then sublet to the peasants. Rarely were day laborers paid only in money.[11] In the United

States, however, they confronted different conditions. Italian government officials, alarmed by the cases of ill-treatment and peonage originating mostly in southern cotton regions, insisted that immigrants could not be "Negroes with white skin."[12] This provocative phrase suggests how Italian officials redefined Sicilians in America. In Italy, Sicilians were viewed by the primarily northern elite as racially other. Many northern Italians gave credence to the newly emerging positivist school of anthropology and sociology which argued that "backward" social and economic conditions in the southern Italian provinces were evidence of the inhabitants' racial inferiority. American employers, policymakers, and others, elaborated upon these perceptions and thought Sicilians physically distinctive from northern Europeans and therefore well-suited to working those low-wage jobs generally reserved for African Americans. Some scholars suggest that this legacy of racism in Italy prepared Sicilians for the racism they encountered in the United States.[13]

How did the Louisiana experience differ from life in Sicily? Racism in Italy created imposing socioeconomic barriers for most peasants. At least on Louisiana sugar plantations, poor and exploited peasants believed they could possibly earn enough money for their personal objectives, which they could not do in Sicily.[14] However, in Louisiana the immigrants became a target of a racial system that applied prejudice at two levels. The first level associated those who worked or mingled with blacks as inferior and suspect. The second level condemned Italian immigrant behavior that did not fit the expectations of a capitalist society.[15]

On the plantations, Italians lived and worked alongside African Americans. In this setting they developed a way of living that was neither intimate nor hostile. Planters entering operation costs in their time books often relegated the immigrants to an "in-between" category, separating Sicilians from both blacks and whites. There were no obvious pay-scale differences between groups doing the same tasks, as is noted in this 1896 newspaper account:

> . . . it is a mistake to assert or assume that these Italians are willing to work for lower wages than are paid to colored laborers. Inquiry of several of the leading planters of this section elicits the information that in no instance have the wages of their Italian hands been less than those of their colored employees, and the only case where any distinction was made was the granting of a small advance on one plantation to a gang of choice Italian cane shed hands who were particularly industrious and efficient.[16]

However, not all comparisons between the two groups of workers were favorable for the Italians. One planter, Rudolph Comeaux, speaking at a meeting of the Sugar Planters' Association in 1900, preferred "Negro labor to dago." However, since he had "no choice" but to work with "dagoes," he hoped to train the younger ones to use plow teams. Other planters at this meeting disagreed with Comeaux's belief, and maintained that Italians learned to plow if they were taught.[17]

It seemed only natural that the combination of an increase in the number of Italian workers on the plantations and sugar planters' praise of their work habits would arouse resentment and hostility among African Americans. In this context, they might have regarded the immigrants as a wage depressant because of their reported high productivity rate. If African Americans believed that this difference would encourage planters to "speed up" the work routine, open conflict might have occurred. Yet no such labor conflicts on the sugar plantations surface in the literature. Instead, the evidence indicates that both immigrant and African American workers moved in and out of the cane fields. For example, Donna Gabaccia discovered that not just unattached men from Sambuca, but also year-round employees moved every year or two, even after 1900. In addition, considerable numbers of sugar parish workers returned to Sicily, including those who had worked year round in family groups.[18] A somewhat similar pattern of mobility characterized African American cane workers, who moved from one sugar plantation to another or from adjacent cotton-growing and rural regions. This fluidity of labor developed during Reconstruction, when African Americans exercised their option to move about freely.[19]

Rather than vie against each other for jobs as plantation workers, African Americans and immigrants responded to the U.S. economy's highs and lows, as well as to the attractions of higher wages in other industries and locations. While black workers moved to urban areas such as New Orleans or to lumber mills in Louisiana, Mississippi, and Texas, Italian immigrants responded to geographically broader labor markets that funneled European immigrant workers to jobs in the Northeast and Midwest.[20] The depression in wages that occurred in 1895, in part as a result of the repeal of the McKinley Tariff's sugar bounty provision, also motivated Italians to quit plantation work, and their departure appeared to forestall tension and competition in a shrinking labor market. According to one local newspaper—which often referred disparagingly to both African Americans and Italians—the remaining African American labor force had no alternative but to accept the cut: "Sambo has contented himself with the 20 per cent cut in his wages; not so the Dago.

The latter is not in great demand this season and a number are returning to their "Sunny Italy," others are being replaced by Negroes wherever possible."[21] This migration accelerated after 1900, when planters observed the tendency of Italians to desert the cane fields when the crop was laid out in the summer, to secure employment on railroads and in the cities of the North and Midwest, where there was a big demand and higher wages of $1.80 per day, and often prior immigrant settlement. By 1910, fewer immigrants, representing only 35 percent of the state's Italians, lived in the sugar parishes.[22]

Italian immigrants often voted with their feet when faced with unsatisfactory working conditions. With family and ethnic networks to jobs in northern and eastern U.S. locales, Italians were able to exercise an option the native black southerners in sugar regions were less able to follow, at least before 1910. Certainly the fact that many Italian workers were males separated from families in Sicily gave the immigrants a greater range of options compared to native African Americans with long established family ties in Louisiana. In addition, the Sicilians who remained in rural Louisiana often followed the same incentives as those who stayed behind in Sicily: they moved out of the landless category by using sharecropping or leasing arrangements as a means to proprietorship with the purchase of land or a small business.[23] While most of the planters continued to praise the productivity of the immigrants, Sicilians never outnumbered and only supplemented their native black American coworkers in the cane fields, even though contemporaries noted the out-migration of blacks from rural to urban/industrial areas.[24]

Sugar planters in the 1870s and 1880s also complained about African American resistance to the employer-dominated wage system, as plantation workers initiated strike actions that disrupted cane harvesting. In 1881, accounts of black and white rioters demanding higher wages in St. Bernard Parish led Louisiana Governor Louis Wiltz to instruct the sheriff to use all legal means to stop rioters. Again in 1887, a larger, more violent, and integrated sugar workers' strike organized by the Knights of Labor resulted in the massacre of thirty African Americans in Thibodeaux. Unfortunately, we do not know if Sicilians participated in these organized labor actions.[25]

We do know that Italian immigrants did have a tradition of protest on sugar plantations. In 1891, for example, Planter Thomas Supple of Iberville Parish discharged his Italian workers who were trying to organize in order to control the cane shed work. In 1895, when the manager of Coulon Plantation in Lafourche Parish told his Italian workers that he could not pay their wages because his property was under seizure, the laborers first threatened, and then burned down, the sugar house. In addition, Italians working for Hermitage Planting Company in Ascension asked for higher wages in 1896. When turned down, they quit. Other forms of retaliation arising out of work grievances resulted in personal attacks by Italians against the overseers who mistreated them.[26]

In terms of interethnic alliances among workers, we know that in the lumber fields of northwest Louisiana, Italians, African Americans, Mexicans, and others participated in the Industrial Workers of the World-affiliated Brotherhood of Timber Workers' strike actions in 1912 and 1913. Covington Hall, a labor organizer and editor of the union journal, described a labor demonstration near Carson, Louisiana, in which African Americans and members of the "Latin race"—which included Italians and Mexicans—"put Southern whites to shame with their militancy."[27] South Lumber Operators Association member John Henry Kirby viewed this demonstration from the corporate side and observed that the Brotherhood received support from "negroes [*sic*], dagoes, and other foreigners who are socialists made at heart through the oppressive institutions of the countries from which they come."[28] This episode in multiethnic solidarity suggests that collective action across divisive lines did occur.

On the plantations, Sicilians and African Americans lived and socialized together, and they appear to have accommodated to each other's lifestyles without difficulty. They lived side by side in quarters provided by the planters. For example, the Brocatos, who came to Louisiana from Cefalù, Sicily, described Italian, African American, and French workers eating and living together without any hostility on Raceland Plantation at the turn of the twentieth century. In addition, the squads working in the fields contained both immigrants and blacks. Sometimes an African American served as hoe gang boss without incurring any resentment from the Italian workers in the crew. The Brocatos also noted that it was not unusual for a black family to live next to an Italian family. Similarly, a 1900 account of roommates Charles Morana and Salvadore Ricza, noted that they lived in a double house with African American workers at Deer Range Plantation on the lower coast.[29]

Moreover, an outbreak of smallpox among African Americans in 1900 on the Germania Plantation in Ascension Parish did not frighten their immigrant Italian coworkers. Although the two groups worked and lived together on the sugar plantation, the immigrants had been vaccinated before arriving in the United States. However, five years later, during a yellow fever epidemic, medical observers maintained that Italian workers in the sugar region, considered "carriers" of the disease, infected their black coworkers because both groups practiced the social custom of visiting their sick neighbors. In the sugar parish towns, these same observers believed that Italian fruit vendors, who employed a staff of several "Negro boy hangers-on," provided other sources for the spread of the dreaded fever.[30]

Indeed, it appears that Italian immigrants and African Americans often supported each other in times of trouble and loss. When three Italians were lynched in Hahnville on August 6, 1896, by a mob of sugar planters, African Americans expressed sympathy for the victims: "A large number of Negroes and Italians were present at the burial, and went home from the scene almost terror-stricken," one scholar has noted. Some whites even feared that African Americans would aid Italians in seeking revenge.[31] The concern that whites had for what they called a "co-mingling" is evident in many documents. For example, on the Belair Plantation, Ignacio Cogmen, a Sicilian immigrant and "model laborer" of fifteen years in the cane fields, earned a reputation among whites of "[mingling] in the cane field with other laborers and [being] friendly with the Negroes and his countrymen." Local whites also noted when Italian Alfred Belloni attended a "Negro ball" held at Crescent Plantation near Houma in 1900.[32]

African American views reveal another layer of the story. When an Italian immigrant family enrolled its two children in a private school for "Negroes," Mary Cook, the Monroe, Louisiana, African American schoolteacher, said that she did not know that she was doing anything wrong in letting "white" children attend school along with the black pupils. Cook's use of "white" to describe the Italian children suggests a number of meanings. While African Americans often shared some common ground with immigrants, they were also fully aware that the newcomers were in many ways "white on arrival."[33] In addition, some African American leaders and newspapers reacted negatively to the efforts of southern states to attract laborers from Europe, and specifically Italians, to the South. Their concerns seem to echo the "racial" prejudices of the southern and northern native white community, which did not value southern Italians, and depicted Sicilians as an inferior race—unclean, illiterate, disease-ridden, and inclined towards violence and crime.[34] It is important to note that the African American press very often represented middle-class attitudes and did not always focus on the opinions of the mass of the semiliterate working class. Many of the views expressed in studies of the African American press have relied on papers far removed from Louisiana or even the South.[35] Moreover, there are contrasting accounts. Alfred Stone, for example, "documented" the superiority of immigrant labor over African American labor on cotton plantations and reinforced the planters' belief that the Italian worked harder and sacrificed everything to accumulate savings. His writing provoked responses from the black press urging white southerners to support their traditional, seasoned, and hardworking pool of black workers.[36] African American spokesmen also countered this image of the Italian "model" work ethic with reminders to white southern planters that blacks worked harder for less money and spent it locally, in contrast to Italians, who sent "all" their money home.[37]

Overall, black plantation workers appear not to have been threatened by their Italian coworkers. Unlike in the cotton-producing areas, where all workers faced the dangers of peonage and other forms of control, which created a setting of competition between groups of laborers or tenants, in Louisiana's sugar fields black plantation workers did not compete with Italians. This was partly due to the fact that the immigrant labor flow at its highest point did not come close to replacing black labor and because of the lack of daily hostility between the groups.[38] This absence of conflict between native black Americans and Italian workers seems striking in the context of Louisiana's rural labor market.

In part, this appears to have been the case because Italian immigrants had less to gain by following the parameters of racist behavior in Louisiana. Instead, they chose to follow enlightened self-interest in all things, including race matters. They sought neither complete intimacy with African Americans or native-born whites, but they did not reject either. Studies that document the odyssey of European immigrants from racial others to white ethnics have stressed an evolution of cultural and racial assimilation in which the immigrant group chooses to "become white" in order to reap the benefits of a racist America. While there is evidence that Italian government officials and some Italian American politicians made a point to distance immigrants from African Americans in Louisiana's social system, Italian laborers in Louisiana seemed to believe differently, at least before 1910.[39]

Italians in 1880–1910 rural Louisiana did not view their social world as white and black, but identified themselves instead as members of Sicilian towns and regions with a nationality, gender, class, and race, as distinct as Irish or Polish.[40] In this period, Sicilian immigrant marriage and residence patterns in Louisiana followed an internal ethnic village and regional preference. Since nine out of every ten immigrants during this period were Sicilian and originated in a cluster of towns in the central and western provinces, the newcomers re-created a close-knit social setting.[41] In Louisiana, then, the Sicilians' world remained focused on their village. Relations with other groups were secondary, albeit interactive. Immigrants chose to walk a fine line between full adherence to native white values and similar caste status with African Americans as a largely landless proletariat. As long as Sicilians remained in the migratory workforce, they were vulnerable to both class prejudice and xenophobia. This surfaced during the outbreaks of crime involving Italians in Louisiana during the 1890s; in the vigilante violence of white southerners against Italian immigrants, which continued into the 1920s; and during the yellow fever epidemics of 1871 to 1905. Many whites also condemned certain aspects of the foreigners' lifestyles, values, and economic achievement, and they expressed their negative opinions publicly or in the veiled actions of socioeconomic exclusion.[42]

However, as Italian plantation laborers moved up the socioeconomic ladder into private enterprise between 1900 and 1910, they left behind much of the low status they had shared with their African American coworkers. Their own experience with racism led the immigrants to modify their foreign habits and adapt to the outward rules of white southern prejudice.[43] The first phase of this movement into private enterprise coincided with planter efforts to stabilize the labor supply by establishing tenantry systems. In fact, the Louisiana Agriculture and Immigration Association in 1907 translated and published pamphlets such as "An Invitation to Louisiana for Italian Tenant Farmers and Agriculturists," which stressed the potential of a farmer becoming his own boss in exchange for half the harvest.[44] In December 1901, John Pharr, a St. Mary Parish planter, wrote to Ciro Lampo of Patterson, Louisiana, requesting Italian tenants who had been in the United States for some years, spoke English, and had money to finance their tenantry.[45] Immigrants who were members of the landless proletariat in Sicily viewed tenantry as a step toward the self-determination and landownership status they sought in coming to the United States.

The 1900 census listings documented another important shift for immigrant laborers as plantation owners preferred families as permanent employees. Families, occasionally with a boarder, substantially outnumbered all-male households in sugar parishes by 1900. The planter Rudolph Comeaux, who had earlier scorned "dago" labor, contracted in 1902 with several Italian families to work part of his Medora plantation in cotton, furnishing the land, teams, implements, and getting half of the produce. He thought the arrangement would succeed, since he observed how all members of the Italian family worked their land.[46]

Yet another shift in plantation economic arrangements during this period occurred as planters seemed ready to offer the immigrants tenantry options and outright purchase, in order to guarantee a stable and adequate labor force. As planters increased their profits by mechanizing sugar processing to produce a higher-quality product, they could sustain financial solvency only by operating their sugar mills on a round-the-clock basis, fed by large plantations and smaller farms. For example, planter Jules Godchaux, owner of a number of plantations in St. John, Jefferson, Orleans, and Lafourche parishes, encouraged Italian laborers on his Reserve Plantation to become tenants. They raised cane and sold it to the Godchaux family's sugar mill. As soon as they saved enough money, Godchaux's tenants purchased land. The immigrant landowners eventually formed a colony called Virgin Mary, located at Bonnecarre Crevasse. This community even received acclaim from official Italian observers.[47]

Numerous references to successful Italian tenants and farmers in the sugar-growing area of the state raises the question if any such opportunities were available to African Americans. We do know that white violence against African American private enterprise became more ongoing and widespread during this period.[48] Rodrigue's study of labor in sugar country during Reconstruction mentions the existence of both white tenant farmers and black sharecroppers who employed black labor. In both cases however, planters reserved the right to decide how to harvest the crop. Sitterson also mentions that white tenants in sugar country hired African American workers during the 1880–1910 period. In addition, most scholars note that land in the sugar region was too expensive for anyone with limited means to purchase, and that planters preferred to retain their holdings.[49] To date, no in-depth study that focuses specifically on African American laborers on sugar plantations during the 1880–1910 period is available to give us a glimpse into their experience.

It appears, however, that Italian immigrants were able to move into commercial enterprises, particularly as peddlers, shop owners, and saloon keepers, in a distinct manner. Enterprising individuals like Bernard Mistretta, peddler and importer in Ascension Parish, sold olive oil and some foodstuffs to Sicilians on plantations. Mistretta reciprocated this favor by supplying laborers from Corleone for the sugar planters.[50] Many other sources document the proliferation of Italian businesses in sugar parish communities. Moreover, references in newspapers from towns throughout the sugar region document that Italian saloons; fruit, produce, confectionery, and grocery stores; restaurants; boardinghouses; hotels; and tailor shops prospered.[51]

The Italians who filled a market niche by selling supplies to their conationals and other workers on the sugar plantations did not experience opposition from planters. Typically in the sugar regions, plantation-owned stores did not operate as monopolistically as such enterprises did in much of the cotton-raising sections. In 1902, sugar planters complained that it was difficult to keep Italians in the cane fields for more than two seasons, for "by that time they have laid by a little money and are ready to start a fruit shop or a grocery store at some cross-roads town."[52] Thus, by reaching out to consumers in the larger community, Italian businesses established a broad-based clientele. Italian entrepreneurs in turn encouraged agricultural enterprise among their co-nationals. Interestingly, the same Bernard Mistretta who peddled products to immigrants on the plantations served as first vice president in 1910 of the truck growers' association in Donaldsonville. Most of its members were Italian.[53]

One is particularly struck by the large number of "colored saloon" licenses granted Italians in the sugar parishes, revealing that Italian immigrant businesses generally serviced both Italian immigrant and black patrons.[54] Italian immigrants who did not have the capital to establish themselves as store proprietors, one observer noted, "strap packs and peddle blue-jeans, overalls and red handkerchiefs to the Negroes."[55] An observer from Plaquemine, Iberville Parish, noted in 1890, "Our town is flooded with melons, but strange to say none have been raised about here. They are imported by the 'dago' fruit vendors, who find ready sale for them among the darkies."[56]

Targeting his trade to African American customers served two purposes for the Italian retailer/peddler. A "colored" establishment might not rate much prestige in a segregated society, yet it provided a market niche for the immigrant willing to maintain socioeconomic ties with the black community. In addition, native whites, for the most part, might not consider such enterprises competitive and threatening to their commercial hegemony, and may have granted the foreigners this inroad in a noblesse oblige fashion.[57] Sicilian laborers in rural Louisiana often followed this trajectory from wage-earner class to sharecropper and tenant, and then sugarcane or truck farmer, saloon keeper, and retail store owner. While some remained in the sugar parishes, others by the turn of the century settled into the truck-farming and berry-growing enterprises located in parishes adjacent to or along railroad routes linked to New Orleans.

Migration of Italian laborers into the berry-growing areas of the Florida parishes of Louisiana, especially Tangipahoa, began in 1890 when a native white farmer in Independence brought an Italian family in to harvest his crop. Soon a pattern emerged of Italian laborers leaving the cane fields at the end of the season in March and moving into Tangipahoa Parish to pick berries. Some African Americans from Tangipahoa Parish also followed the harvest season from cane to berries. Once the berry harvest was over, Italian workers returned to New Orleans, the Midwest, or northeastern cities, until the cane harvesting season began again in December.[58]

In contrast to the sugar region, Italian immigrants in Tangipahoa had access to marginal and cutover lands where they established their own farms. Also, work in the strawberry fields allowed children of both sexes, from at least the age of eight, to earn money for the family. By 1910, the end of the in-migration period, both native-born whites and blacks, as well as immigrants, employed black labor. [59] The dynamics of Italian farm owners supervising African American employees in both the sugar and the berry growing regions remains unexplored. Yet, we do know that as more Italians engaged in strawberry cultivation, the industry became Tangipahoa's major agricultural enterprise. Ice factories, canneries, box and veneer factories, banks, and truck farmers' and growers' associations formed as ancillaries to this burgeoning industry. In areas such as Independence, the majority of storekeepers were Italians by 1910.[60]

The road to success was not always smooth for Italian entrepreneurs. In July 1899, five Italians were lynched by local whites in the rural town of Tallulah, Madison Parish. While the immediate cause of the trouble developed from tensions between a white doctor and his Italian neighbors (whose goat frequently climbed up on his porch, disturbing his sleep), some observers saw other motives. A report by the Italian consul agent N. Piazza noted that a plot hatched against the Difatta brothers, "among rival storekeepers and others, from a spirit of rivalry in trade, and from a desire to prevent the Italians from voting," worked to incite angry townspeople to violate the law. In addition, the Difattas' brother-in-law, Guiseppe Defina, who ran a store a few miles distant in Millikens Bend, was also threatened with violence if he did not leave town. It seems that whites in Louisiana permitted Sicilian immigrants their own businesses only when they did not threaten white interests. [61] When Italian officials investigating the lynching spoke with Joe Evans, an African American who had been formerly employed by Frank Difatta, he said he could identify the lynchers. However, Louisiana Governor Murphy Foster chose not to follow up upon Evans's testimony, and Secretary of State John Hay told the Italian authorities that he was unable to overrule the U.S. dual system of state and federal jurisdiction and intervene in the matter. The grand jury of Madison Parish later declared its inability to discover the names of the lynchers.[62]

African Americans in the South did not benefit from a proactive government intervention on their behalf in times of trouble. The Italian government petitioned U.S. authorities under treaty rights to obtain indemnities for the Italian nationals' wrongful deaths. Yet Italian officials could not claim indemnities for immigrants who had filed their papers for U.S. citizenship. As *The Crisis*, the newspaper published by the National Association for the Advancement of Colored People, noted, the privilege of American citizenship gave to all African Americans and to some Italian immigrants "the inalienable right of every free American citizen to be lynched," without recourse to redress.[63]

Italians faced numerous kinds of discrimination that could be designated as racially as well as economically motivated. When a recession in the lumber industry brought a drop in work and wages in the Tangipahoa town of Kentwood, fifty to sixty white men "decreed that the Italians would have to leave Kentwood under pain of death." They sent a committee of twelve to the Italian section to convey the message and to threaten to blow up the homes of Italians who did not leave town. About twenty families left for New Orleans.[64] Native-born white farmers also acted to exclude "outsiders" from their associations. In 1914, the White Farmers Association of Ponchatoula specifically forbade membership to Italians, Sicilians, Japanese, Chinese, Mongolians, Asiatics, Africans, or descendants of African farmers.[65] With only an incomplete picture of the Louisiana experience, scholars have failed to understand how Italians occupied a status that was neither black nor white, even as they moved out of the class of wage earners to become entrepreneurs.

Louisiana's sugar parish politics provides yet another example of the way in which the complexities of citizenship and civic participation impacted Italian immigrant and African American voters differently over time. Much has been made of the political activity in Louisiana that culminated in 1898 with the disenfranchisement of African Americans and the retention of the Italian immigrant vote. An 1879 state law granted the vote only to those immigrants who had declared their intention to become citizens. Both this earlier law and the 1898 constitutional action could be seen as additional evidence that Italian immigrants benefited from American racism. However, the story is more complex. A review of the literature shows variations in urban and rural voting patterns. Louisiana's candidates courted votes from both Italians and African Americans. While one African American newspaper condemned the New Orleans Democratic Club's voting the "dagoes" for their candidate Francis Nicholls in 1887, other "colored" Democratic clubs and black-operated Democratic newspapers also supported Nicholls.[66] In the sugar parishes, planters used their "influence" and money to induce Italian and African American workers in the 1884, 1886, and 1888 elections to support Democratic candidate Edward Gay, a prominent Iberville planter who chose to run against the Republican incumbent, William Kellogg, for the 3rd Congressional District seat. This coalition, sweetened with planters' money, also rallied immigrants and African Americans to support the candidacy of Murphy Foster, a sugar planter from St. Mary's Parish, and a reform Democrat for governor, in 1892.[67] Once in office, Murphy Foster proposed a suffrage amendment as early as 1894, to use educational and property qualifications to eliminate the African American vote, and thus eliminate the "tool" that divided whites into "bitter camps."

Louisiana voters decided the issue in 1896.[68] Italians joined with Populists to protest the disfranchisement of both themselves and African Americans. In March 1896 they paraded under the Italian flag in New Orleans. Foster's opponent for governor, John Pharr, a Bayou Teche sugar planter who had Italian tenants, supported an antilynching plank that appealed to African Americans and Italians still reeling from the Hahnville lynchings of that year, in which three Italians met their deaths at the hands of angry planters.[69] Despite Pharr supporters' charges of election irregularities, Foster won. Although Louisianans failed to approve the voter restrictions, the state legislature passed a law in June 1896 that for all intents and purposes established a mechanism to deny blacks the vote; it also called for a constitutional convention in 1898 to establish this system permanently. While Foster opposed African American suffrage, he made no attempt to eliminate the urban Sicilian vote that had supported the Democratic machine and its ward politics in New Orleans. Therefore, a special provision was introduced to protect the foreign vote. Louisianans named this loophole the "dago clause." No foreigner "who was naturalized prior to the first day of January, 1898, shall be denied the right to register and vote . . . by reason of his failure to possess the education or property qualifications." [70]

The public expressed views that illustrated conflicting opinions concerning Italian immigrants' political participation. Some, like the editors of the *Daily Picayune*, questioned the value of allowing uneducated and unpropertied immigrants to vote. They lumped the corrupt and ignorant "dagoes" together with African Americans: "If there is any difference between them it is largely in the 'darkies' favor, if we may judge the quality now being imported here as plantation laborers."[71] On the other hand, John Dymond, a

Plaquemines Parish sugar planter who served in the state legislature, defended the "dago clause." Dymond claimed the distinction of being the first planter to employ a Sicilian laborer, Antonio Masacha, on his Belair Plantation in 1870. He noted that "They [Sicilians] nearly all voted the Democratic ticket, and were good citizens. They came from Sicily, which had been the battle ground for liberty for thousands of years."[72]

The concept of "in-between" has been used most recently by scholars to explain this complex position that not only Sicilian immigrants, but others from southern and eastern Europe, occupied in the U.S. racial structure. This understanding draws upon John Higham's classic study *Strangers in the Land*, which viewed the interaction of ethnic groups from the outside in by analyzing contemporary theories of race and nativism. Higham ably described the ebb and flow of America's attitudes toward newcomers within the context of economic conditions, social and scientific theories, and political ideology, such as imperialism. His synthesis, published in 1955, before the bulk of in-depth case studies of southern and eastern European immigrants, searched for common threads in disparate locales and circumstances.[73] Since then, scholars have examined how European immigrants first encountered, and then accommodated to, U.S. racism. The analyses of historians such as James Barrett and David Roediger argue that overall, immigrants generally distanced themselves from African Americans as they gained privileges reserved for native whites. In searching for a broad overview, their theory leaves unexplained the complicated way in which Italians experienced race in Louisiana and reinforces the importance of looking closely at local conditions to measure the relevance of this concept.[74]

In Louisiana, while Italians did move along the trajectory from "in-betweeness" toward social acceptance by shedding some of their outwardly different cultural practices,[75] their conformance to the dominant system was one of compliance to the outward forms, and not necessarily the full weight of racism.[76] While Italian immigrants left wage labor behind, they did not achieve full social equity until the early 1960s, when they discontinued their Virgilian Society of New Orleans because they had been finally invited to join American Carnival Balls with native white membership during Mardi Gras celebrations.[77] The complex history of relations between Italians and African Americans in rural Louisiana invites scholars to reexamine immigrant adaptation to U.S. racism.[78]

Contemporary observations of how Italians in the South modified social behavior toward their black neighbors appear to span the time period from the early 1900s to midcentury. Charles Johnson's classic *Growing Up in the*

Black Belt, published in 1941, described the cross-ethnic interactions along the Yazoo River in Bolivar County, Mississippi (which borders Louisiana). There David Freeman, an African American who sharecropped from an African American farmer renting from a white man, lived across the road from an Italian renter family. Mr. Freeman noted that their families were "'good friends." They often ate together "right in their own house," and their two little boys "play fine." Yet Freeman also sensed a limit to this openness. He did not allow his son to go alone to the Italian neighbor's house, even though it was acceptable for the Italian boy to come to his house. He explained: "They treat us good so far, but we don't know what is to come. If the boy goes over to the Italian's house and something happens . . . maybe the Italian man might say something he didn't like. I'd know what to do . . . I'd come home, but the boy, he wouldn't know what to do." Freeman understood that these rural Italians had not adopted native white identities fully, but that such a process was very possible.[79]

Italians forged a path of enlightened self-interest and self-identification that modified their development of discrimination in their personal, everyday interactions with African Americans that extended well into the twentieth century. African Americans in Miss Jane Pittman's Louisiana continued to make distinctions between "every day dagoes" and white folks as they had in plantation days. How did Sicilians learn race in Louisiana? James Barrett has demonstrated how European immigrants learned racial attitudes from "older, more Americanized workers."[80] It is clear that rural Louisiana offered two sets of "teachers": both blacks and whites educated immigrants about what it meant to become American. We can hope that future scholars will continue to explore these local nuances which suggest that Italian immigrants in Louisiana did not always behave like "white folks."

PART II

RADICALISM AND RACE

CHAPTER FIVE

MAKING THE ITALIAN OTHER

Blacks, Whites, and the Inbetween in the 1895 Spring Valley, Illinois, Race Riot

CAROLINE WALDRON MERITHEW

In August 1895, African American newspapers across the United States focused their readers' attention on Spring Valley, Illinois, a small coal-mining town one hundred miles southwest of Chicago. On August 5, a mob of Spring Valley's new immigrants (Italians, Poles, Germans, French, Lithuanians, and members of other ethnic groups) attacked the African American community. The rioters ransacked homes; assaulted men, women, and children; and fired shots at residents who fled in fear. At a moment when Reconstruction era rights were recoiling and Jim Crow segregation became entrenched, blacks were particularly concerned with the "race conflict" at Spring Valley. Collapsing the nationality of the rioters, an incensed reporter for the *Richmond Planet* wrote, "The Southern bourbon Negro-hater is not present in Illinois, but the Italian has arisen in his stead."[1] Topeka's *Weekly Call* stated that the "dago rioters, anarchists, rebellionists and assassins" had taken over the town. Even more troublesome to the editors was the fact that Governor John P. Altgeld refused to protect "the rights of citizens of his state" after blacks in Chicago had telegrammed him demanding that he do so. "The wolves have killed all the sheep, congratulate the wolf," the paper sarcastically stated. The *Weekly Call* made a clear distinction between citizens and the immigrant "other" to formulate a type of nativist hierarchy that, the editors hoped, might undermine the black/white race paradigm that was at the root of African American oppression in the United States:

> We believe we should welcome every good citizen from the old world among us. But when the slum of scum of the old world lands on our shores and brings with him low, vicious murderous habits, and attempts to strike down the rights of American citizens, whether black or white, he should be put behind the bars or exiled and sent back to his native country if it takes the whole United States army to do it. The rights of American citizens who love their country and obey the laws thereof, are more sacred than the rights of any murderous lawbreaking dago the Almighty has ever made or ever will make.[2]

Just as blacks were challenging racism by attempting to shift focus away from race to citizenship after the riot, Italians were categorizing themselves both ethnically and racially. Chicago's Italian-language newspaper, *L'Italia*, depicted the community by combining national identification (Italianness) with a pan-European whiteness. Highlighting the bonds between new immigrants, the paper reminded readers that blacks "threatened the life of not only the Italians but of all the whites and their families" in Spring Valley.[3]

This essay takes the Spring Valley race riot and observes how blacks, Italians, and other new immigrants attempted to empower themselves and lay claim to status at the "nadir" of race relations in this country.[4] The events leading up to the riot, the assault on the African-American community, and the aftermath of the attack led to vocal outcries against oppression. What constituted oppression, however, was open to interpretation. Furthermore, no group defined itself, or its other, in isolation. Rather, each side responded to the rhetoric of its "opponents" as well as of middle-class whites who became involved in the episode. The riot, then, became a type of social prism in which the meaning and consequences of racial prejudice refracted into clusters of nationality, ethnicity, and class.

Though scholars have overlooked the Spring Valley race riot—perhaps due to the dominance of large urban spaces in social history as well as the failure to incorporate foreign-language sources in the studying of race relations—the violence, in what today seems like a remote coal town, resonated with U.S. residents (native- and foreign-born) across the country.[5] Spring Valley's race riot provided the medium through which distinct groups, inside and outside the mining community itself, identified themselves and others, as well as expressed what belonging to the Republic meant in the last years of the nineteenth century.

The riot is important because it alerts us to the fact that, in the 1890s, the constellation of racial divides in the United States were not fixed. Italians and new immigrants racialized themselves in opposition to the racialization of blacks. Their racial position was complicated by the fact that the meaning of race was both intensifying and fracturing at the turn of the century. As Linda Gordon has argued, "The idea of race was becoming sharper and more stable—what varied were the meanings, numbers, and labels of these 'races.'" By 1911, the Dillingham Immigration Commission defined forty-five different racial groups based on what today we would term nationality.[6] The multitiered racial hierarchy allowed men and women many others.[7] Moreover, groups that shared a negative reference group did not automatically view each other as equals. For example, middle-class whites and new immigrants in the region viewed blacks as their other (though for different reasons). These two groups did not view each other as the same. Blacks may have dubbed new immigrants as white, but foreignness, not whiteness, is what made ethnics the others of the African American community. These oppositional identifications influenced the outcome of the events surrounding the riot.

The multiple and malleable definitions of the other allowed African Americans, native-born whites, and new immigrants to have a hand in defining racial boundaries, suggesting that becoming white and becoming American were closely connected but not inseparable at this historical juncture.[8] By problematizing race and citizenship and acknowledging that these constructs had unique, though certainly indelibly linked, historical trajectories, we are better able to understand how and why racial and ethnic groups divided themselves, and what caused them to come together.[9] Because race was not always constructed as a duality—the opposite of black did not always mean white—African American and ethnic residents were each able to take advantage of prejudice for momentary power.

In analyzing the riot episode, I incorporate four fundamental tools. First, timing, though not everything, placed the event on the cusp of two sweeping chronological moments in American history: the end of the post-Civil War era, when racial justice and integration seemed possible and the beginning of the twentieth century, which marked a long period of increased racial violence and the abrogation of rights lasting for half a century.[10] Second, place and location were also crucial elements in the evolution of the episode. Italians had considerable political power in Spring Valley, which made them fairly unusual among first-generation immigrants, and the town distinctive compared to other immigrant-receiving cities. This political control, however, neither extended beyond the municipal boundaries nor translated into economic power. Through place and location, I focus on the significance of the local, because residents' experiences were inseparable from it. The riot episode did not end in the geographic space where the violence had begun. It quickly moved from a local incident, with limited repercussions, to a national and international phenomenon, with uncertain consequences. Third, demography influenced this transformation from the local and pushed events from the "village-outward." Spring Valley's population included men and women whose ties reached far beyond this small mining hamlet into America's rural South and urban North as well as around the world. The majority of blacks here had been born in the South during Reconstruction to parents who had been slaves. African American residents had strong beliefs about freedom, citizenship, and their position in American society. In turn, many of the immigrants in the region, though of the same generation as their black cohort, had no family or national connections with the crisis over slavery or the revolutionary moment that the Civil War engendered. This, in part, meant that they had vastly different experiences with American racism. Fourth, as noted above, group identification—racial, ideological, and national—rooted in past experiences also conditioned responses. Italians and other new immigrants, blacks, and native-born whites each categorized themselves in relationship to others. Groups made temporary affiliations as well as more lasting connections based on newly formed common ground created by the riot.[11]

Incorporating these four analytic tools underscores the central theme of this essay and also extends recent scholarship that has begun to periodize the formation of racial consciousness. I argue that we cannot understand the meaning of whiteness—whether it was the culmination of a stage beyond the inbetween or a continuation of a racial identification after arrival—without taking account of black voices and African American reactions to new immigrant violence.[12] In turn, we cannot fully discern what racial categorization meant to Italians if we do not explore their own self-understanding of race and how that understanding changed over time.

PRELUDE TO THE RIOT

Events during the summer of 1895 were a product of the well-formed antagonism between Spring Valley, a booming coal community in north-central Illinois, and the county seat of Princeton. Spring Valley was dominated by working-class immigrants whose primary reason for being in America was to mine coal (or, in the case of women and children, to support a male head of household who worked underground). In the 1880s, the Spring Valley Coal

Company (SVCC) advertised for labor nationally and internationally. Families and single men alike migrated to the valley from other U.S. coal regions including places all over Illinois, Iowa, Colorado, and Pennsylvania, joining an earlier generation of skilled miners from Britain. By 1900, twenty-six different nationalities (Italian, French, Belgian, German, Polish, Lithuanian, Russian, Austrian, Slovenian, and others) worked in Spring Valley's mines. Italians—most from Italy's northern provinces—were the largest of these groups. Twelve percent of the mining town's inhabitants were born in Italy, and eighteen percent of the population had two Italian-born parents.[13]

Spring Valley was not only an immigrant working-class town, it was a union stronghold. By the time the riot took place, the area had become a haven for militant trade unionists from Scotland and anarchist-socialists from Italy, France, and Belgium.[14] With so many distinct groups of radicals, there were always ideological disagreements. During labor upheavals, however, Spring Valley miners worked together for a common goal—the unionization of their field, which would ensure better working conditions. The coal strike of 1894, which will be discussed shortly, was one such occasion when this diverse community came together.

The county seat of Princeton housed a vastly different culture than Spring Valley. Both charmed by the importance coal mines played in increasing the wealth of the county and alarmed by the militant activities of its new immigrant residents, Princetonians constantly tried to reform the immigrant coal miners who dominated the town.[15] Princeton's residents were predominately farmers and merchants whose New England and Eastern ancestors migrated to the area in the 1830s. By the 1850s, the houses built here were "more or less pretentious" and suggested "luxury."[16] This aspect of Princeton had not changed much when the Federal Writers' Project compiled the town's guidebook: "Princeton is a rich town—rich in lands and houses, and rich in ways of living."[17] The political affiliation of much of the ruling class was the Republican Party, whose ties reached back to Lincoln's early career in the state (which may explain the tolerant, albeit paternalistic, attitudes toward blacks in 1895).[18]

Political and cultural differences between Spring Valley and Princeton were exacerbated by the 1894 strike. The labor upheaval was one of the most important causes of the riot, and it shaped the way in which county officials responded to the racial violence. While immigrant miners had proven that class cohesion could overcome ethnic differences, the defeat had demoralized the community. The SVCC managers underscored their power by forcing miners who wanted to work again to sign a nonstrike agreement. Then, despite the promises, SVCC's manager hired blacks to replace union activists.[19] *L'Italia* explained the betrayal: The company had rehired "Italians because it wanted to use them as long as they needed them and until they secured [African American] miners who worked for less."[20] In a letter to the *United Mine Workers Journal*, an Illinois miner explained the sequence of events and marked the bitter feelings against the black newcomers: "The majority was opposed to suffer any reductions and the result was as usual, scab labor, military power, strike ended, men discouraged, men victimized, operators employ whom they choose, while our best union men are allowed to walk the streets."[21] Though native-born shared such sentiments, when the rioters eventually came to trial, it was the immigrants on whom the defense attorney focused his argument: "Ill feeling . . . existed on the part of the foreign miners against the colored miners."[22]

Rank-and-file strike behavior, and authorities' response to it, inflamed the deep-seated prejudice between Princeton's elites and Spring Valley's workers. While the strikers included immigrants and native-born miners, newspaper reporters picked up on tactical differences and defined them in ethnic terms—"dagos and huns" confronted an older generation of union leadership as well as the coal company.[23] Slurs against new immigrants and "alien" political ideology continued after the strike was over. County papers never tired of reminding readers of the anarchist threat to American political ideals: "The sidewalks of Spring Valley were Monday night decorated with large red letters extolling anarchy and calling on the workingmen to turn out May 1 and celebrate with anarchists." Immigrants and noncitizens had clearly become the other here.[24]

The same things that drew class-conscious immigrant miners to Spring Valley made the place an affront in the eyes of Princeton's predominantly white Anglo-Saxon Protestant community. During a month when Billy Sunday held his religious revival meetings in the area, Princeton residents were particularly conscious of the differences between the county seat and its eastern neighbor. One newspaper reported, "There is to use a common phrase, a queer feeling pervading the English speaking community."[25] Those feelings were inflamed by an article that called on "good citizens of this county" to root out evil in Spring Valley. The paper insisted that the "better element had, in a word, to humanize, socialize, Americanize and moralize, the baser sort of this almost cosmopolitan population, in order to obtain and maintain a reasonably fair existence." To the Princeton elite, Spring Valley's immigrants were a demon other—"forces of vice and anarchy"—whom

American citizens should "beat down . . . though they may face death in the very attempt."[26] Others in Illinois agreed. A *Chicago Tribune* editorial told readers that "the largely alien and lawless" miners had made Spring Valley "a curse to this state."[27]

In the mid-1890s, blacks were depicted in a less ominous light. One writer compared African Americans to new immigrants to illustrate the point: "The colored people of the 'Location' are orderly and law abiding, and are disposed to attend strictly to their own business. If as much could be said of some other nationalities, Spring Valley would have a much better name."[28] A coal company representative told the *Chicago Tribune* that he would protect African American workers because he had "more faith in them than in the Italians"—blacks, quite simply, "make better miners."[29] In another comparison that tied racial fears with sexuality and suggested that immigrants could be both white and other, the *Bureau County Republican*, reminded its readers that "During the year four men ravished girls in Bureau county . . . all four of the wretches were white men." The article's purpose was to condemn the era's rampant lynchings but it also revealed ethnic prejudice. The paper was "not yet prepared to say that it believes in the shooting and lynching of the Italians or Polanders," but it was reminding them to stay in their place.[30] After the riot, as blacks moved back to the Location, the SVCC was advised to "let the mob gang go in order to give them [blacks] steady work."[31] Ethnic prejudice and racism, then, were rooted in the demographic contours and socioeconomic distinctions within Bureau County.

My argument here is not that Princeton's American-born middle-class white residents perceived blacks as their equals, but rather that they employed a racial hierarchy that included both new immigrant and African American others. Moreover, though some Princetonians described unassimilated ethnics as whites, the two populations were not the same. This suggests that, at the close of the nineteenth century, race and ethnic prejudice was based on intensely local experiences that mimicked, but did not necessarily mirror, the broader contours of American racism.[32]

At the same time that middle-class whites were interpreting events through this multilayered race hierarchy, Italians and blacks invoked their own race evaluations. Italians, for example, used the riot to reinforce their common bonds as "*connazionali*" (co-nationals) while also categorizing themselves as white (a categorization that was not always confirmed by others). Investing in these dual identifications was the project of *L'Italia*. The paper combated "the lies" Princeton's newspapers sent out to the nation and supported their ethnic kin in Spring Valley. In one editorial, a Professor G.

Tonnello stated that Chicago's American reporters must have "stomachs made of bronze which were solid and robust enough to digest the carrots [sent by the Princeton] clowns." "Shame on you," Tonnello scolded, "for all the bad humor and race hatred. . . . [and] all of the infamy directed against the poor Italians."[33] The paper was battling prejudice and fomenting racism at the same time, as it drew ties between Italians and other Europeans. "All of the white element that populated the town" had "chosen to unite to run out the Blacks by force," one article stated.[34]

Despite the Italian efforts to build strength through whiteness and nationality, American Blacks came out ahead in 1895 because they had a more nuanced comprehension of the U.S. race hierarchy.[35] African Americans successfully brought the most violent of the riot perpetrators to court and waged a bold and successful battle against the aggressors. Their actions must be viewed in the local and national historical context. During the 1890s, Jim Crow racism was solidifying and legalizing racial segregation. Spring Valley blacks, who had recently migrated from the South, were closely connecting to the losing battle to keep the Fourteenth Amendment the law of the land. As the famous *Plessy* v. *Ferguson* case was being fought in the U.S. Supreme Court, blacks held that "Citizenship . . . has no color."[36] African American Illinoisans also focused their legal challenges on the rights of all Americans, regardless of race, to equality before the law. In so doing, they utilized the county's nativism, contrasting their own citizenship with the foreignness of the upper Illinois valley's Italian population.

During the 1894 strike, immigrant and native-born white miners also used prejudice to define their place in the community, codifying their plight with stereotypes about race and slavery.[37] "Our condition is worse than the black slave," one strike flyer announced, continuing, "Let us then be prepared to enter this struggle . . . and put an end to this infernal system of monopoly, oppression and wage slavery."[38] In the summer of 1895, Spring Valley's miners again used the concept of chattel to express their frustration. The earlier comparison had served as a positive call to action. A year later, slavery was a metaphor that expressed their economic and psychic condition. In August 1895, the defeated men sent out a press release to convey their desperation. Just four days before the riot, the *Journal of the Knights of Labor* published their plea, which concluded: "Chattel slavery is preferable to industrial slavery." The *Journal* noted that miners in Illinois had "mounted the auction block and begged to contract themselves into slavery for the common necessaries of life."[39] Just like antebellum workers, Spring Valley's activists clearly had race and slavery in mind.[40]

It is important to note that while most miners believed class ties could not mitigate racial difference, there were a few (whites and blacks alike) who disagreed. At a rally before the riot, Jean Brault, a Belgian immigrant and anarchist, urged class solidarity. Brault "declared what is the duty of every anarchist to declare, that it was not black workers who deserved to be shot at—they were driven by hunger to work for lower wages. Rather, Dalziel [the SVCC manager] was guilty of offering black workers a lower wage so he could exploit them."[41] In an attempt to forge an interracial union, one Spring Valley correspondent to the *United Mine Workers Journal*, almost certainly black, claimed that "the colored men here are all good practical miners." This writer argued that if the coal company manager "thinks he is living in slavery times he will be disappointed."[42]

This last effort to unify black, white, and immigrant workers in 1895 failed. In the wake of the riot, African Americans combated oppression by capitalizing on their citizenship rather than their class. Italians and other new immigrants heralded their whiteness for power. As *L'Italia* put it, Spring Valley miners could not spend another day facing "the new nephews of Uncle Tom," who, they claimed, undermined wages and weakened their union efforts.[43]

RACIAL VIOLENCE

The summer of 1895 was a rough one for Spring Valley residents. Coal mining, always slow during the warmer season, was in a particularly deep slump.[44] Within five years, the United Mine Workers of America would become one of the strongest interracial and interethnic organizations in the country, but in 1895 it was a defeated union without a contract.[45] The event that sparked the riot fed fears, antagonisms, and prejudices that were well entrenched in the community. In turn, the riot reinforced power relations and the racial order on the town and the county levels.

On Saturday, August 3, 1895, Barney Rollo, an Italian miner, was mugged by a group of men, who may have been black. The attackers stole the weekly wages the miner had just picked up, took his watch, and shot Rollo, leaving him on the side of the road.[46] The next morning, city police arrested five African American men "without warrant and carried [them] to the City Hall." At a preliminary hearing, the men pleaded not guilty. Before the court proceeding was over, the sound of the fire bell had called together a mob that gathered in the town center. The crowd included people from a multitude of nationalities but Italians led the throng and were, most likely, in the majority.[47]

Authorities freed the prisoners after the crowd had gathered. At some point that morning, police returned to the Location and searched blacks' homes.[48] "Plainly," a later investigation argued, the police were "searching to see how many colored homes had firearms."[49] In other words, the officers, in cooperation with the rioters, had planned the attack ahead of time.

The riot embodied the entanglement of economic circumstances, racial violence, and status in the community. The timing of the attack, midmorning, suggests that the rioters viewed themselves as powerful citizens of Spring Valley who thought that they could get away with an invasion in broad daylight. The multiethnic make up of the crowd indicates that, despite Rollo's Italian nationality, various ethnic groups felt wronged by the robbery and were able to come together despite their language and cultural differences. *L'Italia* reported that "Italians and people from other nationalities [were] indignant," and that they believed that blacks had given "the ultimate and most terrible provocation" for violence.[50] The German-language paper *Vorbote* echoed the sentiments, highlighting the pan-European white connection: "Yes, in less than two hours, 5000 battle-ready white miners would be assembled. The workers say that they had silently endured the infringements of the negroes long enough."[51] The *Chicago Tribune* stated that "the polyglot foreigners" together determined to keep their town white.[52]

This is what the mob had in mind when, at ten o'clock in the morning, it set out for the Location, led by a band that played renditions of the American national anthem.[53] On their way, the crowd stopped at the home of S. M. Dalzell, SVCC manager, and "demanded the immediate discharge" of all the African American workers as retribution for the Rollo robbery. Dalzell refused because "They are American citizens."[54] Arriving at the Location, some in the mob stopped at a saloon before beginning the house raids. Rioters "poured through the village," wielding miners' picks and clubs, and firing "old, rusty guns."[55] They broke down doors, "went into the cellars, [and] pushed their rifles in windows," capturing and beating several blacks as they fled for their lives.[56] Women and children "screamed, and fled terror stricken, while the men, equally helpless, were savagely driven into the woods."[57] Rioters invaded homes and dragged residents outside, into the middle of the mob. On the street, men, women, and children were "knocked down" and "kicked unmercifully."[58] The Norman Bird family was attacked just as they finished breakfast. Mr. Bird was "repeatedly struck" while his wife and daughter headed for the woods to hide. Unable to outrun her attackers, Mrs. Bird "begged upon her knees for mercy, but her only reply was a shot in the face from the revolver of one of the men."[59] By the end of the raids, there were at least fourteen casualties and six missing. All of the victims survived—a rare conclusion in the history of American race riots.[60] For the moment, black residents took refuge in Seatonville, another mining town about six miles west of Spring Valley.[61]

The attack was not yet over. The Monday after the riot, miners held a mass meeting of more than a thousand people who vowed to keep blacks out of the town and out of the mines. One speaker told his audience "he would not stop with the negroes but would settle it once and effectively with Manager Dalzell of the coal company, who . . . deserved all the blame, as he had brought the negroes here."[62] The meeting adopted a resolution that gave African American inhabitants and their families until five o'clock Tuesday evening "to leave the city, and to carry off their effects." Anything left would "be declared confiscated and destroyed."[63] On Tuesday afternoon police were stationed near the Location to deter "destruction of property." The guards were joined by the mayor, but no one made any attempt to stop the evacuation or to temper the crowd that had gathered there. "Women and children were driven from their homes, were abused and insulted and their trunks and belongings were dragged about and despoiled. Wagons were hurrying about gathering up household goods and carrying them off on all the principal highways."[64]

African Americans did more than flee; they fought back. At the same time that miners in Spring Valley had gathered and resolved to racially "cleanse" their union town, blacks were holding their own meeting. The race riot coincided with a camp meeting that brought more blacks to Seatonville.[65] Victims of the riot and religious leaders worked together. At one o'clock in the morning on Monday, August 5, blacks met at Union Church, where participants agreed to remain in Seatonville until they could organize armed resistance. A committee was appointed to go to Princeton "to secure supplies and the 300 repeating Winchester rifles."[66]

Spring Valley's African American residents were not alone in their outrage. All over Illinois, blacks expressed indignation and tried to assert their power. In Peoria, African Americans tendered an offer to "assist in the protection of the colored men." Galesburg's blacks were "terribly incensed over the action of the miners." Seventy-five blacks in Evanston denounced the sheriff and the mayor, and sent a telegram to Governor John Altgeld "praying upon him to give the colored people of Spring Valley adequate protection."[67] At a mass meeting in Elgin, blacks passed a resolution lambasting county and state authorities for failing to punish the rioters. "Colored people in East St. Louis held an indignation meeting to denounce the failure of

Illinois authorities to protect the Spring Valley negro miners."[68] In Rockford and Moline, groups met at each town's African M.E. church. In the former city, they commended coal mine manager Dalzell for his "declarations that he knows no man by color and only by American citizenship." The latter sent word that "200 men can be readily secured" here for help and said they would work "in conjunction with those from Chicago."[69]

Chicago's African American community did the most for the riot victims. At Quinn Chapel, in a meeting that included Ida Wells Barnett, her husband, F. L. Barnett, and other prominent members of the community, there was "a prolonged and heated discussion" about whether or not to "take the law into their own hands." By the end of the night, there was a compromise that included the formation of a riot investigating committee. They also resolved to press the authorities to protect the "lives, liberties, and homes" of "these exiles," and they called on the governor to ensure that all Illinois residents could "earn an honest living in a lawful manner in any part of the state." Finally, the meeting's participants rendered "every possible assistance in the protection and defense of our unfortunate brethren in the exercise of their lawful rights."[70] Within a week, the Quinn Chapel committee had raised fourteen hundred dollars and finished their investigation. Besides the details of the riot, the committee assessed Illinois's blacks' ability to prevent and respond to this type of violence. "We are compelled to admit that we have no cause to congratulate ourselves for our share in the settlement of this affair."[71] The committee believed that help had not arrived as quickly as it should have because "of all nationalities upon this continent the most persecuted and yet the most helpless is the negro." They vowed to formulate a "plan of action which will make us less dependent upon white people and more capable of defending ourselves."[72] Despite this harsh assessment, African Americans had made a difference by helping to focus national attention on the riot, thus undermining Spring Valley officials' tacit approval of events.

African American community organizing had a ripple effect that reached supporters of the rioters and victims alike. The Italian consul general in Chicago reacted to the Quinn Chapel meeting and other signs of African American indignation by sending telegrams to Governor Altgeld and meeting with Chicago Mayor Swift. The consul urged the governor to "reestablish peace" by preventing blacks from going to Spring Valley. He repeated his concerns to Swift, demanding that police arrest the black delegation before they left for the riot scene. Swift refused, but allayed some of the consul's fears. Cook County's branch of the American Protective Association (an anti-immigrant organization) called Spring Valley's mayor a "coward, disloyal and anti-American" because "he did not use his authority to quell the recent riot."[73]

Indeed, Mayor Martin Delmagro clearly knew about the attack at the Location on Sunday morning, but he did not notify County Sheriff Atherton Clark until noon.[74] Before Clark got to the scene, Delmagro had countermanded his request for assistance. The sheriff thought the mayor's change of mind was odd, and he, along with five other county men, decided to investigate. In Spring Valley, they met with the mayor and manager Dalzell. The county group found the mayor unwilling to help because "he thought it would be a dangerous venture for him to offer interference." There were no further official decisions made that day. The sheriff, however, was suspicious of Delmagro's intransigence and he continued to probe. On his way back to Princeton, Clark stopped in Seatonville to visit the refugees. "They wanted the sheriff to furnish them arms for self protection." Clark declined, saying he had to "proceed according to law." Two days later, Governor Altgeld sent a telegram to Clark, inquiring about the situation.[75]

The response that Altgeld received pushed him to send state Assistant Adjutant General Bayle, who arrived in Spring Valley on Wednesday. Bayle found a community divided. Immigrants had met before Bayle's arrival and, *Vorbote* reported, "The miners, who don't speak English, about 200 in number . . . made a resolution whereby no colored person (not excluding women and invalids) would be permitted to remain inside the town borders after this evening."[76] The assistant adjutant general attended another mass meeting with approximately six hundred people present. The presence of two prominent local United Mine Workers of America members, James O'Connor and John Mitchell, suggests that the union was involved. In fact, it was the first time that the miners' organization took a public stand on the riot. About the meeting, one Chicago reporter stated, "Every nation in Eastern and Southern Europe was represented. Every motion that was made, and every speech, had to be repeated at least six times, and each time in a different language." [77]

The main order of business at the meeting was a motion which indicated that some members of the organization opposed the riot violence.

> Resolved, That we, miners of Spring Valley, in mass meeting assembled, declare it to be our belief that all men regardless of race, color, or creed, are born with the same equal rights and should enjoy the same opportunities in pursuit of life and happiness. Resolved, That we denounce any attempt at the suppressing of these rights as unjust and barbarous and pledge ourselves to maintain law and order so far as . . . in our power. Resolved, That we are

> ready now to resume work providing the Spring Valley Coal Company is ready to start the mines.[78]

The sentiments are among the clearest indications of organizer's commitment to interracial unionism for which the United Mine Workers is so well known. The discussion that followed shows that not all were inclined to agree with this type of inclusion. After reading the resolution, the chair asked for debate. Many of those in attendance asked whether passing this resolution would allow blacks to return to the city. "Through various interpreters," the chair evaded the question. When the resolution finally came up for a vote, the chair "declared it carried," though some accounts noted a tie.[79] Union miners were split and the fault line seemed to divide new immigrants from an older generation represented in the local union leadership.

After the meeting, Bayle conferred with city officials, journalists, and union representatives O'Connor and Mitchell. The latter two used Bayle's presence to press the company to rehire men who had participated in the 1894 strike—one of the union's main concerns from the beginning. Manager Dalzell told them that he was willing to "take back all of the miners who had quit work save those who had committed crimes." O'Connor responded that we "expect that all shall be allowed to return to work." Dalzell, in turn, reminded him that the blacks were also "anxious to come back," and added that he had already promised that the company would allow them to work again. Dalzell believed that, under the miners' resolution, SVCC could do that. O'Connor agreed, but stated that the company "must not hold us all responsible" if African American workers were "stabbed in the back." The union representatives then implored Dalzell to wait at least a few days before blacks were brought back—he was clearly balancing the wishes of the racist immigrant rank and file, whose numbers were key to a strong organization, and the ideology of interracialism that was essential for union success nationally. The manager refused: "I take this to mean that the miners have withdrawn their resolution [and] that only white miners shall be employed in the mines." He then turned to Mayor Delmagro and said, "The colored people who were driven out of Spring Valley told me they were ready to come back. Are you ready to protect them?" Delmagro agreed to try. The settlement may have been "amicable," as one report noted, but it was certainly a delicate agreement.[80]

Under the watchful eye of Governor Altgeld, who had threatened the town's officials with a militia invasion, the mayor "swore in 50 conservators of peace." Less than a week after the riot, black miners returned to work in Spring Valley.[81]

RACE, CITIZENSHIP, AND THE SEARCH FOR JUSTICE

With the violence over, Spring Valley blacks fought back by successfully using the legal system and incorporating the language of citizenship to argue their case. As the defense lawyer put it: "He had heard the expression 'American citizen' used in this trial to a considerable extent until it now rung in his ears."[82] Their court victory was, in part, the result of several factors. Illinois's blacks' swift reaction to the riot, one that included setting up a statewide organizational network, was key. The 1895 response fits into the larger pattern of African American resistance to subjugation. For example, a dozen years later, after the 1908 race riot in the state capital, Blacks founded the NAACP.[83] But, in Bureau County, residents won their legal fight also because they were able to tap into prejudice against ethnic others that was so much a part of the relationship between Princeton and Spring Valley.

In addition, Spring Valley blacks were prompted to action, and succeeded in their fight, because of the assistance they received from African American communities around the nation. The Quinn Chapel committee, which had urged the victims to bring a civil suit against the city to recover damages, organized a "relief fund to be used in supplying food and necessaries to the victims of the riot" because, as they put it, "they are in distress, and we should aid them."[84]

African American newspapers around the country also assisted their Spring Valley brethren publishing reports to help bolster the prosecution. Many stories incorporated language that highlighted the distinctions between southern and eastern European immigrants and American citizens, a tradition that had begun with Frederick Douglass.[85] The 1895 accounts tended to group together immigrants and singled out Italians for the brunt of their criticism. The lumping of ethnic populations may have been a reflection of early reports about the demographic makeup of the rioters. It might also have been a product of black–Italian relations in the cities where the newspapers were published. *L'Italia,* for example, helped readers justify the violence by drawing on familiar stereotypes and making connections between African Americans from one of Chicago's multiethnic neighborhoods and Spring Valley's Location. Describing the latter, the paper noted, "Together with the miners there were also jailbirds ... who used to infest South Clark street in Chicago ... [T]hey lived off of the Italian miners principally plundering the streets and their homes."[86] The black press fought these racial caricatures by contrasting Italians and citizens. The Baltimore *Afro-American* wrote: "The Italian outrage on colored laborers in Spring Valley, Ill., will result in no benefit to the foreign labor element in the United States ...

the verdict of the public is against the Italians."[87] The *Langston City Herald* called the Spring Valley Italians, "a band of lousy, dirty, despicable, low bred, treacherous dago miners."[88] To the *Richmond Planet*, "the Italians of Spring Valley" were "misguided foreigners" who did not understand "the right to labor is a right guaranteed by our laws." The paper questioned how anyone could "have so mistaken the spirit of our institutions." It urged Spring Valley blacks to "Purchase Winchester rifles," ending the article with "Lynch-law must go!"[89] If anyone had missed the message, the next issue of the *Planet* stated, as noted in the introduction to this chapter, "the Southern bourbon Negro-hater is not present in Illinois, but the Italian has arisen in his stead."[90]

With this type of backing from all over the United States, blacks in Spring Valley were enabled to heed the Quinn Chapel committee's advice. In September, residents of the Location "presented a claim to the city council for damages," asking for two thousand dollars "for injuries and loss of property . . . sustained by them in the recent riot."[91] Later in the fall, Spring Valley residents joined other Illinois African Americans in a conference in the state capital—an "outgrowth of the late mob violence against the colored people." Here, blacks continued to castigate the "band of outlaws and red-handed midnight assassins" involved in the riot.[92] The assembly pledged itself "to do all in our power to bring the guilty perpetrators of these atrocious acts to justice."[93]

Blacks also started a criminal case against their attackers. On Thursday, August 15, a group of men and women from the Location, accompanied by Representative Buckner of Chicago, went to Princeton and "made complaints before Justice A.M. Swengle."[94] They argued that the violence was "contrary to the statute and against the dignity of the people of the state of Illinois."[95] Sheriff Clark issued thirty-six warrants and he, along with ten of the victims, went to the SVCC No. 3 mine to make the arrests. As the miners came up on the cage, the victims of the riot "would take hold of certain of them, saying to the sheriff: 'This man broke in our door,' 'that man struck me with a club.'"[96] Clark arrested somewhere between twenty-three and twenty-five men. At the preliminary hearing on Saturday, Justice Swengle split up the defendants into two groups to be tried separately, setting bail at three hundred to five hundred dollars each.[97]

Most of the defendants were recent immigrants unlikely to receive fair treatment in Princeton.[98] Because many of these men could not speak English, the court was required to find Lithuanian, French, and Italian translators.[99] To be sure, the defendants understood their standing in the county seat. Many had been harassed and a few had been arrested during the 1894 strike. For example, Jean Brault, the Belgian miner who had counseled solidarity in 1895, had participated in looting a company store during the 1894 strike.[100]

While blacks could rely on county officials for help, Spring Valley's city council was on the immigrants' side. During the arrests at the mine, Mayor Delmagro and several aldermen appeared at the shaft and did all they could to protect the accused rioters. Their presence was another indication of the interethnic ties of this community's population—the city council was composed of English, Irish, Russian, Polish, and Scottish aldermen.[101] The town's elected representatives had asked Sheriff Clark to try the men in Spring Valley, but the sheriff told them that this "would be impossible as the warrants were made in Princeton."[102] The defendants then tried to get a change of venue, claiming obvious bias on the part of the assigned judges.[103] Their request was approved, and the trial was heard by another judge.[104] By November the proceedings were over. The jury found eight of the defendants guilty of riot and criminal assault.[105] Seven were sent to the state penitentiary; the eighth was under twenty-one and could not, under state law, go to jail. The nationalities of those sentenced were Italian, Polish, and French. Those who were set free were French, German, Belgian, and U.S-born. The mix of nationalities, of the guilty and nonguilty groups, is one of the most telling illustrations of the bonds that immigrants had created. These ethnics were not only willing to live and work in the same community, their violent actions show that they had created a common identity based on boundaries of consciousness, outside of which were African American others. Despite similar economic circumstances among Blacks and new immigrants—and, more important, immigrants' willingness to bridge cultural divides for union power—this hybrid community was formulated upon the desire for white privilege.[106]

The rioters had misjudged their position because they did not fully understand the multiple identification of others in the community. African American plaintiffs won because they were able to highlight the foreign other of American citizens and downplay racial difference. They also succeeded for two other reasons: (1) they had the emotional and monetary support of blacks around the country; (2) Spring Valley blacks understood the rift between city and county officials, and used it to build an alliance with Princeton residents. To be sure, this was a tenuous and temporary partnership. We should not, however, ignore its implications if we hope to understand how and when immigrants' became white.[107] Blacks were able to combat racial violence by emphasizing their citizenship.[108] As one group of black observers pointed out in the riot's aftermath, the "mob must be taught that the American people will not tolerate any such outlawry."[109]

Just as blacks triumphed because of their insight into relations between immigrants and native-born, immigrants failed because they had misjudged their position as one of multiple others. Responses to the verdict suggest distinct perceptions of the relationship between ethnicity and race.[110] The way they reacted to the guilty verdict underlines a burgeoning race consciousness. This consciousness melded with their own understanding of class. At one point, the defense lawyer tried to explain this relationship. Blacks had been used as strikebreakers in Illinois's coal mining district, he told the jury, and they were naturally the "silent enemy" of the "white miners."[111] During the closing arguments, the lawyer repeated claims about prejudice in the court. This time he played upon the connection between ethnicity and American identity. In particular, he "thought the people were too much prejudiced against the Italians because they were not American citizens."[112] The jury was not swayed by these arguments. Immigrants had transgressed ethnic lines and attempted to fuse ties as whites.

Finally, the rioters' decision to ask for a retrial illustrates that they had a new understanding of their position in the community. Their nine reasons for a new hearing included the use and misuse of evidence as well as the prosecution's failure to show intent. But what was particularly unbearable to the defendants was that "the counsel for the prosecution . . . indulged in remarks and gestures and exclamations calculated to influence the minds of the jury . . . and to rouse race prejudice and passion."[113] Immigrant miners had become more aware of America's racial order and their uncertain position in it. Over the next months, they worked hard to strengthen white ties and gain racial power. For example, in December, the community held a musical benefit (likely to raise money for the rioters). "There will be music for all . . . la Marsellaise [*sic*] for the French, the royal march and the Hymn of Garibaldi for the Italians; 'Last Rose of Summer' for the Irish, 'Home Sweet home' for the Americans and for all, a short number one program."[114]

CONCLUSION

The violence of August 1895 reveals the multiple dimensions of racial formation and prejudice in the United States at the end of the nineteenth century. The Spring Valley riot also alerts us to the way in which local circumstances affected the American race paradigm and, moreover, how native-born whites, new immigrants, and blacks each had a hand in cultivating the relationships within this paradigm. Italians and other new immigrants had begun to self-identify as white though their own classification did not automatically create ties to the middle-class white power structure, which continued to view them as other. African American residents in this coal community used citizenship and the precarious racial placement of new immigrants to define the other and to challenge racial violence in the courts. The successful battle they waged was both a part of their rapid and cohesive organizing in response to the attack, and their capacity to exploit the white power structure's perception that Spring Valley ethnics were a greater threat to the community than were its African American residents. The riot history, then, helps to untangle the complex connection between racialization and citizenship, clarifying a struggle in which new immigrants' assimilation into whiteness was molded by black resistance to race-based nationality.

Chapter Six

"IT IS PROVIDENTIAL THAT THERE ARE FOREIGNERS HERE"

Whiteness and Masculinity in the Making of Italian American Syndicalist Identity

Michael Miller Topp

In a debate on the status of Italian Americans that erupted in the summer of 2000 on H-ITAM (an Italian American Studies online discussion board), several participants argued that they don't consider themselves part of a white society that oppresses its minorities because they are still themselves members of an oppressed minority. This argument is not without merit. Participants on both sides of the debate, for example, argued convincingly that portrayals of Italian Americans in the media and popular culture generally are dominated by images of the Mafia and characterizations of criminal behavior.

What was unexpected about this debate was that some participants couched their arguments in explicitly—and anachronistically—racial terms. Italian Americans, one argued, are victims of a "virulent and multipronged racism in this country."[1] Another insisted that an NPR panel discussion dealing with Italian Americans and the miniseries *The Sopranos* was "an intentional and choreographed racial slur . . . a true racist event."[2] Although this member became something of a pariah on the list, his calls for Italian Americans to be considered "minorities" in the distribution of federal grants received considerable support.[3]

Nor was this debate the only place where one can find the language of race and racism deployed in discussing Italian Americans' experiences. David A. J. Richards makes a similar argument in his *Italian American: The Racializing of an Ethnic Identity*. Richards, a legal and constitutional scholar, argues that Italian Americans have been treated in the United States as "nonvisibly black." Declaring that "The same terms of cultural degradation apply to all victims of racism, whether visibly or nonvisibly black—the demand of supine acceptance of an identity unjustly devalued," Richards asserts that Italian immigrants, like African Americans, have historically faced the "double consciousness" that W.E.B. Du Bois described in *Souls of Black Folk*.[4] This holds true, he argues, both in the present day and in historical terms. He thus joins other scholars who have argued that at the turn of the twentieth century, southern Italian immigrants at times experienced attitudes and treatment that were more comparable to nonwhite groups than to other European immigrants, and that their experiences were linked closely—at times physically—to those of blacks.[5]

Despite the plausibility of this latter claim, Richards's broader claim is indefensible, and points to the great need for further investigations into the ways Italian Americans' identity was racialized historically. This essay starts from the premise that "blackness," either visible or not, is not an apt metaphor for the Italian American experience. Certainly this is true in the present day. It is inaccurate at best to liken the ways Italian Americans and nonwhite populations are currently treated in American society. In historical terms as well, the comparison between Italian immigrants' experiences and those of nonwhites—the assertion that Italian immigrants were "nonvisibly black"—is simplistic and flawed. During the peak years of their migration to the United States, Italian immigrants occupied a far more complex place in the nation's racial hierarchy.[6]

The complexity of their position can be seen even in the experiences of some of the Italian American community's most marginal members—in this case members of the Federazione Socialista Italiana (FSI).[7] In 1911 and 1912, members of the FSI responded to two disparate events—Italy's war in Tripoli and the Lawrence textile strike—by positioning themselves in the racial hierarchy in the United States in ways that at once reified and challenged, aligned with and complicated, that hierarchy.

Seeking to build on the insights of scholars like Matthew Jacobson, David Roediger and James Barrett, this essay examines the consequences of challenges to Italian Americans' racial identity and particularly how they responded to them.[8] I argue two things here. First, the racialization of Italian immigrants in the United States historically was an intricate process: one that emerged out of more than one context simultaneously, and one in which these immigrants themselves participated. Italian Americans—in this case

Italian American syndicalists—constructed their own sense of place in the racial hierarchy to the extent they could, both in opposing Italy's war in Tripoli and in contributing to the strike at Lawrence. Second, the ways in which Italian immigrants contested their perceived racial inferiority could have dire consequences. Italian American syndicalists fought racial assumptions at Lawrence in two ways: by evoking national pride (rather than whiteness) and by asserting their masculinity. Their masculine ethos—their willingness to face and even provoke violent confrontations—enabled them to answer racial challenges, but also severely limited their capacities as labor organizers. Their experiences at Lawrence reinforced the syndicalist "cult of the woman," a profoundly circumscribed view of women's roles in society that rendered them unable to recognize women workers' increasing numbers and importance in this era.

The FSI, established in 1902, was by 1911 and 1912 experiencing a much-needed redefinition and rejuvenation. A number of scholars of the Italian American Left—Salvatore Salerno, Bruno Ramirez, and Elisabetta Vezzosi among them—have been critical of the Federation, and not without reason. Its first years especially were chaotic and ineffective.[9] When Carlo Tresca, early and briefly an FSI leader, arrived in the United States in 1904, the organization was in a state of considerable disrepair. Years later, he joked about its dire condition. His first meeting with the executive committee of the FSI was held in a basement on Bleecker Street in Greenwich Village: "What a meeting! A big barrel with two lighted candles on it and four men seated around it, seriously . . . urging the necessity of marshaling the power of the Italian workers for the general, coming battle against capitalism."[10] The organization in its first years was not only small, but also rent with political disputes, as factional tensions rooted in both Italian and American left politics erupted frequently among its members. Vezzosi analyzes these battles very effectively in her work on the history of the Federazione Socialista Italiana of the Socialist Party of America (FSI/SPA), an offshoot organization from the FSI formed by reformist socialists who by 1908 had rejected the FSI's increasing enthusiasm for syndicalism.[11]

In 1911, the FSI officially declared itself a syndicalist organization. This was a move that necessitates some explanation. Syndicalists generally sought to use militant labor unions as vehicles to foment ever larger and broader strikes that would culminate in a working-class revolution. In tactical terms, they advocated the use of the general strike, direct action, and industrial sabotage (defined in broad terms rather than simply as violence at the workplace). But the lines between various radical factions—between syndicalists, socialists, and anarchists, for example—were not always easily discernible. They could at times be extremely rigid at time: disagreements between syndicalists and socialists (who advocated revolution through the ballot box and cooperation with mainstream labor unions) had split the FSI; anarchist Bartolomeo Vanzetti issued diatribes against syndicalism from his prison cell even as Italian American syndicalists fought to save his life. But as Salerno's work on anarchist influences in the Industrial Workers of the World (IWW) makes clear, the lines between factions could also be incredibly fluid. Certain Italian American radicals wrote regularly both for the FSI's *Il Proletario* and for Luigi Galleani's *Cronaca Sovversiva* (the anarchist newspaper Vanzetti read and occasionally wrote for). Though FSI syndicalists and FSI/SPA socialists remained at odds for years after their split, by the end of World War I certain of them were again seeking out ways to work together. These complications notwithstanding, in 1911 FSI members declared their intention to make syndicalist ideology and tactics central to their pursuit of revolution.

This culminated a trajectory begun in 1904 and 1905 when Tresca and others began working to popularize the ideology in the organization and voiced support (if from a distance) for the newly formed IWW. The FSI's connection to the IWW would grow increasingly strong in coming years. It would work side by side with Wobbly leaders in the Lawrence strike in 1912, and the FSI would become a foreign-language branch of the IWW in 1921. It may well be, as Salerno and especially Ramirez have argued, that the FSI's affiliation with the IWW was largely opportunistic and fruitless. Certainly this is clear in hindsight: by 1921, as Rudolph Vecoli has noted, the FSI's decision to become a branch of the IWW linked a disempowered organization to a faltering one.[12]

But in 1911 and 1912, the years on which this essay focuses, the syndicalist FSI was imbued with an optimism that was not at all unreasonable. Its decision to fight against Italy's war in Tripoli would introduce it as an oppositional voice in Italian American communities. Its participation in the successful Lawrence strike would propel it into a position of prominence in these communities and in the American labor movement as a whole. Even Edwin Fenton, a scholar very critical of the FSI, noted, "Not since the lynching of the eleven Italian laborers in New Orleans in 1891 had the community united with such solidarity. After Lawrence and the Ettor and Giovannitti case, Italian-America was never quite the same."[13] The future would be less kind. As Vezzosi describes, by the end of World War I the FSI would become isolated and largely stagnant.[14] But to dismiss the organization too quickly is to overlook the moment—if only a moment—when the FSI's advocacy of syndicalism seemed neither opportunistic nor ineffective, but rather a potential blueprint for the future. And it is at this moment, when its impact on Italian American communities and the American labor movement was arguably greatest, that it makes the most sense to examine its members' attitudes about racial hierarchy and about the importance of their own masculinity.

By 1911, the syndicalist FSI had built a number of small but extremely active locals in cities throughout the northeastern, midwestern, and, to an extent, western United States. That year, Italy embarked on yet another effort to enter the ranks of imperial powers by invading Libya through the port of Tripoli. Though embarrassingly unsuccessful in past attempts to seize a colonial possession in Africa, the Italian government hoped to take advantage of the crumbling Ottoman Empire.

What is interesting for our purposes about the FSI's largely unsuccessful effort to generate antiwar sentiment in Italian American communities is that in opposing the war, Federation members criticized Italy's claims to be "civilizing" Libya, and even the idea of "civilization" itself—but not the racial hierarchy on which Italy's civilizing efforts were based. Arturo Giovannitti (soon imprisoned and the focus of the defense campaign at Lawrence) was among several FSI members who critiqued Italy's rationale for the war. He argued the war was nothing more than a means to capitalist exploitation, noting, "The excuse is always the same: Civilization—an elastic and malleable word which may mean . . . the Bible or the public school, the cannon or the locomotive, but which [*sic*] ultimately signifies nothing but capitalism, whether it be investments, taxation or pure and simple highway robbery."[15] Another argued that in modern times "civilization" signified little more than sophistication in methods of killing. "Between a barbarian who doesn't kill anybody, and a 'civilized' man who kills hundreds of his brothers," he asked, "who is civilized and who is the barbarian?"[16] If civilization was defined in terms of robbery and conquest, and in terms of increasingly potent weaponry, it would be difficult to argue the superiority of Italy over an African nation it was able to conquer.

Despite these attacks on the underpinnings of Italian imperial ambitions, however, FSI members ultimately subscribed to the same notions of racial hierarchy as the government they criticized. In one particularly jarring example, an FSI member reproduced in the FSI weekly *Il Proletario* an article from a patriotic Italian newspaper titled "The Africans of Calabria," which speculated that some Calabrians might have been descendants of immigrants from Africa.[17] The original author of this article hedged, stating,

"As far as the question of their origin is concerned, we do not wish to address it because we are not professional historians." But he concluded, "We can simply say that Darwin proved this year that the inhabitants are more closely related to the chimpanzee than they are to Adam and Eve."[18] The Federation member delighted that this Italian conservative was arguing about the dire state into which the Italian government had let southern Italy fall—a point the FSI had been stressing for years. But of course, he and the author agreed not only upon this assertion, but also on the racist presumption that Africans and certain Calabrians were closer to apes than to humans.

Nor was he the only FSI member who equated Africans with animalism and savagery. Another member condemning the state of southern Italy in *Il Proletario* described a feast of St. Alto during which the population of an entire town in Sicily ran nearly naked through the town to a church, in the hope that they would be visited by a miracle. He lamented, "If any strangers happened upon this town and saw the hordes of naked men and women running through the streets they would think they were not in Italy, but among the cannibals of central Africa."[19] Once again, the most desultory comparison an FSI member could make in discussing the state into which southern Italians had fallen was to Africans. Despite their efforts to destabilize the definition of civilization, for Federation members the continent of Africa evoked a distinct set of images. Africans were savages, cannibals, closer to apes than to humans.

This racially based commentary on the state of southern Italy implicated not only Africans but also southern Italians themselves. The Federation member had mocked the feast of St. Alto participants, for example, by likening them to Africans. While he did not racialize southern Italians, he used a racial metaphor—they were behaving and dressing like "cannibalistic Africans"—that he clearly assumed would have resonance with his readers. The other FSI member who reproduced the article on southern Italy took a dramatic step further. The author of the article—and by implication the Federation member who reprinted it—racialized southern Italians themselves by arguing that at least certain Calabrians were linked biologically to Africans.

This was a shocking racial positioning—FSI members in one breath describing Africans as cannibalistic and primitive, even less than human, and in the next breath speculating that certain southern Italians might be themselves descendants of Africans. Even more surprising was the fact that these two Federation members were themselves from Sicily and Calabria. These authors' criticism of southern Italians—their self-criticism—may have reflected an overly enthusiastic denunciation of the Italian government's failings, or divisions, religious or geographical, for example, in Calabria and Sicily. As

Thomas Guglielmo and Donna Gabaccia argue elsewhere in this collection, this racialization of southern Italians was by no means unprecedented. Positivist anthropologists in Italy like Cesare Lombroso, Giuseppe Sergi, and Alfredo Niceforo (the last himself a Sicilian) had argued racial distinctions between southern and northern Italians in the late nineteenth century.[20]

Regardless of the source of the criticisms, once the Lawrence strike began, FSI members' perspective on southern Italians would be much different. Not only their vantage point on southern Italians, but also on violence—critical to their often gendered response to their status in the United States—changed dramatically from the early days of protesting the war in Tripoli.

To understand these shifts, one has to take into account the context within which they occurred. At Lawrence, they were no longer responding as Italian migrants to a distant war being fought by their country of birth. They were no longer criticizing Italy (and Italians) as fellow Italians. In Lawrence they were maligned immigrants, "inbetween" peoples who were "inconclusively white" in American society. They now had to defend themselves against mill owners, conservative labor leaders, judges, and legal authorities—the very people who contested their identity as whites and their right to be in the United States.

They did this not by insisting that they were white, or that they shared a racial identity with Lawrence authorities, but through implicit and explicit assertions of national pride. It is far too easy to assume that southern and eastern European immigrants responded to racial challenges in this era with immediate assertions of their whiteness. As Jacobson has pointed out, however, certain of these immigrants asserted their own national identity in response. In doing so, they thus helped to create and solidify racial distinctions between white populations.[21] Evoking their *italianità*, Italian American syndicalists contributed to the construction of these distinctions. But they refused to accept the hierarchical notions that normally followed from them.

FSI members responded to racial affronts at Lawrence not just by evoking a sense of *italianità*, but also by asserting their masculinity to defend themselves. This was hardly a new impulse. The environment in and around the FSI had long been fiercely masculine, and its members had long placed enormous emphasis on courage. In Lawrence, the attacks they endured exacerbated these tendencies, which extended during the strike and defense campaign to an enthusiasm for violent rhetoric and confrontations. Pierrette Hondagneu-Sotelo, in analyzing machismo and bravado in the late twentieth-century Mexican-American community, has argued that men's public "masculine gender displays" are indicative of "marginalized and subordinated masculinities."[22] In other words, very visible manifestations of bravery and physical prowess produced by working-class Mexican American men reflected and confronted their ethnic and class oppression by other men in society. Italian American syndicalists in 1912 responded to similar imperatives in like ways. Their ability to face their enemies without fear was an essential response to the racial challenges they faced.[23]

The details of the Lawrence strike are well known. At the height of the strike, upward of twenty thousand textile workers representing over twenty different nationalities were on strike. Italian immigrants and women from a range of nationality groups each constituted sizable proportions of the strikers. Working with the IWW, the Federation sought to organize a population long considered unorganizable.[24] They won two enormous victories at Lawrence: the strike itself and a defense campaign waged on behalf of strike leaders arrested in the course of the strike. IWW leader Joseph Ettor and FSI leader Giovannitti were arrested with striker Joseph Caruso on a fabricated murder charge, but were acquitted in November 1912.

Both the strike and the defense campaign would be extremely hard-fought battles, in large part because of the notions of racial hierarchy FSI members and Italian immigrants confronted in Lawrence. Southern Italians, like the antebellum Irish, were the most maligned migrants of their time.[25] Sociological works in the first decades of the twentieth century defined southern Italians as the lowest of the European races, and warned against intermarriage with them.[26] It bears repeating, though, that as bad as their experiences were, they did not make Italians or any other southern and eastern Europeans "nonvisibly black." They may have been racialized as other, but by their own reckoning—the debate on Tripoli is telling here—they considered themselves superior to nonwhites. If the lines between various European immigrants were drawn in stark—and racialized—terms in these years, the distinctions between those whose whiteness was "inconclusive" and those who could not lay claim to whiteness at all were even sharper.

Nonetheless, within the realm of European populations, Italian immigrants, and even Americans of Italian descent, were considered a distinct and inferior race. This was made all too clear when Joseph Ettor, a second-generation Italian, was arrested with Giovannitti on the fabricated murder charge. A Boston paper enthusiastically reported, "The passing out of Ettor means the ascendancy of the white-skinned races in Lawrence."[27] Italian immigrants (and their descendants) were seen as, and saw themselves as, superior to nonwhites. But authorities in Lawrence—and beyond—indisputably saw them in racialized terms. The FSI and the strikers faced racial discrimination throughout the strike and the defense campaign. FSI members bristled when Italians were called "Dagoes," and recognized the racial implications of the verbal and physical assaults they endured. They warned protesters repeatedly, "These police are racists and because of this are treating the prisoners with brutality."[28]

FSI members responded to the racially based challenges they faced in Lawrence by asserting not whiteness, but their shared sense of *italianità*—a pride in the very national identity that made them the targets of so much contempt and suspicion.[29] They did this not only by maintaining transnational connections with allies in Italy (I have analyzed this at length elsewhere), but also by encouraging and evaluating their fellow immigrants in terms of nationality and "Latin-ness."[30] During the pivotal children's exodus—a tradition of removing strikers' children from harm's way carried over from Italy—an FSI member proudly declared, " . . . we Italian radicals have given a totally Latin stamp to the demonstrations in the streets."[31] After the strike, Italian immigrants flooded the streets of Lawrence by the thousands to attend demonstrations for Ettor and Giovannitti organized by Italian American radical Carlo Tresca and FSI members. One FSI member praised their efforts, declaring, "They possess an enthusiasm and a passion that are unknown to other nationalities that don't have our temperament and our fervor for combat."[32] The FSI and fellow Italian American radicals even garnered the support of certain *prominenti* in Lawrence (and beyond) through appeals as fellow Italians.[33]

FSI members' sense of national pride was central to their efforts to combat their desultory place in the racial hierarchy in the United States. One incident that highlighted this pride and resolve occurred far from Lawrence, during a May Day demonstration for Ettor and Giovannitti in New York City. During a fiery speech given by an FSI member, fellow Federation members and their supporters tore down American flags hung around the podium. When American socialists who had helped organize the meeting responded angrily, one Federation member praised the demonstrators who had removed the flags, arguing, "It is providential that there are foreigners here to inject the proper spirit into the workers, to maintain the traditional uncompromising attitude of international socialism"[34] Unlike the employers and state authorities they battled, FSI members did not see their "foreignness" as a source of shame or a badge of inferiority.[35]

At Lawrence, FSI members drew not only on their shared sense of national identity, but also on their masculinity. An aura of masculine bravado surrounded their presence in the textile town. They were firmly united by the imperatives of ardor and fearlessness, and by their contempt for those who did not meet these standards. Federation members routinely accused Lawrence authorities and mill owners of cowardice in their dealings with the strikers and their leaders. Their greatest act of cowardice, of course, was locking up Ettor and Giovannitti. One FSI member stated bluntly: "You are cowards. . . . You are afraid of admitting you are thieves protected by the law. You fear letting the world know that you put to trial[,] you condemn and you kill by raising the gallows to safeguard your privileges and your rights."[36] In the FSI, there were few accusations worse than lack of courage.

To Federation members, bravery in the violent environment of Lawrence—in the face of arrests, death threats, and vigilantes—was of the utmost importance. According to his son, told stories of the strike by his mother, Giovannitti had been worried about his own safety in Lawrence when first called. When his woman companion, a Russian Jew named Carolina Zaikener, offered to go with him, however, he said no. He would not assuage his fear through the reassuring presence of a woman. Giovannitti went to Lawrence alone and withstood nine months in prison facing a life sentence, defiantly translating Emile Pouget's *Sabotage* into English and writing poetry in his cell.[37] (Despite their enormous emphasis on courage in the face of physical confrontation, there was clearly room within the Italian American construction of masculinity for artistic and intellectual expression.) Tresca remembered, "Giovannitti was more powerful and manly than Jesus"—a comment that reinforced the connection between masculinity and heroism.[38]

For Carlo Tresca and many FSI members, courage at Lawrence extended to enthusiasm for violent opposition to the imprisonment of Ettor, Giovannitti, and Caruso. As with their perspective on southern Italians, the contrast between their approaches to violence at Lawrence and during discussions on the issue just months earlier in opposing the war in Tripoli is telling. When the use of violence was raised during the war in Tripoli, there was considerable disagreement among FSI members. Giovannitti, for one, warned against an indiscriminate celebration of violence for its own sake. He argued, " . . . in the haste of exaggerating proletarian violence [certain syndicalists] have united in sentimentalizing violence so that today there is no difference between brute force and conscious force—instead they praise all violence, from wherever it comes."[39]

He later spoke much more enthusiastically about the use of violence in the context of the strike and defense campaign. Just after his release from jail, he explained, "If Syndicalism does not openly advocate violence, as some anarchists do, it is neither because of a moral predisposition against it, nor on account of fear, but simply because, having a vaster and more complex conception of the class war, it refuses to believe in the myth of any single omnipotent method of action."[40] Giovannitti still did not romanticize violence, or embrace its use in every situation. But he and other FSI members came away from Lawrence regarding violence and physical confrontation as necessary, if not singular, tools and as essential displays of courage.

Their stance on violence was not simply rhetorical flourish. During the strike IWW leader Bill Haywood began receiving death threats almost daily, and Tresca began carrying a gun when he walked through Lawrence. He later wrote, "It was civil war, and in war time guns play their part."[41] At one point a friendly reporter informed Haywood that vigilantes were planning to lynch him and Tresca the next day. The two men spent the night in an Italian section of Lawrence called Il Forte Makalle, known for being impenetrable by the police. Haywood slept surrounded by six young armed Italians. Tresca summoned allies from nearby towns to help protect him and Haywood, and armed sympathizers began pouring into town, prepared to take the offensive. A lawyer for the prisoners ultimately convinced Tresca to intervene. Arguing they would fare poorly in an armed battle, he talked the protesters into declaring a truce.[42]

FSI members' willingness to face and even encourage violent confrontation, forged by its members' experiences at Lawrence, distinguished them not only from their earlier ambivalence but also from the IWW. From the beginning of the conflict, IWW organizers discouraged the strikers from using violence to gain their ends.[43] Ettor told the strikers, "By all means make this strike as peaceful as possible. In the last analysis, all the blood spilled will be your own."[44] By contrast, when police tried to arrest Tresca during a protest for Ettor and Giovannitti, Italian immigrant workers encouraged by Tresca and FSI members tore him from policemen's hands. They beat several of members of the police force so badly they required hospitalization. One of them later died from his wounds.[45]

FSI members' "masculine gender displays" united them through the shared imperative of courage as they faced challenges to their racial identity, but their consuming effort to assert their masculinity was a double-edged sword. Elizabeth Faue and other scholars of working-class masculinity have recognized that an embrace of masculinity can easily lead to the gendering of working-class solidarity, and even the working class itself, as male.[46] Hondagneu-Sotelo, too, has warned of the danger inherent in viewing masculine gender displays only as a liberatory form of resistance, without regard for their implications for men's relations to and perspective on women.[47] FSI members' enthusiasm for violence and their assertions of masculinity constituted a profound challenge to their proscribed place in the racial hierarchy, but also rendered them unable to recognize the distinctive contribution women workers were making at Lawrence and in the American labor movement in general.

They had long perceived of women's capacities in extremely circumscribed ways. Their perceptions of women were explained most clearly by an FSI member who had written an open letter to the queen of Italy asking her to intervene and stop the war in Tripoli. He sought to appeal to her by explaining, "We revolutionaries have the cult of the woman. The woman always exerts a fascinating charm over man, a charm that is sweetened when the woman becomes a mother. And you, your Majesty . . . are a woman, a mother, a sister, and a daughter."[48] FSI members' "cult of the woman" meant that they saw women as mothers, sisters, or daughters—and little else. Giovannitti underscored this perspective in an article he wrote on women's rights. Insisting "I am not a feminist," and admitting to ambivalence on the issue of the "so-called emancipation of woman," he concluded, "but . . . a woman who has five children has the rights of five lives and . . . one who doesn't have the right to make a law doesn't have the duty to submit to it either."[49] This critique of women's lack of suffrage, a comfortable fit with the syndicalist dismissal of electoral politics, camouflaged his embrace of the "cult of the woman." To the extent that women had a claim to any rights in society—Giovannitti enumerated the five lives of the children, but not her own—they were again derived primarily, if not solely, from their roles as wives and especially mothers.

During the strike and defense campaign, driven by the compulsion to prove their masculinity, Federation members' myopia rendered women strikers all but invisible to them. Their particular construction of womanhood meant that women textile workers were not merely subsumed into the masculinist working-class identity FSI members used to protect themselves; they existed outside the category of workers virtually altogether. There is no evidence to suggest that this construction was shaken at Lawrence, despite the central importance of women to the strike, and despite the numerous violent confrontations women initiated during the strike. Over half the strikers were women, and as Ardis Cameron has argued, the work they did both before and during the strike was critical to its success. The links and networks they formed across ethnic lines meant that the strikers were not a chaotic mass waiting to be unified by strike leaders. Indeed, Cameron asserts they deserved most of the credit for creating ties among the strikers from various immigrant groups. Numerous women strikers also contributed to the violent atmosphere in Lawrence by confronting and often assaulting scabs and the relatives of scabs. There were numerous cases of women who were arrested for battling with the police, throwing red pepper at them and even swinging an occasional lead pipe. [50] FSI members' attitudes toward the women strikers are all the more compelling in this context.

Several scholars, Francis Shor foremost, have analyzed the gender politics of the IWW, and argued that it, too, was characterized by a masculinist ethos.[51] IWW leader Bill Haywood's comments about victory in the strike are telling here. He boasted of the role women played in the victory, stating flatly, "The women won the strike."[52] He added, celebrating the IWW's ability to curtail the amount of violence initiated by the strikers, "Passive, with folded arms, the strikers won."[53] Haywood thus erased women's capacity for violence in his assessment of the strike—though arguably for good reason. IWW leaders generally were trying to downplay their organization's reputation for violence. Nonetheless, he also recognized how vital women workers were to the strike's success.

By contrast, FSI members were consumed in Lawrence by the need to defend themselves through assertions of their masculinity. Their attitudes toward violence stood in stark contrast to Wobbly attitudes; they would eventually criticize IWW leaders for cowardice and failure of will during Ettor and Giovannitti's trial. And during the strike, they hardly realized women were involved at all. The only time women in Lawrence were addressed specifically in *Il Proletario* during the entire strike and trial was in a condescending filler piece titled "Women Praying," which mocked a group of women seen praying for Ettor and Giovannitti's release.[54] Not until years later, after the end of World War I, would this group of Italian American syndicalist men take up the issue of organizing women—either simply as fellow workers or as a set of workers with particular needs.

The examination of Italian American syndicalists during this critical era underscores the absolute necessity—both historically and in the present day—of understanding the racialization of Italian immigrants in the United States as an intricate process, in which they too participated. It also suggests that Italian immigrants responded to racialization not only by asserting whiteness, but doing so through ideologies of gender and class as well.

Chapter Seven

I DELITTI DELLA RAZZA BIANCA (CRIMES OF THE WHITE RACE)

Italian Anarchists' Racial Discourse as Crime

Salvatore Salerno

In the large and sophisticated literature on ethnic consciousness and Americanization among European immigrants, very little is known about how Italians thought about race or about how they came to see themselves and their interests as white. What we know about the period between 1880 and 1920 is largely anecdotal. In his work on Italians and racial identity, Robert Orsi has drawn on folklore as a means of introducing the complexity of Italian immigrants' experience with race in America. He tells the following story:

> The children and grandchildren of Italian immigrants to the United States all seem to know a story, which they insist is true, about a greenhorn just off the banana boat who is walking one day down a street in New York (or Boston or Chicago or St. Louis) when he sees a black man. The poor greenhorn is mesmerized. He has never seen a black person before. What is this? Stumbling to keep up, he trots along side the black man, staring in consternation and incredulity at the strange sight. But what can this be? the greenhorn asks himself. Finally, he can't take it anymore. He runs up to the stranger, grabs the startled man by the arm, and starts rubbing his skin furiously to see if the black color comes off.

Orsi then compares the experience of this racially unconscious Italian immigrant with that of the five Sicilian shopkeepers lynched in Tallulah, Louisiana, for violating southern protocols of racial interaction in 1899.[1] These two stories portray Italian immigrants as either unaware of racial difference or oblivious to America's racial hierarchy. Racial unconsciousness, however, does not explain the violent reaction by Tallulah whites to these immigrants. This essay looks at this supposed absence of racial discourse among Italian immigrants. The history of the Italian immigrant left in America, particularly the anarchist sectors of that movement, challenges this view.[2]

The first and second generation of Italian immigrant radicals developed a discourse that was deeply critical of the American racial hierarchy, one that the Justice Department came to view as criminal. This essay participates in the recovery of this discourse to argue that the activism of Italian immigrant anarchists problematizes our understanding of the racialization process during the period from 1880 to 1920. During this period federal authorities drew on their own racialized fears to construct immigration law, which created a new class of criminals to justify its developing system of surveillance of oppositional political practices.

My exploration into the Italian anarchist movement began in Paterson, New Jersey, through the newspapers published by one of the more popular Italian immigrant anarchist groups in the New York metropolitan area, Gruppo L'Era Nuova (New Era Group). In the first quarter of the twentieth century, this group made Paterson a key center of the international anarchist movement. It was instrumental in bringing unionism to "Silk City" (Paterson's primary industry was the manufacture of silk) and it was among the first foreign-language locals to join the Industrial Workers of the World (IWW).

In spite of their importance to the international anarchist community and U.S. labor history, little information exists about the group or any of its members.[3] Early in my research I managed to locate a study by Sophie Elwood that explained part of the reason for this lack of information. Elwood looked at the Italian anarchist community in Paterson through oral histories. She found that the movement's descendents and community members no longer remembered those active in the group as anarchists. "I found it interesting," she wrote, that "today those who were children or adolescents in the early 1900s in the Paterson area almost universally describe their fathers and mothers as socialists in the interviews I conducted. None are portrayed as anarchists."

Only one respondent, Angelena, remembered Paterson's past differently. In the interview, Angelena told of an "unmentionable" event, one Elwood argued has shrouded the community's radical past in silence. Angelena told Elwood of three Haledon men, her uncle among them, who were arrested in 1920 and taken to Ellis Island. "Suspected of plotting to plant a bomb on Wall Street, they were held on the island and threatened with deportation. Angelena recalled her mother and aunt carrying food to her uncle on Sundays, but no other details were ever learned by her." The three Italian anarchists were held for several months, and then released without being formally charged with any crime. Following his release, Angelena's uncle described the event as *finito*—finished. Finished meant "no possibility of reopening the subject." Elwood discovered that Angelena's defense of her uncle against the charges of anarchy was echoed in the words of the others whom she interviewed. Her respondents were equally traumatized, and came to view anarchism as a negative force that would destroy order. "To their children anarchism carried the dread that terrorism does today."[4]

I then located another study that also commented on Paterson's historical amnesia. Nina M. Browne found that the city's radical past had been collapsed into a generalized event meant to equate the community's labor activism with a generic radicalism that not only failed but dealt the death blow to Paterson's silk industry. This event is the 1913 strike. The strike began as a walkout at the Doherty Mill over the introduction of the four-loom system. It soon became a general strike under the leadership of the IWW in which twenty-five thousand workers participated, many of them women and children, from almost all of Paterson's 300 mills and dye houses."[5]

What happened to the histories of these women who organized the mills? In spite of recent scholarly accounts to the contrary, this strike and the decline of Paterson's industry generally have been linked in the city's official and unofficial histories.[6] Among Paterson's local historians and residents, opinions remain varied and often bitter concerning the role of the strike in Paterson's history. In fact, three public museums who collaborated on the critically acclaimed exhibit "Life and Times in Silk City" entirely avoided confronting the issue of the strike. A documentary video on Paterson recounts the 1913 strike alongside tales of the devastating 1902 fire and the 1903 flood "as if," in the words of one critic, "it were another natural disaster."[7] "Time and chronology," Browne concluded, "fade within Paterson's official history, narratives end or skip where bad news begins. Most commonly, details give out around 1920," the date that coincides with the raids by the Justice Department on Paterson's Italian anarchist community.[8]

Were the Haledon anarchists whom Angelena talked about an anomaly, or were their arrests part of a larger pattern? What was their crime, if no charges were brought against them? Following Browne's lead, I consulted the available histories of Paterson's Italian anarchist community. The most I found was an unpublished manuscript by George Carey. His study unfortunately stopped with the suppression of the group's first newspaper *La Questione Sociale,* in 1908. My research supported Browne's conclusions. The historical record no longer accorded a place to the memory of Paterson's radical past. The record stopped sometime around 1920, and the events that occurred in that year had also effectively erased the years leading up to 1920 as well as the community's struggle against fascism.

I contacted the New Jersey Public Library and the State Historical Society, only to learn that neither had material on this period. The Newark Public Library's massive clipping files, created by WPA workers in the 1930s, had nothing relating to the arrests of the Italian anarchists. I looked at the New York newspapers, and to my great surprise I found a story not about the Haledon arrests but about another raid. On February 14, 1920, over one hundred federal agents, assisted by volunteers from the American Legion, descended on Paterson and raided the homes of more than thirty members of Gruppo L'Era Nuova, as well as those active in another anarchist group called Gli Insorti (The Insurgents), and those involved in Paterson's Ferrer School, an anarchist-inspired place for the children of workers to study, directed by workers from the community.

Armed with deportation warrants and suitcases, agents from the Bureau of Investigation made arrests, gathered evidence from the homes of these Italian anarchists, and then delivered the activists to Ellis Island to await possible deportation. The raid had been more successful than Special Agent Frank Stone, who was in charge of covert operation, had imagined possible. In an interview with *The Evening Mail,* Stone speculated that the IWW headquarters in Chicago was in the process of being moved to Paterson. The *New York Call* estimated that in total, over a ton of material was confiscated in the raid. Among the material seized was what the government thought to be "the most complete anarchist library in the United States," a library no one has seen since the raid.[9]

The Justice Department believed that among other things, the Paterson anarchists had been involved in a series of earlier bombings. On June 2, 1919, there were explosions in eight cities: New York, Paterson, Boston, Philadelphia, Pittsburgh, Cleveland, and Washington among them. The most sensational and tragic of the bombings occurred at the home of Attorney General Palmer in Washington, D.C. The bomb thrower stumbled on the stone steps that led to the front door of Palmer's home and blew himself to bits. From the fragments of his body and clothing, police determined that the bomb thrower was an Italian alien from Philadelphia. What caused great suspicion within the left community was the fact that the suitcase he supposedly carried was only slightly damaged. In addition to clothing, leaflets were also found, bearing the title "Plain Words" and signed "Anarchistic Fighters." At the same time the bomb at Palmer's went off, another exploded at the home of Koltz, the president of the Suanaha Silk Company in Paterson. When agents learned that two known members of Gruppo L'Era Nuova had been recently discharged by the company on account of labor trouble, and that characteristics of the explosion were similar to those that occurred at the homes of government officials, they came to view the Paterson's anarchists as part of a nationwide plot.[10]

The events that led to the raids on Paterson's Italian anarchist community are a complicated story that involves a dizzying array of factors. Some of these factors include the connections between Italian anarchism and this rash of bombings that took place in the late 1910s and early 1920s. However, the radical community saw these bombings as a deliberate frame-up on the part of authorities to legitimate repression against the labor movement. The leftist press pointed out that as time passed, the bombings continued in spite of ongoing arrests, deportations, and the secret emigration of anarchists who left the country rather then face arrest. The question of who in fact was responsible has been the subject of a number of theories, none of which are satisfactory.

Though the federal government opened hundreds of deportation files on Italian anarchists, they rarely filed formal charges and very few ended in actual deportation. In fact, no formal charges were ever brought against the Paterson anarchists in connection with the bombings, though a number of them were detained for lengthy periods of time, and placed under surveillance for months and in some cases years. This suggests the possibility that the bombings might not have been orchestrated by Italian immigrants at all. Since they were used by the Bureau to justify campaigns of surveillance, detention, arrest, and deportation of those seen as in opposition to the U.S. government, some have suggested that perhaps the Bureau orchestrated the explosions themselves. Indeed, evidence that the federal government used such tactics to crush the resistance movements of other marginalized citizens from the 1940s to the present, through such illegal campaigns as the FBI's COINTELPRO, suggests that this was entirely possible.[11]

Following the outbreak of World War I, an atmosphere of wartime hysteria colored all decisions from the local to the national level. In his study of the federal suppression of radicals, William Preston summarized the situation faced by labor activists:

> One hundred per cent Americanism, with its demand for conformity and distaste for dissent, savagely resented any threat to national unity, especially of a class and radical nature. Nativist anxieties increased this tension. Such an irrational and emotional atmosphere encouraged patriots, businessmen and politicians to indoctrinate official Washington with exaggerated accounts of a treasonable IWW conspiracy. Convinced of its own helplessness in the face of Wobbly [IWW] solidarity, each locality hoped that the federal government would resolve an intolerable industrial crisis.[12]

The Paterson anarchists fueled these fears. They were key to the IWW's campaign to organize all workers, regardless of race, nationality, gender, or skill, in the northeastern mass-production industries, and had organized several effective campaigns and strikes among workers asserting their right to a livable wage, safe working conditions, and humane hours. Italian immigrant anarchist groups like L'Era Nuova joined the IWW immediately after it was founded in 1905, and they remained active throughout the period from 1905 to 1909, when bitter factional disputes threatened to tear apart the movement. During this critical period, the bulk of the early membership abandoned the IWW because it embraced anarchism and syndicalism, which condoned the use of direct action tactics such as the general strike and sabotage rather than the parliamentarianism of the Socialist Party and the Socialist Labor Party.[13] Following these factional disputes, the IWW membership was limited to a handful of foreign-language locals in the East and a few hundred migratory workers in the West. During these lean years, the bulk of IWW activity occurred in the northeastern textile industries, where the majority of workers were Italian. Gruppo L'Era Nuova became an official local of the IWW in March 1906, and its newspaper, *La Questione Sociale,* was one of the first foreign-language papers to carry the IWW logo.

The Italian anarchists continued to be of strategic importance to the IWW in the 1910s. When federal agents raided Gruppo L'Era Nuova, they found E. F. Doree, Philadelphia Secretary of the IWW, at the home of Andre Graziano, a member of Gruppo L'Era Nuova and IWW organizer, showing the depth of L'Era Nuova's ties to what the Bureau of Investigation considered among the most serious threats to the nation. The *New York Times* reported that among Doree's records were the "bulky membership rosters and ledgers showing financial transactions all over the eastern half of the country."[14] In tracking the government surveillance of the Paterson anarchists, I began to unravel a labyrinth of material scholars have been unable to locate since 1960. Indeed, it was in the files kept by the Immigration and Naturalization Service, which had been closed to the public for the last forty years, that the significance of race to repression against the immigrant left was revealed.[15]

During the widespread raids on the immigrant Left during and after World War I, Bureau linguists made extensive translations and analyses of material published by Gruppo L'Era Nuova. Among the reports that have survived is one that focuses on an article that appeared in *La Jacquerie*, the final newspaper that Gruppo L'Era Nuova published and attempted to circulate during the Red Scare. Titled "Race Hatred" and published in the September 13, 1919 issue, the essay appears to have been part of a series or an irregular column dating back to *La Questione Sociale*. In his report to J. Edgar Hoover, director of the Federal Bureau of Investigation, Special Agent Frank Stone cited the following passages as those he considered most troubling: "In the United States, this land of the free and the home of the brave, it is a crime to kill a dog but an honor to lynch a Negro. During the war, while the American Negro soldiers were allowing themselves to be massacred at the French front in behalf of the triumph of democracy, their relatives were being murdered in their own houses by the democratic rabble."[16] The article called attention to the fact that patriotic sacrifice had not ensured that African American soldiers would return to an improved social and political status in the United States. Rather, lynchings by whites increased after the war, and 1919 witnessed the most intense racial rioting in decades.

Black activists such as W.E.B. Du Bois and Ida B. Wells routinely pointed to the increase in lynching and race riots as evidence of the white majority's refusal to accept changes in the racial status quo in this period.[17] In fact, Department of Justice files show the Bureau of Investigation singling out a related article that appeared in *The Crisis*, September 1919 issue, titled "Returning Soldiers." They quoted, "We Sing! This country of ours, despite what all its better souls have done and dreamed, is yet a shameful land. It lynches *** It disenfranchises its own citizens *** It encourages ignorance *** It steals from us *** It insults us." The parallels between these two Italian and African American papers are quite interesting, but I have not yet found evidence of whether Italian anarchists read African American papers like *The Crisis* or *The Messenger*, or if they were in contact with black militants. But it does appear that Italian anarchists were aware of the kind of arguments that African American writers and activists were making to demand that the United States live up to its democratic ideals.

To the Justice Department, however, Gruppo L'Era Nuova's writing on "Race Hatred" was evidence of its involvement in another diabolical plot. In a lengthy report concerning the department's investigations, Attorney General A. Mitchell Palmer warned that America stood at Armageddon: "Practically all the radical organizations in this nation have looked upon the Negro as a fertile ground for spreading their doctrine. These organizations have endeavored to enlist Negroes on their side, and in many respects have been successful. [As a consequence,] the Negro is seeing red."[18] Such overtures to interracial solidarity reawakened fears among elites of what class-based social and political relationships across lines of race might mean for the racial order. The Justice Department's greatest fear was that radicals were intent on breaking down the social barriers that separated blacks from whites.

When the United States entered World War I in 1917, the U.S. Army developed a counterespionage division known as the Military Intelligence Division (MID), which, like the Bureau of Investigation, redirected its energies from combating domestic subversion by enemy aliens to attacking economic and political radicalism. The Army's domestic intelligence efforts focused on radical labor unionists in the IWW, particularly those with connections to anarchism and communism. Convinced of the growing possibility of a "race war," following the race riots in 1919, MID's weekly summary report ominously noted: "IWW and other radical organizations, both white and black, have played their part in inciting the negroes [*sic*] to the recent outbreaks in Chicago and Washington. It is stated that agitators have played on the feeling of resentment against injustices or fancied injustices suffered by the negro [*sic*] soldiers during the war."[19]

Since IWW activists and all anarchists were believed to be chief among the offending radicals, and a significant portion of the IWW membership was foreign, the Justice Department pressured Congress to make changes in immigration law. They amended legislation to make membership in the IWW by noncitizens grounds for deportation, and were thus able to disrupt and eventually destroy what they saw as a major menace. At the same time the Justice Department managed to convince Congress of the necessity of this change, it argued for further amendments to immigration law that would facilitate the arrest of foreign anarchists: "In this class of cases," it was asserted, "the courts and the public have too long overlooked the fact that crimes and offenses are committed by the written or spoken word. We have been punishing offenders in other lines for words spoken or written, without waiting for an overt act of injury to person or property. Individuals can be punished for words spoken or written, even though no overt act of physical injury follows. It is the power of words that is the potent force to commit crimes in certain cases."[20]

One man in particular was singled out for this offense from the thirty members of Gruppo L'Era Nuova who were arrested in the 1920 raid: his name was Ludovico Caminita. Considered by the Justice Department to be the group's leader, he was also identified as the editor of *La Jacquerie*. Caminita had a long history with the group. He was born in Palermo, Sicily, in 1878 and immigrated to the United States in 1902. Upon his arrival he worked as a printer in Barre, Vermont, on *Cronica Sovversiva*, a militant anarchist newspaper edited by the well-known Italian anarchist agitator Luigi Galleani. Sometime later Caminita relocated to Paterson to help Pedro Esteve, a Spanish anarchist, edit *La Questione Sociale*.[21] When Esteve began his propaganda tours among the hard rock miners in the western part of the United States, Caminita took over editing *La Questione Sociale*. He edited the newspaper from November 1905 until he was discharged from his responsibilities in April 1908, by the Paterson-based Italian anarchist group Gruppo Diritto all'Esistenza. (Right to Existence Group)[22] The group discharged him following a series of his articles that resulted in the removal of the paper's postal privileges under obscenity statutes. The first of these articles appeared in 1906, shortly after Caminita had assumed editorship of the paper. The article, entitled "Race Hatred" (like the 1919 essay, which would arouse the fears of the federal government) was intended as a crushing condemnation of racial and ethnic stereotypes, which he argued divided the working class into hostile camps:

> Instead of joining together, workers in this large cosmopolitan nation fight for their existence, according to the laws baptized by Darwin, instead of joining together to mutually defend their class interests against the common enemy: the capitalist. They instead participate in a painful phenomenon which profoundly destroys the proletarian class in its most vital social interest: in a war, that is to say, which is fought fierce and without truce between Blacks, whites, Chinese, Europeans, Americans, Indians.[23]

Unfortunately, Caminita chose to build his case around Czolgosz. Leon F. Czolgosz, a self-proclaimed anarchist who was not a member of any anarchist group or well known within the anarchist movement, assassinated President William McKinley on September 6, 1901.[24] As Caminita observed, "When Czolgosz killed McKinley, it was not enough to shout against anarchy, it was shouted that he was of Polish nationality." The combination of the emotionally charged subject of political assassination coupled with Caminita's caustic wit and Italian sense of irony made the careless reader jump to the conclusion that it was a defense of Czolgosz and not a condemnation of race hatred.

Caminita disappeared from Paterson in May 1908 after a grand jury indicted him for authorship of illegal editorials. Many rumors surrounded Caminita's disappearance, ranging from his joining Emma Goldman and Alexander Berkman's group at *Mother Earth*, a prominent anarchist journal, to having eloped with the young wife of a tavern keeper.[25] Caminita would eventually return to Paterson and reconnect with the Italian anarchist group but details of his life are sketchy. In the 1910s we find Caminita editing the Italian-language column of *Regeneración*, the newspaper of the Mexican Liberal Party (PLM), an anarchist organization responsible for initiating the Mexican Revolution. That the paper included a column in Italian is explained in part by the observations of historian James Sandos. He writes that Ricardo Flores Magón found the deepest support for the PLM and the plight of the Mexican working people among Italian and Spanish anarchists.[26] From Caminita's column it appears that some of the Paterson anarchists fought in the Mexican Revolution on the side of the PLM.

While the details of association between Italian, Spanish, and Mexican anarchists are still obscure, these influences are evident in the movement's expressive culture. In addition to his Italian language column, Caminita contributed many of the graphics that became emblematic of the Mexican Revolution. This can be seen especially in a poster printed as part of the newspaper in 1910. The top part of the poster displays the *Regeneración* masthead. Over a picture of the sun are the portraits of five anarchists: Peter Kropoktin at the center; to his right, the famous Italian anarchist Errico Malatesta and the French anarchist Charles Malato; to his left, the Spanish anarchists Fernando Tarrida del Mármol and Anselmo Lorenzo. These portraits are set against an open book upon which are written two titles, Malato's *Philosophy of Anarchism* and Malatesta's *Conversation Between Two Workers*. Below them are the portraits of the most prominent Mexican anarchists, the Flores Magón brothers, Librado Rivera, Angelmo Figueroa, and Antonio de P. Araújo.[27]

Following the suppression of *La Questione Sociale* in 1908, the Paterson anarchist group began publishing another paper, *L'Era Nuova*. In 1909, an article titled, "I Delitti della Razza Bianca" (The Crimes of the White Race) appeared. The article began by stating: "Since the most ancient times the white race has acted against all the other races like a predatory animal." The article appeared on the front page, but like many of the articles that would appear in this paper on race and antipatriotism, it was written anonymously. The article discussed the many crimes whites had committed, and continued to commit, against Native Americans, African Americans, and Asian immigrants.

> The discovery of America marks the beginning of a period of destruction, which lasts even today for the shame of humanity. The white race continues its systematic destruction of the races of color. When it cannot succeed with violence, it adopts corruption, hunger, alcohol, opium, syphilis, tuberculosis—all weapons—as good as guns and cannons.

In addition to recounting the horrors of colonization, the writer(s) discussed how whites have denied the humanity of those they sought to colonize. To Gruppo L'Era Nuova, the greatest tragedy was the "loss of human variety, the beauty of the entire human species, deprived of its very beautiful and powerful branches." The writer(s) then closed the essay with a reminder of the transformative potential of the resistance movements that were developing among the oppressed:

> We believe that within a short time what they call the Negro Problem will give more trouble to the United States, more than they have already had from any other serious issue, even bigger than the Civil War. Maybe even the destruction of the United States will result from this problem because at this point the Negroes are not willing to be considered the descendents of slaves, and are developing a pride of race . . . we don't know what it will bring. . . .[28]

Another article, titled "Razze Superiori, Imparate!" (Superior Races, Learn This!), attested further to the long history of resistance of colonized people to the European domination. This essay provides further evidence of the breadth of the group's solidarity with worldwide struggles for liberation. In "Guerra di Razza" (Race War), an article that appeared some months later, the Paterson anarchists addressed the topic of patriotism and militarism. The writer focused the critique on modern sociology and called into question the notion that race was based in natural science. Rather, they argued, race should be seen as a historical notion and nationalism the result of secular struggles of the state. The author then addressed the work of Italian anthropologist Alfredo Niceforo, who used statistical data to demonstrate that the southern Italian poor were a race apart from the northern Italian wealthy elite, with specific physical, psychological, and ethnographic deficiencies: "Even if the theory were not correct and the differences of class would not correspond with differences of ethnic origin, the race of the rich and the race of the poor would only have antagonistic interests. That struggle of race, it seems to many, is the propagator of the progress of history." Leaving aside this allusion to the amalgam of race and class, the writer went on to discuss formulas used by the press to whip up jingoism and inspire in every citizen the "duty to cooperate for the triumph and definitive victory of the superior race." After a while, the writer continued, "one perceives that the formula was empty of content, was absurd, was false but, when the game is revealed, it is already too late."[29]

In his examination of the Italian radical press, Rudolph J. Vecoli has found that Italian socialists, unlike other Marxist groups, did not fail to protest wrongs against blacks. Rather, Italian socialists analyzed the causes of racism and attempted to incorporate an analysis of race into their critique of capitalism.[30] However, the Italian socialist press privileged class over race. One of the few articles to appear in the socialist Italian-language paper *Il Proletario* summarized the perspective of the Italian Socialist Federation in the United States. In "Not a Race Issue, But a Class Issue," the writer pointed to the reprehensible way racism was practiced in American society:

> Who do they think they are as a race, these arrogant whites? From where do they think they come? These blacks are at least a race, but the white Americans . . . how many of them are bastards? How much mixing is in their pure blood? How many of their women ask for kisses from the strong and vigorous black slaves? Like the white man who wants the hot pleasure of the black women with big lips and sinuous bodily movement. But the white knights care little for the honor and decency of the black woman, whom they use and abuse as they please. For these, race hatred is a national duty.

In this example the writer fails to analyze the concept of race itself or to problematize the sexual stereotypes associated with race. Instead, the writer ends the article by collapsing race into class: "The producers must unify against the exploiters of their product. The struggle isn't about race but class."[31] Vecoli goes on to quote Luigi Galleani, who "mocked the self-righteousness of Americans who expressed indignation at the persecution of the Jews in Russia while they 'denied blacks work in their factories, justice in their courts, protection in their laws, and pity in their hearts.'"[32] While we find the occasional article in other newspapers of the Italian Left, the anarchist press in Paterson contains the most sustained and detailed critique of race in United States. This was one of the main reasons that these anarchists were targeted during the Red Scare of the late 1910s and early 1920s. The absence of this critical discourse from the narrative of Italian American experience was a carefully orchestrated campaign on the part of the U.S. federal government. It is perhaps a final irony that this history was not entirely lost as a result of the work of federal agents and their team of linguistic experts.

Those Italians who challenged the color line faced the wrath not only of the federal government but also of vigilante whites (who often included political and religious leaders). Italian immigrants were lynched by whites in Louisiana, Mississippi, West Virginia, Florida, and some western mining towns, for alleged crimes that included violating local racial codes.[33] In the summer of 2001, I traveled to a small town on the outskirts of New Orleans to interview the aunt of a friend about a lynching of Italians that took place there in the 1920s. "They will kill me if I tell you," was the first thing that she said when her nephew asked her to tell me the story. "Are you sure that you are Italian?" she asked repeatedly. After many assurances she finally told me the story. There were six, she said, one was only a boy. In her version someone in the group had stood up to the Klan, and in turn a crime was fabricated; the men were tried twice; and all were hanged in a special prison constructed for the executions. My friend's aunt and other members of the African American community considered it a lynching.[34] My friend then took me to a grocery store down the highway owned by Italian Americans. It was a store patronized by African Americans because the owner had been driven out of New Orleans for his consistent business with the African American community. Unfortunately, the owner had little time for someone from the North asking probing questions. I was greeted with the same silence Elwood had encountered in her oral histories with the descendants of the anarchists in Paterson. I knew that it was the kind of story that would take a great deal of time to unravel. What unites the histories of lynching with repression against the Left is not only the refusal of Italian immigrants to regard African Americans as the enemy, but also the heavy consequences of their attempts to join forces. Such transgression challenged the foundations of white supremacy at its core, and for this reason they were attacked, murdered, and silenced.

CHAPTER EIGHT

SURREALIST, ANARCHIST, AFROCENTRIST

Philip Lamantia Before and After the "Beat Generation"

FRANKLIN ROSEMONT

A great poet in a society "too busy" for poetry, Philip Lamantia is not a household name. Far from MTV and the talk shows, however, his reputation is assured and growing. At least to the "happy few" he is well known as the first major surrealist poet in the United States. He was in fact recognized as such at the age of fifteen, in a 1943 letter from André Breton, surrealism's principal founder, who went on to publish several of Lamantia's poems in the New York journal *VVV* (called Triple-V) the following year.[1]

Also known—far more in some circles than his surrealism—is Lamantia's pivotal role as pioneer and exemplar of the San Francisco (literary) Renaissance of the 1950s, and consequently as inspirer of, mentor to, and sporadic participant in the so-called Beat Generation. Readers who try to keep up with the U.S. "poetry scene" are aware that he is one of the principal poetic voices of the late twentieth century, well represented in prestigious anthologies, widely translated, and held in particularly high esteem by other poets. The African American poet Ted Joans, who fully shares Lamantia's surrealist perspectives, has gone so far as to call him the "American Rimbaud." But even those whose poetry is antithetical to his, and whose work he himself has sharply criticized—Kenneth Rexroth, for example, and Allen Ginsberg—have expressed high praise for Lamantia.[2]

Much less acknowledged is Lamantia's crucial part in the resurgence of organized surrealism in the United States from the late 1960s into the 1990s, as coeditor of the journal *Arsenal/Surrealist Subversion* and as contributor to many other surrealist publications. During this period, by far the most productive of his life, he published five books of poems and a number of remarkable articles on poetics. Especially vital are his contributions to the development of surrealist theory and polemics in those years, most notably his profound critique of the "New American Poetry" in 1976 and his impassioned appreciation of the magic and the Marvelous inherent in the mystery and adventure radio shows of his childhood, published in 1979.[3]

Almost never mentioned in the literature about him is Lamantia's passionately *revolutionary* outlook, inseparable from his surrealism: his lifelong commitment to anarchism, antimilitarism, radical ecology (including wilderness preservation and restoration), and his vehement rejection of the "white mystique" and other Eurocentric myths and ideologies. In addition to an unswerving opposition to white supremacy in all its forms, he long ago openly declared himself an Afrocentrist, and since his teenage years has consistently manifested, in his writing and in his life, an active solidarity with the "colored," "tribal," and "primitive" peoples of the Earth. His politics are of course those of a poet rather than of a politician, but they definitely involve sweeping social and cultural transformation—the global supersession of capitalism, no less—and are by no means restricted to the "spiritual" realm. Lamantia's revolutionary views, and especially his "race politics"—which go far beyond mere "antiracism"—distinguish him radically from the majority of U.S. poets and other intellectuals of his time.

Critical literature on Lamantia is far from copious, and 90 percent of what little there is has concentrated on what he himself regards as a relatively minor episode in his life: his much-debated relation to the Beat movement.[4] Unlike most poets and writers of his generation, he has rarely cooperated with—nay, has most often aggressively discouraged—would-be biographers or interviewers.[5] In an age of celebrity overproduction, he has preferred to shun the limelight. Now in his mid-seventies, he remains defiantly "underground," and has often been described as a hermit. This essay explores the distinctive phases of Lamantia's life and work as well as the various interconnections between them, focusing on the various ways in which his critical view of "race matters" in the U.S. helped shape—and were in turn shaped by—his active intervention in "poetic matters."

A SICILIAN AMERICAN SURREALIST TEENAGER

Philip Lamantia was born October 23, 1927, in San Francisco's Mission District, and continued to live in that city until his mid-teens.[6] After a decade and more of wandering in many lands, in 1969 he returned to San Francisco, and has remained there ever since. His parents, Nunzio and Mary Tarantino Lamantia, had emigrated to the United States from Sicily as children. Of his own early childhood, the most crucial formative influence was his paternal grandmother, whose narration of Sicilian folktales was an admirable introduction to the Marvelous.

In grade school he discovered poetry via Edgar Allen Poe, and immediately began writing imitations of Poe's works. Soon afterward he also found his way to the weird fantasy tales of the reclusive and then little-known H. P. Lovecraft. Rebellious by nature, in junior high he became aware of the revolutionary movement, and was briefly expelled for "intellectual delinquency." Retrospective exhibitions of the work of Miró and Dali at the San Francisco Museum of Modern Art opened his eyes to surrealism, and in a matter of weeks he had read David Gascoyne's *Short Survey of Surrealism* (London, 1935), and begun exchanging letters with Charles Henri Ford and Parker Tyler, editors of the surrealist-oriented magazine *View*, published in New York. The publication of four of Lamantia's poems in the June 1943 issue of *View* brought him an enthusiastic letter from André Breton, author of the *Surrealist Manifestos*, who, with other surrealist painters and poets, was then living in New York as a refugee from Nazism. In his letter, Breton hailed Lamantia as "a voice that rises once in a hundred years." The next issue of *VVV*, the bilingual journal of the Paris Surrealist Group in exile, featured three of Lamantia's poems, along with a letter to Breton declaring his wholehearted solidarity with the surrealist movement, all published under the title "Surrealism in 1943."

Like Lamantia himself, surrealism in 1943 was still in its teens. Organized in Paris in 1924—the year of Breton's first *Surrealist Manifesto* and the debut issue of the first surrealist magazine, *La Révolution Surréaliste*—surrealism from the start superseded the narrow frameworks of the various "avant-gardes" that preceded it.[7] Refusing to limit themselves to art or literature, surrealists took up the myriad problems of "human expression in *all* its forms," including social criticism and politics, and situated themselves unreservedly "in the service of Revolution."[8] Despite its European origins, moreover, surrealism from day one was vehemently anti-Eurocentric, and has never ceased to elaborate its merciless critique of European values and institutions.[9] Unlike fauvism, cubism, and Dada, which acknowledged the influence of African and/or Asian art but remained exclusively white movements, surrealism was multiracial. Similarly, while other "avant-gardes" were all male, or admitted only a few "token" women, the surrealist movement has welcomed the active participation of several hundred women poets, artists, and theorists.[10]

Surrealism quickly spread all over Europe, and by the mid-1930s also counted flourishing groups in North Africa, South America, and Japan. Banned in countries under fascist or Stalinist rule, the movement continued to expand during World War II—"underground" in the war-zone countries, but openly in Mexico, Martinique, Cuba, Haiti, and (a little later) Quebec. The New York group, although dominated by refugees and thus only to a limited degree a vehicle for U.S. poets and artists, nonetheless organized a large International Surrealist Exhibition in 1942 as well as several notable smaller shows, and issued an impressive number of significant publications.[11] Apart from Lamantia, however, the U.S. contributions were mostly in the plastic arts, not in poetry. Indeed, of the English-language poems published in *VVV*, his alone can truly be called outstanding. Here, truth to tell, was a startlingly bold and original voice. With lightninglike freedom and verve, his insurrectionary imagination opened the way for a poetry *fundamentally different* from the inhibited and inhibiting puritanical/positivist conventions of the U.S. literary mainstream:

I stamp the houses of withering wax
Bells of siren-teeth (singing to our tomb
refusal's last becoming)
. . .
Every twisted river pulls down my torn-out hair
("Islands of Africa")

The mermaids have come to the desert;
they are setting up a boudoir next to the camel
who lies at their feet of roses
("The Touch of the Marvelous")

Lamantia's letter to Breton, too, is a text of special importance. A veritable mini-manifesto, it is at once a concise statement of the poet's own youthful vision and a key document of international surrealism during World War II. Starting with the proclamation of his "formal adherence to surrealism . . . since it is of a purely revolutionary nature, which even before my knowledge of surrealism, was part of my own individual temperament," he goes on to argue that

> A true revolutionary poet can not help defying every appalling social and political instrument that has been the cause of death and exploitation in the capitalistic societies of the earth. If he is one for the transformation of the world, as he should be, and if he is not stupid, in relation to a method of approaching these vital issues, the poet will not be opposed to the surrealist attitude.

He further indicates his intention "to express a revolt, and a contempt in my poetry or otherwise, for any system or form that stands for mechanistic thinking and the enslavement of man!" Drawing to a conclusion, he stresses the need

> To rebel! That is the immediate objective of poets! We can not wait and will not be held back by those individuals who are the prisoners of the bourgeoisie, and who have not the courage to go on fighting in the name of the "idea"! The poetic marvelous and the "unconscious" are the true inspirers of rebels and poets!

Thus a second-generation Sicilian American teenager threw in his lot with the international surrealist movement in its quest to make a revolution, a *surrealist* revolution: that is, to emancipate humankind not only from wage slavery but also from the slavery of ideology and the Reality Principle by resolving the immobilizing contradictions between the subjective and the objective, the real and the imaginary—in short, between poetry and everyday life.

Clearly, in Lamantia's youthful commitment to the surrealist cause, there is nothing that could be called "dabbling," or "flirtation," or any sort of cynical opportunism. On the contrary, his self-identification with the adventure was so deep and thoroughgoing that he simply and naturally, without even trying, "made it his own." A few months after his exchange of letters with Breton, the sixteen-year-old San Franciscan left home and high school to go east and join the Surrealist Group in New York. He met Breton, the painters Yves Tanguy, Max Ernst, and Kurt Seligmann; Greek poet/critic Nicolas Calas; and a young French poet and Harvard student named Charles Duits. He also became acquainted with several American writers and artists who took part in the group, including sculptor David Hare (managing editor of

VVV) and painter Gerome Kamrowski, as well as the critics Lionel Abel and Harold Rosenberg.[12]

Despite this seemingly auspicious beginning, Lamantia's early participation in the surrealist movement proved to be frustratingly limited, and lasted barely half a year. Even before the newcomer's arrival in New York, the group had ceased to hold regular meetings, so that his firsthand encounters with surrealists were few and far between—and almost entirely with individuals. After the publication of the last issue of *VVV* (no. 4) in 1944, the essentially *collective* character of surrealist activity was scarcely apparent in New York. With the defeat of Nazism in France in May 1945, the group of surrealist exiles in effect disbanded. Breton and the great majority of the surrealist refugees returned to Paris, and most of the U.S. participants—including Abel, Rosenberg, and the painter Robert Motherwell—moved on to new careers with no relation to surrealism, or even openly hostile to it. The stubborn few who remained true to the movement's revolutionary principles and goals—most notably Kamrowski, the photographer Clarence John Laughlin, and Lamantia—soon fled New York, and survived as subterranean "loners" for much of their lives.[13] As Lamantia later recalled:

> I had awakened to something that had been dreamed earlier, but the tremendous abyss between my expectations and reality was never greater than in 1945. It was a time of almost immeasurable anguish, and I felt I was absolutely isolated and living in a vacuum.[14]

IN THE ANARCHIST SCENE

Back in San Francisco, he frequented a small, informal, surrealist-oriented group around the painter Charles Howard, who had taken part in the Surrealist Group in London during the war. A few other painters were involved, including the Greek artist Jean Varda (who had participated in the 1936 International Surrealist Exhibition in London), but the group proved ephemeral and nothing came of it.[15] It was in the Bay Area anarchist scene that Lamantia found not only kindred spirits but also an outlet for his revolutionary fervor and imagination. In the absence of any form of organized surrealism, it was a natural choice. In a 1982 interview he recalled that at his first meeting with André Breton, "I told him I felt close to the anarchist position [and] he told me that he did, too."[16]

He made his way into the largely Italian-language anarchist group in his hometown, and soon he was good friends with several Italian and Sicilian old-timers, including Tony Martocchia, who before immigrating to the United States in 1920 had been closely associated with the celebrated Errico Malatesta. As an anarchist, Lamantia was strictly a rank and filer. He did not put himself forward. He organized no groups, wrote no manifestos, started no anarchist magazines of his own. But he regularly attended meetings and rallies; distributed leaflets; took part in group discussions; lectured occasionally (at least once on the theories of Wilhelm Reich); and corresponded with anarchist comrades in the United States and abroad. He also kept up with, and sometimes collaborated on, the U.S. and international anarchist press. Above all, he lived an anarchist life. Notwithstanding his self-effacing role, the eighteen-year-old poet was the subject of a year-long investigation by the FBI.[17]

Although his direct participation in organized anarchism lasted only half a decade, Lamantia's devotion to anarchist aims and principles remained intact in later years. Indeed, in 1981 he told me he felt he was "becoming more and more of an anarchist every day." His sympathetic interest in the whole gamut of history's heretics and heterodoxies; his perception of a strong anarchist dimension in Native American cultures; his prescient awareness of the urgency of ecological issues (it was from him that I first learned of Earth First! in the 1980s); his passion for the works of such proto-ecosocialists as John Muir and Mary Austin; his Afrocentrism; and his overall emphasis on poetry and love as humankind's surest methods of knowledge convey something of the scope and depth of his anarchism, which the revived anarchist movement of today is just beginning to discover.

COLD WAR, ADDICTION, AND MYSTICISM: A POET'S ECLIPSE

Most people I know who lived through the postwar 1940s and 1950s, the first third of the Cold War, recall them as I do—as bleak years, full of foreboding and fears galore. Red scares, drug scares, Pachuco scares, and UFO scares were the order of the day. For the U.S. ruling class, however—the prime victor of the war—those years meant vast capital accumulation and imperialist expansion, which inevitably also meant global (U.S.-sponsored) counterrevolution. On the domestic front, both major political parties, aided and abetted by the then-new television craze, fostered the myth of an all-pervasive national (as well as nationalist) self-satisfaction underscored by a paranoid antiradicalism that upheld white supremacy, union-busting, Christian fundamentalism, misogyny, and all the other staples of an exploitative social system. The defeat of European fascism did not prevent Senator Joseph McCarthy's rampage against the Bill of Rights, or the passage of fascist-inspired legislation (Taft-Hartley, the McCarran Act, etc.), or even an imbecile war on comic books, right here in the United States.

For true poets and artists, and for surrealists in particular, it was an especially traumatic time. The atomic bombing of Hiroshima and Nagasaki, accounts of the massive concentration camps in Hitler's Germany and Stalin's Soviet Union, and the rise of a mass whites-only, feel-good American chauvinist conformism cast a pall over the whole period. In intellectual circles, as timid, pragmatic, rationalist conventions regained ground, hopes for revolutionary change evaporated. What passed for a literary "avant-garde" was dominated by southern reactionaries and a small New York group of repentant ex-Trotskyists around the journal *Partisan Review.* Together with the multimillionaire promoters of "abstract expressionism" and their "pop art" and "conceptualist" successors in art, this neonationalist bloc, who were not averse to accepting funds from the CIA, fomented a widespread hostility to surrealism that lasted through much of the Cold War.[18] Surrealism was misrepresented, trivialized, and ridiculed in the daily press, the Sunday supplements, the photo weeklies, and academic quarterlies; reduced to the narrow realm of aesthetics in the art magazines; and ignored or condescendingly dismissed in the traditional U.S. Left press. It also had the distinction of being denounced in the halls of Congress.[19]

No wonder, then, that in such calamitous times, demoralization, depression, and despair increasingly defined the prevailing mood among so many free spirits. To cite just a few examples from the former Surrealist Group in New York: Arshile Gorky's suicide, Sonia Sekula's nervous breakdown, and Gerome Kamrowski's retreat to the obscurity of Ann Arbor, Michigan, were signs of the times, indeed!

Lamantia himself, largely under what he later called the "baleful influence" of Kenneth Rexroth, drifted away from surrealism for several years. Unlikely as it may seem, it was Rexroth who wrote the preface to the poet's first book, *Erotic Poems* (1946). "Some commit suicide at eighteen," Lamantia said in 1992. "I didn't commit suicide—I met Kenneth Rexroth."[20] As he explained further, Rexroth's longstanding antipathy to surrealism turned out to be based entirely on "the standard critical pabulum"—that is, the common but mistaken notion that surrealism is nothing more than the "glorification" of the unconscious or the irrational. At the time, however, the young poet—depressed and disoriented—found the older writer's arguments persuasive. "Caught up in the mood of the time," as he put it later, Lamantia entered the most disheartened and desolate period of his life, which he eventually came to call his "eclipse."

This "retreat" from surrealism (I put the word in quotation marks because he never really repudiated his youthful surrealist ideals) was a reckless plunge into nomadism, narcotics, and mysticism. Physically, he all but disappeared—always seemed to be Somewhere Else, far away, out of reach. For extended periods he lived in Mexico, and spent five years in Spain, Morocco, Italy, Greece, and France, with brief, intermittent returns to the United States. In a "Biographical Note" for Donald Allen's anthology, *The New American Poetry* (1960), he described his present whereabouts as "mostly underground, and traveling."[21]

His "interior odyssey" during those years was a harrowing and labyrinthine adventure that led him down many painful detours and to more than a few dead ends. Like many bop musicians, he found in marijuana, heroin, cocaine, and other intoxicating substances not only a temporary escape from an unbearable "reality," but also a means of forcing hallucination, awakening illumination, exploring what is normally invisible and inaudible. "Getting high" was an attempt, in the spirit of Baudelaire's "Anywhere Out of the World," to elude the clutches of the military-industrial-nuclear horror, and the ideological myths built upon it—the systematization and rationalization of misery that Breton designated *miserabilism*.[22]

Opposition to bourgeois society's ruling values, including what André Breton designated as the infamous trinity of "God, Fatherland, and Family," was central to surrealism from the very beginning.[23] In the surrealists' view, the Church was a bastion of the very *worst* in the Old Order: white supremacy, colonialism, misogyny, and other manifestations of psychological, sexual, and social repression as well as brutal political reaction. In Lamantia's youth, Church support for Mussolini's and Franco's fascism, its servile accommodation of Nazism, and its complicity in imperialist genocide and plunder in Africa were especially notorious. It is no accident, therefore, that a vehement anticlericalism and blasphemy, via the blackest "black humor," have been recurring themes of his poetry:

The children who are ten feet tall are wet. . . . .
They play their games as a steeple topples, as a clown's laugh is heard in church.
("A Civil World," in *Touch of the Marvelous*)

Crab gore To give capitalism its due duck-cracker the head of a christian fart
graveyard of sanctimonious filth
("West," in *Meadowlark West*)

Let fly the churches of memory they're only prisons anyway
("Open Your Head of Cisterns," in *Blood of the Air*)

His Sicilian background notwithstanding, Lamantia was not brought up in the Catholic religion; his occasional exposure to its rites, however, provoked a deep revulsion reflected in many poems of later years, most powerfully in "Ex Cathedra" (first published in the journal *Arsenal/Surrealist Subversion* in 1989), which he described to me as a kind of "revenge" against the nuns and priests whose authoritarian words and ways were among the gloomiest memories of his youth.

To weave garter belts with chaos and snakes, the nun's toenail of crimson phallus. . . .
snake oil on a eucharistic tongue

plagues of scripture blown to smithereens

The absolute pulverization of all the churches will be the grace of love's freedom!

HIP VERSUS BEAT

It was as a world-wandering junkie and self-described "bum in tatters" that Lamantia, in New York around 1948, became "associated with"—to use his own carefully chosen words—what later came to be known as the Beat Generation.[24] The locution suggests casual proximity rather than active participation, and it is a fact that he never considered himself one of Allen Ginsberg's coterie, or in sympathy with the neo-Poundian ideology of the "New American Poetry." Apart from the celebrated Gallery 6 poetry reading in San Francisco in 1955, he tended to keep his distance from the media-focused Beats. Even at the Gallery 6 reading, Lamantia significantly did not read his own work, but rather poems by his friend John Hoffman—seaman, longshoreman, hipster— who had died shortly before, at the age of twenty-five. According to Lamantia, Hoffman was "the silent cool one," the very "type" of the "cool" hipster—and indeed, *the* model of the "angelheaded hipsters" saluted in the third line of Ginsberg's *Howl*.[25] Lamantia, who memorialized him in a poem (titled "John Hoffman") in *Ekstasis*—

road that announced him
road that did not see him
eyes that circled the sun

. . .

there's a sign
the sun circles the air
. . .
a road becomes an eye[26]

—recalls him warmly as "the only really close friend I had in my youth . . . the only one who was also a great poet." Nearly half a century later he continues to regard Hoffman's "really marvelous poems" as "much better" than the poetry of Rexroth, Duncan, Spicer, Ginsberg, Kerouac, and other San Francisco Renaissance and/or Beat writers.[27]

It is important to realize that Lamantia was himself a hipster—"hip" rather than "Beat," and the distinction, far from being trivial or frivolous, was in truth vital and visceral, involving radically opposed views of life and the world. For Lamantia, hip was a radical *moral* outlook, grounded in the age-old and fundamentally African American ethic of disengagement from the "mainstream." According to linguist David Dalby, the word is derived from the Wolof *hipiti* (signifying *awareness*), and was introduced to North America in the earliest years of black slavery.[28] By the 1910s it had spread to other "disengaged" sectors; at the start of that decade the IWW-oriented *International Socialist Review* featured an article titled "Get Hip."[29]

In the 1940s, however, the term took on a deeper and more provocative significance with the rapid rise of the new black music known as bebop, or bop. The boppers' unheard-of rhythms, high-speed tempos, and dissonant chords, and the sparkling magic of what Charlie Parker called "internal hearing" broke through thick walls of time and created exhilarating free spaces for the revolutionary imagination.[30] Refusing to "entertain," the bop musicians—Parker, "Dizzy" Gillespie, Thelonious Monk, Babs Gonzales, Max Roach, and many others—developed a defiant stance, "cool" and confrontational. As Robin D. G. Kelley has pointed out, boppers and the hipsters of all colors who made up the bop community came to exemplify a wide-ranging "culture of opposition."[31] In their eyes, World War II was incontestable proof that "white" so-called civilization stood irredeemably self-condemned. The "American Dream," as Malcolm X remarked a few years later, had proved to be a nightmare, and those who really dug Parker's "Warming Up a Riff" and Monk's "Round Midnight" wanted no part of it. To be hip involved a struggle for personal integrity and group solidarity in the face of advanced capitalism's ruthless depersonalization and repression, as epitomized in that daily horror of horrors, the "work ethic." In *Black Talk*, Ben Sidran describes hip as "a reversal of norms wherein the social deviant sees the greater public as not only uninformed but potentially dangerous."[32] For the hipster, says Sidran, the "game" of conformity is "not worth playing."

Bop, nerve center of the hip life, was one of Lamantia's key passional attractions during (and after) his long "eclipse." It would not be going too far to say that the improvisations of Charlie Parker, Thelonious Monk, and others were decisive factors in keeping him alive in this precarious period "on the edge of the abyss . . . marked by psychic and somatic excess."[33] For him, as for many surrealists at the time, these new black sounds were the musical equivalent of "pure psychic automatism" (André Breton's original definition of surrealism)—an auditory experience of the Marvelous.[34] In his desperate battle against misery and the mundane, bop provided him with what poet Aimé Césaire called "miraculous weapons."[35] In spite of excruciating agonies and confusions on all sides, *here*—in the new jazz—was authentic *awareness* at its hottest and brightest.

Clearly Lamantia's sense of "hip" has more than a touch of surrealism in it, but it nonetheless corresponds closely to the original Wolof meaning. Notably, too, his usage has nothing in common with Norman Mailer's once-influential but hopelessly inept notion of the psychopathic "White Negro."[36] The "Beat," however, in Lamantia's view, was entirely something else: an external observer of the hip, a kind of tourist whose "disengagement" from the dominant order he had found to be superficial and calculated. Lamantia, as a hipster, was fully aware of what Chester Himes called America's "highly organized system of reputation-making," and its infinite supply of self-serving ruses.[37] Most Beats, in his view, were basically ambitious bohemian types who used a posture of rebellion to pursue such unhip goals as critical acclaim, official recognition, and otherwise "making it" on the "square" world's terms. Later, as vilification of the Beats by "old guard" conservatives such as Norman Podhoretz backfired, and countless rebellious youngsters swelled the Beat ranks, Lamantia's original criticism no longer seemed to apply.

Interestingly, Lamantia was the only hipster Ginsberg allowed at the Gallery 6 reading; evidently his notorious surrealist past and one-time closeness to Rexroth somehow made him acceptable. Excluded was Lamantia's friend Gerd Stern ("Jack Steen" in Kerouac's *Subterraneans*), who, as it happens, was the one who had notified him that their New York acquaintance "Ginsy" was now in San Francisco trying to organize a poetry reading.[38] What is important is that Lamantia's friends in those days were not the Beats-to-be on the well-lit road to success, but rather the haunted hipsters on the darker path to Nobody Knows Where. (One of Hoffman's texts is titled "Journey to the End.")

What clinched Lamantia's own reputation as a Beat writer were mostly factors over which he had no control: the inclusion of his work in various Beat magazines and anthologies, and his appearance as a character in Kerouac's novelized chronicles of the time. Unlike most writers, who eagerly submit their work to all manner of publications, Lamantia has always had a strong aversion to such "submission," and in truth has actively collaborated on relatively few journals over the years. Significantly, to cite but one instance, he refused to be included in the "San Francisco Renaissance" issue of *Evergreen Review*, considered by many to be the publication that, more than any other, brought the Beat poets to wide public attention.[39]

Lamantia did not disagree with the Beats' opposition to academic classicism, middle-class conformism, complacency, censorship, and sexual repression. His surrealism, however, as well as his experience as a hipster, set him apart from the "crowd-pleasing" Ginsberg and others. To put it simply, Lamantia demanded vastly *more* from poetry. And with rare exceptions from the time of his "eclipse," his own work as a poet, and later as an essayist and a theorist, is light-years away from Beat literature. As Nancy Joyce Peters noted in a standard reference work on Beat writers:

> Lamantia's work, rooted in another tradition, never quite fit the Beat canon. His erudition and eclectic intellectual pursuits were alien to the often semiliterate, populist conventions of the Beats. While much Beat writing was spontaneous reportage and meditation on daily life, Lamantia concentrated on hermetic, symbolic, and magical themes. . . . Many Beat poets made an immediate impact through direct political statement and appealed to unrealized American ideals. Lamantia, on the other hand, never abandoned hope for a world revolution of the greatest magnitude but shunned topical political poetry as had the European surrealists.[40]

BEATS AND "WHITENESS"

The "hip" scene remained small and self-occulted; many found it impenetrable. Eventually, as "modern jazz" became more popular, the once close-knit "hip" community dispersed. The *word* "hip" survived, of course, and is still bandied about today, primarily by the advertising industry, which uses it to promote two of the most unhip activities in the world: buying and selling!

The "Beat" ferment, meanwhile, especially in the years 1959–1964, became a mass movement of sorts, with eager recruits in every high school and home for juvenile offenders in the country—and in many other countries as well. Historians, commentators, and memoirists have insufficiently emphasized the role of minorities in the rise of the Beat movement. This is all the more surprising in view of the fact that so many of the best-known Beats were themselves ethnically a long way from the smug, self-consciously "white" American "mainstream"—or, as the African American surrealist poet Jayne Cortez has renamed it, the "whitestream."[41] To mention just a few: the French Canadian Jean-Louis "Jack" Kerouac; the African Americans Bob Kaufman, Ted Joans, and Leroi Jones (Amiri Baraka); the Jewish Allen Ginsberg; the Russian-Romanian-Jewish Jack Micheline; and a whole bevy of Italians, including the Calabrian Gregory Corso, the Sicilian Diane di Prima, and Lawrence Ferlinghetti, who, besides being Italian, also happens to be of French and Portuguese-Sephardic Jewish descent.

Racial/ethnic diversity was especially visible among the Beat "rank and file"—the thousands of high-school and college dropouts and runaways of all ages who turned their backs on white, middle-class ambitions and took to the road in search of a life worth living. As I can attest from my own experience during 1960–1962, as a hitchhiking teenager and frequenter of Beat cafés in Venice, California, San Francisco's North Beach, and New York's Greenwich Village, the then-booming Beat Generation was decidedly *not* a WASP affair. In North Beach, for example, at the Co-Existence Bagel Shop—where I spent several hours a day for some two months in the fall of 1960, digging everything—the regular clientele (not to be confused with the weekend tourists, almost all of whom were lily white) included numerous African Americans, Japanese, Chinese, Filipinos, Central and South Americans, and many whose ethnic identities I did not know.

It should not be overlooked that the whole Beat saga, including its curious Beatlemania, New Left, hippie, and yippie sequels, coincided with the rapid growth and intensification of the African American civil rights movement. If the Beats' nonwhiteness—or rather, their unwillingness to act "white"—made them an inevitable target for the police, judges, journalists, landlords, and other racists, it was nonetheless one of the qualities that made them so appealing to youthful rebels.

A few individual exceptions aside, the Beat Generation was not much of an intellectual movement, and its politics—anything but coherent—were rarely radical—indeed, they were more often conservative and sometimes blatantly reactionary. Kerouac proudly proclaimed his admiration for President Eisenhower; Ginsberg, whose role in the 1968 Democratic Convention protests was emphatically antirevolutionary, ended up a supporter of "free enterprise"; and William Burroughs, at the Naropa Institute in the 1970s, declared that "communism is an obsolete philosophy," and clarified the statement by adding: "Democracy, shit! What we need is a new Hitler."[42] Most of Kerouac's and Ginsberg's pronouncements on African-American culture and politics, or on race issues generally, would be laughable if they were not so embarrassingly ignorant and wrongheaded.[43] And yet, however naive and misinformed the Beats undoubtedly were, in race matters and in so much else, the fact remains that most of them—and especially the throngs of young people who rallied to the Beat banner—outspokenly opposed white supremacy and promoted a broad solidarity with people of color. A crucial lesson learned from their bopper and hipster models, Philip Lamantia among them, this rejection of the "white mystique" remains the most vital element in the Beat legacy.

THE PROMETHEAN GESTURE: POETRY AND DIRECT ACTION

The specifically *poetic* legacy of the Beats, in Lamantia's view, is quite another matter. To put it bluntly, his own uncompromisingly surrealist poetic praxis has *nothing in common* with what he considers the lifeless neo-Poundian, post-Olson, or Ginsbergian-populist trends that have mystified and manipulated so many would-be U.S. poets over the past several decades. One of his major critical essays, "Poetic Matters" (1976), subjects these retrograde literary fads and vagaries to a merciless revolutionary critique that is just as urgent and compelling today.[44] In full agreement with Hegel that the "unfettered imagination" is the basis of poetry, he finds that

> Most American poets have mistakenly subordinated the imaginative faculty to the predominance of perception conjoining a slavish reduction of language to "speech patterns" and pragmatic usages.[45]

Such "literary practitioners," he continues, have been utter

> failures on the imaginative and lyrical planes of true poetry, preoccupied as they are with a self-conscious acquiescence to the debasement of language characterizing its reification by technicians and mind-managers of later-day capitalism. This direction is glorified specifically in those false poets who pride themselves on a formalized "handling" of "ordinary American speech" which is, in effect, nothing other than a rhetorical camouflage for the betrayal of poetic exigencies in the service of cultural chauvinism and the oppressive "reality principle."[46]

Tracing the weakness and hollowness of much American poetry to the dolorous influence of Pound, Lamantia offers a passionately dissenting opinion of the author of the *Cantos*:

> Contrary to the consensus of American literary "authorities" who decided to separate Pound "the man" from "the poet," deploring his fascist politics and hailing his literary achievements, I believe Pound's poetics are as anti-human as his politics. . . . Fascism's claim to "revolution" by the cult of "youth" and "newness" while resuscitating the classicist values of Greco-Roman civilization and concretized, laughingly so, in the architecture known as "Mussolini modern," is a neat similitude to Pound's exclusive and scholastic insistence on Aristotelian logic and his aping of the "classics" while cinematically employing linguistic idioms of a political ward-heeler in the United States of the 1920s.[47]

From the surrealist point of view, as summed up by Lamantia, Pound was basically a white supremacist, militarist, fascist, idolator of Mussolini and Hitler, one of the most misogynous U.S. writers of the twentieth century, apoplectic enemy of workers' revolution, surrealism, anarchism, feminism, wilderness—in brief, an unregenerate miserabilist and *therefore* also the enemy of authentic poetry. Amazingly, this admittedly severe critique is supported to a large degree not only by much subsequent critical scholarship, but also by Pound himself, in an interview with Allen Ginsberg published in the *City Lights Anthology* in 1974.[48] In that remarkable interview, Pound defined his own work as

> stupidity and ignorance all the way through . . . doubletalk . . . preoccupation with irrelevant and stupid things. . . . My worst mistake was the stupid suburban prejudice of antisemitism, all along, that spoiled everything. . . . I found out after seventy years I was not a lunatic but a moron.

Ginsberg of course objected, pointing out that Pound had been "a model for a whole generation of poets." A short editorial in *Arsenal/Surrealist Subversion* no. 3 (1976) commented:

> Shortly before his death, Ezra Pound . . . expressed his essential agreement with the surrealists' evaluation of his work. . . .
>
> We have said it before, but from a standpoint very different from Ginsberg's: A whole generation of poets in English have derived their work from stupidity, ignorance, doubletalk, and stupid suburban prejudices.[49]

Lamantia's ringing indictment against the great bulk of U.S. poetry at the time left room for several notable exceptions. As precursors of a resurgent surrealism he singled out Samuel Greenberg, Mina Loy, and Harry Crosby, all of whom exemplified another, more daring and wildly imaginative path for poetry than the heavily patrolled superhighway chosen by Pound and his acolytes. Elsewhere he also indicated his appreciation of the work of the African American poet Melvin B. Tolson, one of the first to write in the "hip" argot in the 1940s, and of two Italian-born poets who lived in the United States and wrote in English in the 1910s and 1920s: Arturo Giovannitti, who had taken part in the strikes of the revolutionary Industrial Workers of the World (IWW), and Emanuel Carnevali, one of the "regulars" at Chicago's quasi-Dada Dil Pickle Club.[50] Among his poet contemporaries, too—apart from the surrealist movement—Lamantia also acknowledged "a number of exceptions":

> Both morally and poetically, for example, there is Bob Kaufman, pre-eminently; Gregory Corso, who can also be commended for his public disdain of "the Black Mountain School"; and Daniel Moore of *Dawn Visions*. All of these poets share the distinction of having, at certain times, expressed themselves honestly and intensely in a language with real affinities to surrealism.[51]

In the struggle for what he called the "disalienation of humanity with its language," Lamantia has resolutely maintained that "surrealism offers the sole challenge and viable alternative to what amounts to a conspiracy of poetic degeneracy in this country."[52] In words recalling the abolitionists of old, he declares surrealism's poetic aim to be nothing less than "the full flowering of each individual personality by a permanent annihilation of the interior slavocracy." Despite miserabilism and its apologists, *poetry continues*, forging ahead via surrealist *direct action*: "the Promethean gesture, the gesture that supersedes the cultural commodity."[53]

AN AFROCENTRIC PERSPECTIVE

Surrealist anti-Eurocentrism began with a radical questioning of the Greco-Roman heritage, and more particularly with the rejection, by André Breton and his friends, of what they regarded as France's bankrupt Cartesianism, rationalism, and logic. Soon, however, they were openly affirming their enthusiastic interest in the poetic/philosophical heritage of African and other non-European cultures. What Breton called the "explosive contribution" of "primitive" art from Africa, Oceania, and the Americas was a real force in the development of surrealism.[54] It is also important to realize that Africans—the Riffian rebels in Morocco—had precipitated the world's first Surrealist Group into revolutionary politics as early as 1925.[55]

It was Philip Lamantia who first made me aware that surrealism itself is, in part, the result of a long Afrocentric tradition *within* Europe—a current exemplified by such Renaissance figures as Marsilio Ficino, Giordano Bruno, Pico della Mirandola, John Dee, and the alchemists. This "occultist" counter-tradition, focused on Egypt—the land of Hermes and legendary birthplace of alchemy, where so many of the ancient Greek philosophers went to study—was a determining influence on the poetic "underground" that the first surrealist generation acclaimed as their principal inspirers: Nerval, Lautréamont, Rimbaud, Saint-Pol-Roux, and Jarry.

Lamantia's own Afrocentrism—and he was the first nonblack person I knew who adopted that label—naturally drew on these early surrealist and presurrealist sources. But he was also deeply influenced by the Negritude movement, especially as developed by Aimé and Suzanne Césaire and their comrades in the Martinican surrealist journal *Tropiques* (1941–1945). In a tribute to the Guyanese poet Léon Damas, a cofounder of the international Negritude movement, Jayne Cortez has defined Negritude as

> a force that exists to help forge a new world . . . a step used in literature to fight the slave master, to defend oneself against negative images, distorted information, cultural and spiritual imperialism. . . . Negritude as Black life, Black thought, Black attitude, and multiculturalism . . . a link between the past, present and future.[56]

A forerunner of the Black Pride and Black Power movements of the 1960s, Negritude was and is above all a lyrical affirmation of blackness and *africanité*, and therefore—sometimes directly and otherwise by implication—a revolutionary critique of "whiteness." The masterpieces of Negritude include Aimé Césaire's long poem, *Return to My Native Land* (1939), and his later theoretical/polemical study, *Discourse on Colonialism* (1950).[57] Interestingly, although Lamantia and Aimé Césaire never met, they did "meet" in the pages of *VVV* in 1944, in which Lamantia's three pages are immediately followed by six pages of poems (in French) by Césaire; a full-page photo of the Martinican poet faces the last page of Lamantia's poems.

During the early 1960s, in Europe, Lamantia's Afrocentric orientation was extended further by his meticulous study of the three-volume work, *Le*

Temple de l'homme, by R. A. Schwaller de Lubicz, the French hermetist and nonconforming Egyptologist.[58] The magnificent poem "Egypt," in *Bed of Sphinxes* (1997)—dedicated "In honor of R. A. Schwaller de Lubicz"—reflects this study as well as the poet's own sudden trip to Egypt after the San Francisco earthquake of 1989:

Reading images around papyrus-fluted colonnades
—these moments wonder the world—
the hermetic secret Plato Pythagoras Moses
. . .
Music! perfumes! magic!
. . .
These moving realities appear on the Nile
as if a postcard view of it held up a hieratic bird
silent tonalities a secret passage the beginning of language

From his first poem in *VVV*, titled "Islands of Africa," Lamantia's poetry has abounded in references to Africa and African places, from Cairo and Tangier to Timbuktu. I know of no other nonblack poet in the United States whose work reflects a deeper or longer-lasting kinship with Africa and the African diaspora. America's black counterculture, especially the bop scene that he frequented so intimately for years, has affected him profoundly. Charlie Parker, Thelonious Monk, Slim Gaillard, and other black musican/magicians are movingly invoked in his work. The impact of "Bird" Parker is particularly evident in two examples of the surrealist game Time-Travelers' Potlatch, in which the players imagine *gifts* they would present to various figures of the past.[59] The first is

> *For Charlie Parker:* The materialization of his old green jacket re-forming the future republic of desire and dreams.

The second recipient is the great surrealist poet of Haiti:

> *For Clément Magloire-Saint-Aude:* The cinematic projection from a hummingbird's eye of Charlie Parker's spontaneous musical session at Bop City, San Francisco in 1954, fixed in an order of black, white and red crystalizations volatilizing the human brain on the brink of an evolutionary mutation through a circle of blazing rum.

Significantly, too, few nonblack poets of Lamantia's generation have been anywhere near as familiar with African American poetry as the author of *Becoming Visible.* Bob Kaufman, whom he esteemed as one of the greatest of all U.S. poets, was among his closest friends for years. Ted Joans and Jayne Cortez are also long-standing friends as well as collaborators on joint surrealist poetry readings and publishing ventures. One notable reading with Joans celebrated the life and work of Charlie Parker. During the 1976 World Surrealist Exhibition in Chicago, Lamantia took part in surrealist word games with jazz pianist and poet Cecil Taylor.[60] It was also at that time that he urged me to read the poetry of Melvin B. Tolson. As recently as February 2002, Lamantia made it a point to attend a public meeting in San Francisco honoring the memory of Langston Hughes.

A poet of remarkable erudition and incredibly far-reaching interests, Lamantia is also a multiculturalist in the finest sense, and his surrealist "frame of reference" embraces many other cultures, from the Far East and Oceania to the Australian Aborigines. His affinities with black culture, however—and with many Native American cultures—are especially pronounced in his poetry and essays. Indeed, his relation to African and African diasporan culture—and especially to jazz musicians, poets, and revolutionists, French- and Spanish-speaking as well as English—surely merits a special study. In the present context, what is crucial is the degree to which Afrocentrism has remained central to his life and work. Having early on rejected what he once (on the telephone) called the two-hundred-year-old European tradition of "bad-mouthing the Egyptians," Lamantia since his teens has recognized not only that ancient Egyptian civilization was African, but also that Egyptian thought and culture exerted a strong and enduring influence on Greek philosophy—in short, that much of what is best in Western thought is in truth African in origin.

Aimé Césaire said that surrealism for him was a confirmation rather than a revelation. For Philip Lamantia, as he told me in the late 1980s, reading Martin Bernal's *Black Athena* (1987) was a "highly pleasurable" confirmation of the Afrocentrism he himself had regarded as "second nature" for decades.

Chapter Nine

THE FRONT LINES

Hip-Hop, Life, and the Death of Racism

Manifest

I found my medium and recognized my calling the moment I heard a beat and started rhyming. *Uphold, uplift, master of the riff, don't hesitate to migrate to manifest the gift I'm blessed with . . . revealed at birth, brought to earth, came forth from the source—Spirit—the sole force in the universe. First born, burst out bustin', crushing every beat, bumrushin' . . . complete trust in creativity, practice humility, bonafide emcee to the enth degree.*[1] An odyssey ensued that brought me from the quiet suburbs straight into the toughest ghettoes, from stage fright to stage might with a beat and a mike.

I was born in 1970 in Elmhurst, Queens—the same day the Spirit of Jimi Hendrix ascended to the Heavens. My father, the oldest of eleven, had grown up in a huge, working-class Italian family in Corona, Queens. A brilliant, independent, and enterprising young intellectual, he left the enclave at an early age in search of big open spaces. My mother, from a large, blue-collar Irish family, came from Flatbush, Brooklyn, and joined him as they set to the task of raising their children. The third and last child, I grew up a few miles north of the Bronx, hip-hop's legendary birthplace, a long way from the poverty they left behind.

Back then my neighborhood was an even mixture of working-class and white-collar folks, but there weren't many people of color. To our neighbors, we seemed like a normal, newly middle-class, white, suburban family. In reality, we were something very different. In early 1973, at the same moment the four elements of hip-hop—deejaying, emceeing, breakdancing, and graffiti—

crystallized into a culture, my twenty-eight-year-old mother returned to the Creator after a yearlong battle with cancer. Just two-and-a-half at the time, I was shell-shocked. So was the rest of my family. We all spiraled into intense pain, depression, guilt, confusion, and neglect. Our house filled with a deep, dark misery.

> Back at home, it was all wrong
> Sad song after Mom died
> It was like the love was all gone /
> Oh no! Two years old, low blow
> With my bro and my sis, had to roll with the sitch /
> And my Pop gone mad
> Took a wrong turn, got burned real bad, make ya hate Dad /
> On the surface, nervous, I deserve this
> Hurt, this dirt, this worthless purpose /
> Heard this voice say, "Join Mommy, and desert this Earth,"
> On my third birthday /

We each did our best to adapt while my father struggled to hold it all together, working full time and raising us alone. In desperate need of help, we escaped to Flushing every weekend to grandma and grandpa's house, my father's parents, themselves the children of immigrants from Naples and Basilicata. Still filled with youngsters, it became our home away from home and a safe haven from the raging storm. Every Sunday, the whole group of boisterous *paesans* gathered for scrumptious meals, joyous celebrations, raucous debates, and good times. The tremendous outpouring of love we received there renewed our faith and rejuvenated us for the week ahead. It was in my grandparents' home, in the midst of these weekly gatherings filled with magic, mystery, and mist from all the cigarette smoke, surrounded by first, second, and third cousins, aunts, great aunts, uncles, uncles' girlfriends, boyfriends, in-laws, neighbors, neighborhood priests, weary travelers, vagabonds, and con men, that I became more aware of "race" and racism.

We're an elaborate, passionate, often irascible bunch and sometimes can agree on only one thing: to disagree. Before, during, and after dinner—an all-day event—debates large and small raged on about myriad issues. Popular topics included food, fashion, relationships, Hollywood, sports, and national and local politics. Locally, the concerns centered on "the neighborhood" and its changing racial and ethnic make up, who was "taking over," and whether or not the area was being "ruined" because of it. A common complaint was that newer immigrants "don't even speak English," conveniently forgetting that my great grandfather Giuseppe, who migrated to America in 1890, lived over eighty years in New York and stubbornly refused to learn, let alone speak, a word of English. Even so, I overheard remarks of how "they're rude" and "unfriendly." Many wondered aloud why "they" couldn't uplift themselves "the way we had." Stories of the backbreaking work earlier generations had to endure just to get by always had a way of silencing us, ending the debates, and making us grateful for the food on our plates. Still, as children, we sensed there was more to the story.

> Illegal hero, heave-ho, eager get this dough
> Regal dago, payroll, wrote this so they know /
> See I came with a bang, traveled overseas
> Had no thang, but my game, had to move them ki's /
> Or that booze, all that weed, hustle bustle feed my seed
> Muscles bleed lugging bricks for stuck up lunatics /
> Soon to fix, sly fox, sewing up ya blocks
> Got them cops in the Bronx
> Got them crooked-boogie Brooklyn-woogie /
> Bookies, hooker rookies never look us in the eye
> They shook, they book, they quick to take a dive /
> I survive, thrive, stay alive, get my piece of pie
> Piece of mine, piece of yours, ain't no peace in do or die /
> Means war, hardcore, come knocking atcha door
> Greasing these indecent whores in all ya courts of law /

I first discovered hip-hop on the streets of New York thanks to my father. A true lover of diverse cultures, he introduced me to "The City" and its people on many a wild adventure: the Fulton Fish Market before dawn, Chinatown after dark, gospel churches in Harlem, butchers and bakeries on Arthur Avenue, whirling dervishes in Astoria, and the weed-infested upper deck of Reggie Jackson's Yankee Stadium, to name a few. Huge, colorful murals consumed the walls of abandoned, burned-out buildings like wildfire. Subway trains transformed into living, breathing canvases, tattooed serpents slicing through the labyrinth of steel and concrete chaos. Flattened cardboard boxes on dusty street corners became the site of classic b-boy battles. Crushing beats and rugged rhymes rose through the dense, hot air like great wafts of incense. I was transfixed, mesmerized. Hip-hop struck like a molten bolt of lightning. With it came a lifelong opportunity to transform my pain into something positive. Far more than a mere genre of music, hip-hop became a way of life for me and an outlet to vent pent-up frustration and rage; to work through anger and fear; to express joy, love, and sorrow; and to imagine and manifest a world free of suffering.

From the late 1980s to the early 1990s, during a renaissance for the art form, New School groups like Public Enemy, Boogie Down Productions, Eric B & Rakim, X-Clan, The Jungle Brothers, Queen Latifah, Paris, NWA, Ice Cube, Sistah Souljah, Stetsasonic, A Tribe Called Quest, De La Soul, and Brand Nubian used hip-hop as a platform to raise social awareness. Many eschewed the popular European and white American designer clothing and gold jewelry preferred by much of rap's elite, opting instead for Kente-cloth, Africa medallions, head wraps, dreads, and beads. Legendary New York radio deejays like Red Alert, Marley Marl, Mr. Magic, and Chuck Chillout brought these new, conscious artists and their messages to the masses by putting their records in primetime rotation. They used Afrocentric, often militant, messages to blow the whistle on the establishment and uplift Black people. They reached me in the process.

> Opposition magician, Survivor Soul's efficient with foes
> Vesuvio will send you politicians packin' /
> It's the fast track enforcer, Mr. Rap Minister
> Mad professor, regulate the sinister /
> Maestro of flow, revolt like Castro
> Draft the blueprints to mastermind the overthrow /
> Cock the bow release the arrow, straight and narrow
> Pharoah like Ahkenaton upon a throne at thirteen /
> Inshallah, shining star, shoot far, son of Jah
> Shed light, blind ya eyesight, bright like rays of Ra /
> The Czar by coup d'état, holy Roman emperor waging war
> Shogun yogi while you bogeying par /

Indeed, what I was learning in school—the glory and supremacy of western/white civilization—and what I was learning in life, and through hip-hop, was diametrically opposed. One had to go. And so, out the window went anything contrary to the wealth of knowledge I was receiving through hip-hop. With profits from my paper route, I bought every tape I could find. In the mid-1980s you had to search for the measly rap section; many record stores didn't have one. Back then, there were only a few of us in my entire high school into it. We even caught flack for it. Many claimed it wasn't "real music" and called us fools for following a fad. Unfazed, I linked up with three of my homeboys and formed a group. We recorded our first rap song when I was sixteen. The moment I heard my voice over the beat on the playback, I was hooked.

The 1989 tragic murder of Yusuf Hawkins at the hands of a racist Italian mob in Bensonhurst, Brooklyn, marked a turning point in my life. I was eighteen and highly impressionable, and already knew I was destined for a lifelong career in hip-hop. Yusuf's murder went against everything I believed and held sacred. The haunting front-page photos of meaty Italian American men taunting Black protesters with raised watermelons and racial slurs revealed a seething hatred so deep it shook me to my core. How had we gone from persecuted victims of lynching to proud leaders of bloodthirsty lynch mobs? The message was clear. We Italian Americans have long sought to distance ourselves from Blacks and Blackness to be accepted as white and "make it" in America. My path would be the opposite.[2] I drew the line there, forever deciding to honor my mixed ancestry, bridge the gap between our communities, and contribute to healing the wounds, ignorance, and bigotry in my own self, in my community, and in my music.

It's the valiant stallion, New York Italian
My style's caliente, One Love to my gente /
Plenty of support from those that sport Kente
For rappers that produce I up the ante /
Squash that beef, Yusuf rest in peace
Let the hate cease, stop worshiping the beast /
Start praying to the east, give thanks for this feast
My increase happened after seven years of famine /
It's apparent you believe movies and TV
Still can't see the fantasy they throwing atcha /
They gotcha, check your history, know your culture
Been shackin' up since Antony and Cleopatra /
The hat trick hero, fear no evil
Catch the fever like DeNiro, Power to the People /
Love to see unity in my community
One race, one heart, one place, one great God /
It's the ramblin' man, arrived on a whim
Banned from the land of the mandolin /
In a strange land, scrambling, hustling, gambling
Neopolitan gold /

After graduating high school, my crew disbanded and I headed off to Haverford College outside Philly, with no real plans. One day I returned to my dorm room to find that Grover Andrew Zinn, my new roommate, had moved in. Alongside my immaculate, lifesize posters of LL Cool J, EPMD, MC Lyte, Stetsasonic, and Run DMC, hung even larger ones of Depeche Mode, New Order, The Cure, and Bryan Ferry. I was horrified. In the corner, to my surprise, there was a keyboard, a four-track, a mike, and a drum machine. Growing up in Oberlin, Ohio, he, too, caught the music bug as a child. Descended from poor southern white laborers, Zinn followed his parents' lead to academia. We immediately began making music together.

As two collegiate, white, suburban kids, we had virtually no example to follow. Even though the Beastie Boys, 3rd Bass, House of Pain, and Vanilla Ice had all enjoyed commercial success in rap by the early 1990s, the waters were still uncharted. Indeed, dozens of "manufactured" white rappers had cropped up over the years as pure business ploys to make a quick crossover buck. But as a rule, white rap acts, famous or not, quickly disappeared. The Beastie Boys, originally a punk rock band, burst onto the scene doing frat-boy rap and touring alongside superstars Run DMC, found their niche, and returned to their more alternative roots. 3rd Bass, the most legitimate white crew at the time, earned the respect of Black and white audiences alike, but broke up and vanished after their second album. House of Pain, who scored big with the song "Jump Around," never had another hit and disbanded, with front man Everlast going in a more rock-influenced direction. And one-hit-wonder Vanilla Ice has received far more ridicule than respect in the long run. Ultimately, none of them had staying power.[3] We endured on blind faith, instinct, and brotherly love.

Living adjacent to a Black working-class area, deejaying parties and a weekly college radio show, and falling in love for the first time with an African American woman from the neighborhood, opened my eyes, and my heart. It also surrounded me with a diverse community of friends on this quiet, elite, suburban Quaker campus. In class, I devoured treatises by Marcus Garvey, Alain Locke, Ralph Bunche, Booker T. Washington, and W.E.B. Du Bois. Back at the lab, Zinn and I continued writing and recording. My growing awareness and thirst for knowledge were surpassed only by my dream of hip-hop stardom.

Compared with life back home, my college years brought an independence and distance that tested the strength of my family. As we got older, we got wiser. When important pieces of our past returned to our collective memory, each of us responded very differently. Still, nothing could have prepared me for the news I received senior year while home for the holidays. After a vicious argument with my father, my sister pulled my brother and me aside. She told us in the months following my mother's death she had been sexually abused—by my father. Blindsided, I listened in awe as my repressed anger and pain, unexamined since childhood, came rushing to the surface. I returned to college in a daze, a burning rage, frequent alcohol binges, and a deep crease in my brow, the most visible signs of crisis. At a time when I lacked adequate tools and a support system to deal, hip-hop was my salvation. On the advice of a Latin homey, already a master beat maker, I purchased my first keyboard sampler. Amidst the insanity, discord, and dysfunction, I found harmony inside my headphones, converting emotions into sound. With each rhyme, I squeezed out the pain of my insane frame of mind.

> What soon came was even harder
> Being brought up by a father trying to play the martyr /
> His refusing to get some help, well, led to hell
> And my sister getting sexually abused /
> Sleepless nights as a tyke, fights over gripes
> Getting lectures on my rage over bites /
> Crying to myself, lying to myself
> Been so reckless with my life almost killed /
> 'Til I chose to feel, to heal
> What made me ill, made me real, deal /
> To see concealed in the heartache and pain
> There's a hard way to gain the type of ruff n' tuff love that sustains /

Six months later, I graduated, got a job at a local deli, and threw my lot in with Zinn. We decided we needed another rapper in the crew and spent months looking. Finally, we gave up. One autumn morning, I came face-to-face with Oakland-born emcee Jabari "Able Body" Gray, and knew he was the one. He had responded to a "DJ for hire" flier I had hung up on his college campus. A Black kid of African and Irish ancestry, he took one of my beats home and wrote a magical verse to it. Likewise, his rhymes revealed a quiet rage hidden beneath a calm exterior. From the day we joined forces in the fall of 1993 until we all went solo in early 2001, we kicked thousands of raps, cowrote and recorded a hundred odd songs, rocked over eighty live shows, freestyled, philosophized, realized, dreamed, laughed, argued, and cried together. We rewrote history with *our* story. Only now do I realize the work we unknowingly did to eclipse race and racism. To us, it's always been about the music. It's what brought us together in the first place and what's kept us together since. People felt this unity of purpose. It ran deep.

Our careers began in earnest the day we left Philly to go for gold out West. We arrived in Los Angeles; set up shop in Venice; pressed our first album *Swells of Abstract* (1995) to cassette; and took our act to any stage that would have us. Combing the streets, we played hole-in-the-wall clubs where our pay was anywhere from a swift kick in the ass to a small plastic cup and easy access to the keg. We worked our way onto numerous urban music "showcases" after surprising the judges in the auditions. One particular promoter had been so impressed by our performance that he invited us back to headline his next event.

In the days leading up to the gig, things in L.A. started to heat up. Just hours before the show, a few miles from the venue, O.J. Simpson was declared "not guilty," sending shock waves throughout the City of Angels that were felt across the country. The atmosphere was charged. A thick sense of distrust, injustice, self-righteousness, and bottled-up rage spewed out onto the streets. Folks carried huge signs along freeways and sidewalks. Bumper stickers and T-shirts declared one's allegiance. Heated arguments erupted. Sides were clearly drawn along racial lines. Many people feared violence would set off another riot. We hit the stage smack dab in the middle of a powder keg.

The place was packed, though I couldn't see anything past the blinding spotlights at the front of the stage. It was hot. Every single person in the joint was Black except for Zinn, toting a purple bass guitar and dressed like a grunge rocker, and myself, sporting long hair and a goatee. Jabari, bless his soul, has always been down for a good time, especially when it comes to people's misconceptions about race. He was ready to rock, and so were we. The comedian emcee took one look at us and immediately ripped into Zinn who simply walked by him and plugged his bass into the amplifier. "And who do we have here? Oh, you guys about to play some country music for us?" The crowd, recognizing the spectacle, livened up at the sight of us. We took the stage silently. I remember looking directly into the beams of light and realizing that no one, no matter what, was gonna come between me and my mike.

The beat hit, and we launched into one of the most inspired performances of our lives. We were possessed. All hell broke loose the moment we dropped the mikes. The place erupted as everyone rose to their feet and gave us the loudest standing ovation of our careers. Shouts of "Hallelujah!" and "Praise the Lord!" rang through the club. I walked into the crowd a changed man. In thirty minutes we went from subjects of public ridicule to honored and respected masters of the ceremony. Hip-hop created this opportunity. At the height of racial tension, we transformed the hate.

> Guinea, Dago
> Honkey, Mick
> Limey, Faggot
> Nigga, Spic /
> It's the land of the free, home of the brave
> Where we live to get fat off the sweat of a slave /
> Glued to our TVs, locked in our te-pees
> Watching repeat replays in our peejays /
> Fuck PG! Lyfe's rated X
> High tech, high tax, hijacks, and sex, getcha hit of Ex /
> The average American is living arrogant
> Married again and if we can /
> Control the whole world
> Fill factories with boys and girls, make toys and pearls /
> It's a damn shame
> I don't even know your name
> If you're Black then you're strapped, if you're rich then you rap /
> If you're Irish, I bet you drink like a fish
> If you're Asian, you're patient, got a small dick /
> If you're Jewish, you're cheap, and love to bitch and moan
> If you're white trash then you crash in a mobile home /
> They're called stereotypes
> They're called what?
> Stereotypes of a type y'all misunderstood but it's still all good /

Looking back, it makes perfect sense that we were constantly tested. As a "white rapper," I stood in a long line of fair-skinned impersonators and thieves of Black culture. Everyone remembers Elvis. And yet, I half enjoyed the scrutiny; it kept me on my toes. My work had to blow people away without fail. Otherwise, I'd be written off as a fake and a biter. Working odd jobs to pay the bills left me little time for anything else. I felt redeemed, even triumphant after many of our shows, but worn out as well. Sometimes I even thought about giving up.

Crowds booed us, fans cursed us from the front row, and even rushed the stage once, trying to pry the mikes from our hands and turn our performance into an all-out emcee battle. Before our first performance in New York,

I was physically paralyzed with fear for ten minutes before slowly making my way to the stage. Every show felt like an exorcism, and I was the devil. I internalized voices of doubt, looks of disgust, and hoots of mockery. I began to resent my own skin color. "I'm not white," I reasoned, "I'm Italian!" Many of my Black and Latin friends had told me this. Still, it was never enough. Slowly, I began to accept the notion that these hecklers, second guessers, and dis-masters, whose seemingly sole purpose was to throw salt in my game, were actually there to train me for the pros.

I got insufficient funds, no submissive huns
And sophisticated puns to make ya shake ya buns /
I got 'nuff light to smite the bright sun
Got enough cheap brews to cruise and get the runs /
I refuse to lose, get bruised, and be abused
Mr. Fool Proof, the newest improved, the Who's Who /
Fuck the rules, I paid dues but never got paid
Heavily slept on but barely got laid /
I display night and day, never decay
Clever while you fakes said I'd never make the grade /
I done paved this road, prayed afraid to grow
Ashamed to show, laid low but stayed in the flow /
Instigate, state facts, react, and rake dough
Take roll, owe no back tax, and letcha know /
I make sure to be the first dayglo dago
Check my stage show, you know I told ya so /

While I often felt alone facing the rap world, having Jabari on my squad made it that much easier. He gave me encouragement, credibility, and a Black perspective. We were the front men. Side by side, we offered a vision of the new face of hip-hop. Before long we developed a small, loyal following as our tenacity began to pay off. We signed our first recording contract less than a year after arriving in L.A. and released our second album *Weep No More* (1996). With a fledgling, one-man record company owned by a young Italian American, a Black female firefighter-turned-publicist, a vigilante Black street promoter, and a $30,000 budget, we finally had a team and some cash behind us. Our record, now reaching a national audience, received rave reviews in the press but a mixed response almost everywhere else. People either loved our ingenuity and maverick approach or thought it was wack. To do it right, we realized that we'd have to replace Zinn on bass with a real live deejay for shows.

Jabari and I met Rastafarian DJ Drez at a rave one night in the summer of 1996 while out late promoting our first twelve-inch vinyl single. A white kid, he grew up in a blue-collar, single-parent home in suburban Orange County. His love of hip-hop and faith in Rastafari merge in the music he reveals to the people. We began recording, rehearsing, and performing together, quickly developing a close friendship. Together, the four of us explored the temples of underground hip-hop, meeting hundreds of artists along the way. We come in all creeds, colors, shapes, and sizes. Indeed, commercial rap, as seen through the eyes of mainstream media, is largely a one dimensional, thugged-out, Black male-dominated world. In reality, it's much more complex, conscious, and compelling.

Rap's glorification of violence, greed, materialism, and misogyny, which so many criticize, is a direct reflection of good 'ole amerikan values. Many cast us as criminals, yet hip-hop epitomizes the capitalist success story we're all raised to respect and desire. As white suburban youth have replaced urban "minorities" as rap's largest consumer segment, the music and its messages have reflected their tastes. In addition, white-owned major labels backed by multinational corporations have supplanted Black and independently owned record companies. Our once equally commercial and visionary culture has been reduced to reinforcing oversimplified stereotypes of Blackness for mass consumption. Coming in beneath the radar of pop culture, underground hip-hop remains a multi-ethnic, autonomous, grassroots movement and a powerful voice of youth opposition and insurrection. And while rap stars grace your TV OD'd on ego like Liberace, 99 percent of hip-hop artists survive on modest incomes, relatively unconcerned with mainstream popularity.

Hip-hop was born from the vicious street gang culture that ruled the Bronx and much of New York City's bombed-out neighborhoods of the early 1970s. As an antidote to the warfare, visionary Bronx deejays like Kool Herc, Afrika Bambaataa, Grandmaster Flash, and Grand Wizard Theodore offered a creative, peaceful alternative to running the streets at their late night jams.[4] The news spread fast. Soon, rival crews sprang up all over the city as hip-hop replaced gang culture as the "in" thing to do. Simultaneously, Afrika Bambaataa founded the Universal Zulu Nation, today the largest hip-hop organization in the world with more than ten thousand members and chapters in over twenty countries, "dedicated to music and, above all, peace." Naturally, one of the first deejays Jabari and I met in L.A. was Mark Luv, the West Coast chapter president of the Zulu Nation. An African American from South Central, Mark has long been a fixture on the scene, as deejay for everyone from KRS-One to Freestyle Fellowship and The Pharcyde. We fast became family, collaborating, sharing, and making hip-hop history. A legend in his own right, Mark joined Drez behind the wheels of steel as the fifth member of our group The Anonymous, the motliest crew on the planet.

Just as soon as we gained momentum, our record label went bankrupt (after selling only two thousand units), and we lost our team and backing. I took it upon myself to make it happen and began writing and producing tracks for our next album. On weekends, we set up shop on the Venice boardwalk, bumping our songs, peddling our CDs, freestyling with passersby, and networking with local industry types, gang bangers, and street urchins alike. The result: *Green and Gold* (1998). Our third studio album, it featured an up-and-coming battle emcee and fellow race rebel by the name of Eminem (I met his manager on the boardwalk), and twenty other highly respected underground artists including Nikko, E-Rule, Medusa, Divine Styler, Mystik Journeymen, Grouch, Neb Luv, Jizzm, Awol One, Zaire Black, Tony da Skitzo, and Iriscience of Dilated Peoples. Our single climbed the rap charts for eight solid weeks, peaking at #9 in the nation, while our record, recorded and mixed in my living room, went on to sell over twenty thousand copies. Now at the center of the West Coast community, we built alliances based on musical integrity, not race. The exposure earned us widespread acclaim and brought me the acceptance I had longed for since childhood.

> I grew up in the 'burbs, heard a grip of big words
> Kickin' verbs to birds, gettin' drunk, smokin' herb /
> Curbside, no ride, used to walk or take my bike
> Hoping one day that I could be like Mike /
> And take flight writin' tight rhymes, hit the big time
> Toys wanna bite every rhyme I recite /
> But in the meantime I find myself in a bind
> Paperboy, busboy, people pay me no mind /
> Try my best to get signed, shopping crates of tapes
> Combing the States, I'll do whatever it takes /
> Aches and pains, insane, styles change but I remain
> Thirteen years in the game, still ain't heard of my name /
> It's Manifest homey, it's a shame you don't know me
> Only one life to live so I ain't gon' spend it lonely /

As our relationships developed and our conversations deepened, the subject of spirituality became central to our collaboration. One Christmas, Drez gave Zinn and me each a red, gold, and green Rasta-colors shoelace, and from that point on, I began checking for Selassie. Jabari and Zinn did the same. I quickly found myself walking in heavily Rasta-influenced social circles, consulting and discussing spiritual texts of all faiths, digging deep into dub and roots reggae, and smoking lots of green herb. It was one of the most productive, illuminating, and transformative periods of my life. Through Selassie, I began to examine, accept, and celebrate the divinity of the entire human family and the interconnectedness of all things.

Years of soul-searching yielded these simple realizations. I went deep to heal the "wounds" of my youth and erase a lifetime of false teachings. Hip hop provided me with a conscious, Afro-centric community in which to deconstruct my illusions of racial and cultural superiority. My need to expose and cut off the root of racism, subvert white authority, absorb and sanctify hip-hop, hail Selassie, and wail my truth in raps over beats at the top of my lungs, was connected to my childhood. As a kid I was powerless and speechless in the face of a sometimes ferocious and out-of-control single parent in crisis. My mother died before I fully learned how to speak. My voice was silent through it all. Inside I roared.

> I flip songs like David writ the psalms
> Give alms, right the wrongs, hold this world in my palm /
> Remain calm, come correct, collect respect then jet
> The Resurrector, protector, rule your sector /
> Get corrected by the rod, guard the Holy Sceptre
> Supreme style perfector, chief Elect of God /
> Livin' large sarge, lead the charge against darkness
> They heartless, I'm leavin' heathens scarred irregardless /
> My finger's on the bounty, Queens County king
> Do my thing righteous despite the vice that surrounds me /
> Can't confound me, fade me, take me down or drown me
> Babylon to Zion, iron like a lion, hail Selassie /
> Tribe of Judah, awake the Buddha within
> Lyrical Zen swordsman, wield a ballpoint pen /
> Conquerin', eliminate the demon
> Royal defender with the strength of forty men /
> Shaman, beat farmer, big game performer
> Dalai Lama, my rhymes affect your karma /
> Causin' harm to serpents, snap necks, check your armor
> Bronx Bomber Manifest steps up, prepare for drama /

What began as the artistic practice of a handful of impoverished Black and Brown New Yorkers has fast become the most powerful youth movement of our time. Critics fail to recognize that a sacred, open space to express and heal human suffering lies at the center of hip-hop, a culture in constant metamorphosis. It is this common ground that continues to galvanize the world's children. Italy is no exception. In 2000, I spent four months traversing the Italian peninsula, performing, writing, producing, recording, and collaborating with Italian hip-hop artists. Starting in Milan, I worked my way down through Rome and Naples to Sicily and back again. I found the scene vibrant, vast, and extremely visible. I met many accomplished artists, such as Turi, Esa and Polaroide of Gente Guasta, Dumbo, Muhammed, Rodney, Fritz da Cat, Malaisa, Ice One, Polo and Sha-One of La Famiglia, DJ Skizo, Pooglia Tribe, Vigor, Vez, Kiave, Bassi Maestro, DJ Enzo, Master Freez, Fede, Wehad, Phil, DJ Gruff, and Ghedda. Many are from poor Southern Italian families who migrated to the industrial North for economic opportunity. In a country so invested in its past, hip-hop represents a clean break from convention and a chance for this generation to distinguish itself.

Arab North Africans, Black Africans, and even African Americans frequent the scene as well. For them, confronting the tremendous racism they have faced living in Italy is a primary concern. My friend Muhammed, Afrika Bambaataa's younger cousin, enjoyed a career in the States as a Bronx b-boy before moving to Milan a decade ago as a model and hip-hop entrepreneur. His cousin, rapper Rodney, also a native of the South Bronx, has made his home in Como, an hour north of Milan, for ten years, and is married to an Italian woman. A passionate, skilled wordsmith, he kicked me molten verses filled with ire and venom for a people and culture he feels have never embraced nor respected him. He even began to rap in Italian to better communicate with his audience.

In the underground, amidst legions of supporters and practitioners, Italian hip-hop develops by leaps and bounds.[5] From the back alleys to the ornate *piazze*, jet-set clubs to *centri sociali*, all four elements are well represented. Graffiti, the most prominent, is thriving. Tags and pieces adorn almost every block of Milan. Italian subway trains are covered head-to-toe. It looks like New York during graffiti's heyday. So much so that Milan city officials held a special summit, consulting then New York City Mayor Rudolph Giuliani, on ways to prevent "bombing" from covering their metropolis—to no avail. The movement cannot be stopped.

The universe, planet Earth included, is at a critical juncture. Spiritually, we are being asked to uplift ourselves out of habitual patterns of behavior based on fear. We are being called to seize the present moment and realize an empowered existence rooted in faith, trust, and love. Hip-hop is a major focal point where this evolution is taking place. In cities across the globe, diverse groups of God's children congregate to work it out creatively. Nonviolent, antiestablishment, Goddess-conscious, Rasta-loving, street-level revolutionaries are healing the cuts and scars left on our hearts from generations of trauma, war, and oppression—at home and abroad. We do it through graphic art, dance, and music.

Until the philosophy which holds one race
Superior and another inferior
Is finally and permanently discredited and abandoned
Everywhere is war
—Bob Marley[6]

The true revolutionary is guided by a great feeling of love.
—Che Guevara

Africa is not only the cradle of the human community,
it is the mother of Civilization itself. . . . And until the West—
and the rest of us—knows Africa, we can never truly know ourselves.
—Henry Louis Gates, Jr.[7]

PART III

WHITENESS, VIOLENCE, AND THE URBAN CRISIS

CHAPTER TEN

WHEN FRANK SINATRA CAME TO ITALIAN HARLEM

The 1945 "Race Riot" at Benjamin Franklin High School

GERALD MEYER

New York City's worst racial incident within the public school system in the immediate postwar period erupted on September 27, 1945, at Benjamin Franklin High School, an all-boys school located on Pleasant Avenue between East 114th and 116th Streets in Italian Harlem. The neighborhood was, at the time, one of the largest Little Italy's in the city, with approximately sixty thousand residents.[1] The school's 1,162 students reflected the multiethnic neighborhood, 37 percent of whom were Italian American, 13 percent African American, 9 percent Puerto Rican, and 41 percent "other" which included a large number of Jewish students.[2] Over a span of two months, this incident generated more than eighty articles and editorials in New York City's press as well as mention in the black press outside of New York City.[3] Some of these newspaper accounts, and the accompanying photographs, gave the impression that a full-scale riot had occurred and that the Italian community was populated by violent racists. By implication, these reports communicated that the school, its principal, and its underlying educational philosophy had failed. All of this had taken on heightened importance because the high school had gained a national reputation as a center of intercultural and interracial education, so of all of New York City's eighty high schools it seemed to be one of the least likely high schools where a racial incident would occur. This essay recreates these events and presents the remarkable campaign—which concluded one month later, when America's most famous

Italian American, Frank Sinatra, visited the school—that healed the racial breach caused by this incident and restored the reputation of the school, its principal, and the Italian Harlem community.

Leonard Covello, New York City's first Italian American high school principal, had gained national recognition for his leadership as the founding principal of Benjamin Franklin High, which was widely viewed as an experimental community for the implementation of Covello's educational philosophy.[4] Among other things, his perspective (which he termed "community-centered education") celebrated the contributions of immigrants and advocated the maintenance of their cultures and specifically their languages; in 1939, for example, 553 students, almost one-half of Franklin High's enrollment, were studying the Italian language.[5] Course materials and lessons in every subject area as well as frequent student assemblies celebrated the contributions of all nationalities and races in the construction of a pluralistic culture and society.[6] Covello insisted that public schools reflect a "reciprocal relationship between the good things in both foreign and native cultures. . . . For this purpose the community-centered school does not want to suppress the traditions of foreign cultural groups. . . . The appreciation by the school of such values leads to a fuller integration between itself and the community; it gives recognition and prestige to foreign cultural groups. . . ."[7] According to Covello, the goal of Franklin High was to "make the school the training ground for democratic living."[8] In recognition of this, the Office of War Information (OWI) produced a documentary about the school, *A Better Tomorrow*, which was screened in a score of countries that depicted the school as an exemplar of "democracy in action."[9] At Franklin, the recognition and celebration of ethnic diversity was consciously extended to include full racial equality.

On Thursday morning, September 27, a dispute over a basketball broke out in the gym between a small group of African American and Italian American boys, and later spilled over into the locker room. The boys challenged one another to fight it out after school. When news of this incident reached Covello, he assigned William Spiegel, the basketball coach, and Salvatore Pergola, the dean of boys, to stand outside the building at dismissal in order to quell the threatened fight. No two better people existed to carry out this task. Spiegel was the attendance officer for the school and, much more important, he had led the winning (and integrated) basketball team. The *Benjamin Franklin Year Book* for 1942 was dedicated to Spiegel, and under his smiling photograph, a student journalist asserted: "He may act tough at times but he is only fooling. He gives unselfishly of his time to us in the community."[10] Dean Pergola also had a unique rapport with the students. In his autobiography, Covello describes him as "a stocky, colorful, energetic man . . . born in New York City of Neapolitan parents, with an instinctive affinity for problems relating to tough East Side boys."[11]

Covello's intervention was sufficient to ensure that the African American students exited the school without incident; however, when they reached the bus stop, which was two blocks north of the school, a mob—primarily made up of local toughs armed with sticks—randomly attacked them. The police were called; and within ten minutes, peace was restored. Although many of the African American boys had been hit, none had been injured sufficiently to require medical treatment. The next morning, a group of African American boys, while marching down East 116th Street (Italian Harlem's major east–west artery), began chasing a white boy. Upon being alerted to this development, Covello raced from the steps of the school, where he had been standing to meet the group. Covello arrived at the same time as the police, who searched some of the African American students and arrested two of the boys for carrying weapons. Later, in school, the police questioned and searched other African American boys from this group and arrested three more for carrying weapons. (The charges against the five African American students were ultimately dropped.) During the day, some of the African American students became very much alarmed when a crowd from the Italian American community began gathering outside the school. Covello allowed those African American students who felt threatened to remain together as a group within the school library. The schedule of the day, however, including a student assembly at which African American and Italian American students performed, proceeded normally.[12]

Under Covello's guidance, the faculty and staff acted to protect the African American students from any potential harm when they left the school building. The city buses that most of the African American students used to reach their homes in central Harlem were rerouted so that they stopped directly in front of the school. The buses, which were escorted by police cars, did not stop to pick up passengers until they had reached Lexington Avenue, the informal western border of Italian and Spanish Harlem.[13] Significantly, the African American students who opted to walk through Italian and Spanish Harlem to reach the subway line, four long blocks from the school, arrived there without incident.[14]

After dismissal, a faculty conference was held, but unfortunately there is no documentation of its deliberations. On Saturday, at the school, Covello conferred with John Ernst, associate superintendent of the Board of

Education, and Edward Lewis of the Urban League.[15] It was not unreasonable, therefore for Covello to state to reporters: "There is no need to worry. Everything's all right now."[16] However, major New York City newspapers did not concur with this version of these events.

On Saturday, five of New York City's daily newspapers covered the Benjamin Franklin story. In a four-inch article printed on an inside page, the *World-Telegram* reported that "Street fighting broke out twice with five hundred white and Negro students and their elders battling each other and eighty uniformed and plainclothes policemen."[17] The article in the liberal Republican *Herald Tribune* focused on the measures taken at Franklin High to ensure order. It reported that the Italian American mothers who had escorted their children to school were ushered into the school auditorium where Covello and John de Martino, the chief inspector in charge of the ninety-five police officers assigned to the school, assured them, in English and Italian, that they had no cause to fear for their boys' safety.[18] Contrasting with these reports were articles that sensationalized and grossly misreported the events by the *New York Times*, the city's most prestigious newspaper; the *New York Daily News*, a tabloid with the largest circulation; and the *New York Post*, the (then) liberal tabloid.[19]

Most damaging was the *Times*'s front-page story, whose headline blared "Student 'Strikes' Flare into Riots in Harlem Schools: Knives Flash in Street Fights as Elders Join Pupils in Battling the Police: Coaches' Row a Pretext." The use of "Riots" to describe these events associated Franklin High, Italian Harlem, and Covello with the most disreputable forces in American society. The subtitle of the *Times* article tied the disturbance at Franklin High to student strikes organized by the Communist-led American Youth for Democracy that were in progress in other high schools in support of a city-wide boycott organized by the public schools' physical education teachers who were demanding additional pay for after-school supervision of student activities. However, Franklin High did not have a chapter of the American Youth for Democracy, and no student strike was ever proposed—or carried out—at any time there. The *Times* also extensively reported on assaults on African American students who had boarded buses after school, an occurrence about which no other newspaper reported and for which no evidence was proffered. Covello insisted that the *Times* reporter, Alexander Feinberg, whose byline appeared on this article, was not present at any of the flare-ups, and had culled emotion-laden testimony after the fact.[20]

The headline of the *New York Daily News* article–"2,000 High [School]

Students Battle in Race Riot"–epitomized the single most inaccurate and incredible reportage of this incident. First, the figure 2,000, which was cited in no other report, grossly overestimated the number of participants in a dispute in a high school with an enrollment of twelve hundred. Most disturbing, of course, was the appending of "race" to the term "riot" in the headline. Those terms were contradicted by the text of the article, which reported that "Almost miraculously nobody was seriously hurt, although there were battered heads and bruised faces."[21] The *New York Post* published two similar stories in its two editions; one of the headlines used the term "riot," and the other, the milder description "school race strife." In contrast to the articles' headlines, the texts of both articles characterized the incidents in Franklin High as "flare-ups" and a "free-for-all." [22] Both articles, however, linked the Benjamin Franklin incident to the much more serious racial disturbances simultaneously occurring in Gary, Indiana, and Chicago.

On Sunday, September 30, the city's press published more balanced reports on the incident.[23] For example, a short article published in the left-leaning daily, *PM*, characterized it as an "outbreak of street fighting . . . among several hundred white and Negro pupils [in which] no one was injured." In closing, the article quoted Covello: "The real trouble is not the school. The trouble is that adults mix into the situation."[24] The Italian-language paper *Il Progresso Italo-Americano* described the incident in its headline as a "tumult," and in the text as an "uproar" among "more than five hundred students."[25] The only new perspective on the event came from the *Sunday Worker*'s article, whose headline broadcasted an "Anti-Negro Riot," which was part of a "Nationwide Racist Plot." The text of the article pointed out two neglected facts: "two Negro lads" had suffered injuries, and although five African American boys had been arrested, "No whites were touched by the police."[26]

Covello understood that the sensationalizing of this incident in segments of the press threatened to discourage boys from enrolling in Franklin High. In an unpublished article, Covello revealed that "Today, families in the areas adjoining the East Harlem area, particularly from Yorkville [a predominantly Irish and German American community south of East Harlem], use every subterfuge to send their boys to schools other than Franklin."[27] The capacious, almost palatial, edifice that had been erected to house the school had been designed to accommodate three thousand students.[28] Nonetheless, even after James Otis Junior High School, with its enrollment of one thousand, was located within the building, there were still far too few students to fill this monumental building. However, Franklin's evening adult enrollment had swelled from fifteen hundred in 1938, to as many as four thousand during the war years, in courses as varied as Russian, advanced English, and vocational courses such as "doctor's office assistant" and "switchboard."[29]

At his home, on Sunday evening, September 30, Covello convened a meeting with seventeen well-chosen people, who developed a strategy and tactics to combat this assault on their school and their community.[30] William Spiegel and Sal Pergola were invaluable liaisons to the student body. Abraham Kroll, a reliable and close associate, had served as Covello's administrative assistant from the founding of the school in 1934. The four names that are illegible on the minutes were most likely members of the high school's faculty. Rose Russell, the leader of the Teachers Union (CIO) represented both the faculty and the left.[31] Fred Kuper, the law secretary to the Board of Education, provided a direct link to Franklin's governing body.[32] Daniel Dodson, the executive director of the Mayor's Committee on Unity, would ultimately write the key report on this incident. Rose Covello (née Accurso) a mathematics teacher, assisted Covello in every aspect of his work.[33] Miriam Sanders (Mrs. Vito Marcantonio) was the "head worker" of Harlem House,[34] and one of the local community directors of the East Harlem League for Unity, an organization formed in 1943 for the purpose of developing "better understanding among nationality and racial groups."[35]

Most important was the presence of the most prestigious member of the community, Vito Marcantonio, who represented the community in Congress from 1934 until 1950. Marcantonio's reputation rested in part on his sponsorship of civil rights legislation in the House, where he led the fight against the poll tax, fought to make lynching a federal crime, and to ensure the funding of the Fair Employment Practices Commission.[36] In the House, he had achieved a national reputation as a spokesman for the Left. In the city, he was the leader of the American Labor Party (ALP), and in East Harlem he forged its multiethnic, multiracial population into an unchallenged political coalition. The childless Covello and the orphaned Marcantonio were lifelong collaborators.[37]

The group agreed to draw up a fact sheet to counter the biased reportage. It then focused on returning the school to normal, which more than anything else meant students learning in classes. Marcantonio recommended that "teachers visit homes of absentees [and that] Negro organizations send out representatives to all Negro students' homes—if absent." There was also discussion of the creation of a brochure, "mimeographed copies to be sent to leaders in [the] community for their signatures."[38] Someone suggested using the newspaper articles about the racial incidents in social science classes as "an example of how bad reporting is done." The minutes of this meeting then bluntly stated: "Plan for parade—very carefully planned—try to have it come from students." It was recommended that the "student suggestion for parade" come from "VO [Varsity Organization] leaders," and that the "boys responsible for incident on Thursday . . . take initiative." Marcantonio committed to contact Mayor Fiorello LaGuardia to obtain permission for the parade. He was also charged with convincing "Joe Lewis or Frank Sinatra" to attend a rally.[39] Remarkably, except for a proposal that a filmstrip be created for use in local movie houses, everything that was proposed in this one meeting was actually carried out.[40]

Covello and Marcantonio knew that the attitude and actions of the Italian American community were key to repairing the damage caused by the racial incidents that took place on September 27 and 28, as well as enhancing the long-term prospects for racial harmony in and around Franklin High. The content and thrust of the brochure that came out of the September 30 meeting reflected that conviction. Titled "Who Gets Hurt?/*Chi ha Sofferto da Tutto Questo?*," its text responded: "The Italo-American Community; the Negro People; Every Group in the Fight for Liberty!" Clearly, the key assertion that this leaflet had to sustain was that an attack on the African American boys outside of Benjamin Franklin also hurt Italian Americans. The flyer supported this premise by making three points. First, it reminded its readers that "The same people who hate us, also discriminate against us, also hate the Negro people, the Jews, the Catholics, the foreign-born. They hate everyone who wants America to be free for all the people." The flyer stated that "Benjamin Franklin High School is an example of how the people can unite and live peacefully together." It also pointed out that Franklin was "one of the most beautiful, most modern, best equipped of any school in the city." Finally, it reminded the readers of the OWI documentary: "The Government was proud of us—proud enough to show us at work to the Italians, to the French, to the British, and many others." The text then attacked "the reactionaries, who would divide us, including some traitors among our own people. . . . our own 'Bilbos' [who] are as dangerous as the Bilbos of Mississippi." It closed with these slogans: "Stop Hate Talk"; "Build the People's Unity"; "Keep Our School Free of Discrimination and Hate—Free to Grow."[41]

Theodore Bilbo (D., Miss.) was perhaps the single most virulent racist in the Senate. His name was current in the Italian American community because two months before, he used the salutation "My Dear Dago" when he responded to a letter written by Josephine Piccolo, a resident of Brooklyn, castigating him for attempting to block the appropriation for the federal Fair Employment Practices Commission. From the floor of the House, Marcantonio demanded an apology from Bilbo (which he did not offer) on behalf of Piccolo, who had three brothers in the armed forces—one of whom had died while in service.[42] Covello and Marcantonio seized upon Bilbo's slur as the linchpin of their effort to engage Italian Americans in a campaign affirming interracial cooperation.

Clearly, the flyer was intended for circulation solely in the Italian American community. After all, the African American people did not need to be convinced by anyone that Bilbo was an abomination and a threat. The translation of the leaflet into Italian was done not only to accommodate the Italian immigration generation, many of whom could not read English well, but also because Covello believed that "The familiar language must be used. It is the idea and not the language itself that is important."[43] The brochure was used to enlist the support of Italian Harlem's *prominenti* (community leaders), who received letters from Covello requesting that they join the campaign by adding their signature to the leaflet.[44]

On Monday morning, October 1, Covello conferred at the school with a number of people who could credibly verify his version of these events. They included Walter White, the executive secretary of the National Association for the Advancement of Colored People; Walter O'Leary, the director of the Bureau of Attendance; Assistant Chief Commander John De Martino; Ed Lewis of the Urban League; Edith Alexander, an African American, who was the associate director of the Mayor's Committee on Unity; and Saul Battle, the first African American New York City patrolman, who was then city parole commissioner.[45] Directly and indirectly, these individuals lent their reputations and influence to the cause of defending Covello and Benjamin Franklin High School. That same morning Covello convened a general assembly to enlist the students in the fight-back campaign. Covello laid down the law. He explained to the students: "Our student body represents forty-one nationalities or races, yet we never had such an outbreak as the one that occurred Friday." He then intoned his mantra: "We must not have intolerance here." Sal Pergola, who followed, admonished the students: "We don't want Bilboism here. . . . A few days ago we slipped. Let's not do it again."[46] On Tuesday, October 2, the faculty was armed with information: A chronologically organized fact sheet, which was prepared by a "committee of teachers," was presented at a faculty meeting. This document established that the scope and consequences of the events were far smaller and much less virulent than depicted in the press coverage.[47]

The tone and content of Monday's newspaper articles reflected the beginning of a turnabout. The *Times* quoted Covello to the effect that "the battles" at his school were "merely a boys' fight," and that "outside elements, unorganized but vicious, might have contributed to the difficulty."[48] The removal of the racial conflict from the school—after all, the fights did take place outside the school and school operations were not interrupted—distanced the incident from Covello and Franklin High. On Tuesday, Covello's voice was widely heard in the city through reports on Monday's student assembly. The archconservative *Journal-American* (an afternoon paper) printed in bold type this terse quote of Covello: "We must not have intolerance here." It also reported that attendance at Franklin on Monday reached 60 percent,[49] which, in view of the lurid press coverage, was evidence that Franklin was returning to normal. The most dramatic change occured in the coverage of the *Post*, whose African American journalist, Ted Poston, endorsed Covello's "contention that three slightly related racial incidents had been magnified into sensational stories of racial conflict." Poston added that Covello's version of these events was "strongly supported by eyewitnesses and community leaders. . . . [as well as] several teachers, including two of the five Negro members of the staff." The second edition of the *Post* also published a photo of two Franklin students—an Italian American boy with his arm around the shoulders of an African American boy—studying together. The article closed by quoting Covello to the effect that: "Stories . . . which smear a community unjustly play right into the hands of Bilbo and his ilk."[50] The shift in the *Daily Worker*'s coverage was hardly less dramatic. The headlines on Monday's paper blandly stated, "'One of Those Things': Cops Call School Riot."[51] The same issue of the *Worker* reported a Teachers Union proposal that the Board of Education reduce class size at Franklin to twenty-five students and hire at least twenty-five additional teachers, especially trained for remedial work.[52] In a somewhat different vein, a third article prominently printed a joint statement issued by Marcantonio and Benjamin Davis, Jr., a city councilman elected on the Communist Party ticket from Manhattan, calling on "the parents of all children, both Negro and white, to see that the children attend school today."[53]

The press's affirmation of Franklin High continued in the following days. The *Mirror* printed Covello's pledge that "positive action will be taken to prevent future outbreaks." It further cited his assertion that "in the eleven-year history of the school, the multiracial student body had gotten along like members of one family."[54] The *Daily News*, *Il Progresso*, and the *Daily Worker*, (which focused on Pergola's speech excoriating Bilboism) spoke favorably of Monday's student assembly. The *News* described it as the beginning of a "campaign for cooperation between white and Negro students."[55] The most thorough and thoughtful coverage, however, appeared in the *Herald Tribune*. It elaborated on White's crystal-clear declaration, "What happened on Friday was not a riot," in greater detail than other papers, and described visible signs of racial harmony and cooperation. Uniquely, the *Tribune* account quoted at some length Saul Battle, the African American parole commissioner, who stated that "it seemed rather unfair that only Negroes were arrested in a flare-up that involved both Negroes and whites."[56] White's interpretation of these events, as the leader of the preeminent African American organization, carried great weight. However, Covello also knew the importance of Battle's presence. In a seventeen-page unpublished manuscript, "The Community School and Race Relations," he wrote: "We are not living in a fool's paradise. When necessary, police action will definitely be taken. We have already had Negro policemen assigned near our school, and in fact more than one, to give our Negro students a feeling of greater security. [This decision has also been taken in order to] point out to the neighborhood that Negro police and Negro teachers have been accepted by the city and school authorities on the basis of equality."[57]

The best news of all was first carried by the *World-Telegram*: "On Tuesday all except 10 percent of normal attendance showed up for classes."[58] Hence, the first goal of the fight back—normal attendance—had been achieved. In addition to all the other measures enacted, the normalization of attendance had resulted from a letter Covello sent to the parents of absent students that stated: "It may be that this absence was caused by an expression of fear that your son might receive personal injury. We wish to assure you that the majority of the boys of this school were in classes today; everything was peaceful, and at no time was there any hint that anyone might be injured. Accept this assurance that conditions in this school are completely normal. I urge that you have your son return to school at once."[59] Articles in other city papers were also supportive of Benjamin Franklin and its administration. For example, the *World-Telegram* reported that a telegram sent by Algernon Black and William Andrews, the co-chairs of the Citywide Citizens Committee, to LaGuardia, placed the blame for the racial incidents on "adult attitudes which are aimed at segregation and inequality," and criticized the Board of Education for the overcrowding of classes.[60]

This dramatic reversal in reporting was brought about by the personal and immediate intervention of both Covello and Marcantonio. A lifelong resident recalled that in the evening following the racial outburst, Marcantonio approached a group of older boys with whom he was hanging out near Franklin High and asked them not to loiter around the area of the school.

One of the boys shouted out to Marcantonio: "If you had a sister, would you want her to marry a n———?" He then recalled that without saying a word, Marcantonio turned on his heel and walked away.[61] Covello also talked to the members of a social club whose headquarters, on East 118th Street and Pleasant Avenue, faced the site where the attack on the African American students had occurred.

The major event of the fight-back campaign took place on Monday, October 8, at 8 P.M., in the auditorium of the high school. Billed as a "community mass meeting," it clearly intended to bring together the leadership and residents of Italian Harlem for the single purpose of reaffirming and manifesting the commitment of the Italian American community to Franklin as an integrated school. Covello and Marcantonio conceived of this assembly as a means of demonstrating the unanimity of the community's leadership on this issue, as well as providing a way for enlisting the community members in the fight-back campaign.

On Saturday, October 6, Covello made a special effort to reach Italian-speaking members of the community by speaking on the radio in Italian in order to give "a very brief and very exact exposition of the facts" of what had occurred at Franklin on September 27 and 28. He closed his talk by inviting his listeners to attend the meeting at the school in order to join together with "eminent citizens of our community who will present to you, in English and Italian, the true and fair exposition of the facts."[62] Covello appealed in a letter to the parents as someone who "for eleven years [has] worked all year around, day and night, seven days a week," asking them "[to] assume your share of the duties as citizens of this Community" by attending the assembly, where, he noted, he would report to them in English and Italian.[63] On his congressional stationery, Marcantonio sent a letter of invitation to community residents that exhorted them to remember that "The Benjamin Franklin High School belongs to the people. . . . and we must defend it. American democracy is based on the principle of equality. We cannot permit the ugly head of race hatred to rise in our midst."[64]

Gathering the *prominenti* of Italian Harlem was the next task. On October 1, letters of invitation were sent to forty-three leaders, thirty-four of whom accepted. Covello and Marcantonio had succeeded within one week in assembling: State Senator Richard Costanzo; State Assemblyman Hamlet Catennacio; Democratic Party chieftain Frank Rossetti; judges; labor leaders; heads of veterans clubs; and morticians. Most important, the local clergy endorsed this effort. Catholic clergy attended from every Italian national church—Our Lady of Mount Carmel, St. Lucy's, Holy Name, and St.

Anne's.[65] The pastor from Jefferson Park Methodist Church, of which Covello was an active member, also accepted the invitation. Among the minority who did not respond were Joseph Piscitello, a functionary from the International Ladies Garment Workers Union, whom Marcantonio had defeated in the 1940 ALP primary; Frank Ricca, his defeated Democratic opponent from 1942; and Joseph Cioffi, the Democratic Party candidate in 1944 for state assemblyman who had been defeated by the Republican—ALP candidate, Catennacio. Within one week, Covello and Marcantonio had successfully summoned the political, social, and religious leadership of Italian Harlem. In addition, four non-Italian Americans were among the thirty-four attendees—two Irish American Catholic priests, who served at local parishes, one social worker, and one medical doctor who worked in Italian Harlem.[66]

One thousand parents ("mostly Italian American," *PM* reported) attended the community mass meeting.[67] The headline "Who Gets Hurt?" and the responses "The Italo-American Community!" appeared on the top of the assembly's program along with this slogan: "No man is safe, unless all men are safe; no group is safe, unless all groups are safe." The program was highly ritualized. It started with the color guard of James Otis Junior High School marching into the auditorium, while the audience stood to sing the "Star-Spangled Banner." This was followed by *A Better America*, the OWI-produced documentary, and then Covello's introductory statement, the text of which is not available. The program ended with "brief statements by leading citizens of East Harlem and sponsors of the Community Mass Meeting." *PM*, the only newspaper to cover this event, published this excerpt of Marcantonio's address: "[The street fighting] would delight Bilbo and [Rep. John] Rankin [Congressman from Mississippi]. We've got to fight the Bilbos and Rankins all over the world. We, of Italian origin, know the meaning of discrimination because we have been exploited, so we refuse to discriminate against others. We have no quarrel with any people; we have no quarrel with Negro people." (*PM* noted that the audience booed the names of Bilbo and Rankin.)[68] Although we have no copies of the other talks, we do have a message from A. Salimbene, a business representative of a local of the Excavators and Building Laborers Union, who, because he was unable to attend due to illness, wired Covello this statement: "In the highest form of democracy, tolerance is the greatest need. To live together, work together, and study together regardless of race, creed, or color is what our fighting men gave their lives for. . . . In a democracy such as ours, this must be our daily creed. I urge this meeting to resolve that we will always fight for freedom for all peoples regardless of race, creed, or color."[69] Following the speeches, a resolution was presented and unanimously accepted that reaffirmed "our profound belief in the American principle of racial equality and tolerance [and] pledged to go forward in unity and solidarity in an ever-expanding program of better understanding among all racial and cultural groups in our community."[70]

The morning following the community mass meeting, Covello distributed a letter to the faculty and students that reproduced the resolution, which he asked be discussed in every English class. He further urged the faculty and students "to take positive action by signing the pledge [card] to march in the Columbus Day parade on Friday. . . ."[71] This reminder was reinforced by a letter from Covello to the parents, requesting that they sign consent cards so that their children could march. He closed by urging their "cooperation in this manifestation of unity among all our people, by the participation of your son, and if possible, yourself, in this parade." The faculty also received a letter from Covello seeking their participation in the Columbus Day Parade, which closed: "Let us affirm by positive action how deeply we feel on the question of segregation, discrimination, and the fomenting of race hatred."[72]

Actually, preparations for the parade were under way in advance of these missives. At an all-day student conference held on Wednesday, October 3, the *Herald Tribune* reported, "A Negro boy proposed a resolution that all the boys of the school march *en masse* in the city's Columbus Day parade, to demonstrate their unity to the entire city."[73] In addition, students developed a series of slogans, including "Christian, Jew, Negro, White—Americans All—Unite and Fight Race-Hate." The chair of the English Department, Robert Shapiro, requested that the English teachers work together with the students to create "slogans that are brief and dramatic. They should be expressions of: 1) the democratic spirit of unity of races; 2) respect for all individuals; 3) our school unity."[74]

Benjamin Franklin's participation in the Columbus Day Parade became news even before it happened. Columbus Day morning, the *Mirror* reported that "A feature of the parade will be the participation of the student body of Benjamin Franklin High School in East Harlem, scene of recent racial disturbances. The students voted to take part as a demonstration of American unity and solidarity, their principal announced."[75] The following day, four New York City dailies published stories that included mention of Franklin's participation in the parade. The *Times* remarked that a "delegation of five hundred students of Benjamin Franklin High School, led by their principal, Dr. Leonard Covello, and flanked by parents . . . marched in a demonstration of unity, signalizing the restoration of interracial harmony and good-will at the school, where disorders occurred on September 27 and 28."[76] The *Times* did not, of course, here or any other place, note that on the day following these "disorders," it had published a headline terming them "a riot." Noting that the Franklinites marched behind a huge banner that proclaimed that they were "Americans All," the *Tribune* increased the estimate of the Franklin delegation to six hundred, which, it noted, constituted "fully half of the student body of the school, [who marched] . . . as a demonstration of its 'American unity and solidarity.'"[77] The *Mirror* stated, "Notable among the ten thousand students who took part was a large group of white and Negro pupils from the Benjamin Franklin High School. . . ." The article also noted, "A burst of applause greeted a float on which one of the girls from the high school personified the Statue of Liberty. She was flanked by banners reading: 'Americans All—Negro, Jewish, Catholic, and Protestant.'"[78] *Il Progresso* printed the Franklin story under the subheading "Every Race, Every Faith." After relating some background, it described how "[The students] were marching together one after the other—the whites, the Negroes, the Catholics, the Protestants, and the Jews—with Prof. Leonard Covello, the principal, at the head. The public comprehended the significance of this 'fusion' and applauded from the heart."[79]

On October 23, 1945, the finale of this remarkable campaign took place. The most popular singer in the United States (who, not inconsequentially, happened to be Italian American) came to Benjamin Franklin High School to add his voice to the chorus demanding "unity and solidarity" across racial, national, and religious lines. From 1944 until 1948, Sinatra was very involved in supporting a wide variety of progressive organizations and causes, but most especially the fight against racism. In 1945, for example, he made thirty appearances around the country speaking against prejudice.[80] *PM* published an article on the morning of the event in which Sinatra (who was described as toying with a gold St. Christopher medallion, on the back of which was engraved a Star of David) said that he was "going to lay it on the line" during his talk at Franklin.[81] In the middle of a program that started with an organ prelude, flag salute, Bible reading, and band selections, and ended with "expressions of our School's thanks to Frank Sinatra, Ambassador of good will,"[82] Sinatra told the students that hate groups had sent "delegates and agents among the kids to talk up race prejudice. . . . This country was built by many people of many creeds, so it can never be divided. . . . No kid is born and two days later says: 'I hate Jews or colored people.' He's got to be taught."[83] The *Daily News* reported that Sinatra pointed out that there are no discernible "biological differences between races. He also asked the high school students to serve as "neighborhood emissaries of racial good will."[84] The *Daily Worker*, the only other city daily newspaper to cover this event, reported that the boys liked Sinatra because as one boy said, "he speaks our language." Curiously, Sinatra did not sing "The House I Live In," a Popular Front anthem that Sinatra had recently dramatized in a ten-minute documentary, but one of his least memorable songs, "Aren't You Glad You're You?," which was totally devoid of social or political content.[85]

Covello and Marcantonio's success in leading this movement depended on their deep roots and prodigious service to this community. Covello had arrived in Italian Harlem from Italy at the age of nine; Marcantonio spent his entire life within a four-block radius in Italian Harlem.[86] Subsequently, they lived in adjacent brownstones at 229 and 231 East 116th Street, three blocks from Franklin High, and on the same block as Marcantonio's political headquarters, 247 East 116th Street.

In the House, Marcantonio was a singular voice defending the rights of the foreign-born, Puerto Ricans, African Americans, and specifically Italian Americans. Marcantonio's delivery of service to his constituents was legendry. Every Sunday at his East Harlem headquarters, he listened to the petitions of his constituents until the last was heard. Annually, thousands upon thousands of residents in Italian Harlem had some problem resolved or at least attended to by Marcantonio and his staff. One of his biographers has stated: "Few men in public life have been so intimately linked with a particular urban neighborhood . . . the man was the product and personification of the neighborhood."[87]

Contemporaries described Covello as "almost a little god in East Harlem," and as "the dean of East Harlem. He is undoubtedly the most experienced person in the community and his activities were more widespread and extended over a longer period than any other person."[88] His involvement with East Harlem extended far beyond Franklin High. For example, when he identified its lack of a newspaper as both a reflection of, and a contributing factor to, the disunity of East Harlem, he spearheaded a group that in March 1941 founded the *East Harlem News*, an eight-page tabloid that appeared monthly until 1943. It featured articles in Italian and Spanish, and published announcements and news about the community's numerous social clubs, churches, and of course schools. Under the headline "Towards Building a Better Community," the front page of its first issue, for example, announced the monthly "community night" at Franklin where readers had the opportunity to join community committees. These committees, which both afforded services for the community and linked the school to the community, included: Housing, Health, Juvenile Aid, Racial, Adult Education, Parents Association, Citizenship, and Naturalization.[89]

Covello and Marcantonio had led the campaigns first to found the school, which was initially housed in two antiquated public school buildings, and, some years later, to obtain a new facility for the school. When its new edifice was opened in 1944, Marcantonio stated at its dedication: "[Franklin High] is interracial in character and community-wide in the scope of its work. . . . It can truly be said that this great building is indeed a monument to democracy in education."[90]

Their highly visible and tangible service to Italian Harlem gave them enormous prestige and credibility. Therefore, the community, its leaders, and its residents accepted both their evaluation as to the gravity of this situation and the course of action they proposed. Their actions had also given them enormous credibility and trust among African Americans, Puerto Ricans, and other residents in the community.

Covello and Marcantonio built this fight-back on the ideology of the New Deal, especially as articulated by Henry Wallace and the Congress of Industrial Organizations. This political perspective insisted that democracy (social democracy, if you will) was dependent on working-class unity, which was endangered by racism, anti-Semitism, and nativism. Therefore, they did not try to shame or bully the Italian American community, but to appeal to its best instincts and sense of self-interest. They succeeded in convincing the Italian Americans that what was at stake was their reputation, the viability of their school, and a connection with others who had been systematically left out of the American dream.

Unfortunately, this racial incident became the single most publicized, and remembered, incident in the history of Franklin High. In *The Heart Is the Teacher,* Covello acknowledges that despite the creative and comprehensive fight-back, "Damage was done to the prestige of the school, making it less effective as an educational institution and stigmatizing the community and the students." Nonetheless, this campaign helped prevent a recurrence of racial incidents, reinvigorated Benjamin Franklin's progressive mission, secured Covello's reputation, and helped perpetuate Marcantonio's leadership.[91]

CHAPTER ELEVEN

FRANK L. RIZZO AND THE WHITENING OF ITALIAN AMERICANS IN PHILADELPHIA

STEFANO LUCONI

In the 1980s, the Dougherty Irish Dancers, a fraternal group active in the Philadelphia area, dropped nationality requirements for enrollment and came to include not only members of Irish extraction but also individuals of German, Jewish, Polish, and Italian ancestry. It was initially established as an ethnic association that intended to use Irish dances to distinguish Irish Americans from other immigrant minorities. However, the Dougherty Irish Dancers progressively reached out to different national groups and eventually turned into a social club for Americans of European backgrounds, regardless of the country of birth of their forefathers.[1]

Notwithstanding the willingness of the Dougherty Irish Dancers to open their doors to people who were not of Irish background, the presence of Italian Americans within this association may apparently seem quite strange against the backdrop of an extended history of a troubled relationship between Irish Americans and Italian Americans. Indeed, like almost all major U.S. cities, Philadelphia had long been the setting of conflicts and animosities between these two ethnic groups. For instance, Irish Americans' enduring control of the great bulk of positions with the city's police force brought up charges that Irish officers enjoyed harassing Italian Americans out of ethnic intolerance. Likewise, Irish politicians restrained Italian Americans' political rise on both the local and the federal level. This acrimony affected religious life as well. Although most members of both nationality groups shared the Catholic faith, the prevailing Irish hierarchy of Philadelphia's archdiocese tended to antagonize worshipers of Italian extraction in the attempt to uproot the latter's allegedly unorthodox and superstition-prone religious practices. And ethnic strife sometimes extended into the postwar years. In politics, for example, Philadelphia's First Congressional District remained almost an Irish preserve until Thomas M. Foglietta won election to the U.S. House of Representatives with the support of the city's Irish American mayor, William J. Green III, in 1980.[2]

It can be hardly suggested that Italian Americans' membership in the Dougherty Irish Dancers was a belated confirmation of Ruby Jo Reeves Kennedy's 1944 "triple melting pot" theory, according to which the disparate national identities of immigrant minorities would eventually merge into only three groups made up of the three major confessions practiced in the United States: Protestantism, Catholicism, and Judaism. Actually, while Irish Americans and Italian Americans are Catholics, this is not the case of Jews and German Lutherans, who nonetheless joined the Dougherty Irish Dancers. Rather, one may more reasonably argue that the white membership of this club, regardless of national extraction or religious affiliation, epitomized one of the vertices of the "ethnoracial pentagon," or "quintuple melting pot," of European Americans, African Americans, Asian Americans, Hispanic Americans, and Native Americans, which, in David A. Hollinger's opinion, represents the great divide in the elaboration of identities in present-day U.S. society.[3]

Of course, Italian Americans' adherence to the Dougherty Irish Dancers is nothing more than a mere metaphor of the broadening of their sense of group affiliation. This essay intends to highlight the process by which and the reason why Philadelphians of Italian descent renegotiated their nationally based ethnic identity and developed a racially oriented white self-perception that led some of them to feel comfortable in joining what had been an Irish club. To pursue such a goal, this essay will focus primarily on the political experience of Italian Americans and, specifically, on their response to the deeds of Frank L. Rizzo, a former policeman of Italian descent-turned-politician who came to personify European American Philadelphians' whiteness between the 1960s and the 1980s. The political focus of this analysis is not accidental. Actually, in sociologist Albert James Bergesen's view, the reshaping of ethnic consciousness since the late 1960s has resulted mostly from defensive political protest. Likewise, according to historian Anna Maria Martellone, politics has been central to the formation and the redefinition of the self-images of ethnic minorities in the United States, especially Italian Americans.[4]

Examining ethnic relations in New York City in the 1960s, sociologists Nathan Glazer and Daniel Patrick Moynihan identified a demise of major differences between Irish Americans and Italian Americans in that decade which was not different from the collapse of those ethnic barriers which long contributed to preventing the transformation of the Dougherty Irish Dancers in Philadelphia. They argued:

> Whether we say "Italian" or "Irish" is not important, and yet we know we are talking about roughly the same people. . . . the people are the same, and the issues are the same: their feelings that they have been ignored, have received little from government in recent years, and have borne the brunt of the costs involved in the economic and political rise of the Negroes.[5]

In other words, Italian Americans and Irish Americans developed a common identity out of their tendency to hold African Americans responsible for the deterioration of their own standards of living. Actually, as George Lipsitz has contended, the consolidation around whiteness among European Americans resulted primarily from their demonization of blacks for most social and economic problems of postwar United States.[6]

Animosities between African Americans and Italian Americans broke out in Philadelphia as early as the mid-1930s, following the impact of the domestic repercussions of the Italian–Ethiopian War. While most Italian Americans rushed to support the successful Fascist invasion and subsequent annexation of this African country, black Philadelphians mobilized to prevent Italy's military and diplomatic victory in eastern Africa. Although physical clashes characterized the relations between these two communities in the months of the war, from October 1935 to May 1936, such enmity failed to make Italian Americans acquire a white self-image. Rather, Italy's achievements under the Fascist regime in the 1920s and 1930s made Italian Americans proud of their national ancestry and contributed to strengthening their Italian ethnic consciousness as opposed to their sense of racial affiliation.[7]

Italian immigrants to the United States were long considered by many white Americans as "nonwhite" or "less than white," and held an "inbetween" color status. However, it has been argued that the Italian–Ethiopian War helped initiate the process by which Italian Americans eventually attained a white self-image. Scholars have also pointed to the race riots, the segregation in the military, and the hate strikes against African Americans' access to jobs previously beyond their reach as other rites of passage that fostered the development of a white identity on the part of the European minorities during World War II. However, this was not the case for Italian Americans in Philadelphia.[8]

The Fascist regime did use racialized language in its propaganda efforts to justify Mussolini's colonial venture in Ethiopia. Nonetheless, while immigrant groups in Philadelphia struggled with one another over access to political patronage and recognition, cheap housing units, and shrinking job opportunities in the wake of the Depression, the ensuing tensions with Irish Americans and Jews continued to make Italian Americans shy away from other white minorities. The spread of Fascist anti-Semitism in the city's community further separated Italian Americans from Jews. As a result, in the mid-1930s, Italian Americans rallied against an urban renewal project that would bring new residents, most of whom were also descendents of European immigrants but not necessarily of Italian ancestry, into South Philadelphia's mainly Italian Second Ward. The project's opponents feared that such a development would consolidate the overwhelming white presence in the area and dilute the Italian majority. In addition, Italian Americans did not play an active role in the strike of the roughly six thousand white employees of the Philadelphia Transportation Company who protested against the promotion of African American fellow workers from maintenance jobs to positions such as conductors and bus drivers in order to cope with the wartime personnel shortage in August 1944. No riot split Philadelphia along racial lines in the war years, and the lack of such opportunities for the mobilization of the white population as a whole helped the city's Italian Americans retain an ethnic identity based on their national ancestry. After all, the latter survived even after Italy's declaration of war on the United States, although Italian Americans rushed to show off their unqualified allegiance to their adoptive country. Ethnic associations such as the Order of the Sons of Italy in America launched the major drives to encourage the purchase of war bonds in Philadelphia's "Little Italy," and did so on the occasion of traditional Italian American festivities, such as Columbus Day. The Italian-language press also made a point of focusing on the U.S. servicemen of Italian origin who had been killed in action or awarded military decorations, and joined the immigrant organizations in stressing that the members of the community supported the war efforts of the United States not just as Americans but also as Americans of Italian descent.[9]

It was only in the tumultuous 1960s that Italian Americans began to join forces with other immigrant groups from European backgrounds and to develop a white consciousness in the common effort to curb African Americans' claims and alleged encroachments. As blacks rose from about one tenth of the city's population in 1930 to roughly one third in 1970, they were increasingly associated with crime, social disruption, and urban blight in the eyes of the city's white residents who could not afford to move to the suburbs. Against this backdrop, adopting a "law and order" view of the functions of the municipal government, which regarded the protection of citizens rather than the expansion of social services as being the chief purpose of the city administration, Rizzo became the champion of white Philadelphians. Even his own following among Italian Americans resulted less from his Italian ancestry than from his ability to whiten the ethnic identity of his supporters of Italian descent.[10]

The son of Italian immigrants, Rizzo joined Philadelphia's city police in 1943 and in a few years made himself a reputation for his heavy-handed methods against African Americans. A thirty-one-year-old district captain in the predominantly African American community of, West Philadelphia under the liberal administration of Mayor Joseph S. Clark, Jr., and District Attorney Richardson Dilworth, Rizzo did not refrain from adopting a storm trooper approach to hunting down the local black-operated and -patronized illegal speakeasies, where numbers playing was widespread. As a result, Police Commissioner Thomas J. Gibson rushed to move his rough-riding captain to the Center City district in less than five months after appointing him to West Philadelphia. While rising from deputy police commissioner in 1965 to head of the city police two years later, Rizzo intensified his tough tactics against African Americans. He arrested Malcolm X and his bodyguards when they came to Philadelphia. He ordered his men to charge African Americans who protested against the exclusion of nonwhite students from Girard College arrested black members of the Student Nonviolent Coordinating Committee on charges of storing explosives. He disrupted a relatively peaceful demonstration of African American teenagers, who called for more courses in African American culture and the permission to wear African-style clothes in high schools, in front of Philadelphia's School Administration Building, which resulted in the hospitalization of fifteen black activists. In 1970, in a major display of his own determination to repress black protests, Police Commissioner Rizzo raided Philadelphia's headquarters of the Black Panthers Party and had its members strip naked to search for concealed weapons in front of photographer at 2 A.M.[11]

While racial riots had plagued U.S. cities since the 1965 African American revolt in the Watts district of Los Angeles, the brutality of Philadelphia's enforcement officers against black activists earned ironically Rizzo the credit for preventing mayhem. Philadelphia experienced only one major racial uprising—which caused two deaths, the injury of 339 people, and the destruction of property worth about three million dollars—in late August 1964, when Rizzo had not yet reached the top ranks in the police hierarchy. Democratic Mayor James H. J. Tate proudly boasted on the eve of the 1967 mayoral election in praise of Rizzo's work during the previous summer, "While other cities were being burned, sacked, and pillaged, Philadelphia has had law and order." Indeed, despite forty-two minor and short-lived incidents, there was no major outburst of large-scale violence in those months. Rizzo's terror policy even managed to inhibit the African American violent response to the assassination of Martin Luther King, Jr., that broke out in most major urban centers in April 1968.[12]

In the words of then District Attorney Arlen Specter, the brutality of the police under Rizzo made black Philadelphians feel "written out of the social contract." However, it also turned Rizzo into "the hero of the city" among residents of European descent because he helped them to assert their white identity. In her work on the history of lynching, historian Grace Elizabeth Hale has maintained that the blatantly public spectacle of lynching not only was intended to reverse African Americans' emancipation but also contributed to the consolidation of whiteness across class lines in the South. One might suggest that the public humiliation of black activists by Rizzo served a similar purpose. As a result, he easily became the symbol of white Philadelphians' backlash against African Americans. Indeed, when Mayor Tate endeavored to strengthen his political following among white voters in view of his 1967 bid for a second term, he announced the appointment of Rizzo to the position of police commissioner. Tate proved to be right, not only because he won reelection, but also because support for Rizzo in the aftermath of the School Administration Building incident cut across the lines of national descent and brought together white Philadelphians regardless of their ancestry. While the Philadelphia chapter of the National Association for the Advancement of Colored People called for Rizzo's "immediate" replacement as police commissioner because of his "Gestapo-like tactics," the congratulations of readers of the *Philadelphia Inquirer* with such Jewish-sounding names as Frank Burnstein, on how Rizzo had quelled the African American protest outside the School Administration Building, echoed an editorial of the Italian-language weekly *Sons of Italy Times* that wanted to "strongly commend the effective action of the uniformed police under the able command of Commissioner Frank Rizzo in bringing under control an unruly crowd of 3500 people [who] had become inflamed and threatening to the safety of innocent persons and property." In addition, a wave of "hate letters" signed "a white man" or "a disgusted white tax payer" attacked the chairperson of the Philadelphia Board of Education, Richardson Dilworth, who had criticized Rizzo's handling of the demonstration.[13]

Most Italian Americans were particularly sensitive to school-related matters and intended to restrain blacks' claims in the field of education. For instance, after casting 58.5 percent of their ballots to let Democratic Mayor Richardson Dilworth win a second term in 1959, Italian American voters let Republican James T. McDermott carry their community by 52.9 percent in his unsuccessful 1963 bid for City Hall against Tate. Unlike his Democratic opponent, McDermott opposed busing and campaigned on this issue. Similarly, in 1969, the electorate of South Philadelphia's Italian American districts joined voters from other predominantly white wards in rejecting a referendum held to authorize the city administration to borrow ninety million dollars for the construction of a number of new public schools in Philadelphia. Since white attendance at public schools had undergone a significant decline in the previous years, it seemed that the project would be funded mainly by white taxpayers but would benefit primarily African American students. Consequently, in a referendum that saw the electorate polarized along racial lines, a coalition of white voters defeated the loan issue by 56.6 percent.[14]

In the aftermath of the 1969 referendum, Tate—whom the City Charter prevented from seeking a third consecutive term in 1971—handpicked Rizzo as his successor because he thought that his police commissioner was the best candidate to keep white voters in the Democratic column and avoid their bolt to the GOP that his own party had experienced in the 1968 presidential race at the federal level following the pledge of the Johnson administration to African Americans' integration. As political scientist Ivor Crewe has pointed out, candidacies like that of Rizzo were the response of the Democratic Party "to the blue-collar white 'backlash'" against blacks. Indeed, Tate himself argued in his memoirs a couple of years later that "the old Democratic coalition of . . . organized labor, the working-class whites, liberals, blacks and other minorities was breaking down. The working-class whites . . . were developing increasingly Republican tendencies. . . . I felt Rizzo could bring the white working-class vote back into the Democratic Party."[15]

Tate was right once again. In the 1971 mayoral contest, working-class Italian Americans, lower-middle-class Jews, and middle-class Irish set aside their previous ethnic and class differences to elect Rizzo to City Hall. In particular, Rizzo obtained a large following in South Philadelphia's "Little Italy." Italian Americans, who had cast only 43.1 percent of their ballots for

Democratic presidential hopeful Hubert H. Humphrey in 1968, contributed to Rizzo's 1971 victory with 86.1 percent of their votes.[16]

It is likely that Rizzo's "law and order" approach gratified many Italian American voters as a partial redress for the ethnic stereotypes that had long associated people of Italian descent with organized crime. Yet it was Rizzo's racial characterization as the champion of whites' claims, rather than his national ancestry, that enabled him to win the support of most Italian Americans. According to KYW news anchorman Larry Kane, Rizzo embodied "the interests of middle- and lower-income Philadelphians who didn't have the economic power to move to the suburbs." That his Republican opponent, W. Thacher Longstreth, was the self-proclaimed representative of those members of Philadelphia's Anglo-Saxon Protestant elite who, from their own suburban residences, advocated the racial integration of African Americans in the center city's neighborhoods and school system further contributed to turning Rizzo into the candidate of the white voters who belonged to European immigrant minorities. As a Democratic committeeman of Italian descent pointed out, "If there is one issue on which white voters of South Philadelphia agree on [sic], it is their dislike of racial conflict. Any political candidate who associated himself with the prevention of racial conflict would be sure to command wide support."[17]

A major plank in Rizzo's 1971 platform was his opposition to the Whitman Park Project of the Philadelphia Housing Authority and the U.S. Department of Housing and Urban Development, which aimed at building 120 low-cost public houses in a southeastern section of South Philadelphia of 6.15 acres, and at integrating the area racially. On December 18, 1970, the groundbreaking triggered the protest of the white residents in the district, who feared that the arrival of blacks would both cause an increase in crime and make the real estate value of their own homes collapse. They also resented the idea that their hard-earned tax money would be used to subsidize housing while they had to purchase their homes with their savings and loans. Unlike the urban renewal project of the Second Ward in the 1930s, this time Italian Americans joined Polish American, Russian American and other Euro-American residents in taking to the street to picket the site of the project in April 1971, and in testifying against the Philadelphia Housing Authority in court. Hearings before Philadelphia's Court of Common Pleas described the Whitman area as "familial" and "a very tight, closeknit community," in which the white self-image of the residents was the glue that united Italian Americans and people from other European backgrounds. Indeed, the common efforts of white Philadelphians against the Whitman

Park Project transcended their national origins and revealed the development of a racial consciousness that replaced ethnic identities based on different ancestral countries. As Rizzo himself would remark a few years later about the presence of Italian Americans among the opponents of the project, "When I was first married, I wanted to buy a house in a really nice neighborhood, Germantown. They got a petition with 400 names not to sell it to me because I was Italian. So we have come a long way." Ironically, however, Rizzo used the case of his own discrimination in housing to justify the efforts to exclude prospective African American residents from the Whitman area.[18]

Larry Kane has argued that Rizzo interpreted his election to City Hall as "his calling to preserve the neighborhoods." Indeed, on April 29, 1972, after taking over as mayor, Rizzo let the contract of the Philadelphia Housing Authority with Multicon Construction Corporation, the developer for the Whitman Park Project, expire. The decision cost the city administration $626,000 in damages, but it stopped the construction of the 120 public houses and pleased Rizzo's white constituents. In the mayor's view, "open warfare" would result if the construction continued. Yet, according to federal Judge Raymond J. Broderick, who eventually ruled against the city administration in November 1976, in a suit filed by an organization of public housing tenants, Rizzo "felt that there should not be any public housing placed in white neighborhoods because people in white neighborhoods did not want black people moving in with them." Rizzo also curbed the rise of African Americans in the city administration. As one of his biographers has written, "By the fall of 1975, there was only one black deputy mayor, two black assistants to the mayor, no black cabinet members, and one black department head."[19]

Rizzo's support for the claims of white Philadelphians paid off at the polls, and he won a second term with 57 percent of the vote in 1975. Among Italian Americans, however, his plurality was much larger; he carried their community by 83 percent. A majority of Italian Americans cast their ballots along racial rather than national lines. The Republican mayoral candidate, Thomas M. Foglietta, was of Italian descent, too. Yet, although 31 percent of the city's eligible Italian American voters were registered as Republicans, Foglietta's following among Italian Americans failed to exceed the 18 percent that he obtained citywide. With an African American, Charles W. Bowser, running for mayor as an independent candidate, most Italian Americans did not cast their ballots for Foglietta because they feared that splitting the white vote would result in the election of a black politician to City Hall. As Foglietta recalled, Rizzo's supporters "made some 40,000 phone calls to people who were solid Republicans and they said to those people, we know that Tom Foglietta is a good guy, a competent guy; however, Charles Bowser is going to win this election if we divide the white vote."[20]

Rizzo's second administration placed further emphasis on the mayor's pro-white bent. Most notably, besides resisting attempts to revitalize the Whitman Park Project by means of lawsuits, on August 8, 1978, Rizzo had the police storm and raze the headquarters of MOVE, a back-to-nature, mainly African American, counterculture group that had settled in West Philadelphia.[21]

As Philadelphia increasingly polarized along racial lines, Italian Americans consolidated their identity as white ethnics in 1978. That year, Rizzo promoted a referendum to amend the City Charter so that he could serve more than two consecutive terms. His campaign endeavored to cash in on his long, though controversial, advocacy of the interests of white Philadelphians, and drew racial lines for the alignment of voters on the amendment issue. After suggesting that "whites must join hands" at a press conference, Rizzo directly asked for the support of the white cohort of the electorate for the change to the City Charter before the leaders of a civic organization called the Northeast Coalition for Community Problems. With reference to the charter amendment, Rizzo observed that "black leaders want to make it a black and white thing." In order to counter his opponents' call for African Americans to "vote black," Rizzo urged his backers to "vote white" by ratifying the amendment that would enable him to run for City Hall in 1979. Once again, Rizzo resorted to a double standard. On the one hand, he criticized African American leaders' supposed efforts to racialize politics. On the other, he himself fostered racial polarization by endeavoring to turn white Philadelphians into a cohesive voting bloc. However, Italian Americans' favorable response to Rizzo's appeal to their racial identity was overwhelming. Sixty-six percent of the city's total electorate rejected the proposed amendment. African Americans cast 96 percent of their ballot against it. Conversely, 85 percent of Italian Americans voted to remove the two-consecutive-term limit. Such a percentage meant a 2 percent increase over Rizzo's following in the 1975 mayoral contest. Not even class affected the outcome significantly, since 86 percent of Italian Americans in lower-income voting precincts endorsed the amendment, as opposed to 79 percent in upper-income districts. Remarkably, support for the repeal of the term limit was lower than two thirds of the ballots cast in none of the eighty-nine precincts that were predominantly Italian American, and ranged from a low of 67 percent to a high of 92 percent. Such data is particularly meaningful because Italian American turnout was 75 percent, seven percentage points higher than voter participation in Philadelphia as a whole.[22]

Italian Americans' support for Rizzo underwent an additional increase as the white-versus-black cleavage became more evident even in symbolic terms in Philadelphia. Conversely, it was subject to a significant decline when race was no longer a paramount factor in election campaigns. As political scientists Jack Citrin, Donald Philip Green, and David Sears have argued, Rizzo was "an established symbol of hostility to blacks." The ups and downs of his following among Italian Americans matched this picture.[23]

After four years out of office, Rizzo made a political comeback in 1983 to challenge African American leader W. Wilson Goode for the Democratic nomination for mayor, though to no avail. Undaunted by his defeat, Rizzo went over to the GOP, secured the 1987 Republican mayoral nomination, and vainly faced Goode again in the November election. Even if both of Rizzo's bids for City Hall were unsuccessful, he received 97 percent of the Italian American vote in 1983 and 92 percent in 1987 while he ran against a black politician. In 1987, Goode made a fruitless effort to reach out to the white electorate, but he also made a point of stigmatizing Rizzo's racial insensitivity while he had been mayor in the 1970s. In addition, with an incumbent African American mayor, an African American school superintendent, an African American president of the City Council, and an African American managing director of the municipal administration, many Italian Americans feared that white Philadelphians had lost all political power to the black community, especially after the Goode administration had benefited this latter disproportionately in the allotment of city contracts, jobs, and patronage. Indeed, in 1987, the chairperson of the Democratic City Committee, Robert Brady, who had endorsed Goode, could hardly rely on the votes of his own ward leaders, district committeemen, and their relatives in South Philadelphia.[24]

In 1991, Rizzo ran for mayor one more time. He won the Republican nomination again, but died from a heart attack before the general election. In the GOP primaries, both of Rizzo's opponents—District Attorney Ronald Castille and Samuel Katz, a former member of the Philadelphia Board of Education—were white, and racial issues played no major role in the campaign or in its coverage by the media. The lack of a black candidate who challenged Rizzo and the marginality of race in the political discourse caused the Italian American vote to scatter, and the support for Rizzo among Italian Americans fell to 62.5 percent that year.[25]

In other words, it was Rizzo's whiteness, rather than his Italianness, that attracted Italian American support. The presence of a black candidate enhanced such a characterization and helped him win votes. To the contrary, the absence of an African American opponent turned Rizzo into one of the white politicians on the ballot and weakened his appeal to the Italian American electorate. Indeed, Philadelphians of Italian ancestry were responsive to the increasing salience of race in voting behavior that has generally characterized northern cities such as Chicago and New York City, besides Philadelphia, since World War II. As a result, they thought of themselves as white voters when the choice of a candidate and the issues at stake had racial implications. This phenomenon offers further evidence that Italian Americans did vote white rather than Italian in 1978 and that, therefore, their racial identity replaced their ethnic sense of affiliation based on their national ancestry in the wake of the racial strives of the 1960s and 1970s.[26]

Of course, not all Philadelphia's Italian Americans supported Rizzo and thought of themselves as white European Americans. The search of *Esquire*'s senior editor Bill Tonelli for his own Italian roots, for instance, gives evidence that some still cherished an ethnic identity based on their national origin in the 1990s. Similarly, as early as 1971, author and University of Pennsylvania professor Jerre Mangione established an Arts Committee for Green that backed William J. Green III's bid for the Democratic mayoral nomination against Rizzo. Yet, as the election returns listed earlier demonstrate, Rizzo's foes were a minority within the Italian American community. After all, when a drive to recall Rizzo was launched in 1976, criticism of this campaign came mostly from Italian Americans. Once again, however, most of Rizzo's supporters of Italian extraction read the recall referendum, which was never held because the petitions were eventually ruled invalid, through racial lenses. For example, Leonora Riccinti wrote to the editor of the *Evening Bulletin* and verbally assailed former African American mayoral candidate Bowser, one of the promoters of the anti-Rizzo drive, on the grounds that he allegedly sought political revenge for his own defeat in the 1975 race for City Hall.[27]

Other Italian American politicians capitalized on the antiblack resentment of the voters of Italian descent elsewhere in the nation. In 1969, for instance, in Newark, New Jersey, Hugh J. Addonizio—the city's first mayor of Italian descent—won 87.5 percent of the Italian American vote in an unsuccessful reelection bid against Kenneth A. Gibson, an African American highway engineer. Such voting patterns reflected the growing racial fears of the local Italian American population that followed black rioting in the summer of 1967.[28]

The case Stephen Adubato, one of the leaders of the protest against the supposed encroachments of African Americans in Newark, provides an additional example of the transformation of Italian Americans' identity in the wake of the outburst of racial tensions in the United States. While giving voice to Italian Americans' resentment of the alleged pro-black attitude of the Gibson administration, Adubato—an urban affairs specialist of Italian descent at Rutgers University and the chairperson of Newark's North Ward Committee of the Democratic Party—did not refer to his own fellow ethnics as a national group. Rather, he made himself the spokesperson of "white ethnics":

> Blacks have got all these special programs to help them get to college, or to rehabilitate their houses, or to help them find jobs. *We white ethnics* don't get any of these things. All we want is equity. . . . A lot of people confuse us with white Americans, which we are not. We are the working-class people who haven't made it in America, like the blacks, and we are still in the inner city competing with them.[29]

Interestingly enough, in Adubato's opinion, Italian Americans were "white ethnics," but not "white Americans," a category he reserved for those groups which had "made it," namely Anglo-Saxon Protestants. Indeed, less than one year later, Michael Novak, the leading theorist of the white ethnic movement, would contrast the socially established white Anglo-Saxon Protestants of northern European ancestry to the "PIGS." This acronym referred to the working-class and lower-middle-class white underdogs of eastern and south ern-European descent, among whom Polish, Italians, Greeks, and Slavs were the largest ethnic groups.[30]

Yet an Italian-sounding last name was not enough for a politician to build up a considerable following among Italian American voters unless he or she disregarded the national ancestry of his or her constituents and appealed directly to their white identity. Joseph R. Paolino Jr.'s 1996 campaign for the Democratic nomination in Providence's heavily Italian American Second Congressional District offers a case in point. Paolino's campaign manager argued that since this constituency had "one of the highest percentages of Italian Americans in the country," it was about time the electorate of Italian descent sent "one of its own" to Congress. Such a statement was intended to secure Paolino the Italian American vote. Yet it eventually backfired. Lieutenant Governor Robert A. Weygand won the Democratic nomination with 49.2 percent of the vote, as opposed to

Paolino's 36.6 percent and scattered votes for two additional candidates. However, not only was Paolino defeated, but he also failed to receive significant support within Providence's "Little Italy." Indeed, many Italian American voters got angry at the blatant appeal of his campaign manager because they were more worried about the increasing number of Hispanic immigrants in their district than with the national ancestry of their congressman.[31]

Conversely, even politicians who were not of Italian extraction managed to receive large majorities of the Italian American vote when they played on the white identity of their constituents of Italian background. For example, in 1966, Democrat George P. Mahoney capitalized on antiblack feelings to capture almost 75 percent of Baltimore's Italian American vote in his unsuccessful bid for governor of Maryland against Spiro Agnew. Likewise, after Louise Gay Hicks came out against the municipal administration's resort to busing in order to cope with racial imbalance in Boston's public schools, the share of her votes in the general elections for the city's School Committee in the district comprising the largely Italian American North End jumped from 26.0 percent in 1961 to 56.1 percent in 1963, which meant a 30.1 percentage increase in support for her in just two years. When Boston's schools were eventually desegregated eleven years later, Italian American Connie Maffei expressed the racially-based sense of frustration that characterized her community as she remarked, "There's a general depressed feeling that we don't count anymore. Everyone has a feeling it's a black city. Nothing is going our way. Even our husbands are coming home from work saying that every promotion goes to a black, Spanish-speaking or woman." Although fellow Italian American Tracy Amalfitano was not against school desegregation, she agreed that, in the wake of the enforcement of busing in Boston, "the community basically was talking about kids not being safe going into the minority communities."[32]

Italian Americans resented busing in cities such as Bridgeport, Hartford, and New Haven. Bostonians of Italian ancestry, however, were not alone in their fight against busing. While opposing school desegregation, they joined forces with Irish Americans although intense ethnic conflicts had separated these two immigration groups before World War II. Indeed, residents from the Irish South Boston and the Italian North End bulked large among the members of Restore Our Alienated Rights, the city's leading anti-busing organization. Likewise, resistance to residential integration with blacks brought together Italian Americans and Jewish Americans in the Canarsie district of Brooklyn even though prewar strife had similarly divided these groups in New York City.[33]

Historians Van Gosse and Kavita Philip have contended that access to police departments "is literally the mechanism that whitened up generations of Europeans who otherwise were despised immigrants." Resorting to a "law and order" approach and strong-arm methods to curb African American claims, second-generation immigrant and former policeman Rizzo perfectly fits this interpretation. But his large following among voters of Italian extraction in the elections that polarized Philadelphia along racial lines clearly demonstrates that Rizzo's whitening was the epitome of the acquisition of a white identity on the part of most members of the Italian American community as a whole. Actually, sociologist Richard N. Juliani has remarked that the opening of a Wal-Mart store in South Philadelphia's "Little Italy" in November 1994 was the symbol of the "erosion of the social and cultural system that defined the Italian-American character of the area." The adoption of a consumer culture mentality by the local residents not only persuaded Wal-Mart to establish business in a community whose members had long shunned chain stores in order to make their purchases in neighborhood shops operated by fellow ethnics of Italian ancestry. It also highlights Italian Americans' definitive entry into mainstream white U.S. society. However, the shift from an ethnic self-perception based on national ancestry to a racialized identity was not confined to Philadelphia. Rather, it extended to Italian Americans nationwide as they responded to the economic crises of the 1960s and 1970s by moblizing against rather than with working-class people of color.[34]

Chapter Twelve

"ITALIANS AGAINST RACISM"

The Murder of Yusuf Hawkins (R. I. P.) and My March on Bensonhurst

Joseph Sciorra

The city, however, does not tell its past, but contains it like the lines of a hand, written in the corners of the streets, the gratings of the windows, the banisters of the steps, the antennae of the lightening rods, the poles of the flags, every segment marked in turn with scratches, indentations, scrolls.
—Italo Calvino, *Invisible Cities*

There is no agony like bearing an untold story inside of you.
—Zora Neale Hurston, *Dust Tracks on a Road*

There I was, a typical New Yorker, alone in the crowd. I was standing in the streets of Bensonhurst on August 27, 1989, four days after a group of some thirty men, predominantly Italian American, accosted four African American youths looking to buy a used car and fatally shot seventeen-year-old Yusuf Hawkins on Bay Ridge Avenue. I traveled from northern Brooklyn to denounce and express my outrage, along with others, at this violent act of racial hatred. I took part in this organized demonstration as an Italian American, informed by a sense of *italianità* that consciously stood in opposition to ethnic chauvinism and racial violence. Although I couldn't think of another *paisan* I could ask to join me in the black-led march through the streets of Bensonhurst, I carried a handmade, poster board sign that read

ITALIANS AGAINST RACISM. My use of the plural was a simple expression of hope.

The day before marching in Bensonhurst, I watched in disgust and with profound sadness the televised images of neighborhood residents staging a shameful spectacle of overt racism in response to the first of many demonstrations. It was a blatant exhibition of xenophobia in defense of parochial village values.

I was also deeply distressed by the excruciating silence emanating from the self-proclaimed leaders of the Italian American community. The city witnessed the utter lack of leadership as cautious politicians, out-of-touch academics, and aloof *prominenti* were invisible and ultimately ineffective in participating in the public discourse surrounding the unfolding events. I desperately searched for, but did not find, an Italian American of public stature who stepped forward in those early tense days to make an unequivocal repudiation of racism and violence, and to speak out against its manifestation in Bensonhurst among the Italian community. A clear and authoritative Italian American voice was absent from the public sphere where the city's citizens could turn for understanding, resolution, and healing. The so-called leadership was struck by deep denial and paralysis.

The demonstrators met at the murder site—Bay Ridge Avenue and the corner of 20th Avenue—for a prayer service. We then marched up 20th Avenue toward St. Dominic's Roman Catholic Church, five blocks away. That was when things started to heat up. The sidewalks on either side of the avenue were packed with white men and women, young and middle-aged, jeering, laughing derisively, and screaming insults at us from behind wood barricades and the line of police officers. One newspaper estimated there were 100 marchers, 400 counterdemonstrators, and 250 cops. "Fuck you, niggers!" "Niggers go home!" The tirade was incessant. Faces were flushed red with rage; I could see the veins bulging on men's necks. People held up watermelons to taunt the African American protestors, and waved Italian and American flags in some perverse expression of ethnic pride and patriotism. It was a grotesque performance of collective hate from my community, folks I had grown up with and documented as part of scholarly research on Italian New York.

I watched with trepidation as clusters of young men followed us, hugging the storefronts as they scrambled behind the crowd of counterdemonstrators. Where were they going? What were they up to? At one point, a loud explosion rang out, startling us in the street as we flinched in unison in fear of a gun. Someone had tossed a firecracker into the marchers. Young women with their boyfriends laughed from behind the barricades.

My sign and whiteness in the midst of the predominantly black demonstrators got the attention of the Italians lining the sidewalk. People pointed in my direction, laughing, cursing, spitting. Some clearly thought it was a ludicrous proposition: Italians against racism. Others were incensed. My cardboard placard called into question the popular notion that joined Italian American identity and racial hatred in some natural and essentialist union. I was a race traitor, the internal threat to the prevailing local rhetoric.

The taunts and tension increased when we stopped at the church steps to hear a series of speakers. To the left of the church, a group of men screamed repeatedly in my direction. One man—middle-aged, mustached, and balding—whose photograph was reproduced months later in *Harper's Magazine*, directed his malice at me, screaming "Fuck you!" and spitting out the ultimate Italian curse, "*Sfacimm'*!" (sperm of the devil). I screamed back "racist" and "*razzista di merda*," with a mix of anger and fear. I pulled my verbal punches, afraid to incite their anger and provoke retaliation later when I would make my way to the subway alone. One guy screamed that he was "going to get" me.

At one moment, a young woman stepped from the crowd and headed right toward me. Oh, shit, I thought. This is it. Here was this woman, I imagined, so angry with me and my sign that she would leave the safety of the crowd and plunge into a group of black demonstrators in an attempt to punch me. And I knew that if she swung, all hell was going to break lose. How the hell did I get here?

THE PATH TO BENSONHURST

Born and raised in the Flatlands section of Brooklyn, my family had intimate ties to Bensonhurst and the surrounding southern Brooklyn neighborhoods of Gravesend, Dyker Heights, and Bay Ridge. It was where my parents bought the orthopedic shoes we kids hated, and discovered as adults we never really needed, where we shopped for Italian food products along Avenue U and under the elevated subway tracks along 86th Street. It was where my mother's *paesani* and our *compari* Gianni and Levia Liberace lived, almost exclusively in their wood-paneled basement.

My parents, while born in New York in the 1920s, were raised in Italy and returned to the city as adults in the early 1950s. My mother, Anna Anniballe, who joined her siblings in New York after World War II, worked in the downtown Brooklyn needle trades before getting married. She displayed the tough and feisty antiauthoritarianism associated with southern

Italy's laboring poor. I remember her storming the Catholic school I attended from first to fourth grades to berate the feared Irish nuns about corporal punishment. "Don't you ever lay a hand on my child," she'd warn them. (That was *her* job.) When I was a kid, she would answer back a cop without hesitation. The notion that you should fight for what you think is right has been my mother's greatest legacy to me.

While my mom only completed the compulsory fifth grade in Italy, my father, Enrico, graduated from the University of Naples as a veterinarian and worked for the U.S. Department of Agriculture for forty years. My dad is the family historian, keeping us connected to our past, to our Italian relatives, and to the American branches of both sides of the family. It is my dad who diligently engages in the "work of kinship," what anthropologist Micaela di Leonardo noted was the domain of Italian American women.[1] His repertoire of stories, which he has told repeatedly for decades, include the Nazi occupation of his hometown, the trials of war-ravaged Italy, and his first impressions of the United States. He would recount how second-generation, working-class Italian Americans treated him dismissively, a dumb greenhorn with an accent, unable to accept a literate and university-educated immigrant. During the 1960s, with the increase in black militancy, my dad told us of his shock at seeing racially segregated public facilities while working in slaughterhouses and meatpacking plants in the South during the 1950s. Once, he absentmindedly drank out of the black-designated water fountain at a meatpacking plant in Florida, and was quickly reminded of the Jim Crow laws by his white colleagues. These stories were told as an expression of empathy set against the background of the civil rights movement. Growing up under my parents' roof, I never heard them hurl the word "nigger" as a racial epithet.

This is not to say my parents were not burdened by racism. I remember distinctly my mother yelling at us kids about her "working like a nigger" when she became frustrated with domestic chores and our lack of support. Her angry outbursts stemmed from her aggravation with working so hard as a housewife doing demanding, invisible, and thankless labor coded by gender and often race, work commonly reserved for a black maid.[2] My father's racism, on the other hand, flipped the race and labor pairing by occasionally spouting pseudoscientific postulations attributing blacks' ascribed laziness to their proximity to the sun, racial theories learned in the Italian fascist school system. When I countered that his hypothesis would suggest that Italians living in the Mezzogiorno (The Land of the Midday Sun) would be prime candidates for similar slothful attributes, and that Anglos had historically attributed such traits to southern Italians, he found himself at a loss for words. Ultimately, we were not immune to racism's repugnant effects.

By my early twenties, I had come to understand that the first two decades of my life were defined by a sense of outsiderness. The block where we lived, Coyle Street, was white Catholic: Italian, Irish, and some German. My earliest memories were of being a skinny five-year-old (my mother worried I had tuberculosis) and being beaten up by kids on the block. These repeated encounters were informed by our "foreign" status, my parents' accent, my use of Italian, and, I am convinced to this day, the elegant Italian wool knit outfits my mother dressed me in. (I didn't own a pair of jeans or sneakers until I was in my mid-teens). On a block lined with Italian American families, I was known as the "spaghetti bender," a term I never understood. (You don't *bend* spaghetti! You twirl it.) I still remember the day I came home from school and told my mother that I would no longer speak Italian. Only English!

My dad was transferred to Connecticut when I was ten. We moved to recently suburbanized farmland in the town of Wethersfield. As an adult, I would tell people that the town's high points included George Washington having slept there and Malcolm X getting a speeding ticket, which he mentioned in his autobiography. Here again the sense of being the Other—this time an Italian New Yorker, the city kid in the suburbs—continued. My mom reinforced this feeling with her growing nostalgia for Brooklyn. She longed for the conviviality of stoop culture and urban life, and dismissed her neighbors as "cold Yankees," despite the fact that many of them were Italian Americans who had recently moved from the "slums" of Hartford. I internalized my mother's cultural dislocation by viewing the suburbs as an antiseptic wasteland and New York as the golden land of freedom and opportunity where civilization thrived right outside one's doorstep.

Although we spent numerous weekends in New York during our five-year hiatus, nothing prepared me for the return to Brooklyn. In September 1970, at the age of fifteen, I entered the newly constructed, "state of the art" South Shore High School, and within weeks the school erupted into a full-blown "race riot." Welcome to New York. Sitting on the edge of the Canarsie neighborhood, South Shore was caught up in the tension surrounding school busing and changing demographics documented by sociologist Jonathan Rieder years later.[3] Police were called in to patrol the corridors. After the climate calmed down, another "riot" closed the academic year.

High school was a culturally schizophrenic experience. Students were divided by ethnicity and race, and sometimes even subdivided by class affiliations and cultural affinities. Initially, I found myself hanging out with one set of friends in school and with another group in the neighborhood. In my first year, I joined forces with Darlene Love, a turbaned African American girl, in a successful petition to oust a senile tenth grade math teacher. She and others soon educated me on the racial politics of the New York City school system—Brooklyn's invisible Berlin Wall rose at 3 P.M. dismissal as black, Latino, and white kids returned to their respective communities. What did I know? I was just some rube returning from the distant white suburbs. After school, I hung out with mostly Italian Americans and some Irish neighborhood kids. In those days, they were referred to as "hitters," and the girls were tougher than me. (Their cultural heirs would be known as cugines, from the Italian word for cousins, *cugini*, and eventually, guidos.) I remember one day hanging out on the corner in our perpetual attempt to escape boredom, when someone suggested we travel the distance of two bus rides to South Shore just to "beat up some niggers." Jesus Christ! I wasn't interested in starting a fight with total strangers! I decided then and there that this was not my crowd.

I soon found myself gravitating toward Jewish kids. My path did not follow the now classic trope of the Italian American from a book-hating family seeking friendship with the "people of the book" for intellectual stimulation and freedom. Our mutual interests were sex, drugs, and rock and roll. I ended up hanging out with two distinct groups of Jews who were identified as "JAPS" (Jewish American Princesses) and "freaks," respectively, with the former favoring expensive clothes and Quaaludes, and the long-haired latter favoring thrift shop apparel and reefer. Speed seemed to bridge the cultural divide. JAPS tended to side with Italian Americans in their fear and hatred of blacks and Puerto Ricans, with some of the males qualifying as bona fide hitters, while the latter were politically liberal, despite that fact that there weren't any blacks or Puerto Ricans in our group.

After surviving high school, I attended Brooklyn College, where I fell in with Puerto Ricans (I discovered salsa music in 1973—*¡Eddie Palmieri es Dios!*) and become involved with a group of political activists in the struggle to save free tuition at the City University of New York. As I soon discovered, this fight was part of a larger agenda for the leadership of the campus-based activists. The Brooklyn College organizers involved members of the Puerto Rican Revolutionary Workers Organization (PRRWO), a group that evolved out of the Young Lords Party. PRRWO members were adherents of "Marxist-Leninist-Maoist thought" and were actively engaged in forming a new American Communist Party. We met in "cells" to read and discuss political tracts ranging from Lenin's *What Is to be Done?* to the Filipino Communist Party's position on "principled" relationships between "revolutionary couples." The movement even had its own cultural contingent in the guise of an a cappella group dubbed the Socialistics. One of their songs began, "The world's in great disorder and that's a good, good thing, because the people all over the world are fighting, are fighting to be free. Yes, they're fighting to be free."

I was dubbed "Serpico" (a nickname I wore with great honor) because of my ethnicity, and long hair and beard, and because of people playfully acknowledging their fear that I just might be an undercover cop. As part of the group's political maneuvering, I was asked to "infiltrate" the two Italian student clubs on campus and assess their receptivity to "coalition building." One club consisted of American-born, English-speaking students who were interested primarily in social gatherings, although the president at the time publicly expressed his support for free tuition. The other group was an informal gathering of immigrant and Italian-speaking students whose main preoccupation centered around eating lunch in the faculty dining room in close proximity to the Italian language professors. The two never met or socialized. At the time, I had no interest in either of them. I was comfortable hanging out with Latinos, with their racial diversity, concern with social issues, and passion for dancing.

The radicals soon started hurling dangerous accusations around campus as sectarian politics heated up. People were publicly denounced and vilified as "opportunists," "reactionaries," "lackeys of the bourgeoisie," and "Trotskyites" in some Brooklyn version of the Stalinist purges and the Chinese Cultural Revolution combined. These accusations often had a threatening street quality to them. One woman (in fact, the biracial daughter of an Italian American father and an African American mother) had her apartment ransacked with only her infant twins' clothes stolen. The message of this intimidating act was clear to all of us. She immediately left the city with her children for the safety of her mother's home in Virginia. My girlfriend at the time was on the short list of "class traitors" and feared that she would soon be attacked. My turn came when a close friend and "comrade" ratted me out to the leadership for making some disparaging remarks the likes of which I can't remember today. It was time to get off campus and maybe out of the city before I was sent off to the gulag or worse.[4]

My Italian cousin Raffaele saved me by arriving in the summer of 1976 with the idea of driving cross-country à la Jack Keroauc. I quit my summer job in a bookstore and headed west in a banged-up "drive away" car. I dropped out of college when I returned to New York and got a job washing pots at a neighborhood Italian restaurant. I didn't have much to lose when first Raffaele, and then a woman from Milan I had met in San Francisco, invited me to Italy.

During 1977, I lived in Bologna and Milan, creating new friendships and getting to know my Italian relatives. It was a time of radical politics that included right-wing and left-wing terrorism. The Italians dubbed it *gli anni di piombo*, the bullet years. It was only later that I fully understood that I had lived through a remarkable historic moment. I participated in many of the defining political activities of the period: endless political debates with friends and family; broadcasts from the pirate "free" radio station Radio Alice (once a group of feminists took over the station, kicking Raffaele and me out of the broadcast booth while we were on the air); the occupation of the University of Bologna; ultra-Left demonstrations; the student protest against the police killing of Francesco Lo Russo under Bologna's Communist-controlled government that brought the city to a standstill; and the subsequent national youth conference in that city.[5] For a twenty-two-year-old, it was a life-defining experience.

A personal tragedy hit my family while I was living in Italy. Angelo Treglia, my mother's *paisan* and family friend, was shot dead by a neighbor. They had been arguing over a sidewalk paving job the neighbor had botched. The killing of this forty-two-year-old plumber in Brooklyn's Gravesend section made the headlines of the city's tabloids for several days in late October. It was not just the murder that was news. Over fifty people witnessed the shooting, yet not a single one came forward to talk to the police about what they saw. When the four shots rang out, kids were playing in the streets, people were washing their cars and gardening in their front yards, and a wedding party had assembled outside. John Kifner of the *New York Times* wrote: "On the street, people looked away when asked by a stranger if they had seen the shooting. No, they said, they were inside, out shopping, in the backyard, in Queens on a job."[6] Only after Italian-speaking detectives initiated an intensive outreach campaign did witnesses break their *omertà*, the code of silence in operation even for this non-mob-related murder. In Italy, I encountered this principle in the (stereo)typical response witnesses to mafia killings in Sicily reportedly gave investigating police: "*Io non c'ero e se c'ero dormivo. E se dormivo, sognavo di non esserci.*" ("I wasn't there and if I was, I was sleeping. And if I was sleeping, I was dreaming about not being there.") After Yusuf's death, an unidentified "Bensonhurst teenager" was quoted as saying, "I didn't see nothing, and even if I did see something, I didn't see nothing."[7]

I found this silencing, this loss of voice, in the face of criminality and injustice deeply disturbing and debilitating.

The erasure of grassroots voices would also become a theme when I returned to the States to study anthropology and art history at Brooklyn College. I found the anthropology teachers' perspective antiquated, as we read ethnographies of dark-skinned Others living long ago and in remote places at the expense of learning about their contemporary descendents. I told one professor that I wanted to study Brooklyn. Pointing out the window, I proclaimed, "Brooklyn's the most tribal place in the world!" The art department was intellectually exciting but it tended to decontexualize non-Western art, my area of interest, reducing the creative process to exotic objects on a museum wall. I wanted to know about living people whose art I could experience directly. In my last year of study, I met a group of scholars trained as folklorists who were documenting the artistic expressions of everyday people in New York and throughout the country. I went on to conduct fieldwork and write about the vernacular cultural expressions of Italian Americans, as well as other communities. After two decades of ethnographic writing, this essay is my first attempt at memoir.

The art of "participant observation," the staple of anthropological fieldwork, involved long-term and sometimes intense relationships with people who invited me into their homes, their social clubs, their churches. I liked the people I met. I had a sense of being part of a community without many of the responsibilities and restrictions that were part of the social group. So when people ("informants") made racist, sexist, or homophobic comments, I ignored it. I didn't want to jeopardize my relationship and ultimately the fieldwork by contesting the "informant." At first, I did not see the relevance of race, gender, or sexuality to the specific folk art we were discussing, the subject at hand. I believed people were drifting, going off on a tangent. But it soon became apparent that when people voiced their fears and hatreds to me—someone who was both an insider and an outsider—it was because those socially based sentiments had everything to do with their notions of identity and cultural reproduction. I just needed to follow the various threads.

American-born Italians and immigrants who arrived after World War II told me about moving from areas of early Italian settlement like Harlem in Manhattan and East New York in Brooklyn, as those neighborhoods underwent dramatic demographic shifts. Others saw their Brooklyn neighborhoods of Williamsburg and Carroll Gardens/Red Hook remain predominantly Italian but become more concentrated and ultimately gentrified.

Many were emotionally scarred and resentful at seeing their communities radically altered. Neighborhoods had been destroyed through a combination of economic disinvestment, banks "red lining" communities in regard to mortgage loans, "slum clearance," highway construction that destroyed viable apartment buildings, and the advent of hard drugs, gang activity, and violent street crime. But they directed their anger at recent arrivals, African Americans and Puerto Ricans, who were vilified as the cause of these social changes.[8] It is not all that surprising that people reacted in the way they did; it is extremely difficult to see and understand how seemingly disconnected economic and political forces shape our daily lives.

While I was waiting for the demonstration to begin, I overheard two young white women, definitely not from Bensonhurst, talking despairingly about the neighborhood Italians, about their racism and conservatism. While I agreed with them, I could not help but think how ignorant these women were, unaware and uninterested in what drove working-class people to such vehement and visceral hatred. I was irritated with their white, liberal self-righteousness that conveniently targeted Bensonhurst's overt racism to veil their own prejudices. In the aftermath of the murder, similar distancing of middle- and upper-class whites from such "barbarism" made racism the sole problem and preserve of blue-collar whites.[9]

After some internal struggle, I began to question people/"informants" when they raised what I deemed ugly statements and gently articulated my position, without being confrontational. I was a guest in their home, their community. I had both a personal and a professional desire to understand why Italians in New York had come to base their identity in direct opposition to people of color.

As part of my research, I culled local newspapers for leads and background information on the city's Italian American communities. I could not help but notice the involvement of Italian Americans in attacks on African Americans and Latinos. I started a clipping file, which soon grew. From Corona, Queens to Fordham in the Bronx, Italian Americans seemed hell-bent on stopping the city's changing demographics by policing the racial borders of "their" neighborhoods. Articles ranged from a single paragraph concerning an attack without any follow-up to front-page stories of homicide that lasted for days as well as being featured on the evening television news. There was the 1982 fatal bludgeoning of African American transit worker Willie Turks in Gravesend, Brooklyn, by twenty men. Four years later, a dozen whites wielding baseball bats and golf clubs chased three black men through the streets of Howard Beach in Queens. Michael Griffith, in a desperate attempt to escape his pursuers, clambered onto the nearby highway and was killed by an automobile. The Rev. Al Sharpton and others organized demonstrations in the neighborhood, assembling at a local pizzeria where the attack began. The charged symbolism of the pizzeria helped linked the attack with the neighborhood's "Italianness," despite the fact that not all the assailants were Italian American.

During the same period, there were incidents reported in the newspapers that gave me hope as everyday Italian Americans opposed racist acts. The papers occasionally featured the work of Gerard Papa, a Bensonhurst native, who created the Flames Neighborhood Youth Association in 1974 with the specific aim of getting young men from South Brooklyn neighborhoods to play on multiracial basketball teams in an organized league. In 1986, thirteen-year-old John DeMarco testified in court that he witnessed a white man spray paint a racist and threatening message on a house in northeast Philadelphia that an African American family was considering to buy. "I felt that blacks have the same equal rights as whites, plus I have a lot of black friends, and I think there's really nothing wrong with black people at all."[10] Inspirational! Then in the summer of 1988, Salvatore Taormina, twenty-two, and Jeff LaMartina, twenty-four, came to the aid of a black man who was attacked by six white men wielding bats and sticks outside their pizzeria Café di Sicilia, in the Westerleigh section of Staten Island, New York. "There's too much racial violence going on. I went against six guys for a black guy and I'm glad I did. It's a matter of right and wrong, not black and white," LaMartina stated simply.[11] These people were my heroes.

In the summer of 1989, Brooklyn-based director Spike Lee released his fourth feature film, *Do the Right Thing*, based, in part, on the Howard Beach attack. White journalists expressed their concerns that the film would raise the thermostat for the proverbial "hot summer" and incite blacks to riot. The film had a profound effect on me because it looked at the Italian American version of racism I had experienced firsthand in New York. Pino, the character played by John Turturro, was an incredibly accurate portrayal of the confused and angry youth I had grown up with and interviewed. Lee's film reminded me of *Saturday Night Fever*, an earlier movie that problematized Italian American masculinity and racism. In that film, the character Tony Manero, frustrated by the corner boy lifestyle of turf battles, ethnic vengeance, rape, and a friend's suicide, rejected the provincialism of Bay Ridge, Brooklyn, by escaping into Manhattan—"the City." Was it necessary to physically and spiritually abandon one's community in search of a more complete and holistic self? How did one create an alternative sense of *italianità* that did not discard community ties? People who denounced Lee's film as anti-Italian never spoke out against racism in our communities or suggested how we deal with it. Instead, Italian American spokespeople remained obsessed with the self-serving mantle of defamation expressed each time another mafia movie was premiered or a politician's sleazy past was revealed. A few weeks after *Do the Right Thing* was released, life was about to imitate art imitating life.[12]

BACK IN BENSONHURST

I was living back in Greenpoint, Brooklyn, when Yusuf was killed on Wednesday night, August 23, 1989.[13] I was scheduled to return after Labor Day to Philadelphia, where I was studying toward a Ph.D. in folklore, but I was compelled to do something before I left New York. The words of Rev. Martin Luther King, Jr. rang in my ears: "The tragedy of Birmingham is not what bad people did, but that good people did nothing."

The media reported that Al Sharpton would lead a demonstration in Bensonhurst on Saturday but did not provide logistical information. Newspapers, radio, and television were clearly ostracizing the media-savvy civil rights leader at that time. Sharpton led the Howard Beach demonstrations, forcing the media to pay attention to the racist attack that took place there and the legal system to render justice. His activism took a loopy turn when he became the spokesperson for fifteen-year-old Tawana Brawley from Yonkers, an African American who claimed to have been kidnapped and raped in 1987 by a group of white men. Several months later, the grand jury determined that Brawley's charges were false and might have been concocted in an attempt to protect herself from parental punishment. Sharpton's credibility came under increasing scrutiny when he came to the defense of black and Latino teenagers accused of bludgeoning and raping a white woman jogging in Central Park.[14]

Sharpton later admitted that he demonstrated in Bensonhurst to provoke neighborhood racists into revealing themselves for the television cameras. And they did so with a remarkable lack of self-consciousness, self-restraint, and media understanding. Images of Italian Americans waving the tricolor flags and making incredibly crude gestures and absurd statements ("I'm not a racist, I just hate niggers") were broadcast around the world. For years, friends and family in Italy would ask me to explain how Italians had become so vicious in America. The footage of angry, screaming people was an updated version of the black-and-white images from the civil rights movement that I had seen as a child growing up.

Television reporters announced that a "prayer vigil" would be held the following day, Sunday, August 27, mentioning the meeting time and location. This second event would be led by an alternative group of African American ministers—Rev. Timothy Mitchell, pastor of the Ebenezer Missionary Baptist Church in Queens; Rev. Calvin Butts of the Abyssinian Baptist Church in Harlem; and others. During the prayer service held at the site of the killing, one speaker asked, "Where are the members of this community?" I shouted my reply, "We're here!" The TV cameras whirled around. Everyone looked in silence. Then the clergy and speakers returned to their oratory, ignoring my presence. It was much easier for them, as well as the media, to have a monolithic evil Italian community than to hear or imagine Italian American voices of conscience and possible partnership. In the end, though, whom did I represent other than myself? What political entity could I muster? I never saw my sign in the newspaper or on television, despite the fact that I had been photographed and filmed.

Some Italian Americans pointed out that prominent Italian Americans did in fact condemn the killing, and criticized the media for ignoring these voices of reason. They maintained that the press was enthralled with the dramatic and facile images of monosyllabic bigots. This position was often coupled with the idea that the media were painting Bensonhurst in its entirety as racist, as if the neighborhood had become some hideous, sentient organism. The argument that Bensonhurst residents were victims of media assassination in effect stated, "We deplore the killing and racism but we're being attacked, too!"[15] Years later, I have read or heard that such-and-such Italian American attended Yusuf's funeral; that Politician A issued a press release in the early hours after the shooting to denounce racism, and Clergy B was diligently working behind the scenes toward peace, and so on. It was simply not enough. The Italian American leadership did a horrendous job of speaking clearly and repeatedly against racism and sufficiently representing us in the public eye. Those who did speak out needed to be more forceful, more vocal, and better organized in getting their message to the public. Months after Yusuf's death, Bensonhurst resident Anthony Iacono addressed the repeated demonstrations by poignantly commenting, "There is no one speaking for us. The council people and leaders wait until it is politically safe to say something."[16] As a community, we failed miserably at a crucial moment in the city's history, and we will live with the shame for years to come.

I did notice those within the Italian community who acted conscientiously during this time of crisis. Irene Deserio and her young daughter came to the aid of Yusuf as he lay dying on the sidewalk. Lucy Capezza was part of a crowd of Bensonhurst residents who confronted the arrested suspects—Steve Curreri, Brian O'Donnell, and Pasquale Raucci—outside the 62nd police precinct the night of the killing. "You should be ashamed. You're afraid to show your face. You're a disgrace," Capezza was quoted shouting. One could not help but observe that it was Italian American women who often spoke out against the senseless killing.[17]

So there I was, with my sign, alone in the crowd. And out stepped this woman. I braced for the worst as she approached. Instead of taking a swing at me, she asked, "Can I walk with you?" and then "Who else is here with you?" That is what Stephanie Romeo remembers. For me, it was a bit of a cacophonous blur. Years later, as close friends, Stephanie and I still disagree about the exact place where she distanced herself from the crowd and walked into history.

Stephanie was living in Manhattan's East Village but her roots were in Bensonhurst. She and her family had lived there at various points in her life. It was where her maternal grandmother and great-grandmother, the extended family's anchors, lived. Her parents had an apartment on Bay Ridge Avenue, a mere four blocks away from where Yusuf was killed. Stephanie came back to the neighborhood that Sunday to witness for herself what she had been reading in the papers. She has written about that momentous afternoon on a number of occasions:

> I ended up marching in Bensonhurst—not intending to, but happy for the experience. I was watching the march, observing the people around me, many of them upset that the media were making a big deal out of nothing. As the march passed by, I felt very emotional and very guilty. Guilty because I was a silent objector. Suddenly, I saw a guy pass by carrying a sign that said "Italians Against Racism." It had a magnetic power that drew me to him, and I ended up marching, and staying with him for the rest of the day.[18]

It seemed as if Stephanie's arrival attracted others. Camillo "David" Greco, an immigrant from Calabria who worked in a Brooklyn hospital, suddenly appeared, asking to march with us. A young Puerto Rican man and Bensonhurst resident joined us, as did the two white women I had seen earlier. We were about ten people by the end of the march, all moving under the same banner. We turned left onto Bay Ridge Parkway, with the heckling but thinning crowd still lining the sidewalk. Camillo drove me to the subway, my cardboard sign safely curled under my arm.

I never participated in any of the subsequent demonstrations. I went back to Philadelphia soon afterward to prepare for my qualifying exams, returning in November to a devastating recession under the first Bush administration.

BEYOND BENSONHURST

Yusuf's murder was a turning point in the city's political history, ultimately influencing the outcome of that year's mayoral election; David Dinkins became New York City's first African American mayor. It also had a dramatic impact on New York's Italian American community, as it fueled a tremendous amount of critical thinking and activity by Italian American scholars and artists, ultimately contributing to a more expansive, self-reflective, and socially engaged sense of identity.

Literary scholar and poet Robert Viscusi was deeply affected by the silence that hovered over Italian Americans in the aftermath of Yusuf's murder. "Al Sharpton posed a real categorical challenge to Italian-Americans, and Italian-Americans came up short," Viscusi noted. "The problem wasn't that people were ignoring us. The problem was that we weren't saying enough."[19] Viscusi and other writers joined together to form the Italian American Writers Association (IAWA), an organization that creates venues for Italian American authors to meet, read their work, and add thoughtful Italian American voices and commentary to public discourse.

The New York musical and theatrical troupe I Giullari di Piazza's "folk operas," based on the Italian devotion to the *Madonna Nera* (Black Madonna) have dramatized the affiliations between southern Italian spirituality and pre-Christian goddess worship, including Native American and African-derived religious devotions. The "multicultural production(s) dedicated to Mother Earth" titled *The Voyage of the Black Madonna* and *1492–1992: Earth, Sun, and Moon* juxtaposed the percusive music and dance of Italian traditional *pizzica* (trance music) and *tammuriata* (tambourine ensembles) with Gypsy flamenco of Spain, West African drumming, Afro-Brazilian music and dance, and the Thunderbird American Indian Dancers. La Madonna Nera di Tindari, Cibele, Yemaya, the White Buffalo Woman, and other sacred personages were evoked through performance in a vibrant and exhilarating vision calling for an inclusive spirituality and multiculturalism that offered a unique, roots-based Italian contribution.[20]

Contemporary culture from Italy also provides rich sources for reconfiguring *italianità* for members of the diaspora living in the United States. The hip-hop nation has firmly planted its flag in Italy and *rap italiano* transformed the Italian cultural landscape during the 1990s by adapting and mixing rap and other world styles with local musical traditions, spoken vernacular, and the everyday concerns of Italian youth. The localizing of a global black popular culture in Italy was achieved through a series of interlocking elements. Hip hop artists rap in Italian as well as various Italian dialects, reappropriating a vernacular voice in opposition to a national trend of flattening language distinctiveness. Italian MCs and DJs create musical hybrids that combine the global pop styles of rap, reggae, dancehall, acid jazz, and trip hop with Italian folk and popular musical traditions. Italian artists address social and political issues, rapping about topics from the historic economic exploitation of the Mezzogiorno to the devastating impact of the mafia. In these ways, contemporary Italian artists are offering Italian Americans, especially the youth, examples of how to cultivate a renewed sense of Italian identity that is local and cosmopolitan, fresh and relevant.[21]

Recent academic scholarship has been instrumental in providing a nuanced understanding of Italian American history and offering a usable past on which to build a viable future. Historian Philip Cannastraro's 1997 groundbreaking conference, "The Lost World of Italian American Radicalism," sponsored by the John D. Calandra Italian American Insitute of Queens College, brought greater attention to left, radical, and progressive traditions among Italian Americans. We have learned much about historic figures such as garment worker and labor organizer Angela Bambace (1898–1975); photographer and revolutionary Tina Modotti (1896–1942), who helped define the vocabulary of Mexican modernism; union organizer and painter Ralph Fasanella (1914–1997); civil rights leader Father James Groppi (1930–1985), from Milwaukee; radical Congressman Vito Marcantonio (1902–1954), who represented New York's East Harlem; longshoreman and labor activist Peter Panto (1911–1939), who led a rank-and-file revolt against the corrupt union leadership on the Brooklyn waterfront; student leader Mario Savio (1942–1996) of the Free Speech Movement in Berkeley; anarcho-syndicalist and labor organizer Carlo Tresca (1879–1943); and many, many others.[22] We are reclaiming this radical and progressive left heritage abandoned in the wake of McCarthyist repression and middle-class assimilation. These historic champions of democracy and the rights of the working poor are a refreshing alternative to the litany of successful businessmen and conservative politicians Italian American *prominenti* endlessly herald as role models.

The reclamation of historical memory is particularly important for Italian American youth who seem bereft of inspirational role models. I will never forget the comment uttered by Charles Gallante, a twenty-year-old from Howard Beach, Queens, when *capo di tutti capi* John Gotti was convicted in 1992: "I love this man. He's a beautiful Italian-American. How more beautiful do you want?"[23] In addition to real-life mobsters, media *mafiosi* with their one-dimensional view of Italian American identity and experience, have their own insidious influence. The American fascination with Italian American gangsters can be attributed to the familiar and foreign, the attraction and repulsion these fictional characters evoke. Italian Americans, especially those from the East Coast urban experience, find authentic portrayals of Italian American life in well-crafted and wonderfully acted films like *Goodfellas* and the television program *The Sopranos*. I thoroughly enjoy seeing my comfort foods of *pasta fazool'* and *sfogliatell'* lovingly presented, hearing the earthy phrases in southern Italian dialect, and seeing men kiss each other on the cheek in tender welcome. Just like my family. Too bad everything escalates into baseball bat threats and semiautomatic retribution. Nothing at all like my family. For middle America, on the other hand, East Coast *mafiosi* are slightly exotic, often buffoonish, and comfortably white. There is no rush to convene congressional hearings to investigate these celluloid mobsters, as has occurred with governmental scrutiny of the perceived menace of African American rappers and their use of violent imagery. While the impact of mafia movies and television programs on Italian American youth culture is difficult to quantify, its influence is visible among the emerging Italian American presence in hip-hop. Young MCs like the Lordz of Brooklyn, Jo Jo Pellegrino of Staten Island, Genovese from Yonkers, and Don Pigro from Philadelphia are microphone *mafiosi* inspired by mediated images of the country's "original gangstas."[24]

During the 1990s, Italian Americans for a Multicultural United States (IAMUS) emerged as an organization in which politically progressive Italian Americans could come together to work proactively on issues concerning them. IAMUS was founded in 1992 to protest the quincentenial celebrations of Columbus's "discovery" of America and to stimulate Italian Americans' understanding of American racial history.[25] The annual Columbus Day parade on Fifth Avenue is not part of my childhood memories, and my family members do not conflate the deeds of a distant Columbus with their sense of ethnicity. The organization's "statement of purpose" challenged "Italian Americans to acknowledge the wrongs inflicted on people of color throughout U.S. history, and the privileges from which Italian Americans and other groups of European ancestry benefit." IAMUS activities included writing op ed pieces and newspaper articles; sponsoring study groups, forums, and conferences on Italian American history; and participating in coalitions with other organizations on issues of social justice. For a time, the group organized potluck dinners at which participants discussed the conflict and sense of isolation growing up in politically conservative households and neighborhoods. It offered a progressive Italian American position that stood in marked contrast to mainstream and primarily conservative Italian American political ideology.

The tragedy of Yusuf Hawkins's death engendered an examination of conscience and values among Italian Americans in ways that simply did not exist before. As a result, an alternative *italianità* that ultimately aims to build "forms of solidarity and identification which make common struggle and resistance possible but without suppressing the real heterogeneity of interests and identities" has been set in motion.[26] This new ethnicity is not achieved without struggle, and remains a continuous and dynamic process. A network of self-identified and articulate Italian Americans who stand against racism and other forms of exploitation has been established. We are no longer alone, we are no longer silent.

PART IV

TOWARD A BLACK ITALIAN IMAGINARY

CHAPTER THIRTEEN

SANGU DU SANGU MEU

Growing up Black and Italian in a Time of White Flight

KYM RAGUSA

The last time I slept in the house in New Jersey was the night before my grandmother's funeral. The hush that hovered throughout the house, that hush which is the sound of unknowable loss, was the first thing that struck me as I followed my cousins and my father through the back door and into the kitchen. You have to understand, this was never a silent house. In the more than twenty years that my family occupied it, it was a kaleidoscope of sound: two hard-of hearing grandparents shouting to and at each other in English and Calabrese; at least one television blaring at full volume; my two cousins' stereos in two different parts of the house, one blasting Elton John and the other deep-Mississippi blues; my aunt's oldies radio station ringing out Motown hits; a couple of years of my father and stepmother arguing before their marriage ended; me singing songs to myself upstairs in the bathtub . . . and the most pervasive sound of all, laughter. More than anything, even our common (and uncommon) blood, laughter was the thing that made us a family and literally kept the house from falling apart.

My family moved to Maplewood, New Jersey, from the Bronx in 1974. My father went in on the house with his parents and his sister, Evelyn. The house was already divided into two apartments; my grandparents, aunt, and two cousins would live downstairs, and my father, stepmother, and I would live upstairs. The move was thrilling, a moment of promise in all our lives. There would be more room for all of us, a garden for my grandfather and a swing set for the kids, fresh air, better schools—and the biggest selling point of all—it would be a "safe" place to live. What I didn't understand at the time—what I didn't understand for many years to come—was the historicity of that moment; this was, after all, a classic case of white flight. What was not lost on me even then, as an eight-year-old biracial child, was the absurd complexity of "our" white flight. My African American mother and Italian American father split up when I was a baby, and now my father was getting provisional custody of me. In addition, my new stepmother was Puerto Rican. She and I were exactly what my family was fleeing from, and we were caught up in that flight of fantasy.

The dynamics of race, class, ethnicity, and geography have always been complicated for both sides of my family. Both sides lived in a constant state of physical, emotional, and economic migration. My mother's mother, Miriam, was from Pittsburgh; she belonged to a nominally privileged caste of light skinned African Americans who had been intermixing with their Native American and German neighbors for generations. Their "high color" afforded them a certain amount of respect and even glamour within the community; but at the same time, the family had remained working-class. Miriam was beautiful and ambitious; she dreamed of becoming an actress and seeing the world. When she was still a teenager, she married her acting teacher and had a child, my mother. In the 1950s, the three of them moved to Los Angeles, and Miriam found work as a society reporter for a local "negro" newspaper. A few years later the marriage ended. She took my mother to New York, to Harlem, which for her still held the allure of the Harlem Renaissance, which she had learned about as a child. Miriam made this place her home; she worked as a reporter for Harlem's *Amsterdam News*, and, eventually became a community activist who fought the city for better services and recognition of historically significant sites around the neighborhood.

My father's mother, Gilda, was born in East Harlem; her parents had migrated from their village near Cosenza, in the mountains of Calabria, and had settled into a tenement building on 113th Street filled with their *paesani*. When she was sixteen, Gilda's mother took her out of school and arranged for her to marry Luigi, a man from the village who had recently arrived in the United States. I never knew what effect this upheaval had on her, what kind of life she might have imagined for herself if she had been allowed to finish school. I do know that the marriage was troubled from the beginning, that my grandfather drank, that there were times when she wanted to leave him but didn't. Luigi worked as a day laborer, and later as a bartender; Gilda did piecework at home while their three children were small, and then she became a maid in a downtown hotel. As my father tells it, the family was displaced when the city tore down their crumbling tenement building to make way for a new housing project. In addition, the neighborhood was "changing"—his euphemism for the arrival of newer immigrants from Puerto Rico. The family left East Harlem, following my grandfather's younger brothers, who had been more successful than he, to a predominantly Italian, working-class neighborhood in the Bronx. I learned later that the route of the elevated #6 train was expanded during this time of "urban renewal," and much of the white flight out of East Harlem and into the Bronx took place along the # 6 train line.

My mother and father met in 1964 at Columbia University. They were not students, but low-level clerical workers, and their presence as employees on this campus was the closest either side of the family had come to a college education. My mother worked as a secretary in one of the administrative offices. I have a photograph of her that was taken around that time, a simple black-and-white head shot, maybe from her high school yearbook. Her hair is straightened into a *That Girl* flip, complete with bangs. She's wearing a neat Peter Pan collar, and around her neck is a tiny cross on a thin chain. Her expression is open, even blank, revealing nothing of the person she might have been then, the person she would become. A picture of my father at the same time shows him sly-eyed and goateed, playing a set of bongos, almost like a cartoon image of a beatnik. What they had in common, at least back then, was a certain restlessness, a desire to be something different than what their families and communities had proscribed for them—indeed, a desire to escape these communities and their unyielding ethnic/racial boundaries altogether.

They were young—my father was twenty, my mother, eighteen—and both still lived at home. My father took the #6 train back to Harlem each morning from Westchester Square, passing every day through the mostly black and Latino South Bronx, back through the old neighborhood that was now more *El Barrio* than Italian Harlem. The apartment where my mother and her mother lived was down the hill from Columbia on 110th Street in Central Harlem. Each morning my mother walked up the hill to the university's hallowed grounds, along the tattered northern edge of Central Park and past the dilapidated tenement buildings that gradually gave way to neatly kept dormitories and faculty housing. It was only a few blocks, but Columbia seemed like another world. Clean streets, cafés, people talking about books, the air itself charged with possibility. And although my parents were invisible workers serving young people their own age who had the luxury to study, the little bit of money they earned allowed them a feeling of independence and upward mobility, allowed them to grab a little of that sense of possibility for themselves.

My parents fell (briefly) in love at this crossroads, which marked the space in between their known worlds. And in a way it could have happened only there. Both my maternal grandmother and my paternal grandparents denounced the relationship. My father's parents saw my mother's presence as a personal affront to them, a disgrace against the family, *una vergogna*. Gilda, in particular, felt my father's interest in a black woman as a betrayal against her and against any "progress" the family had made by leaving Harlem. Miriam thought my father was beneath her daughter; she called him and his family "poor white trash" and later blamed *his* African blood for my kinky hair. This denial was my legacy, with each side of the family vehemently refusing their own history, rejecting their own experiences of racial/ethnic discrimination and economic struggle in exchange for silence. Silence and the illusion of purity.

This silence surrounded my birth and the first few years of my life. My parents weren't married, and after I was born, I lived with my mother and grandmother in the apartment in Harlem. On the other side of the family, only my father's sister knew about my existence. She would come by herself to Harlem to visit us as often as she could. I try to envision her, a petite but tough Italian American woman, pulling up in her old white convertible and walking through the building's courtyard bearing toys for me, as our African American neighbors looked on. Those equally tough women sitting on their lawn chairs watching their kids (just like their Italian counterparts) and nodding knowingly to each other as the little white lady strode by. It's only now, writing this, that I can appreciate her courage, her sense of family and her openmindedness at a time when my father couldn't work up the nerve to officially claim me as his own.

The fact that my father kept me a secret from his parents was a huge point of contention between him and my mother, and when I was two, they split up. He began dating the Puerto Rican woman, Mercedes, who would become my stepmother—yet another shame upon the family—and at this point he started bringing me to the Bronx, telling his parents that I was her niece. I guess my fawn-colored skin was a good enough match to hers to keep everybody fooled, for awhile at least. I didn't find out about this masquerade until I was an adult. The story finally came out one day when I asked my father about the family for an oral history project I was working on. His explanation of the situation was so casual, almost as if it were funny, a farce, a comedy of errors. It never occurred to him how painful the news was to me, how devalued it made me feel, as if *I* had been the error, the mistake that threw the wrench into the story of my family's American Dream. No matter how "rebellious" my father may have been in his youth, his position within the family would never be questioned. He would always be on the inside, of the home, the community, and the culture. Yet I would learn, over and over again, how tenuous my own position was.

My first memory of my Italian grandparents is the sound of their voices; even when they were younger, they were loud. Also, they spoke in a mix of dialect and English, and I remember the musical sounds of their words and the ease of the exchange of languages. I also remember the color black: my grandfather's shiny black shoes and my grandmother's voluminous black purse. It's unclear what the catalyst was that led my father to tell his parents the truth about me. All I know is that at some point they became my grandparents, real grandparents and not just people I went to visit every now and then. My father had married Mercedes and was living with her in an apartment above the bar where my grandfather worked; they had decorated a room just for me in little-girl colors, and I began to spend half my time in the Bronx with them and half my time in Harlem.

In Harlem, I lived primarily with my grandmother Miriam. My mother had become a fashion model—this was the height of the era of "black is beautiful," an idea that, once appropriated by the fashion industry, enabled my mother to finally escape the ghetto and, in a way, to escape blackness itself. Ironically, she moved to Italy—of course not to the South, but to Rome—and spent more than a decade there as I was growing up. Her deep love of Italy and my visits to her there, starting when I was eleven, were as fundamental to my sense of Italian American identity as the actual Italian blood that ran through my veins, blood that others seemed so eager to deny. In the meantime, my grandmother Miriam became the rock in my life; she was both mother and father to me at a time when my "real" parents had other priorities. She was the only constant I knew, and her love for me was unconditional. Within our home and among our extended family, which included a group of formidable elderly aunts who visited regularly from Pittsburgh, I had a sense of being enveloped in a secret world of women who, through their protection, made and remade the world that I woke up to each morning.

At the same time, I was thoroughly confused by my grandmother's hybrid racial and cultural identity (and my own), and what that meant for us in relation to our neighbors. On one hand, she had a fierce pride in being a black woman, yet because of her light skin and straight red hair she quietly harbored a sense of difference, or ambivalence, around her blackness. She cooked German food along with soul food and said *gesundheit* whenever somebody sneezed. And like so many of her generation, she had a particular disdain for Africa, which she truly believed was the "Dark Continent." I don't remember her having many friends in the building, notwithstanding her tireless work for the community. I was teased a lot by the other kids on the block, for being light-skinned and for having a white daddy, and she constantly had to defend me against them, which probably made matters worse.

Miriam's frustrations with my father aside, she appreciated the effort he was making to create a place for me in his life, and it was important for her that I know the other side of my family. She also wanted me to spend as much time away from our neighborhood as possible. In the 1960s and 1970s much of Harlem was an embattled territory: increased poverty, decaying schools, burned-out buildings, junkies mugging old women for a dollar—an atmosphere of violence, desperation, and government neglect. After my uncle was stabbed to death on the steps outside our door, and after a little girl was raped and thrown off the roof of a building across the street, Miriam decided that she would do whatever it took to get me out.

Not that the Bronx was such a paradise either. Many of the same forces that were besieging black communities were also taking their toll on working-class white neighborhoods. Heroin was everywhere, and members of my own family were not immune to its lure. There was daily gang violence—the Irish kids against the Italian kids, Germans against the Irish, Italians against Italians, and on and on. There were also stabbings and robberies too close to home, and the combination of drugs and *omertà* added to a palpable sense of helplessness among people, like my family, trying to make sense of what they saw around them. The helplessness turned to blame, and the blame went, again and again, to African Americans and Latinos, for "bringing the drugs into the neighborhood," for moving too close by and "devaluing (white) property," the whole familiar litany.

So it was time to move again. For my family, as for many Italian Americans, white flight was the culmination of an escape from the desperate poverty of southern Italy. It was the last leg in a series of migrations—from Italy to America, from immigrant slum to ethnic neighborhood—and these migrations themselves were inextricably linked to provisional class ascension and the ascension to whiteness. The move from the ethnic neighborhood to the outlying suburbs was the completion of these migrations. It held the promise of assimilation into the dominant white culture, in exchange for a final displacement of the "Old Country" as both home and ideal. The suburbs became a place of forgetting, of leaving history behind.

Without question, my family's move was part of a historical moment of collective racism. Yet my understanding of our move is not simply about Italian Americans deliberately shedding their past to blend in among the white folks in the suburbs. My father, aunt, and grandparents bought a house together in New Jersey not only out of racialized fears and misplaced blame, but also because they saw it as the fulfillment of their dreams. They dreamed of having trees and grass and vegetables growing around them, not because these were things they associated with whiteness but because this made them feel closer to life in the Old Country, closer to something elemental in themselves. It was what they believed they deserved, and what America, after all, constantly held out as its promise. This promise—that they could make something more of their lives, that they could work hard and save their money and buy a house—was of course conditional upon their official recognition as white people. My Latina stepmother, who grew up in the ravaged South Bronx, also dreamed of moving to a better place. And my grandmother Miriam held this dream for me. But both realized that the only way to achieve it was on the heels of my Italian American family's white flight.

The first image that comes to my mind when I think of the day we moved into the house is that of a group of white kids screaming and throwing eggs and tomatoes at the windows of our enclosed front porch. I have asked various family members about this incident, and they have all assured me that it never happened, that I must have made it up. Yet I remember it so clearly. I can still see the kids' hard, taunting faces and the bright red and yellow, like blood and vomit, splattering against the windowpanes. I wonder what stake my family would have in denying an "experience" that has left such a lasting impression on me. If it really did happen, maybe they don't want to remember because it calls into question the ease with which they thought they could assimilate into this neighborhood. Or maybe it never happened, maybe it's no memory at all, but a symbol of my own anxiety about finally becoming a part of the family, after so many years of waiting outside the door.

But there were indisputably real incidents as well. I wasn't allowed to join the neighborhood pool, but my aunt, stepmother, and grandmother Gilda fought the local community board and finally I was let in. I can see them now, confronting the WASP community board members, like three ethnic furies whose righteous indignation was doubtless mingled with humiliation at having been singled out and excluded. At school, I was the only person of color in my class. My classmates couldn't figure out what my story was. Early on, I would get called "nigger" (as I had been in the Bronx), until once one of them came to my house and saw a bunch of "white" people speaking "Italian"; then, one by one, they began to warm up to me. I never understood the terms of their acceptance—it all seemed so arbitrary. How did the sight of my dark-skinned, heavily accented, white undershirt-clad grandfather represent whiteness for them, and how did that whiteness then get conferred upon me?

I knew my friendship with these kids went only so far. Whenever I started to feel like I was beginning to fit in, there would always be something, a joke or comment, that would shock me back into the reality of my difference. There was one Halloween, for example, when I was getting dressed up with some of the other girls on the block, comparing our witches' and fairies' costumes. I was dressed as a princess, complete with a tin-foil crown atop a wig of yellow yarn. One of the girls, from a large Irish American family across the street, showed us how she put razors in apples "for niggers." At nine years old, I didn't know what to say or do except to be quiet and not draw attention to myself. I carried this desire for invisibility with me for a long time. It was tied to my sense that my difference somehow caused trouble for my Italian family, made them stand out in a way that hurt *them*.

I was too young to really see how the move affected my stepmother. She and my grandparents didn't get along; I don't think they ever made her feel welcome at home. Because we were in the suburbs, she was isolated from her friends, from the independence of the urban spaces she knew. There certainly weren't any other Latinos in the area. I know she wanted it to work. She wanted to be a mother to me and have children of her own and live the dream that had for so long been advertised to her. At the same time, my grandparents were experiencing their own sense of isolation. They had left behind their siblings and their families, and all their relatives from Italy who still lived in the Bronx. They had left behind my grandmother's church and my grandfather's bar and the Italian stores where they bought their groceries. The physical and cultural distance between Maplewood and the Bronx (and by extension, Italy) was just too great.

Still, we were a family, in spite of or because of the isolation. And when I think of that house on Boyden Avenue, that's what I come back to. There was very little time for leisure. The adults worked to keep up the mortgage payments on the house; my father and stepmother commuted to the city every day; my aunt and grandmother worked as domestics in the big houses on the other side of town. When everyone had time off, they spent it at home, together. The women of the house would gather at the kitchen table and play cards. I remember us playing gin for pennies and nickels, cracking walnuts and almonds from their shells with the old worn-out Italian nutcracker. My grandfather, who called me *pappano*, showing me how he grew grapes along the outside walls of the garage. Listening to jazz with my father in his attic study, learning so much about black music from him. Sitting on the floor between my stepmother's knees as she combed and braided my hair. And I remember Gilda's laughter. Her laugh was so loud and infectious that it was like a wave which carried us all within its arc. We would do whatever we could to make her laugh, and often that meant teasing her and my grandfather. The laughter was the sound of our voices coming together, of us being together. At times it was even enough to keep at bay the realities of race and class, deception and disappointment, that complicated our ability to love each other and ourselves, without fear, without question.

One day, when I was around fifteen, my grandmother and I were sitting together in the living room, watching through the window as the neighbors packed their furniture and boxes into a moving truck. They had been there when we moved into our house and had been the only people to welcome us into the neighborhood. Now they were leaving, and my grandmother was terrified. I could see the panic in her eyes, I could feel her sense of abandonment in the way she wrung her knotty, wrinkled hands. I asked her who the new neighbors would be; she didn't know, but she told me that she hoped they were white. It was a sentiment that I had come to expect from some Italian Americans, but this was my own grandmother. I was never conscious of her racism, since so much of its outward manifestation occurred when I was too young to understand. She said the words to me, speaking to me, but not really seeing *me*. If she was afraid of black people living next door, who did she think I was, living in her house? Once again I said nothing—where would I even begin? We sat together in silence, watching the movers, and I raged inside. I raged mostly because I loved her. I wanted her to be something more than what she was, and I knew that she would never change, that my presence in her life hadn't really taught her anything. And I understood then that her love for me could only be partial, a love based on an almost acrobatic capacity for contradiction and denial.

It turned out the new neighbors were an African American family. They were almost interchangeable with the previous family: a husband who drove into the city to work each day, a wife who stayed home, a few kids, a dog in the backyard. And as the years went on, my grandmother began to trust them and consider them her friends. She gossiped with them, exchanged cookies with them, baby-sat for their kids. After a while, it was their turn to move. They were concerned that the neighborhood was "changing." Houses were starting to get robbed, and every now and then gunshots could be heard in the tree-lined streets. The drug this time was crack. Eventually most of the families, all white, who were there when we arrived had left; it was like a mass exodus. But my grandmother wouldn't sell the house, wouldn't give it up while she was still alive, though many of us, including myself, had long since moved back to New York. She had worked all her life to get to this place. Her husband and daughter had died here. This was her home. Her days of migration were finally over.

That last night, after dinner, I wandered through the rooms downstairs, where the events of twenty years had unfolded: birthdays and deathbeds, homecomings and divorces, Italian dying into English. Everything was so still now, the cold, slightly stale air, the empty, echoing space within and between each room. The kitchen and dining area seemed much bigger than before and the walls had a yellow cast to them that I never noticed before. There was a huge water stain in the middle of the ceiling like a fresh bruise, and I imagined the whole thing suddenly giving way, giving in, falling down on me. The old television that sat on one of the counters, always on at full volume while we ate, was unplugged and covered with a fine layer of dust. The cabinets were bare, the refrigerator empty.

In the living room, I sat on the frayed plaid couch, where my aunt Evelyn died of cancer five years earlier. Behind the couch were the windows to the enclosed front porch, the panes icy on this October night. This porch, where we would sit with our milky, sugary tea and watch the world outside, where we would decorate our Christmas trees, where more recently a bullet from a random drive-by would lodge itself above the door. Across from the couch was the blocked-up fireplace, inside of which I had hidden on the day we moved in, overwhelmed by the piles of boxes that filled each room. Later it would hold our fake yule log, the one that made the crackling sounds, just like a real fire.

In my grandparents' bedroom, their twin beds lay stripped. On top of the heavy wooden dresser, my grandmother Gilda's altar to the Madonna and Saint Anthony was still there, but there was no candle burning. The only sign of the life that once filled this space was the photograph that hung on the wall over the beds. It is a black-and-white image of my grandparents, seemingly caught off guard. Gilda is helping my grandfather Luigi put on his cardigan; she's smiling at him tenderly, all her attention on this seemingly simple act of caring for him. He looks confused, his mouth open as if in mid-speech, his eyes fixed on something outside of the frame. I can see him telling the person taking the picture to go away and leave him alone. There is such quiet intimacy in this image—I imagine him wanting to hold on to this moment that must have felt rare to both him and Gilda, a moment of peace between them. I see so much love in this image, and some of that love she gave to me.

The next day I would leave this house forever, taking the photograph with me. There would be so much more that I would have to leave behind. "Our" white flight: What was it ultimately a flight from and to? For me, these years created a sense of myself as equally and passionately both African American and Italian American, and an understanding that this dual identity would be something I would have to fight for every day of my life. For my Italian American family, these same years were a time of undoing. My grandmother Gilda's death was the dissolution of a dream, the end of the line. There is no "Old Country" anymore, and no "Old Neighborhood." We are migrants no more. We are simply scattered like stones.

Chapter Fourteen

FIGURING RACE

Edvige Giunta

One boy pointed at me and said to Donna, "There is a nigger here." She said, "No, that's my cousin Kym. It's just dark outside."
—Kym Ragusa, *fuori/outside*

1997. It's a winter evening in New York and I am waiting for Kym Ragusa at Barnes & Noble. I had met Ragusa for the first time a few months earlier: our common interest in Italian American women has brought us together. On this particular night we are going to hear an Italian American writer give a reading at the bookstore. When Kym first walks in, I hardly recognize her. This is only the second time I have seen her, though we have spoken many times; her hair, which during our first meeting expanded gloriously around her face, is now tied back, rather coyly, behind her ears. I wonder about this radical transformative gesture, one she has enacted before, I learn later. In Sicily, too, she felt compelled to turn to this more subdued style, one that will not flaunt her multiple heritage, one that will help her pass. Hiding among your own—passing—when learned as early as Ragusa has, can become a life-long practice, insidious because of the tragic necessity that prompted it in the first place.

The daughter of an African American mother and an Italian American father, Ragusa is a filmmaker whose work centers around a relentless questioning of the boundaries—of gender, race, and class—that have informed her life and the lives of her families and communities.[1] Born in New York in

1966, Ragusa was raised by her grandmothers, though her paternal grandmother did not know of her existence until she was about two years old. Her father had hidden her existence from his mother, who did not approve of his relationship with Ragusa's African American mother. Even when she was finally introduced to the paternal grandmother, she was introduced as the niece of his Puerto Rican girlfriend.

This early "masquerade around [her] . . . origins," as she herself describes it in her video *fuori/outside* (1997), will inform her videos, in which a search for personal roots and identity is always linked to a search for—as well as a questioning of—cultural roots and identities. Her first video, *Demarcations* (1991), can be described as an exploratory visual meditation on personal and cultural boundaries. Demarcations are points of separation and encounter, like those designating her fluctuating sense of racial identification: between the presumed whiteness of her working-class Italian American family and the clandestine blackness of her African American family. Always keeping a keen eye on issues of class, Ragusa exposes the interconnections between class and race in U.S. history, especially in her most recent work, *fuori/outside*, as she recalls the exploitation and the lynching of Italian Americans in the early stages of their emigration to the United States.

Her racial/cultural allegiance is ambivalent and multiple: forced to pass as white in her own Italian American family as a child, Ragusa quickly learned how the dynamics of class and race operate in social as well as familial contexts. Indeed, while all of her work is memoiristic—insofar as it focuses on her personal history as well as the history of her communities—it is also historical because it links her own story with the history of her family, her community, her country. Indeed, the personal is political in powerfully direct ways in Ragusa's work.

In *Passing* (1996), broadcast on PBS in 1997, Ragusa cracks open the question of racial identity. Structured as a dramatic monologue and drenched in a dreamlike aura enhanced by the black-and-white filming, this video features an African American woman's recollection of a road trip to Miami in 1959 and what happens when she stops to buy some take-out food at a diner in North Carolina. Because she is fair-skinned—her ethnic background is African, Native American, German, and Chinese—the racist customers are uncertain about her racial identity. The woman's evocation of the trip foregrounds the ambiguity of racial identity—and identification: the uncertainty of the customers in the diner about her racial identity is articulated through their relentless question: "What side of the tracks are you from?" she recalls them asking. At first, she does not understand what they mean; then, the repetition of the words, spoken again and again, begins to unveil their significance. Repeatedly, she avoids answering the question, having become aware of the possibility and imminence of danger. But before leaving, she turns defiantly towards her questioners and tells them: "Well, you just served a nigger!"

This narrative illustrates one way in which race is socially constructed, as in the exchange between the customers and the woman, who proudly claims as her own that racial identity which stigmatizes her. This woman was Ragusa's maternal grandmother, Miriam Christian. The video, aptly titled *Passing*, represents a crucial moment in Ragusa's investigation of racial/ethnic identity. While Ragusa's voice is never heard—and her face is never seen—in the video, she is clearly the one who through her questions or requests prompts the grandmother's recollection. This recollection indirectly mirrors Ragusa's own experience of passing, as she, too, will be faced with the question of origins and belonging: the question "What side of the tracks are you from?" is one that resonates powerfully for Ragusa. It is significant that the next step in her filmmaking would be an autobiographical exploration of her experience of race—and passing—in *fuori/outside*. Her investigation of race is never linear and has no clear point of departure or arrival.

In Kym Ragusa's work, race does not solidify as a physical reality. It takes shape as a constellation of exploratory moments, all interconnected, all equally elusive. Ragusa's exploration avoids facile answers even as it suggests possibilities for connection and understanding—as in her relationship with her paternal grandmother and the Italian American community she represents—where only rupture and barriers once existed. "I was furious, but I never challenged you. For me, it was just another example of the racism of your people. But your people are also my people" (*fuori/outside*). These words, spoken by the voiceover narrator, Ragusa herself, to the Italian American grandmother who obviously cannot hear, capture the story of her relationship to two cultures, a relationship that follows a trajectory fraught with contradictions.

In her videos, Ragusa is filmmaker, interviewer, and silent witness, coordinating and observing the unfolding of the narrative; she is both spectator and protagonist. These shifting roles, often embraced simultaneously, point to a problematic configuration of identity, one that entails an examination of her relationship to culture(s), family(ies), race(s), and the work that articulates her troubled and troubling interactions with these categories. I ask myself where I stand in relationship to the space Ragusa delineates in her work, a space that cuts across and weaves together race, culture, and age, a space that claims and denies familial and cultural connection.

As I began to follow this trajectory, I found myself in a space I had not envisioned occupying, one in which my own story and Ragusa's intersect. Writing about Ragusa prompted some reflections on what I, as a southern Italian woman, have experienced as race and racism.

As a Sicilian, I have at different times in my life felt myself a potential target of racism. I was born in 1959 in Sicily and thus grew up at a time in which the pressure toward cultural homogenization—enacted through the privileging of Italian language and culture over Sicilian culture and dialect—was particularly strong. The prevailing of Italian culture and language was achieved at the cost of cultural losses. My parents, like most middle-class parents, well understood the interconnections of language/culture, class, and gender: their prejudice was that Sicilian was the dialect spoken by the poor, the uneducated, even though my parents, both university-educated, spoke Sicilian between themselves and with family members. Because they wanted to propel their children into a better, more progressive, and socially and economically advanced world, my parents forbade us—especially the girls—to speak Sicilian dialect. My brother was allowed some flexibility: it was easier for boys than for girls to pick up the rhythms and sounds of the dialect outside the home; girls could move with less ease between cultures, classes, and languages, especially outside the bounds of the parental home. As a result, when I was a child, I spoke with hardly any trace of a Sicilian accent. Yet the first words I uttered as a toddler were in Sicilian dialect. In spite of, also because of, my parents' interdiction, I developed a heightened sense of Sicilian identity. Although my parents strove to instill in us—as the school system did—a sense of national and linguistic identity that transcended and even erased the signs of regionalism, they also managed to transmit to us a passionate pride in our *sicilianità*.[2] If my mother reprimanded me and my siblings whenever a Sicilian word would accidentally slip into our otherwise flawless Italian, she also sang Sicilian lullabies and songs. Sicilian was the language of intimacy, the language my parents would speak between themselves in soft, musical whispers after a late dinner, while I slept peacefully in my mother's lap.

As I grew older, I became increasingly aware that in the national—and international—public imaginary and discourse, southern Italy was often depicted as an economically underdeveloped area, and as a geographical area inhabited by racially inferior people. Racism—that is the term used in Italy —toward southern Italians, pervasive in northern Italy and northern European countries (especially Switzerland and Germany, where southern Italians emigrated in great numbers), spread in southern Italy, generating a sense of rebellion, combined with a most insidious self-hatred.[3] I learned to take pride in the cultural identity that I was supposed to shed. In my cultural roots, I found a source of intellectual and poetical force. This is the cultural identity that, no longer repressed today, informs my work, critical and creative. Now I write of Sicily, though ironically, still in another language.

Summer 1975. I am sixteen years old and traveling to northern Italy, the *continente*, for the first time. There is something momentous about this first departure from the island: it is not so much the geographical distance that causes my excitement, but the crossing and moving into a country, Italy, which is my own and yet, in some strange ways, also foreign. I am traveling with my family by train: a long journey up along the boot that quickly turns into an overwhelming cultural experience, one that enables me to grasp the significance of Sicilian identity vis-à-vis Italian identity. As we move farther away from Sicily, I cannot fail to notice that everything, including the train on which we are traveling, becomes cleaner and more efficient. Once in Milan, my Sicilian aunt's Milanese friends, perfectly at ease with their thick Milanese accent, compliment me on my accent-free Italian, which so well camouflages my Sicilian origins. I feel pride, but also shame, for passing the test—for passing.

This cultural confrontation triggers my first serious reflection on the significance of race and racism. I feel like a trespasser, an outsider who has found a way to be on the inside: I am at once betrayed and betrayer. If I regard myself as Sicilian, I also regard myself as Italian. And these people, who discriminate against my own, are my people, too. Even though I may not be able to articulate it to myself or others, I become acutely aware that passing is a strategy of survival adopted to escape damning racial identification, but one adopted at a certain cost in terms of one's sense of cultural and personal integrity. I may speak Italian, but there is something inauthentic about my Italian identity: I have adopted and adapted, but remain an outsider. Race, I begin to understand as an adolescent, is a slippery concept, part of a story made up by those in charge of language.

During the same vacation in Milan, after observing us with curiosity at the pool in the complex where my aunt lives, a bunch of local teenagers approach me and my sister. They know we are from Sicily. When they learn that my sister is in medical school, one of them exclaims: "Alla faccia delle terrone!"[4] This is supposed to be a compliment: even though she is a *terrona*, my sister is smart enough to be a medical student; she has transcended their expectations of our origins. *Terrona*—from *terra*, earth—can be translated as "creature of the earth," but that hardly conveys the denigrating connotation of this appellation designating southern Italians, which is meant to suggest dirty, poor, ignorant, dark like the earth.[5]

This seemingly minor incident stays with me as one of the few things I remember about that summer vacation. It settles insidiously in the crevices of memory. Other incidents will follow, and as they gel, they will constitute the texture of my cultural identity. Not surprisingly, many years later I will become actively involved in Italian American studies, feeling naturally drawn to the cultural production of immigrants and their descendants.

History, geography, and folklore—the geographical proximity of Sicily to Africa, the Carthaginian presence in the eighth century B.C., the Arab rule in the ninth century A.D., the geographical layout of the boot "kicking" Sicily, but especially the position of colonial subject that Sicily has held at various times—have all contributed to the creation of an ambiguous cultural and racial perception and self-perception. Whether it's Sicily, Africa, or the United States, the positing of hierarchical racial differences provides both a basis and a justification for ruthless economic exploitation.

Southern Italians have variously and ambivalently responded to this racial and cultural identification. "Siamo meridionali," an Italian song of the 1980s, offers, through self-parody, an indictment of the racism that splits Italy apart: "We are from the South"—the song goes—"We are small, dark . . . . we grow tomatoes in bathtubs." "Tenemmu l'Africa vicinu": We are close to Africa. It is no coincidence that Italian American immigrants, many of whom are of southern Italian origin, have recently begun actively to explore the interconnections between race and class.[6]

Kym Ragusa's *fuori/outside* (1997) speaks against silence: a film, letter, poem, biography, tribute, story, history, this video is also a memoir, one that does not subscribe to what Louise DeSalvo has called "the recovery narrative," a narrative that exonerates the reader/viewer of any social or political responsibility.[7] Recovery as a strategy of tracing the past, as an act of remembering necessary to representing the past, is, of course, central to Kym Ragusa's work; it is the patient piecing together of fragments of lives: hers, her grandmother's, her great-grandmother's. Yet "the recovery narrative"—which basically says, as DeSalvo explains, "I was sick, I cured myself, and now I am fine: don't worry about me"—has little to do with this important work of recovery. Ragusa's work does not present a convenient, facile history of emancipation from a past ridden with problems and contradictions, or an unproblematic transition to a relatively conflict-free present.

The dual title embodies not only a dual linguistic and cultural identity (*fuori* means "outside"), but also a separateness of identities as well as a bridging of multiple identities: that the two words are separated by a slash remains a deliberately ambivalent choice on the part of the filmmaker, one that forces the viewer to take an active role in Ragusa's journey. It is also significant that she chooses not to capitalize the initials of either word: capitalizing both initials would have marked, syntactically, a stronger separation; capitalizing only *fuori*, on the other hand, would have established those hierarchies that Ragusa's work brings into question. It is a precarious balance that Ragusa wants to present, one that can be easily tilted, one that, through her artistry, she learns to maintain.

The video's narrative folds on itself, opening with the question, "Do your remember?," addressed to her paternal grandmother, who has lost her hearing, her memory, and her lucidity. Age and illness force a role reversal; the tenderness of the exchanges between adult granddaughter and aging grandmother in need of nurturance offer some of the most moving moments in the video. At the same time, the expression of this love is underscored by the necessity to ask that initial question, which in turn generates a series of other disquieting questions concerning the relationship between the African American granddaughter and the Italian American grandmother who, at one time, rejected Ragusa because of her race.

Ragusa's project foregrounds class and race as complicated markers of personal and social history. The linguistic gap between the terms *fuori/outside* articulates an interrogation of origins, of separateness of family origins, which in Ragusa's case is tied to the racism she first experiences in the safety of the Bronx neighborhood that, twenty-two years later, she still regards as home. Safety and danger overlap in this video, which faces and foregrounds contradictions without claiming to solve them; yet, in the process of confrontation, the seams that divide two people, two families, two communities, two cultures, begin to connect, as in the closing image of Ragusa walking arm in arm with her Italian American grandmother.

Fracture and connection between two worlds, two cultures, two races, is rendered through a series of thematic and visual juxtapositions: Ragusa's life and her grandmother's and great-grandmother's; city and country; the Bronx and Newark; youth and old age. Inside and outside are graphically illustrated through windows—car windows, camera lens, and especially the window of the grandmother's house as Ragusa looks in from the outside and films her grandmother through it. Ragusa's almost ghostly reflection stares back at her (and us) from the window, creating a series of interconnected specular images that put into question a firmly established narratorial position. The family house, a paradoxical site of inclusion and exclusion, represents safety—the house is conceptualized by the family as "a fortress"—and yet one cannot overestimate the danger that this same house posed for the young Ragusa's developing sense of identity, as she finds herself in enemy territory, in a troubling repetition of her maternal grandmother's experience in *Passing*.

The muffled voices, like the frequent silences in the video, express the struggles and complications underlying the articulation of that which has been, thus far, unspoken: the racism experienced by Ragusa within her family and her Italian American community, and what she describes as the "masquerade" around her origins, the domestic violence suffered by her paternal great grandmother, and the oppression suffered by early Italian immigrants.

Ragusa connects the question of origins with travel and movement: the camera itself travels, shuttling the spectator through highways, suburban streets, religious processions, family meals and lore. Travel may offer the promise of something better—economic safety for the first-generation Italian immigrant; physical safety for the second generation that escapes from the city. Travel also contains, always, some kind of threat or disturbance: leaving the city to move to the so-called country—the suburbs of Newark—is likened to another migration, also traumatic, also a rupture of the safety of home, even when that safety has already proven illusory. As a dominant narrative mode of the film and one of its major thematic concerns, travel aptly renders Kym Ragusa's fluctuating sense of identity.

Thematic and visual juxtapositions are contained within the frame of a journey that occurs at multiple levels: first, the migration, voluntary and forced, from Europe and from Africa, a journey that triggers creation and disruption of identity. In an earlier video, titled *Blood of My Blood*, Ragusa juxtaposes the journeys of her ancestors from Africa and southern Italy.[8] Indeed, the original idea for *fuori/outside* was a dual, intersecting narrative of the lives of Ragusa's maternal and paternal great-grandmothers: a Calabrian peasant of Sicilian origin and an African slave. The video that Ragusa actually produced is contained by, and contains, these journeys.

The opening question of Ragusa's video becomes a poignant request: "Do you remember?" That Ragusa's grandmother cannot hear or remember does not diminish the impact of her question; indeed, the determination to speak against secrecy and silence projects that question into a context which is not solely personal. Ragusa's experience of racism and passing transcends the circumstances of her family history and must be understood in the context of the history of race and class in the United States.[9] In addition,

Ragusa's own personal search and questions trigger important revelations: namely, her father's (Ragusa's great-grandfather's) violence. This history of family violence emerges only when Ragusa begins to pose questions to her grandmother: while the old woman seems out of touch with the present, the past powerfully overcomes her and, as she is talking with her granddaughter about her own mother, she lashes out at her father for his violence against her mother. In the background, we hear the voice of Ragusa's father, who remarks that he had never heard this story before. It is only when questions are asked that answers can be given and unspoken histories be written. Ragusa's narrative and her provocative work of excavation thus delve into a multilayered narrative that defies the secrecy enveloping her life, her grandmother's, her great-grandmother's, and the history of her country.

When I began to write this essay in the summer of 1997, Ragusa's words and images slipped through my fingers every time I tried to pin them down and turn them into a subject of investigation, analysis, interpretation. The essay was to be presented at a conference on African American and Italian American communities. As an African American (but also German, Chinese, and Native American) on her mother's side, and Italian on her father's, Ragusa's work proved to be the most appropriate, but also the most problematic, conference topic I could have chosen. Writing about her seemed an elusive, even impossible task, one I was nevertheless determined to pursue.

A number of factors made writing this essay difficult. I did not want to approach it from a solely academic angle. My reservations were rooted in a fear of compromising something—my friendship with Ragusa? my relationship to her work? to my work? My autobiographical approach is rooted in a transformation of the critical discourse that as women—Italian American, Native American, African American, Chicana, Chinese American, Arab American, Jewish American—many of us feel the need to pursue. The memoir is proving to be a literary and artistic form that can collapse and articulate the differences between personal and political, as well as critical and creative, in more direct and compelling ways than any other literary or artistic form; it's that which enables Ragusa "to cross the lines of time, memory, and color that map our relationship and complicate our ability to communicate" (*fuori/outside*).

Being aware of the dangers of exemplary narratives, I did not wish to present Ragusa's story or her work as paradigmatic. The questions and issues that I dealt with in writing this piece at first had to do with positioning myself in relationship to the question of race as an Italian American and a

Sicilian. Kym Ragusa's work addresses the fractures within "Italian American" and within "Italian." My personal history unveils the conflicts within the deceptively simple term "Italian." There are no monoliths facing one another here, but multifaceted and interconnected worlds inhabited by historically situated individuals whose specific experiences of race defy unified and coherent categorizations.

Chapter Fifteen

GIANCARLO GIUSEPPE ALESSANDRO ESPOSITO

Life in the Borderlands

John Gennari

"Giardello, what kind of name is that?" The desperate, gun-toting white man puzzles over the dark features of the FBI agent trying to talk him into releasing the son and daughter he holds hostage in his barricaded apartment. The vowel-heavy name doesn't square with the face: he needs identity clarification. "I'm Italian, Italian and black," Mike Giardello responds. A smile creeps up the face of the embattled white man, and he seizes the opportunity to crack wise at this racial enigma. "Ha," he says, "chitlin' scallopini."

For Giancarlo Esposito, the actor who played Mike Giardello on the acclaimed NBC police drama *Homicide: Life on the Streets*, the confusions of a biracial identity have been personal adventure and professional calling card. Son of an African American mother from Alabama and an Italian father from Naples, now husband of an Irish American woman and father of two mixed-race girls, Esposito is a walking, breathing embodiment of U.S. cultural complexity. Since establishing his career playing straight-up black characters in Spike Lee's early movies, Esposito has gravitated to roles as offbeat, idiosyncratic African Americans whose hybrid backgrounds and complex personalities scramble conventional racial expectations. An actor whose keen mind and taut body vibrate with intensity, Esposito now reigns as one of the most intriguing border-crossing figures in American film and television.

In *Homicide*, Esposito's inscrutably pedigreed Mike Giardello is the prodigal son of Lieutenant Al Giardello (Yaphet Kotto), known affectionately as "Gee," an Afro-Sicilian American who runs the detective squad like a *padrone*, wise in the ways of power, fiercely protective of his surrogate family. In the 1994 movie *Fresh*, Esposito took his own turn as a paragon of Old World manhood—in a more darkly sinister form—as the Latino drug lord Esteban. In *The Keeper* (1996), he played Paul Lamott, a New York City jail guard whose repressed memories of a troubled relationship with his Haitian father leak out as he becomes deeply implicated in the fate of a Haitian immigrant convict. As Yo-Yo in Jim Jarmush's *Night on Earth* (1991), Esposito's jive-talking Brooklyn b-boy undergoes a hilarious and magical bonding with an incompetent East German immigrant cab driver. In Paul Auster and Wayne Wang's *Blue in the Face* (1995), Esposito's virtuoso improvisational sketch of black Italian Tommy Finelli epitomizes indie film hipness.

On-screen mastery of such transethnic experience comes hard by life experience. Esposito's parents met in Italy in the 1950s when his mother, an opera singer, was performing at La Scala in Milan, where his father worked as a stage technician. Esposito lived his first five years in Naples, Rome, and Hamburg, in tow to his mother's career. He was born in 1958 in Copenhagen, where she split a nightclub bill with Josephine Baker. The family later moved to Elmsford, New York, just north of New York City, where Esposito lived on the border between the town's black and Italian neighborhoods.

It's often said that the Irish and Italians gained their passports as full-fledged white Americans when they adopted American racism. For Esposito, the same dynamic was at work, only in reverse: the move from Italy to the United States made him "black." "In Italy," he told me in an interview in June 1999, "I was raised in a household where I never realized my mother was black or my father was white. Once I came to America, things changed."

That moment of realization at age six came, oddly enough, in the men's room of the old Horn and Hardart Automat on 57th Street. "My brother and I went to the bathroom alone without my dad. The urinals, to me they were like incredible things: they were like sculpture, these big porcelain urinals. I liked to go right down the row and hit them all and make a big wall of waterfalls. My dad let us go, but we didn't know he had followed us. Then I went to go to the bathroom, using the last urinal. A very tall white man walked in. There were plenty of urinals, but he walks over and shoves me out of the way—all of a sudden I'm peeing on the floor. I didn't know what the hell was going on. My dad was standing in the doorway and saw it. He went at this guy and beat the crap out of him."

A white man walks past another white man on the way into a public bathroom, can't imagine he's the father of the black kid using the urinal, and assumes by some tacit racial agreement that he can shove the kid with impunity. The enraged father—enraged both by the assault on his son and, surely also by the evident invisibility of his fatherhood—reacts with violence: so transpired the lifting of an immigrant family's veil of racial innocence. "It was one of the most frightening memories I ever had," Esposito says, "and when I understood that it was all about the fact I was the wrong color, it freaked me out. I said, Where *are* we?"

The great Brooklyn Dodgers catcher Roy Campanella ("little bell" in Italian), whose Sicilian father sold vegetables in the Nicetown neighborhood of Philadelphia, is remembered not for his childhood scraps with the black and white kids who called him "half-breed," nor for his years playing winter ball in Mexico and Puerto Rico, where he was able to pass as a native, but as one of a handful of black players who broke the color line in major league baseball in the late 1940s. Giancarlo Esposito is similarly a black man: not because of his love of jazz or his commitment to black progress, but because that's how Americans go about labeling people of "mixed race."

Much as he would prefer not to have to choose between his African American and Italian bloodlines, experience tells him that in America this choice usually will be made for him. Cab drivers, in particular, have made a habit of defining him prima facie by a skin tone several shades darker than his father's deep olive, leaving him curbside with his hand hanging aloft. Esposito's romance in the late 1980s with white actress Fia Porter hit a snag when Porter's parents in Nashville threatened to disown her for dating a black man. Esposito was married in 1996 to producer Joy McManigal. The couple have no illusions that their two mixed-race girls will grow up in a color-blind society. Just the day before I interviewed Giancarlo, he was with his wife and daughters, Shane and Kale, in the waiting room of a pediatrician's office, when a woman who had been staring intently at the family approached him. "They didn't get much color, did they?" she said.

Esposito can regale you with stories of not fitting in. Back in Elmsford, "The black guys didn't understand me. They didn't understand how I spoke. I didn't walk with a little dip. I didn't wear my hair in an Afro and I had a name like Giancarlo Giuseppe Alessandro Esposito. They couldn't relate. Same with those little guinea guys who I so wanted to relate to because of my boyhood with my dad in Italy. I had to wind up telling them, listen, I'm *more* Italian than you are. Look at my name. I lived there. It worked out by the end of my years in Elmsford that I sang 'My Way' at my high school commencement. It made everybody happy."

Esposito found refuge in a friendship with another ethnic outsider named Paul Budish, now a cop in Miami. "His saving grace in high school," says Esposito, "was that he was funny, in a very personalized Jewish way. No one messed with him because he had the gift of lightness. He used to say to me 'mal, mal, mal' [bad, bad, bad in Italian]. Why am I bad? Because I didn't fit in. He didn't fit in either. It was a big joke between us. We went through school together. He made me feel comfortable. We didn't commiserate over the fact that we were both outcasts. It was just known. We never even had to talk about it."

Budish was the only of Esposito's childhood friends who invited him home to meet his parents. "He walks in the front door and he calls up to Sam and Charlotte—he didn't call them Mom and Pop, it was Sam and Charlotte—'don't be afraid of the black guy with me.' That's how we entered the front door. Charlotte came down and I just fell in love with her right away. She starts feeding me gefilte fish. 'You know what this is?' she asked me. Yeah, I kind of did know, because my mother was into Jewish culture. These people were like my family, my second home. No problem with my color."

An unabashed liberal integrationist, Esposito waxes passionate about Jewish participation in the civil rights movement. "I just don't get it," he says about recent tensions between blacks and Jews. "Jews more than anyone else were with African Americans when we were trying to find ourselves, and they still do things that help create unity between their culture and black culture." Esposito and his wife have enrolled their three-year-old daughter Shane in a Jewish nursery school. "I want her to know Jewish people," he says. "I want her to know about that culture. I want her to hear a cantor sing."

If Esposito is black, by choice and by fate, and maybe a little Jewish, by a leap of appreciation, don't think the Italian part doesn't get respect. It's not lost on Esposito that Italian Americans, as a group, not only did not distinguish themselves as supporters of the civil rights movement, but were at the forefront of the 1970s and 1980s white ethnic backlash against affirmative action and other racial justice initiatives of post-1960s liberalism. He's acutely aware that his difficulty making friends with the Italian kids in Elmsford had much to do with the negative stereotypes of blacks they heard in their homes. The irony is that many of these kids's grandparents were Sicilians and southern Italians who *themselves* were subject to the same racial ridicule, both in Italy and America. They were "othered," first by lighter-complected northern Italians and northern Europeans, then by Anglo Americans, as lazy, criminally inclined, intellectually inferior, and overly sensual. And then, when they gained an economic foothold in the United States and secured their status as "white" Americans, they turned the same stereotypes back on the people poorer and darker than themselves.

Of course, this thumbnail sketch of Italian American racism is also a stereotype. It doesn't account for any individual's particular experience; worse, it doesn't explain why Italians and African Americans have shared so much mutually enriching cultural experience. And this is what makes Giancarlo Esposito such a fascinating figure. You need only hear him speak his name—which he pronounces, as they do in his father's Naples, with the "r" languorously rolled and the emphasis in Esposito on the "spo" rather than the "si"—to understand how strongly he embraces the musicality at the heart of his Italian heritage. He proudly tells the story of his paternal Italian grandfather, a man of the opera who worked backstage at Naples's San Carlo Theater. With Mussolini's ascendance in the 1920s, fearful of the Blackshirts running riot over the theater, he hid the sets for the company's operas all over South Italy. It was this kind of commitment to art that Esposito's mother found so bracing when she went to Italy to pursue her singing career in the 1950s. Giancarlo describes her as a "beautiful, dark, stately" woman who "adopted European consciousness," turning to high art as a refuge against American racism. When Giancarlo met his mother's brother, he was stunned by the contrast between diva and downhome. "Uncle Al, whom I love dearly, he's country. *Couuuuntry*. He's a different man. The whole language is different."

Esposito's maternal grandmother played organ in the Pentecostal church; his mother sang in the chorus. With "sisters falling out in the aisles," it was one of those black churches that looks like it might rock off its foundations during a rollicking Sunday morning service. Giancarlo's love of performance owes as much to this vernacular tradition as to the formal vocal training his mother gave him when he appeared in nine Broadway musicals between the ages of nine and fourteen. The Pentecostal church, he says, "was a whole other world for me [than the Broadway stage], and I grew up in that world, too. The lesson was that you can celebrate your God, you can celebrate your happiness, and you can ask it to enter your body."

Spirit reverberating through the voice and the body—one thinks of the bravura virtuosity of Enrico Caruso and Louis Armstrong, of Louis Prima scatting "Jump, Jive an' Wail," of Frank Sinatra crooning bel canto over the limousine swing of the Count Basie rhythm section on "Pennies from Heaven." Song-and-dance Broadway baby Giancarlo Esposito belting out

"My Way" at his high school commencement makes mirth of his identity dilemma, but he also invokes the modern American tradition of racial and ethnic outsiders sparking fresh cultural energy through rhythm, tune, and humor. In particular, Italians, like Jews and Latinos, have turned to African American urban culture to develop distinctive performance techniques emphasizing bodily elegance and stylized emotion.

Leave it to the academics to argue whether this kind of mixing and matching is respectful borrowing or racial theft. For Giancarlo Esposito, the question is a matter of living his life the only way he knows: at the crossroads.

In the late 1970s, after his stage career shifted from Broadway musicals to drama, Esposito won an Obie Award for his performance in the Negro Ensemble Company's *Zoo Man and the Sign*. One night during the show's run, a young man came backstage to introduce himself and compliment Giancarlo on his work. The well-wisher was a recent NYU film school graduate now making ends meet by cleaning films for Maxie Cohen at First Run Features. He was black, and talked with fervor about his vision for making movies that plumbed the depths of black life and culture from the inside. He was working on a script called "Homecoming," a musical that explored fraternity and sorority life at traditionally black colleges modeled on Morehouse and Spelman. His name was Spike Lee.

"Homecoming" became *School Daze* (1988), the first of four films in which Esposito has worked under Lee. Esposito plays Julian, the sadistic fraternity president in *School Daze*; Buggin' Out, the amateur political agitator in *Do the Right Thing* (1989); Left-Hand Lacey, the dandyish jazz pianist in *Mo' Better Blues* (1990); and Thomas Hayer, one of the assassins, in *Malcolm X* (1992). For a fledgling actor of color then paying dues with bit parts as a pimp, thief, and drug dealer in schlocky TV shows and second-rate movies, these roles were like manna from heaven. None were leading-man vehicles, and none showed the full range of Esposito's talent and intelligence. But by hitching his wagon to the rising star of America's hottest young filmmaker, Giancarlo Esposito became a familiar face, if not a household name.

The most absorbingly personal of these roles was Buggin' Out, a hip-hop generation black nationalist who looks and sounds like a hybrid of boxing promoter Don King and rapper Flavor Flav. The movie unfolds on a scorching hot summer day in the predominantly black Brooklyn neighborhood of Bedford-Stuyvesant, where Buggin' Out patrols the sidewalks with an exuberance more comic than menacing. His signature valediction, "stay black," comes with a soul-brother handshake so elaborately choreographed that it suggests parody as much as solidarity. When a white Yuppie wearing a Larry Bird, Celtic-green basketball shirt rudely bicycles over his just-out-of-the-box Air Jordan sneakers, then compounds the insult by repairing to the stoop of his brownstone and intoning about *his* property rights, Buggin' Out stands tall for the 'hood against this especially boorish representative of white privilege. But he stops short of unleashing vengeance, cooling out his posse of b-boys and girls with an appeal to the moral superiority of the "righteous black man" with "a loving heart."

Do the Right Thing was Lee's third movie—after *She's Gotta Have It* and *School Daze*—but it was his first to feature nonblack characters and to foreground interracial relations. Lee, who grew up cheek-by-jowl with Italians in Brooklyn's Cobble Hill neighborhood, turned here to the depiction of New York Italians, as he would in *Jungle Fever* (1991) and *Summer of Sam* (1999). Lee wrote the script partly in mind of the folksy ethnic sociability that distinguishes Italians in the New York imagination. But he was also meditating on the strained relations between blacks and Italians that came to light most tragically one night in 1986 in the Howard Beach neighborhood of Queens, when a posse including Italians wielding baseball bats and tree trunks chased a black man named Michael Griffith onto a highway, where he was struck and killed by a passing car.

The plot of *Do the Right Thing* centers on the fate of a pizzeria, Sal's Famous, owned and operated by the Franziones, an Italian family that commutes to Bed-Sty from Bensonhurst, Brooklyn's Italian fortress. The Franziones park their Cadillac in front of the pizzeria, where it looms large as a parvenu emblem of material success. For Lee, Sal's pizzeria symbolizes not just the persistence of economic colonialism in the postintegration era, the flow of capital out of the black community into the hands of nonblack ethnic entrepreneurs—the Korean grocery store across the street from Sal's carries that theme just as well. At Sal's, the stakes are higher than what the cash register tape reveals; here, the coin of the realm is *respect*.

Buggin' Out is plenty miffed by the two dollar surcharge for extra cheese on Sal's miserly slices, but what really incenses him is Sal's wall of fame, a photographic shrine to Italian American achievement made up of publicity shots of Frank Sinatra, Dean Martin, Perry Como, Liza Minnelli, Al Pacino, Joe DiMaggio, and Luciano Pavarotti. "Yo, Mookie," Buggin' calls out to the character played by Lee, who works as a delivery man for Sal, played by Danny Aiello. "How come there ain't no brothers up on the wall?"

Sal's response to Buggin' Out shows none of the loving heart we see elsewhere in the film, none of the *simpatico* he urges on his son Pino (John Turturro), an unreconstructed bigot who thinks "we should stay in our neighborhood and the niggers should stay in theirs." Sal counters Pino's racist vitriol with touching Mediterranean benevolence—"these kids have grown up on my food, my food. I'm proud of that"—but with Buggin' Out he musters only spiteful defensiveness: "Get your own place, you do what you wanna do. You can put up your brothers and uncles, nephews and nieces, stepfathers and stepmothers, what you want. But this is *my* pizzeria. American Italians only on the wall." To which Buggin' Out sharply responds: "Rarely do I see American EYEtalians eating here. All I see is black folks. We spend much money here, we should have some say."

Lee's romantic depiction of Stuyvesant Avenue leans heavily on representations of black consumer culture: a billboard of Mike Tyson looming over the pizzeria, Magic Johnson T-shirts, Air Jordan sneakers, Afrocentric body ornaments, and the ubiquitous black music sound stream flowing out of Señor Love Daddy's storefront radio station two doors down from Sal's. Against this backdrop, one might hear Buggin' Out's call for a change in the iconography at Sal's as a gesture of "hip black separatism," as Joe Klein, the film's sternest critic, suggested. But as literary critic Tom Ferraro has brilliantly argued, the nuances of the film instead reveal a Brooklyn urbanism founded on the interethnic common ground shared by the Franzione family and its black customers. Ferraro eloquently breaks down the social dynamics at work in *Do the Right Thing*'s interracial contact zone:

> On the strip along Stuyvesant between Quincy and Lexington lies an habitus of stoops and windows, street mingle, store flow, and music float: less a mean street than the boulevard of what Herbert Gans once called an "urban village," its open hydrant the fountain of an elongated *piazza*—and what we see there is the syncopated congress, the *opera* of the streets: where the individual is constituted not so much outside of group interaction as through it—as one or another archetype or ethnic persona, realized in competitive display, in oral inventiveness or eloquent silence, in the airing of family linen, intrablock melodrama, or neighborhood defense; and where the ethical imperative that emerges is a formidable combination of love and irony, respect and suspicion, absorption and wariness.

These Italians and blacks are the most passionate of enemies: familiar enemies, others who are almost the same. Mookie knows how to get under Pino's skin: he intimates that his kinky hair gives away the tar brush hidden in his family history. And biological mixing is just prelude to the cultural weave. The Bensonhurst guidos and the Bed-Sty homeboys inhabit overlapping urban style worlds marked by syncopated streetwise lingo, body posturing, and a visual vernacular of hair, clothing, and ubiquitous gold jewelry. They treat their Air Jordans and their Cadillacs as organic extensions of their bodies, using them for purely expressive purposes. They groom and they strut and they emote.

And they scream. None louder or uglier than Buggin' Out and Sal in the pivotal showdown that grows into the most incendiary racial conflagration in recent American cinema. Buggin' Out storms the pizzeria in league with his homey Radio Raheem, whose signature boombox blasts Public Enemy's "Fight the Power" at ear-splitting volume. Sal yells that he wants the music off. Buggin' Out holds ground. The two start spewing a skein of racial epithets in one another's faces. Sal grabs his baseball bat (a grim reference to Howard Beach) and smashes Raheem's radio to bits. The ensuing melee takes on grisly, tragic proportions when a policeman squeezes the life out of Radio Raheem with a brutal nightstick choke hold. After a moment of eerie calm, the hitherto placid Mookie strikes his blow for the revolution, flinging a trash can through the front window of Sal's, sparking a riot that ends with the pizzeria and the Cadillac in ruins.

Lee's movie was a big cinematic public mural, a broad-stroke representation of ethnic pride hardening into racial conflict. Released the summer before an acrimonious mayoral showdown in which African American David Dinkins bested Italian American Rudolph Giuliani, *Do the Right Thing* triggered more public debate than any film in recent memory. Joe Klein, worried that the film would incite the city's black youth to riot, denounced Lee's work as a reckless threat to public order. Lee expressed outrage at Klein and other critics, accusing them of putting a higher value on Sal's property than on Radio Raheem's life.

For Esposito, there was a devastatingly intimate reality beneath the film's colorful surface and controversial reception. At the time of the Howard Beach incident, Esposito's father was teaching Italian at a public school in that very Queens neighborhood. Giancarlo's parents had divorced years earlier, and while he had grown somewhat estranged from his father, he deeply craved a stronger bond with him. "I didn't know if I was doing him proud as a son, because I could never be as Italian as he is—I can't speak the language as clearly as he does." Curious to check out Howard Beach, but as fearful as any other brown-skinned person of stepping foot there, Giancarlo joked with his father about coming to visit one of his classes. It was one of those jokes that disguises an undercurrent of pain. In Howard Beach, Esposito senior had assimilated into white America, but the son remained persona non grata. "Deep inside me, there was resentment," he says. "He could be accepted in that world and I could never be."

The script of *Do the Right Thing* heightened Esposito's inner conflict. "I started thinking about my relationship with my dad, and about my long journey, having been born the son of an Italian man and a black woman. The movie was part of the catharsis I went through to release a lot of anger that I had built up. Playing an angry black man allowed me to say: 'I refuse to live in that space that says I am not good enough, a world that will not accept me because of the color of my skin.'" Complicating matters was the rapport Esposito enjoyed with John Turturro, Richard Edson, and Danny Aiello, the actors who were playing the Italian characters. The bonding ran deepest with Aiello, a man who "was the same color skin as my dad" and who seemed to be able to relate to Giancarlo in ways that his father had come up short.

This camaraderie worried Lee, who tried to keep the two from fraternizing. "Spike's style," Esposito explains, "is to make his actors enemies [off-camera] because he wants the real thing to appear on screen. In *School Daze*, he separated the jigaboos from the wannabees and even put them in different hotels. It was freaking everybody out because people had friends on the other side, but Spike wanted war. I understood it. He's a new filmmaker, and that's his way of creating the tension he needs. But it was frightening to me because he was manipulating people in a way that's different than just directing. It was about manipulating who people *are*. If you can do that as a director, you probably get a better scene or a better movie. But I didn't agree with it. I felt that what I do is *act*. I don't have to carry that hate inside me."

Whatever the virtues or defects of Lee's approach—call it Method directing—the upshot was a stunningly powerful blowup between Buggin' Out and Sal. Beyond the reach of Lee's directorial hand, however, the scene also served as a poignantly shared personal epiphany for Esposito and Aiello. "We got to that scene and an amazing thing happened," Esposito discloses. "Everyone is going nuts and screaming. All of a sudden I felt all these years and years of rage. And Danny, who I never heard curse—ever—started cursing. I can't remember exactly what he said, but it was something really, really different. Not a typical epithet, not just 'nigger.' It reminded me of what my mother had taught me. She said, 'When someone calls you something, you have to say something back.' Danny had learned that lesson, too. We started screaming at each other, and some of the things that came out of his mouth I had never heard before. I could not believe it. Some of the things that came out of *my* mouth I also couldn't believe.

"It was a really harrowing moment for both of us. We were staring into each other's eyes, and all the anger from all those years came right out. Needless to say, we got an amazing scene. Spike was going nuts. He loves it.

Danny starts to cry. I start to cry, and we start to hug. We hugged each other for at least twenty minutes. We didn't want to take that anger out of the scene, didn't want to take it away with us."

If Lee's resolve to take on the hard issues of race gave Esposito a place to release his dramatic power, other aspects of Lee's filmmaking were in tension with Esposito's betwixt and between sensibility. Despite a strong friendship buoyed by their shared passion for jazz and sports, Esposito doesn't shy from talking about the frictions with Lee. In what he calls a "vehement disagreement," Esposito settled for a minor role in *Jungle Fever*, Lee's 1991 movie about a love affair between Flipper, a married African American architect from Harlem's Striver's Row (Wesley Snipes) and Angie, an Italian American office temp from lower-middle-class Bensonhurst (Annabella Sciorra). Lee's inspiration for the movie was the 1989 murder of Yusuf Hawkins, a black teenager who was attacked by a mob of Italian youths in Bensonhurst. "Harlem and Bensonhurst for me are more than just geographical locations; it's what they represent," Lee told *Newsweek*. "Yusuf was killed because they thought he was the black boyfriend of one of the girls in the neighborhood. What it comes down to is that white males have problems with black men's sexuality. It's as plain and simple as that. They think we've got a hold on their women."

Esposito, whose entire family life has been built around interracial marriages, found Lee's thinking narrow-minded. "I was just crushed about it, crushed. I thought, get smart, get some serious issues out there. When I confronted him, he said to me, 'Look, Giancarlo, it's called "Jungle Fever," that's all it is.'" For Lee, the relationship could only function as a projection of racial mythology: a white woman's fantasies about sexual equipment, a black man's curiosity about forbidden fruit. But the movie fails to develop even this cliché: the relationship has no passion, no frisson. The only energy around it is the hysteria it unleashes in the lovers' families. Implausibly, the black architect's wife deals with her marital crisis not by worrying about the effect it might have on the couple's young daughter, but by convening a talk-show-style caucus of black women to kvetch about white women's obsession with black men. More plausibly, but so impulsive and overheated as to become a parody of Italian hotheadedness, the temp's stone racist father, upon learning of the relationship, beats his daughter to a bloody pulp.

In *Jungle Fever* as in *Do the Right Thing*, Lee does his best to show Italians at their paranoic, loathsome worst. (Those caricatures have now been surpassed by the Bronx primitives featured in Lee's *Summer of Sam*. These are Italians so subhuman that John Turturro, in his off-camera role as the voice of the dog who addles the mind of "Son of Sam" killer David Berkowitz, is just about the most articulate of the lot.) "For Lee," critic David Denby wrote in a description of the Bensonhurst guidos of *Jungle Fever*, "Italianness is mostly a disgrace. These people have no class."

Denby is right that the characters played in that movie by Nicholas Turturro and Michael Badalucco, "local layabouts wasting their days at a candy store pour[ing] out their hatred of blacks," are meant to signify moral shame in Bensonhurst's most xenophobic quarters. But this doesn't quite explain the paradox of why these racists seem so much more interesting and compelling—so much more alive—than Lee's black characters. Lee's black characters in these early films are archetypes; they deliver public manifestos on the problems of the race. His Italian characters are who they are. They live and breathe.

Spike Lee is a race man, but he's also a product of Brooklyn's interethnic cultural milieu. Esposito thinks that in *Jungle Fever* and *Do the Right Thing* Lee "had a better feel for the Italian stuff. It made more sense. It was more natural. It was more flowing than the African American stuff. Maybe it was that Spike grew up around all these Italians and it was in his blood more than he even knew." What saves *Jungle Fever* for Esposito is the Bensonhurst scenes. For all of the odiousness of what's said in the candy store, Esposito sees a social flow there that's not equaled in the Harlem scenes. "I know those guys, and those guys know each other," he says.

For Esposito, the only true romance in the movie is found in Bensonhurst, and it comes in an interracial coupling that seems to contradict Lee's ideological blueprint. Angie's longtime boyfriend Paulie (John Turturro), harassed by the candy-store chorus as a race traitor for craving the education that will get him out of Bensonhurst, falls for Orin (Tyra Ferrell), the black woman who patronizes his store and encourages him to apply to college. She has class, and she sees the gentle soul of this deeply pained man. "That relationship, that was what made the movie for me," says Esposito. "It wasn't about Wesley and Anna. John and Tyra, they were in love. It was beyond anything you can label. That's what life is about, it's about that kind of innocence. It doesn't matter how different people are. Did you ever meet people who don't speak the same language, yet they are in love? It's magnificent. That kind of love is the language of the world."

When Esposito points out that Spike Lee has given John Turturro more parts than himself, he means it as a tribute to Lee, a defense against the critics who accused the director of a "Crow Jim" vision and hiring policy. But the truth is that Turturro has found a niche that still largely eludes Esposito: a hip, edgy ethnic *Italian*. The role Esposito prizes as his "most Italian" was one he created for himself whole cloth in the 1995 indie film *Blue in the Face*, improvising on the situations set up by writer Paul Auster and director Wayne Wang. The movie, like its better-known twin *Smoke*, is a hymn to what Auster referred to in a publicity interview as "The People's Republic of Brooklyn," complete with statistics on the borough's polyglot ethnicity (2.5 million inhabitants, ninety different ethnic groups, 1,500 churches, synagogues, and mosques), and documentary video footage of local characters who reek of authenticity. Esposito's character is one of the regulars who hang out in Augie's (Harvey Keitel) cigar store reading the racing form, copping a smoke, shooting the breeze.

Esposito's climactic riff comes when a black con artist (Malik Yoba) wanders into the store, hawking some Rolex watches. "I got the African price and the European price," he announces. Looking warily at Augie, he says "I deal with the African first. Black people first always." He turns to Esposito, and the two start trading fours:

> Esposito: I'm not from Africa. My name is Tommy Finelli. That's my name.
>
> Yoba: What you doing hanging out in this neighborhood, man? How'd you get the name Finelli?
>
> Esposito: This *is* my neighborhood. I'm from Italy. My father's Italian, my mother's black.
>
> Yoba: You ain't no mulatto, you as black as me. Y'all wanna be white, that's the problem.
>
> Esposito: How do you know what I am?

Whatever else he is, Esposito is an actor who treats his craft like a sacrament, consecrating it with deep knowledge of the rites and practices of the cultural traditions he's inherited and studied. The improvisational format of *Blue in the Face* allowed him to get up a costume from his own wardrobe of antique clothes and "to think jazz." "I'm a big jazz fan, huge, huge," Esposito says. He speaks of friendships with Dexter Gordon, Lee Konitz, Philly Jo Jones, and Russell Procope, and lets on that he's now studying jazz alto sax to "loosen up" a bit from the classical piano he's played since his childhood. "Jazz has no barriers," he says. "It doesn't say that you have to be on Channel Seven or Channel Four. It's a personal expression of who you are. Your history comes out in notes and melodies and chords."

Sporting a porkpie hat and the easy hipster pose of a Count Basie sideman, Esposito takes his solo time in *Blue in the Face* to evoke a person and an experience that remain deeply etched in his memory. The name Tommy

Finelli pays tribute to the man who sold him his first house, one of those Italians whose lovingly tended backyard sings out to the neighborhood like a beautiful melody. "I remember feeling so at home on this little piece of land," Esposito recalls. "It was just a little 75 by 100 foot lot, but every inch of it bore fruit. Cherry trees, a plum tree, a pear tree, an apple tree. You see, the Italians, they love working with their hands. They're about the earth, about nature, and sustaining themselves, by themselves. It's one of the things I've always loved the Italians for, one of the many things." As he talks, Esposito mimics the hand movements of a man working the soil, and the effect is just as expressive as when he demonstrates Thelonious Monk's hand spread on the keyboard and Charlie Parker's fingering of the alto sax. For Esposito, arboriculture meets jazz craft in the laying on of hands.

It was this cultural borderland that Esposito hoped to explore even further in his role as Mike Giardello on *Homicide*: "a guy who could relate to all the guineas with no problem and then could step across the line and go 'Yo, what's up?'"

In writer/producer Tom Fontana, Esposito saw a kindred spirit, a crossover dreamer alert to the myriad ways that lived experience and the imagination refuse to abide the color line. With *St. Elsewhere*, *Homicide*, and the extraordinary HBO series *Oz* to his credit, Fontana is the hottest writer in television. He grew up in a Sicilian family that worked in the bar business in the racially mixed neighborhoods of Buffalo. With Baltimore native Barry Levinson and the show's other writers, he took it as his charge to "write the city accurately." Above all, this meant capturing the city's ethnic character. "Baltimore is a brown city. To pretend otherwise would have been irresponsible. This is where Little Italy rubs right against the projects. We wanted characters who could travel both sides of the street."

Homicide, which was canceled after seven seasons, didn't need NAACP pressure to realize the virtues of a racially integrated cast. Or to portray race as complexly and interestingly as any other television show to date. The show eschewed happy endings and did its best to resist pleas from network suits for more chase scenes. The driving pulse of the show was not so much the plot as the dialogue, zesty repartee that registered the quirks, vulnerabilities, and complicated inner lives of the idiosyncratic cast of characters that made up the detective team.

In hatching Mike Giardello, *Homicide* opened up more opportunity for its clever treatment of black and Italian exchange. In Al Giardello (Yaphet Kotto), Mike's father, the show offered a black Italian who's more Old World than old school: he delivers aphorisms in the original Italian, stares people down with the *malocchio* (evil eye), and condemns the nouvelle pseudo-Mediterranean cuisine on Baltimore's trendy waterfront as an accursed yuppie affectation. A deeply passionate man, he's given to alternating bouts of fiery rage and weepy sentimentality.

Fontana had no trouble seeing himself in Pembleton (Andre Braugher), a Jesuit-trained, black supercop known for his jackknife temper and ruthless interrogation methods, his struggles with his Catholic faith, and his existential raps on personal redemption and the integrity of the soul. "The character was a part of Tom," Esposito says. "He wrote Pembleton as if to say, 'It doesn't matter what color the person is who serves as my alter ego or voice.'"

Yaphet Kotto was just as game to explore the possibilities of straddling racial boundaries. "Yaphet brought so much to the role," says Fontana. "He really captures this guy's schizophrenic personality. He's both an angry black man and a brooding Sicilian. His Sicilian side was incredible. On the set we would say, 'He's out Brando-ing Brando' [as Don Corleone in *The Godfather*]. He was always pushing the writers, 'Give me some more Italian lines.'"

With "Gee" serving as a backdrop, *Homicide* burrowed deeper into the black/Italian theme. When Latino actor Jon Seda joined the cast, he declined the role of the show's first Latino detective: he wanted to be Sicilian. When his character, Falsone, and black detective Stivers (Toni Lewis) investigate a set of murders in Baltimore's West Indian community, Stivers grouses to her partner about West Indian blacks' superior attitude toward African Americans. Falsone nods knowingly: "It's like the northern Italians, they get confused sometimes, think they're Swiss or something, different than Sicilians."

Esposito's Mike Giardello had yet to really take shape when NBC finally pulled the plug on *Homicide*. "I've known Giancarlo for twenty years," Fontana says. "We literally wrote the part for him. We were creating a character who knows the town, but he's also an outsider. There's a lot of stuff he's trying to work out with his father. We wanted to put it all in there: the pain, the reconciliation, all the emotions."

In the two-hour movie that NBC aired in February 2000 to close out the *Homicide* story, Captain Al Giardello, now running for mayor, takes an assassin's bullet while on the campaign stump. Emergency surgery gives Gee a few more hours of life. He uses it well, eschewing his intravenous feeding tube in favor of a dish of gnocci. He chides Michael for settling for a rushed lunch of mediocre Chinese take-out. The essence of *italianità*, the father tells the son, is always—always—to take the time to eat well. Esposito and Fontana "never quite got there" with Mike Giardello, Esposito rues. I ask Esposito where he wanted to go with Mike Giardello. "I wanted him to be more Italian," he tells me.

What would it take for Giancarlo Giuseppe Alessandro Esposito, son of Giovanni Esposito of Naples, to be able to pass as an Italian in America? Will his picture ever appear on a Brooklyn pizzeria wall alongside those of Sinatra, DeNiro, and Pacino? Would it matter that his picture also graces the walls of Harlem barbershops, where he's the son of opera diva Elizabeth Foster Esposito?

Giancarlo Esposito's life story and his art force us to ask just how ready we really are to imagine a truly interracial society that reflects the truth of our race-defying DNA. Esposito knows better than most how far we must go to build such a society. On his recent trips to Italy, he has come to the realization that color matters there in ways he wouldn't have been able to understand as a child. In Naples, he has seen Ethiopian immigrants—a reminder of Italy's colonial history in Africa—struggle against their pariah status. In New York, recent conversations with his father—now married to a Haitian woman—have ruefully noted the case of the Italian American police officer who brutalized the innocent Haitian Abner Louima.

Still, Esposito remains the inveterate crossover dreamer. When I ask him which of his roles teaches his children the best lesson, he barely hesitates: it's Yo-Yo in *Night on Earth*. Costumed as a walking signifier of early 1990s inner-city blackness, Yo-Yo tries desperately to hail a Manhattan cab back to Brooklyn. Spurned by several drivers, finally he's picked up by an East German immigrant who can barely speak English, has no idea where Brooklyn is, and . . . can't even drive the car. "It's the great equalizer—everybody drives," Esposito says. "But he can't drive. (He laughs.) 'All right,' Yo-Yo thinks, 'You don't speak any English, and you can't drive. Let *me* drive myself home.' And I do. Now think about it: what possesses this guy to trust me, an *out* black guy, to take over the wheel?"

In Brooklyn, Yo-Yo picks up his sister, played with sassy ebullience by Rosie Perez, and the two poke fun at this hapless immigrant. But then comes a turnaround, a magical epiphany. "It turns out that this driver, Helmut, is a clown. A *real* clown, I mean. He pulls out his clown's nose: he used to be in the circus." Helmut's innocence, his guilelessness, is so pure that it completely disarms Yo-Yo: he sees clear through to his own prejudice. . . .

"This is what life is really about," says Esposito. "The person that you think you know so well—he's stupid, he's naive, he's a foreigner—well, it turns out that you don't really know him at all. And then he shares with you a pearl, a gift that is so magnificent, it completely changes the way you think about the world. It teaches you to stay open-minded, because you never know where the next pearl will come from."

Chapter Sixteen

ITALIANI/AFRICANI

Ronnie Mae Painter and Rosette Capotorto

Black Madonna

My mother is white but only to me.
She's Italian American not black like me
My black friends say she's white
so what else could she be
Other white folks say hell no
You're Italian American from Sicily
So we all look in the mirror
My brothers and sisters to see
If we're really black or really white
or from Sicily?

Ronnie Mae Painter

Hail Mary

My mother is black I say and the
room goes silent. A simple way
to halt racist talk
My mother *is* black.
Dark hair, dark skin, long legs. *Terrono*

Sicilian is Black is African.
Africani/Siciliani they chant
under my window.
The Black Madonna del Tindari
lives around the corner.
Sicilians have a lot of explaining to do.

Rosette Capotorto

His Hands

My father is black. That's plain by his skin and his pain.
He woke up at 5:00 am. That's when his workday began.
We seldom saw him. To bed by 8:00 pm.
Children should be seen and not heard, Beatrice said.
Sometimes we heard him. With our hands to our ears
trying to muffle the sound of screams brought on by
huge hands. But the morning was always silent.
My father is black. That's plain by his skin and his pain.

Ronnie Mae Painter

Our Father

My father is white. Short. Thick.
Fingers. Hands. Thick.
Punch. A stomach. A window.
Pull a splinter from a baby's foot.
My father is Italian. American.
Upholding the law of a land of his
own making. Harsh, unbendable law.
Not even his own children can be spared.

Rosette Capotorto

HONEY
RONNIE MAE PAINTER

My Black self has always been obvious by the way others perceive me and the low expectations they have of me. But the notion of being white seems ridiculous. I have the so-called "better hair" but still nappy, my skin is brown, and my consciousness follows. What makes me Italian? Surely not the store security guard who follows me up and down the aisles to make sure I'm not slipping the salami down my pants or the tomatoes into my bra. What makes me Italian are my eyes and my mouth. If you look very closely at my eyes, you'll see Italy in them. From my mouth you'll hear my mother, Beatrice. I say what I want, when I want, to whomever I want. If you couldn't tell I'm Italian by those two features, you'd better, because when my mouth starts telling you what I want, watch out for my arms. They'll be flying with such enthusiasm you have to step out the way for fear of a serious injury.

My father worked all the time, some to get away from us, but mostly to put food on the table and clothes on our backs. Have you ever tried to buy shoes for six children? This had to be a job for Superman. Just getting us out of the apartment at the same time required a great deal of skill, never mind money. He worked so hard to provide for us we never saw him, and when we did, he was eating dinner, watching TV, smoking a joint, or drinking. On Sunday mornings he was home though. That's when he would teach me how to cook. Soul food, of course. You see, in his opinion, mother couldn't cook. Her food wasn't black enough. Spaghetti, eggplant, gravy, parmesan, stinky cheese. Not what a black man needs after a hard day's work. So we learned to cook for him. Collard greens, fried chicken, baked macaroni and cheese. The girls, of course. The boys couldn't boil water without burning down the kitchen. Boys should empty the garbage and mow the lawn, but since we had no lawn, all they had to do was take out the trash. And they didn't get that right. My mother had many rules like that. You didn't have to make your bed or clean the bathroom as long as you were a boy.

Did this make me Italian? Or was it that little man in the red velvet gown who stood on her dresser receiving hand-clasped prayers? Or the music? Every so often you would hear it blaring from the Victrola in the living room, which of course no one was to sit in, another rule.

Sola, perduta, abbandonata
in landa desolata! Orror!
Intorno a me s'oscura il ciel.

Ahimè, son sola!
(Puccini, *Madame Butterfly*)

Sneaking glimpses, I'd watch her in the living room. There you could see her singing these songs and sometimes she'd be crying and singing and singing and crying. And sometimes there'd be laughter and talk in a language I could never translate.

Terra di pace mi sembrava questa!
Ah, mia beltà funesta
ire novelle accende
strappar da lui mi si volea
(Puccini, *Madame Butterfly*)

On occasion my father would come from the room, say nothing, shake his head, and with a confused smile say, "That's your mother." My father would clip his fingers and tap his toes so gently to Green Onions or maybe Dizzy. Most Sunday mornings he would take a shot of Seagram's VO. We'd cook in silence and listen to Billie sing,

here is a fruit
for the crows to pluck
for the rain to gather
for the sun to rot
for the tree to drop
here is a strange
and bitter crop
(Lewis Allan, "Strange Fruit")

Maybe that's why they stayed together for more than forty years, until she died in that bed next to him. My father slept on the same mattress with her imprint on it for the next five years. Maybe it was the honey we found when we cleaned the room that morning, right under her head, all fresh and new. Maybe they did understand one another's blues.

MY MOTHER IS BLACK
ROSETTE CAPOTORTO

Call it *omertà*, call it the right to privacy, call it protestant prudery, but I am not going to talk about how racism has destroyed my family. That is a subject too painful and relevant to my everyday life to share publicly.

For myself I start here—my race card is in my little red phone book—rubber bands and all. It's in who comes to my house, to my daughter's birthday parties. My little red phone book cuts through many lines of demarcation. As a girl raised in the Bronx, I am well aware of lines of demarcation. I acknowledge those lines. In some ways I accept them.

I was raised to be a racist. Not the name-calling, dagger-carrying kind but the more subtle, insidious, "some of my best friends," let's uphold the neighborhood kind. Something went wrong along the way. Exactly what that something was, I have never figured out. To be honest, I wasn't always as open-minded as I am now. I tried out many points along the race continuum until I found a place where I am comfortable. For me, inclusive is best. This was not always so.

For many of the people I grew up with, this is NOT so. They are more liberal than their parents, but they do not live inclusive lives. How many of us do?

I went to school, to Hunter College, in the 1980s as a returning woman student. I was privileged to study with Audre Lorde, Johnnetta B. Cole, Blanche Wiesen Cook, and Louise DeSalvo, among others. Desmond Tutu, Jesse Jackson, Geraldine Ferraro, Maurice Bishop, Angela Davis, bell hooks, Toni Morrison all came to speak at Hunter while I was there. I met and worked with many incredible people, mostly women. Many women of color. Always we talked and wrote and read. I attended events where I was one of two or three white women and it's an obvious thing and I have learned a thing or two.

Interracial relationships take longer to form. They are more fragile, less likely to survive. For me, it's a quality of life issue. It's loving the faces of my friends; my daughter dancing with M., little C. asleep on my lap, baby F.'s huge smile when I appear.

Of course racism is bigger than personal relations—when I walk past a "gang," meaning a "group," of black teenage boys I feel the physical tension and I try to acknowledge it, render it real.

I worry about being older, old, and not being able to walk past these boys in the way I can now.

What do they see when they look at me?

I have lived in New York City all my life. I have ridden the #2 train in the dead of night in a miniskirt and lip gloss. I have sat next to a tall black man in white kid shoes and a gold ring as big as a baby's fist. I have shared a subway car with a Latin gang, the girls more treacherous than the boys.

I have traveled safely. Arrived safely.

I have a friend, a guy, who was beaten up many times. Somehow he brought trouble on himself. He was beat up by greasers in a bar, beat up by black kids, by Puerto Rican kids, by junkies in Bronx Park. Unfortunate. Unlucky.

The result: this person has grown less tolerant over time.

Race is more than black or white. Always we simplify, make binary. In this way we limit ourselves, make ourselves dull. Where are our Latin friends, our Lebanese, Pakistani, Korean, Filipino friends? How can we Americans construct a dialogue about race based on black and white? The notion is absurd.

My daughter, just turned nine, thinks it ridiculous to describe skin as "white."

"White skin," she exclaims, "how silly. Look at your arm, my arm. Do you see white?"

Equally she rejects the notion of Black. "Black skin must be called *brown*," she says.

My daughter also believes it's cool to be African American. She got this from TV—Will Smith, Sister Sister, Moesha. And from me.

When I tell her Sicily is a stone's throw from Africa and that in Italy, Sicilians may be considered "black," she dances around the room singing, "I'm African, yeah . . . I'm half Sicilian, yeah, I'm African, Africa and Italy, yeah."

I smile at this response and note that it puts some spin on "politically correct."

I ask my friend E., born and raised in Sicily, to explain again the relationship between Africa, Sicily, and Italy. There are two stories told, she says, to illustrate the relationship between Sicily and Africa. One story is that Sicily was originally part of Africa that somehow moved closer to Italy. The other story is that Sicily was originally attached to Italy, part of the boot, but was "kicked off" for her inferiority. For her small, dark, *terrona* self.

Do I exaggerate my understanding of Italy's attitude toward Sicily, of my father's Baresi people toward my Sicilian mother? If I say out loud to my family, "Sicily is considered 'African,'" or if I suggest a racist attitude toward Sicily, my family goes into spasms of denial. "No," they say. "Absolutely not. You're crazy."

They admit to African influence. The Moors. Those "Arabic-type Africans" as my aunt put it recently.

Always in search of my own Black self, I have the uncanny ability to end up in black neighborhoods. Driving home from Jones Beach one night and looking for a diner, I find one. A black-operated, -staffed and -eaten-at Greek diner. But where were the Greeks? We never found out. Diners, gas stations. My friend K. says it's because I ignore the usual signs that "scare" white people away. But it is also because I am attracted to people of color. The aesthetic—the looks, the talk, the food—is more pleasing and more comfortable for me and my Italian/Sicilian/American self. "White people make good music, too," my aunt chides. But it is not "my" music. When I play Italian folk music, clearly African in nature, the elders say, "That's not Italian." It is, I assure them, it is.

There are times I find myself among white people and the talk turns racist. Subtle or not so subtle. I have developed an effective response. I say loud enough for several people to hear, "My mother is black." The room goes silent. No one says a word.

If I said this among Black folk, the response would be quite different. Talk would be plentiful. Interesting. We would begin to get somewhere. *Punto.*

WE BEGIN WITH FOOD
ROSETTE CAPOTORTO

my grandmothers
arms rolled five pounds of flour
into *cavatelli* on a Sunday morning

labor & love &
the planting of
flowers and fruit

I see your hands she says
the night we meet
a woman who is a contractor by trade
an artist by desire
then we are able to talk

black italian
motherbrothersister

food
taste this

tender long green
bean
kitchen whistle clean

knuckles
nails
skin sun
texture

learned how to cook from my father
the hard way

wooden spoon
red touch of tomato
borough accent specific
as a dime

rooftops come in handy
on hot summer nights

love is thick
                        and painful

fingers forearms fists

slap throw punch
working hands
        sometimes
                        gentle as an egg

mortar brick
        concrete

plaster mixed like dough
        dry white circle
        simple board
        water

toxic she says
I know what I'll die of

callus cramp
muscle

armload of wood
crown of barbed wire
        girl jesus
black and beautiful

rock me in your
arms of stone and steel
let me eat and drink of you

Afterword

DU BOIS, RACE, AND ITALIAN AMERICANS

David R. Roediger

In 1909 Jane Addams described the scholar-activist W.E.B. Du Bois's visit to her celebrated settlement house in Chicago. Addams wrote of the rapt attention paid by the Hull House audience of "Mediterranean immigrants" to the words of Du Bois. They listened with "apparently no consciousness of the race difference which color seems to accentuate so absurdly." And for good reason, according to Addams. Some in the crowd faced physical assaults "simply because they are 'dagoes.'" Addams mused that anti-immigrant hysteria might "be much minimized if we faced our own race problem with courage and intelligence, and these very Mediterranean immigrants might give us valuable help." Southern Europeans, she observed, reflecting on the year Du Bois launched the National Association for the Advancement of Colored People, cared deeply about "the advancement of colored people."[1]

Addams's account doubtless carried a heavy dose of hyperbole, and her remarks concerning race and color were especially curious since Du Bois was doubtless no darker than many of those who heard him. Moreover, Hull House itself tragically joined in the common settlement house practice of accepting Jim Crow, on the theory that bringing in African American residents would cause immigrants to withdraw.[2] Such a policy robbed her projection of pan-"colored" unity of much of its grandeur. Indeed, the position of Du Bois's critics at *The Crusader*, the organ of the African Blood Brotherhood, seemed in some ways a perfect antidote to Addams's romanticizing. In 1920, *The Crusader* unequivocally answered the question that provides a title for the collection of essays you hold:

> Only a super-ass would see even the slightest comparison between the Negro's degraded position in this country and the favored position of the English, the Irish, the Germans, the French, the Italians, and the Russians, all of whom are admittedly within the charmed circle of the dominant race.[3]

Such clarity has merits, both as we think about history and as we frame contemporary debates over affirmative action and reparations. Indeed, on balance I agree with Tom Guglielmo's spirited argument that Italian Americans were "white on arrival" in the eyes of the U.S. state and in other important ways as well.

Surely the recognition of the Italian American as "white," and therefore as legally fit for naturalized citizenship and political participation even before naturalization, set the Italian immigrant apart from Asian immigrants and from African Americans and Mexican Americans. The symbolism mattered, as did the political power. As a historian, Woodrow Wilson could write of Italian immigrants as "sordid and hapless." In the context of presidential campaigning, they became for Wilson "one of the most interesting and admirable elements in our American life."[4] Even on the terrain of naturalization and whiteness, however, complications abound. While Guglielmo's distinction between the certain color status (white) and the uncertain racial position of Italians makes sense of many broad patterns, the courts tried to define whiteness as race in the naturalization cases. Judicial opinions regarded the *color* of southern Europeans as open to question, but their white racial credentials as impeccable. Some expert testimony even placed southern Italians in a "dark white" racial category that resonates with several essays in this volume, especially Louise DeSalvo's wonderful contribution.[5]

Du Bois's own attention to multiplicity and nuance regarding the ways in which Italian Americans were positioned racially offers a chance to reflect more fully in this brief afterword on the astonishing variety of the essays preceding it and on the further questions they raise. Just a year after his Hull House visit, for example, Du Bois reported on an experience Italian Americans and African Americans sometimes shared. He noted the lynching of two Italian Americans and dripped irony in adding, "The Italian government protested, but it was found that they [the victims] were naturalized Americans. The inalienable right of every free American citizen to be lynched without tiresome investigation and penalties is one which the families of the lately deceased doubtless deeply appreciate."[6] In his college days, Du Bois recalled, each lynching "was a scar on my soul." The lynching of Italians in turn-of-the century Louisiana led him first "to conceive the plight of other minority groups." As late as the mid-1920s he would explain astronomical U.S. murder rates partly in light of the nation's record of so long allowing the "killing of Negroes, Italians, Hungarians and Indians . . . with such impunity" as to develop a "habit of killing." In general, Du Bois refused the notion that U.S.-style antiblack racism could mature in Europe. Instead, he held that the United States "trains her immigrants [in the] despising of 'niggers' from the days of their landing, and they carry and send the news back to the submerged classes in the fatherland." The African American novelist Claude McKay applied Du Bois's point specifically to Italian Americans.[7]

Du Bois would again reflect on race and the Italian state in 1935, this time connecting that state to white terror rather than to the investigation of such terror. The invasion of Ethiopia, he maintained in a *Foreign Affairs* essay, clarified the place of Italy internationally. "Economic exploitation based on the excuse of race prejudice is the program of the white world. Italy states it openly and plainly."[8] The important connections of race, violence, diaspora, empire, and national feeling (as both Italian and U.S. citizens) running through so many of this volume's essays are thus far from a present-minded projection of current concerns onto the past. The past often turned on such concerns. Indeed, Du Bois's remarks raise the need for us to consider (as several of the essays do) whether immigrants from Italy were ever white *before* arrival, or at least accustomed to race-thinking *before* arrival.

Similarly, Du Bois charted the labile ways in which Italian Americans were slotted into racial categories, and to some extent how they variously placed themselves. In 1915, for example, he held that "the European and white American working class were practically invited to partake of the new exploitation" structured by race and imperialism. Such white workers, Du Bois added, "were flattered by popular appeals to their inherent superiority to 'Dagoes,' 'Chinks,' 'Japs,' and 'Niggers.'"[9] Nonetheless, Du Bois drew a distinction between new immigrants from southern Europe and African Americans. He wrote of the mobbing of the former as designed to encourage them to join unions, and of the latter to keep them out.[10] Again his insistence, both on being as complicated as real life and on connecting racialization with labor and property, presaged the best of recent critical studies of immigration and race. Du Bois was hardly alone. A contemporary, the economist Robert Foerster, writing in 1919, almost perfectly anticipated Cheryl Harris's recent inquiries into "whiteness as property": "In a country where the distinction between the white man and black man is intended as a distinction in value as well as in ethnography it is no compliment to the Italian to deny him whiteness, yet that actually happens with considerable frequency."[11] At present, it might be added, our knowledge of the specifics of wage discrimination against Italian Americans remains all too impressionistic.

In a remarkable series of articles in the 1920s, Du Bois further elaborated multiple stances on Italian Americans, new immigrants generally, and race. The context was the campaign for immigration restriction, forwarded by eugenicists wielding I.Q. test scores and by a Ku Klux Klan with several million members. The debates culminating in the 1924 restrictions featured racial attacks on the impact of "inferior" (though arguably white) "new immigrants" on the United States. In 1922, Du Bois was testing the waters regarding the possibility of uniting broad forces against "a renewal of the Anglo-Saxon cult: the worship of the Nordic totem, the disfranchisement of Negro, Jew, Irishman, Italian, Hungarian, Asiatic and South Sea Islander."[12] By 1924, he had published *The Gift of Black Folk* in a series of volumes defending immigrant contributions and equality. Issued by the Catholic Church's Knights of Columbus, the book carried a long introduction dissecting proposed restrictions on immigration and particularly coming to the defense of Jews and Italians.[13]

As racist immigration quotas became the law of the land, Du Bois offered a brief commentary that is extremely valuable for our purposes here. "Now everybody knows that a black man is inferior to a white man," he bitterly wrote in 1924. A parenthetical conclusion followed: "(except of course, Jews, Italians and Slavs)."[14] The force of the passage does not lie so much in raising yet again the complex racial location of Italian Americans. More interesting is the studied confusion of the construction of the parenthesis. Du Bois, unequaled in his literary precision even when his sentences stretched to paragraph length, here lets the meaning get fully lost in a brief aside. Is it that new immigrants were categorized outside the sure protections of white supremacy? Or is it that Italian Americans and others didn't know the racial order in the United States and hadn't yet bought into whiteness? Surely the ambiguity suggests that Du Bois intended to make readers grapple with both possibilities. The point matters greatly to many of the best essays in this collection. Those essays remind us that in the United States race has functioned as both category into which laws, employers, realtors, police, teachers, courts, streetcar conductors, and others have placed people and as an identity through which U.S. residents have embraced or contested such categorizations of themselves. (Racism, as legal theorist Patricia Williams argues, is both "aspiration" and "condemnation.")[15] Keeping both sides of this double meaning at play, as Du

Bois did, is central to our tasks. Thus, for example, Tom Guglielmo argues that Italian Americans moved directly into the white category on arrival but (like Luconi) that it was only much later that they mobilized as whites.

The last Du Bois remark to be considered comes from his brutally honest essay in the most celebrated book to come out of the Harlem Renaissance. Closing Alain Locke's *The New Negro* (1925), Du Bois admitted that a broad front against "Nordic" racism had *not* been built. Shrewdly regarding immigration restriction as "born of war," he summarized the many-sided results of the Johnson-Reed Act of 1924. Not only did the law decimate total immigration from Europe, it specifically sought "to exclude the Latins and Jews and openly to insult Asiatics." A confession followed: "Now despite the inhumanity of this, American Negroes are silently elated with this policy." A newly favorable labor market position gave the African American worker "a tremendous sword to wield against the Bourbon South and by means of wholesale migration he is wielding it."[16]

However much we could quarrel over details, the Du Boisian emphasis on asking whether and how political mobilizations might be forged out of the ways in which immigrants from "Latin Europe" experienced both whiteness and racial discrimination seems to me a most useful point of departure. Just as in the present the abstract question of "Who is (or is becoming) white?" gains a grounding when we also ask "What antiracist coalitions can be built?," so, too, for the past. To pose such a question is not to envision only mass movements. As Franklin Rosemont's contribution shows, the generation of individual dreams and of poetry matters. So, too, does Joseph Sciorra's reminiscence teach us that a lonely stand, developed in the contradictory interstices of a racial system, may turn out to be not so lonely after all. The excellent work of Salvatore Salerno and (elsewhere) of Rudy Vecoli demonstrates that the startling critique of racism, whiteness, and even civilization by Italian American radicals did not need to be a majority view to be an important one.[17] But asking organizing questions forces us to be concrete in discussing how race-making experiences differed from group to group and how within groups, class, color, and gender differences made possible at once appreciations of the power of whiteness, illusions regarding its desirability, and creative possibilities of becoming disillusioned with white identity.[18] Confronting the possibilities and impossibilities of solidarities over time forces us, as do the superb contributions to this volume, to ask not only if Italian Americans were white, but when, and in what sense, and in whose eyes, and with what benefits, and at what costs.

Notes

INTRODUCTION

1. See postings on H-ITAM at http://www2.h-net.msu.edu/~itam/ from July 2002 with subject heading "Italians are niggers," especially Dona De Sanctis's comment on behalf of the Order on July 16, 2002.

2. For the writing of W.E.B. Du Bois, see "Afterword" by David Roediger in this anthology. See also James Baldwin, *The Price of the Ticket: Collected Nonfiction, 1948–1985* (New York: St. Martin's Press, 1985), 660–667; Ann Petry, *The Street* (Boston: Houghton Mifflin, 1946), 31–33, 42–43, 53; Ana Castillo, "Dirty Mexican," in *My Father Was a Toltec* (New York: W.W. Norton, 1995), 8; Bernardo Vega, *Memoirs of Bernardo Vega: A Contribution to the History of the Puerto Rican Community in New York* (New York: Monthly Review Press, 1984); Piri Thomas, *Down These Mean Streets* (New York: Vintage Books, 1997).

3. Malcolm X, *Malcolm X on Afro-American History*, enl. and ill. ed. (New York: Pathfinder Press, 1970), 24.

4. Baldwin, *The Price of the Ticket*, 667. My thanks to David Roediger for pointing this excerpt out to me.

5. Baldwin, *The Price of the Ticket*; James Baldwin, "On Being 'White' . . . and Other Lies," *Essence* (April 1984): 90–92, reprinted in David Roediger, ed., *Black on White: Black Writers on What It Means to Be White* (New York: Schocken Books, 1998), 177–180.

6. Among a vast literature see, for example, Cheryl I. Harris, "Whiteness as Property," *Harvard Law Review* 106 (June 1993): 1710–1791; Douglas S. Massey and Nancy A. Denton, *American Apartheid: Segregation and the Making of the Underclass* (Cambridge, MA: Harvard University Press, 1993); Jill Quadagno, *The Color of Welfare: How Racism Undermined the War on Poverty* (New York: Oxford University Press, 1994); Melvin L. Oliver and Thomas M. Shapiro, *Black Wealth, White Wealth: A New Perspective on Racial Inequality* (New York: Routledge, 1997); George Lipsitz, *The Possessive Investment in Whiteness: How White People Profit from Identity Politics* (Philadelphia: Temple University Press, 1998); Grant Meyer, *As Long as They Don't Move Next Door: Segregation and Racial Conflict in American Neighborhoods*

(Lanham, MD: Rowman and Littlefield, 2000); Joe R. Feagin, *Racist America: Roots, Current Realities and Future Reparations* (New York: Routledge, 2001); Eduardo Bonilla-Silva, *White Supremacy and Racism in the Post-Civil Rights Era* (Boulder, CO: Lynne Rienner, 2001); David R. Roediger, *Colored White: Transcending the Racial Past* (Berkeley: University of California Press, 2002); and Manning Marable, *The Great Wells of Democracy: The Meaning of Race in American Life* (New York: BasicCivitas Books, 2002).

7. Innumerable social histories of the United States have made this argument. See, for example, Robin D. G. Kelley, *Freedom Dreams: The Black Radical Imagination* (Boston: Beacon, 2002); Alan Dawley, *Struggles for Justice: Social Responsibility and the Liberal State* (Cambridge, MA: Harvard University Press, 1991); Howard Zinn, *A People's History of the United States: 1492 to Present*, rev. ed. (New York: Harper Perennial, 2001); Edmund S. Morgan, *American Slavery, American Freedom: The Ordeal of Colonial Virginia,* reissue ed. (New York: W.W. Norton, 1995); and W.E.B. Du Bois, *Black Reconstruction in America, 1860–1880* (1935; rep. New York: Simon & Schuster, 1995).

8. Roediger, *Black on White*, 21–22.

9. Baldwin, "On Being 'White,'" 178.

10. Ibid., 180.

11. Audre Lorde, *Sister Outsider: Essays and Speeches* (Freedom, CA: Crossing Press, 1984), 123, 113.

12. bell hooks, *Black Looks: Race and Representation* (Boston: South End Press, 1992).

13. Robert Orsi, "The Religious Boundaries of an Inbetween People: Street *Feste* and the Problem of the Dark-Skinned 'Other' in Italian Harlem," *American Quarterly* 44 (September 1992).

14. Jonathan Rieder, *Canarsie: The Jews and Italians of Brooklyn Against Liberalism* (Cambridge: Harvard University Press, 1985), 66.

15. Micaela di Leonardo, *The Varieties of Ethnic Experience: Kinship, Class, and Gender Among California Italian-Americans* (Ithaca, NY: Cornell University Press, 1984). See also her "White Ethnicities, Identity Politics, and Baby Bear's Chair," *Social Text* 41 (1994): 165–191.

16. Du Bois, *Black Reconstruction*; Alexander Saxton, *The Rise and Fall of the White Republic: Class Politics and Mass Culture in Nineteenth-Century America* (New York: Verso, 1990); David R. Roediger, *The Wages of Whiteness: Race and the Making of the American Working Class* (New York: Verso, 1991); Robin D. G. Kelley, *Yo' Mama's Disfunktional: Fighting the Culture Wars in America* (Boston: Beacon, 1997); Tera Hunter, "*To 'Joy My Freedom": Southern Black Women's Lives and Labors After the Civil War* (Cambridge, MA: Harvard University Press, 1997); Dana Frank, "White Working-Class Women and the Race Question," *International Labor and Working Class History* 54 (Fall 1998): 80–102; Lipsitz, *The Possessive Investment*; Dolores Janiewski, *Sisterhood Denied: Race, Class and Gender in a New South Community* (Philadelphia: Temple University Press, 1985); Bruce Nelson, *Divided We Stand: American Workers and the Struggle for Black Equality* (Princeton, NJ: Princeton University Press, 2001); Noel Ignatiev, *How the Irish Became White* (New York: Routledge, 1995); Theodore W. Allen, *The Invention of the White Race*, 2 vols. (New York: Verso, 1994, 1997).

17. See our posting from April 1, 1997, at http://www2.h-net.msu.edu/~itam.

18. Quotes taken from Samuel Freedman, "In Howard Beach, Pride and Fear in a 'Paradise,'" *New York Times,* Dec. 23, 1986, B4, and Dec. 29, 1986, B3. Cited in Patricia J. Williams, *The Alchemy of Race and Rights: Diary of a Law Professor* (Cambridge, MA: Harvard University Press, 1991), 58, 66.

19. My analysis benefits greatly from Williams, *The Alchemy*, 55–79. See also John DeSantis, *For the Color of His Skin: The Murder of Yusuf Hawkins and the Trial of Bensonhurst* (New York: Pharos Books, 1991).

20. For discussion of this see Jerome Krase, "Bensonhurst, Brooklyn: Italian American Victimizers and Victims," *Voices in Italian Americana* 5:2 (1994): 13–53. For focus on defamation of Italian Americans see the following documents from the Order of the Sons of Italy: "Bensonhurst: CSJ Acts Swiftly," *Goldon Lion* (Sept.–Oct. 1989); "Bensonhurst Tragedy Unleashes Wave of Ethnic Vilification," *Capital Notes* 2:4 (Oct. 1989); "The Tragedy of Bensonhurst: CSJ Responds to Italian Bashing," *OSIA News* (Nov. 1989); Dominic Massaro, "Bensonhurst: An Italian American Perspective," *Capital Notes* 2:4 (Oct. 1989) and *L'Italo-Americano*, (Oct. 19, 1989). See also, Danilo Romeo, "L'Invenzione dell'Etnicità negli Italoamericani della Terza e Quarta Generazione" (Laurea thesis, Università degli Studi di Milano, 2000).

21. See Anti-Defamation League's website, http://www.adl.org/backgrounders/american_knights_kkk.asp.

22. In addition to works previously cited by these authors, see Toni Morrison, *Playing in the Dark: Whiteness and the Literary Imagination* (Cambridge, MA: Harvard University Press, 1990); Cherríe Moraga, *The Last Generation: Prose & Poetry* (Boston: South End Press, 1993); Ronald Takaki, *Iron Cages: Race and Culture in Nineteenth-Century America* (Seattle: University of Washington Press, 1979); Ian Haney Lopez, *White by Law: The Legal Construction of Race* (New York: New York University Press, 1996); Matthew Jacobson, *Whiteness of a Different Color: European Immigrants and the Alchemy of Race* (Cambridge, MA: Harvard University Press, 1998); Tomás Almaguer, *Racial Fault Lines: The Historical Origins of White Supremacy in California* (Berkeley: University of California Press, 1994); Grace Elizabeth Hale, *Making Whiteness: The Culture of Segregation in the South, 1890–1940* (New York: Vintage, 1999); Arnoldo De León, *They Called Them Greasers: Anglo Attitudes Towards Mexicans in Texas, 1821–1900* (Austin: Univeristy of Texas Press, 1983); Michael Rogin, *Blackface, White Noise: Jewish Immigrants in the Hollywood Melting Pot* (Berkeley: University of California Press, 1996); Karen Brodkin, *How Jews Became White Folks and What That Says About Race in America* (New Brunswick, NJ: Rutgers University Press, 1998). See also Maurice Berger, *White Lies: Race and the Myths of Whiteness* (New York: Farrar, Straus & Giroux, 1999); Joe L. Kincheloe, Shirley R. Steinberg, Nelson M. Rodriguez, and Ronald E. Chennault, eds., *White Reign: Deploying Whiteness in America* (New York: St. Martin's Press, 1998); Richard Dyer, *White* (New York: Routledge, 1997); Alastair Bonnett, *White Identities: Historical and International Perspectives* (Harlow, UK: Prentice-Hall, 2000); Ghasson Hage, *White Nation: Fantasies of White Supremacy* (New York: Routledge, 2000); and Thandeka, *Learning to Be White: Money, Race, and God in America* (New York: Continuum, 1999).

23. This question was also posed in an article on Italians and race by Rudolph J. Vecoli, "Are Italians Just White Folks?" *Italian Americana* (Summer 1995): 149–165.

24. Antonio Gramsci, *The Southern Question*, translated, annotated, and with an introduction by Pasquale Verdicchio (West Lafayette, IN: Bordighera, 1995). See also Pasquale Verdicchio, *Bound by Distance: Rethinking Nationalism Through the Italian Diaspora* (Teaneck, NJ: Farleigh Dickinson University Press 1997).

25. Gabriella Gribaudi, "Images of the South: The *Mezzogiorno* as Seen by Insiders and Outsiders," in Robert Lumley and Jonathan Morris, eds., *The New History of the Italian South: The Mezzogiorno Revisited* (Exeter: UK: Exeter Press, 1997), 87; Verdicchio, *Bound by Distance*, 22.

26. John Dickie, "Imagined Italies," and Garbriella Gribaudi, "Images of the South," in David Forgacs and Robert Lumley, eds., *Italian Cultural Studies: An Introduction* (Oxford and New York: Oxford University Press, 1996); Jane Schneider, ed., *Italy's "Southern Question":*

Orientalism in One Country (Oxford: Berg Press, 1998); John Dickie, *Darkest Italy: The Nation and Stereotypes of the Mezzogiorno, 1860–1900* (New York: St. Martin's Press, 1999); Robert Lumley and Jonathan Morris, eds., *The New History of the Italian South*; Gramsci, *The Southern Question.*

27. Donna R. Gabaccia, *Italy's Many Diasporas* (London: UCL Press, 2000), 52.

28. Alfredo Nicefero, *L'Italia barbara contemporanea: studi ed appunti* (Milan and Palermo: Remo Sandron, 1989); Cesare Lambroso, *L'Uomo bianco e l'uomo di colore: lettere sull'origine e la varietà delle razze umane* (Padua: F. Sacchetto, 1871); Enrico Ferri, *Studi sulla criminalità* (Turin: Bocca, 1901); Giuseppe Sergi, *Ari e italici* (Turin: Bocca, 1898).

29. Anne McClintock, *Imperial Leather: Race, Gender, and Sexuality in the Colonial Conquest* (New York: Routledge, 1995), 5.

30. See, for example, Mary Gibson, *Prostitution and the State in Italy, 1860–1915* (Columbus: Ohio State University Press, 2000).

31. Matthew Frye Jacobson, *Whiteness of a Different Color: European Immigrants and the Alchemy of Race* (Cambridge, MA: Harvard University Press, 1998), 57.

32. David Roediger and James Barrett, "Inbetween Peoples: Race, Nationality, and the 'New-Immigrant' Working Class," in Roediger, *Colored White* (Berkeley: University of California Press, 2002), 142–144. See also Roediger, "*Guineas*, *Wiggers*, and the Dramas of Racialized Culture," *American Literary History* 7 (Winter 1995): 654–668.

33. Paraphrased from early dissertation prospectus by Thomas A. Guglielmo. For detailed discussion of this history, see his essay in this collection and his, *White on Arrival: Italians, Race, Color, and Power in Chicago, 1890–1945* (New York: Oxford University Press, 2003).

34. Lipsitz, *The Possessive Investment*, 5. For an excellent study of the effects of these historical economic and demographic shifts on Italian Americans, see Rieder, *Canarsie.*

35. Guglielmo, *White on Arrival.*

CHAPTER 1

1. Quoted in Matthew Frye Jacobson, *Whiteness of a Different Color: European Immigrants and the Alchemy of Race* (Cambridge, MA: Harvard University Press, 1998), 56.

2. And, according to the latest research on race, it appears that my parents were correct. See Natalie Angier, "Do Races Differ? Not Really, Genes Show," *New York Times,* Aug. 22, 2000, F1, F6.

3. David A. J. Richards, *Italian American: The Racializing of an Ethnic Identity* (New York: New York University Press, 1999), 5.

4. Richard Gambino, *Blood of My Blood: The Dilemma of the Italian-Americans* (Toronto: Guernica Editions, 1996), 42–76.

5. See Dominic T. Ciolli, "The 'Wop' in the Track Gang," *Immigrants in America Review* (July 1916).

6. Gambino, *Blood of My Blood*, 316.

7. Jacobson, *Whiteness of a Different Color* 56.

8. Ian F. Haney Lopez, *White by Law: The Legal Construction of Race* (New York: New York University Press, 1996), xiii, 82.

9. Gambino, *Blood of My Blood*, 313–316.

10. The wording of the definitions is mine and is very freely adapted from the *Oxford English Dictionary.*

11. Quoted in Jacobson, *Whiteness of a Different Color*, 36.

12. This, according to Edvige Giunta, is a common term that northern Italians use for people from the South. That people in the United States learned contempt for southern Italians from northern Italians is discussed in Gambino (85). For the political situation in the South at the time of the emigration, see David A. J. Richards, "Promise and Betrayal," in *Italian American*, 76–115.

13. See Haney Lopez, *White by Law*, 14.

14. See Jacobson, *Whiteness of a Different Color*, 43.

15. Ibid., 19.

16. See Haney Lopez, *White by Law*, 16.

17. See Dorothy Hoobler and Thomas Hoobler, *The Italian American Family Album* (New York: Oxford University Press, 1994); Michael A. Musmanno, *The Story of the Italians in America* (New York: Doubleday, 1965).

18. See Jacobson, *Whiteness of a Different Color*, 33.

19. "[I]n denying the petition of Albert Henry Young, an immigrant of half German and half Japanese descent (1912), a Federal Court in Washington state offered that 'Caucasians' referred to 'all European races around the Mediterranean Sea, whether they are considered 'fair whites' or 'dark whites.' . . ." The case is quoted in Jacobson, *Whiteness of a Different Color*, 243.

20. Ibid., 57.

CHAPTER 2

Those who wish to see a more extensive treatment and documentation of the subjects in this chapter should consult my book, *White on Arrival: Italians, Race, Color, and Power in Chicago, 1890–1945* (New York: Oxford University Press, 2003).

1. Leonard Giuliano, Jan. 2, 1980, Box 5, Folder 30, 90; Constance Muzzacavallo, June 12, 1980, Box 16, Folder 102, 54; Joseph Loguidice, July 21, 1980, Box 15, Folder 96, 18; all in the Italian-American Collection, University of Illinois at Chicago Special Collections (hereafter UIC). For evidence that these views extended beyond Chicago, see Richard Gambino, *Blood of My Blood* (Garden City, NY: Doubleday, 1974), 336–337; Robert Orsi, "The Religious Boundaries of an Inbetween People: Street *Feste* and the Problem of the Dark-Skinned 'Other' in Italian Harlem, 1920–1990," *American Quarterly* 44 (Sept. 1992): 319; Jonathan Rieder, *Canarsie: The Jews and Italians of Brooklyn Against Liberalism* (Cambridge, MA: Harvard University Press, 1985).

2. Lillian B. Rubin, *Families on the Fault Line: America's Working Class Speaks About the Family, the Economy, Race, and Ethnicity* (New York: HarperCollins, 1994), 187–188.

3. Eduardo Bonilla-Silva, "Rethinking Racism: Toward a Structural Interpretation," *American Sociological Review* 62 (June 1996): 469–470.

4. Richard Jenkins, *Rethinking Ethnicity: Arguments and Explorations* (London: Sage, 1997), 81, 74–75.

5. Leonard Covello, *The Social Background of the Italo-American School Child* (Leiden: E.J. Brill, 1967), 25.

6. John Dickie, "Stereotypes of the Italian South 1860–1900," 135; Gabriella Gribaudi, "Images of the South: The *Mezzogiorno* as Seen by Insiders and Outsiders," 96; both in Robert Lumley and Jonathan Morris, eds., *The New History of the Italian South: The Mezzogiorno Revisited* (Exeter, UK: Exeter Press, 1997).

7. Reports of the U.S. Immigration Commission, *Dictionary of Races and Peoples* (Washington, DC: U.S. Government Printing Office, 1911), 81, 82.

8. Edward A. Ross, *The Old World in the New: The Significance of Past and Present*

Immigration to the American People (New York: Century, 1914), 95–119; "To Keep Out Southern Italians," *The World's Work* 28 (Aug. 1914): 378–379.

9.*Chicago Record Herald,* June 14, 1910, 2; *Chicago Record Herald*, Oct. 30, 1907, 1; Edward F. Haas, "Guns, Goats, and Italians: The Tallulah Lynching of 1899," *North Louisiana Historical Association Journal* 13 (1982): 50; George E. Pozzetta, "Foreigners in Florida: A Study of Immigration Promotion, 1865–1910," *Florida Historical Quarterly* 53 (Oct. 1974): 175; Willard B. Gatewood, Jr., "Strangers and the Southern Eden: The South and Immigration, 1900–1920," in Jerrel H. Shofner and Linda V. Ellsworth, eds., *Ethnic Minorities in Gulf Coast Society* (Pensacola, FL: Gulf Coast History and Humanities Conference, 1979), 8–10; Charles Shanabruch, "The Louisiana Immigration Movement, 1891–1907: An Analysis of Efforts, Attitudes, and Opportunities," *Louisiana History* 18 (Spring 1977): 217; Rowland T. Berthoff, "Southern Attitudes Toward Immigration, 1865–1914," *Journal of Southern History* 17 (Aug. 1951): 328–360; David D. Mays, "'Sivilizing Moustache Pete': Changing Attitudes Towards Italians in New Orleans, 1890–1918," in Jerrel H. Shofner and Linda V. Ellsworth, eds., *Ethnic Minorities* (Pensacola, FL: Gulf Coast History and Humanities Conference, 1979), 95, 103; Anthony V. Margavio, "The Reaction of the Press to the Italian-American in New Orleans, 1880 to 1920," *Italian Americana* 4 (Fall/Winter 1978): 72–83.

10. *Chicago Tribune*, Aug. 19, 1910, 9.

11. Jerre Mangione, *Monte Allegro: A Memoir of Italian American Life* (1942; New York: Columbia University Press, 1981), 65; Ray Stannard Baker, *Following the Color Line: American Negro Citizenship in the Progressive Era* (New York: Harper & Row, 1964), 268; Gatewood, "Strangers and the Southern Eden," 5–12; Pozzetta, "Foreigners in Florida," 175; Dino Cinel, *From Italy to San Francisco: The Immigrant Experience* (Stanford, CA: Stanford University Press, 1982), 115, 138, 282 nn. 63–64; Orsi, "The Religious Boundaries of an Inbetween People," 313–347; Rudolph J. Vecoli, "Prelates and Peasants: Italian Immigrants and the Catholic Church," *Journal of Social History* 2 (1969): 230, 233, 238, 250, 263 n.160; Samuel L. Baily, *Immigrants in the Lands of Promise: Italians in Buenos Aires and New York City, 1870–1914* (Ithaca, NY: Cornell University Press, 1999), 83–89; Gary R. Mormino and George E. Pozzetta, *The Immigrant World of Ybor City: Italians and Their Latin Neighbors, 1885–1985* (Urbana: University of Illinois Press, 1987), 239–242.

12. Mangione, *Monte Allegro*, 65; Alexander DeConde, *Half Bitter, Half Sweet: An Excursion into Italian American History* (New York: Scribner's, 1971), 111; Jerre Mangione and Ben Morreale, *La Storia: Five Centuries of the Italian American Experience* (New York: HarperCollins, 1992), 153, 162–163; Robert Orsi, *The Madonna of 115th St.: Faith and Community in Italian Harlem, 1880–1950* (New Haven, CT: Yale University Press, 1985), 16; Virginia Yans-McGlaughlin, *Family and Community: Italian Immigrants in Buffalo, 1880–1930* (Ithaca, NY: Cornell University Press, 1971), 112–117.

13. For quotations, see *Skandinaven*, May 8, 1900, Chicago Foreign Language Press Survey (hereafter CFLPS), Reel 63, Immigration History Research Center (hereafter IHRC), University of Minnesota Minneapolis, MN; Harvey Warren Zorbaugh, *The Gold Coast and the Slum* (Chicago: University of Chicago Press, 1929), 160.

14. *L'Italia*, Oct. 15, 1904, 1; *Chicago Tribune*, June 11, 1915, 13. For further evidence of lynchings of Italians, see *L'Italia*, Dec. 21, 1907, 1; *L'Italia*, Sept. 24, 1910, 1; and the following secondary sources: John V. Baiamonte, Jr., "'Who Killa de Chief' Revisited: The Hennessey [*sic*] Assasination and Its Aftermath, 1890–1891," *Louisiana History* 33 (Spring 1992): 117–146; Barbara Botein, "The Hennessy Case: An Episode in Anti-Italian Nativism," *Louisiana History* 20 (Summer 1979): 261–279; Haas, "Guns, Goats, and Italians," 45–58; Robert P. Ingalls, "Lynching and Establishment Violence in Tampa,

1858–1935," *Journal of Southern History* 53 (Nov. 1987): 626–628; John S. Kendall, "Who Killa de Chief," *Louisiana Historical Quarterly* 22 (1939): 492–530; Marco Rimanelli and Sheryl L. Postman, eds., *The 1891 New Orleans Lynching and U.S.-Italian Relations: A Look Back* (New York: Peter Lang, 1992); Matthew Frye Jacobson, *Whiteness of a Different Color: European Immigrants and the Alchemy of Race* (Cambridge, MA: Harvard University Press, 1998), 56–62. On African Americans being the prime targets of lynching violence, see W. Fitzhugh Brundage, ed., *Under Sentence of Death: Lynching in the South* (Chapel Hill: University of North Carolina Press, 1997), 2; and *L'Italia*, Jan. 10, 1915, 7.

15. House Committee on Immigration and Naturalization, *Hearings Relative to the Further Restriction of Immigration*, 62d Cong., 2d Sess. (Washington, DC: U.S. Government Printing Office, 1912), 77–78; William M. Leiserson, *Adjusting Immigrant and Industry* (New York: Harpers and Brothers, 1924), 71–72; Charles B. Barnes, *The Longshoremen* (New York: Survey Associates, 1915), 8; John Higham, *Strangers in the Land: Patterns of American Nativism, 1860–1925*, 2nd ed. (New Brunswick, NJ: Rutgers University Press, 1988), 66. See also Rueben Gold Thwaites, *Afloat on the Ohio: An Historical Pilgrimage of a Thousand Miles in a Skiff, from Redstone to Cairo* (New York: Doubleday and McClure, 1900), 69; Rudolph J. Vecoli, "Chicago's Italians Prior to World War I: A Study of Their Social and Economic Adjustment" (Ph.D. diss., University of Wisconsin, 1963), 320, 322, 330–331, 419; Gunther Peck, *Reinventing Free Labor: Padrone and Immigrant Workers in the North American West, 1880–1930* (Cambridge, Eng: Cambridge: Harvard University Press, 2000), 169.

16. George E. Cunningham, "The Italian, a Hindrance to White Solidarity, 1890–1898," *Journal of Negro History* 50 (July 1965): 34; Paul Campisi, "The Adjustment of the Italian Americans to the War Crisis" (M.A. thesis, University of Chicago, 1942), 83. See also John V. Baiamonte, Jr., *Spirit of Vengeance: Nativism and Louisiana Justice, 1921–1924* (Baton Rouge: Louisiana State University Press, 1986), 15; Jean Scarpaci, "A Tale of Selective Accommodation: Sicilians and Native Whites in Louisiana," *Journal of Ethnic Studies* 5 (Fall 1977): 38–39, 44; Hodding Carter, *Southern Legacy* (Baton Rouge: Louisiana State University Press, 1950), 105–112; Robert L. Brandfon, "The End of Immigration to the Cotton Fields," *Mississippi Valley Historical Review* 50 (Mar. 1964): 610; Mormino and Pozzetta, *The Immigrant World of Ybor City*, 241.

17. By "sustained" I mean color challenges that are not isolated incidents, but occur over a prolonged period of time. By "systematic" I mean color challenges that become entrenched in institutions such as the U.S. census, law, residential patterns, restrictive covenants, hiring policies, union membership rules, dating and marriage customs, and so forth.

18. On the Near North Side riot, see *L'Italia*, Oct. 22, 1912, 3. Asians, like African Americans, also were quite restricted in their marriage options. See Ifu Chen, "Chinatown of Chicago," paper for Sociology 466, 1932, Ernest W. Burgess Papers, Box 128, Folder 8, University of Chicago Special Collections (hereafter UC), 14.

19. Thomas Lee Philpott, *The Slum and the Ghetto: Immigrants, Blacks, and Reformers in Chicago, 1880–1930*, 2nd ed. (Belmont, CA: Wadsworth, 1991), 116–182; Allan Spear, *Black Chicago: The Making of a Negro Ghetto, 1890–1920* (Chicago: University of Chicago Press, 1967), 21–33; James R. Grossman, *Land of Hope: Chicago, Black Southerners, and the Great Migration* (Chicago: University of Chicago Press, 1989); Homer Hoyt, *One Hundred Years of Land Values in Chicago* (Chicago: University of Chicago Press, 1933), 315–319; William M. Tuttle, Jr., *Race Riot: Chicago in the Red Summer of 1919* (New York: Atheneum, 1970), 159–176; Edith Abbott, *The Tenements of Chicago, 1908–1935* (Chicago: University of Chicago Press, 1936), 117–126.

20. On discrimination against Italians by employers, unions, and fellow workers, see Vecoli, "Chicago's Italians Prior to World War I," 342–345, 350, 360, 419–424; *La Parola dei Socialisti*, Jan. 4, 1913, CFLPS, Chicago Historical Society (hereafter CHS). On the far more widespread discrimination against African Americans, see Philpott, *The Slum and the Ghetto*, 119; Spear, *Black Chicago*, 30–41; Grossman, *Land of Hope*, chs. 7–8; Tuttle, *Race Riot*, 108–130; interview with Frank Mead, 1970, Box 25, Roosevelt University Labor Oral History Project, Roosevelt University, Chicago, 44–45.

21. Spear, *Black Chicago*, 42–49; Grossman, *Land of Hope*, 127–128. See also *L'Italia*, Sept. 10, 1910, 2, on some Chicagoans' resistance to one Japanese and two Chinese students attending a local high school. *L'Italia*, Apr. 10, 1909, CFLPS, CHS, talks about a theater owner, Louis Lang, who was on trial for refusing to admit several Italians into his "Nickel Show."

22. I have not discussed Mexicans here because they did not start arriving in Chicago in large numbers until World War I.

23. Gordon H. Shufelt, "Strangers in the Middle Land: Italian Immigrants and Race Relations in Baltimore, 1890–1920" (Ph.D. diss., American University, 1998), 208, 179. On the "Great Fire of 1904," see pp. 127–149; on the first disfranchisement campaign of 1905, see pp. 150–183; on the second disfranchisement campaign of 1910, see pp. 184–209; on the housing segregation ordinances of 1910–1913, see pp. 210–232. See also Shufelt's essay "Jim Crow Among Strangers: The Growth of Baltimore's Little Italy and Maryland's Disfranchisement Campaigns," *Journal of American Ethnic History* 19 (Summer 2000): 49–78.

24. On anti-Italian violence, see Andrew F. Rolle, *The Immigrant Upraised: Italian Adventurers and Colonists in an Expanding America* (Norman: University of Oklahoma Press, 1968), 174–178; Alexander DeConde, *Half Bitter, Half Sweet*, 125; Luciano J. Iorizzo and Salvatore Mondello, *The Italian-Americans* (New York: Twayne, 1971), 67; and Patrick J. Gallo, *Old Bread New Wine: A Portrait of the Italian-Americans* (Chicago: Nelson Hall, 1981), 113. On discrimination in San Francisco, see Cinel, *From Italy to San Francisco*, 115, 138, 282 nn. 63–64; on the "bully" quotation, see Mangione and Morreale, *La Storia*, 192; on the Arizona copper companies, see Linda Gordon, *The Great Arizona Orphan Abduction* (Cambridge, MA: Harvard University Press, 1999), 102.

25. For general histories of the West's particular color structure, see Tomás Almaguer, *Racial Fault Lines: The Historical Origins of White Supremacy in California* (Berkeley: University of California Press, 1994); A. Yvette Hugginie, "'Mexican Labour' in a 'White Man's Town': Racialism, Imperialism and Industrialization in the Making of Arizona, 1840–1905," in Peter Alexander and Rick Halpern, eds., *Racializing Class, Classifying Race: Labour and Difference in Britain, the USA, and Africa* (New York: St. Martin's Press, 2000), 32–56; Gordon, *The Great Arizona Orphan Abduction*, esp. 99–100, 175–195, 305; Richard White, "Race Relations in the American West," *American Quarterly* 38 (1986): 396–416; Peggy Pascoe, "Race, Gender, and the Privileges of Property: On the Significance of Miscegenation Law in the U.S. West," in Valerie J. Matsumoto and Blake Allmendinger, eds., *Over the Edge: Remapping the American West* (Berkeley: University of California Press, 1999), 215–230.

26. On the occasional categorizing of Italians as nonwhite, see note 15 above. On the South's color structure, there is, of course, a voluminous literature. For some general works, see C. Vann Woodward, *The Strange Career of Jim Crow*, 3rd rev. ed. (New York: Oxford University Press, 1974); Joel Williamson, *The Crucible of Race: Black/White Relations in the American South Since Emancipation* (New York: Oxford University Press, 1984); Howard N. Rabinowitz, *Race Relations in the Urban South, 1865–1890* (New York:

Oxford University Press, 1978); John Whitson Cell, *The Highest Stage of White Supremacy: The Origins of Segregation in South Africa and the American South* (Cambridge: Cambridge University Press, 1982); Grace Elizabeth Hale, *Making Whiteness: The Culture of Segregation in the South, 1890–1940* (New York: Pantheon, 1998); Leon F. Litwack, *Trouble in Mind : Black Southerners in the Age of Jim Crow* (New York: Knopf, 1998); Glenda Elizabeth Gilmore, *Gender and Jim Crow: Women and the Politics of White Supremacy in North Carolina, 1896–1920* (Chapel Hill: University of North Carolina Press, 1996). On miscegenation laws, see Peggy Pascoe, "Miscegenation Law, Court Cases, and Ideologies of 'Race' in Twentieth-Century America," *Journal of American History* 83 (June 1996): 44–69; Rachel F. Moran, *Interracial Intimacy: The Regulation of Race and Romance* (Chicago: University of Chicago Press, 2001); Randall Kennedy, *Interracial Intimacies: Sex, Marriages, Identity, and Adoption* (New York: Pantheon, 2003).

27. J. Vincenza Scarpaci, "Labor for Louisiana's Sugar Cane Fields: An Experiment in Immigrant Recruitment," *Italian Americana* 7 (Fall/Winter 1981): 27; Gatewood, "Strangers and the Southern Eden," p. 4. For more evidence on these points, see Berthoff, "Southern Attitudes Toward Immigration, 1865–1914," 334, 356–357; Botein, "The Hennessy Case," 262; Walter L. Fleming, "Immigration to the Southern States," *Political Science Quarterly* 20 (June 1905): 276–297; Emily Fogg Meade, "Italian Immigration into the South," *South Atlantic Quarterly* 4 (July 1905): 217–223; Alfred H. Stone, "The Italian Cotton Grower: The Negro's Problem," *South Atlantic Quarterly* 4 (January 1905): 42–47; Alfred Holt Stone, *Studies in the American Race Problem* (New York: Doubleday, Page, 1908); *Daily Picayune* (New Orleans), Mar. 13, 1898, 3.

28. U.S. Immigration Commission, *Reports of the U.S. Immigration Commission*, vol. 21, *Immigrants in Industries* (Washington, DC: U.S. Government Printing Office, 1911), pt. 24, 242, 295, 305, 353, 367–368. On the rise of anti-immigrant sentiment in the South, see Berthoff, "Southern Attitudes Toward Immigration," 343–360; Gatewood, "Strangers and the Southern Eden"; Higham, *Strangers in the Land*, 164, 166–171, 191, 288.

29. *Daily Picayune* (New Orleans), Mar. 7, 1898, 7; the *Memphis Commercial Appeal* quotation is from Gatewood, "Strangers and the Southern Eden," 9; Meade, "Italian Immigration into the South," 217.

30. James W. Loewen, *The Mississippi Chinese: Between Black and White* (Cambridge, MA: Harvard University Press, 1971), see esp. 1–2, 58–83.

31. U.S. Immigration Commission, *Dictionary of Races and Peoples*, 3.

32. Eliot Lord, *The Italian in America* (New York: B.F. Buck, 1905), 20, 232.

33. For naturalization applications of Italians, see RG 21, National Archives Great Lakes Branch, Chicago, IL. See also Ian Haney López, *White by Law: The Legal Construction of Race* (New York: New York University Press, 1996); Jacobson, *Whiteness of a Different Color*, 223–245.

34. For general information on changes in race/color census categories and related shifts in how enumerators were instructed to fill in such categories, see *200 Years of United States Census Taking: Population and Housing Questions, 1790–1990*, prepared by Frederick G. Bohme and Walter C. Odom (Washington, DC: U.S. Government Printing Office, 1989), 26, 30, 36, 41, 50, 60, 69. On the power of censuses in general to construct social categories, see Benedict Anderson, *Imagined Communities: Reflections on the Origin and Spread of Nationalism*, rev. ed. (London: Verso, 1991), 163–170, 184–185.

35. *Chicago Daily News*, Feb. 9, 1921, 7.

36. Lothrop Stoddard, *The Rising Tide of Color against White World Supremacy* (New York: Scribner's, 1920), 267. On the Immigration Act of 1924, see Desmond S. King, *Making Americans: Immigration, Race, and the Origins of the Diverse Democracy* (Cambridge,

MA: Harvard University Press, 2000); Mae Ngai, "The Architecture of Race in American Immigration Law: A Reexamination of the Immigration Act of 1924," *Journal of American History* 86 (June 1999): 67–92. The Japanese were singled out in 1924 only because the 1917 Immigration Act had already excluded virtually all other Asians from immigrating to the United States.

37. See especially George Lipsitz, *The Possessive Investment in Whiteness: How White People Profit from Identity Politics* (Philadelphia: Temple University Press, 1998), ch. 1.

38. Jacobson, *Whiteness of a Different Color*, 8.

CHAPTER 3

1. Donald Horowitz, "Immigration and Group Relations in France and America," in Donald Horowitz and Gérard Noiriel, eds., *Immigrants in Two Democracies: French and American Experience* (New York: New York University Press, 1992), p. 7.

2. "Week in Review," *New York Times*, May 24, 1998, p. 8.

3. On the contrast among folk, unitary, republican, and plural or multicultural national concepts, see Stephen Castles and Mark J. Miller, *The Age of Migration: International Population Movements in the Modern World* (New York: Guilford Press, 1993), 223–228.

4. David Hollinger, *Postethnic America: Beyond Multiculturalism* (New York: Basic Books, 1995), 3.

5. Werner Sollors, *Beyond Ethnicity: Consent and Descent in American Culture* (New York: Oxford University Press, 1986); Matthew Frye Jacobson, *Whiteness of a Different Color: European Immigrants and the Alchemy of Race* (Cambridge, MA: Harvard University Press, 1998).

6. Donna R. Gabaccia, *Italy's Many Diasporas* (London: University College of London, Seattle: University of Washington Press, 2000).

7. Gianfausto Rosoli, ed., *Un secolo di emigrazione Italiana, 1876–1976* (Rome: Centro Studi Emigrazione, 1978).

8. Gianfausto Rosoli, "Le popolazioni di origine italiana oltreoceano," *Altreitalie* 2 (1989): 3–35; Piero Gastaldo, "Gli americani di origine italiana: Chi sono, dove sono, quanti sono," in *Euroamericani* (Turin: Fondazione Giovanni Agnelli, 1987), 149–199.

9. For a general treatment of the early racial theorists, see Thomas F. Gossett, *Race: The History of an Idea in America* (New York: Schocken Books, 1973), ch. 3.

10. Still useful for the United States is Richard Hofstadter, *Social Darwinism in American Thought*, rev. ed. (New York: Braziller, 1959). For Italy, see Giuliano Pancaldi, *Darwin in Italia; Impresa scientifica e frontiere culturali* (Bologna: Il Mulino, 1983). For Argentina, and Latin America more generally, see Thomas F. Glick, ed., *The Comparative Reception of Darwinism* (Chicago: University of Chicago Press, 1988); Glick, *Darwin y el Darwinismo: En el Uruguay y en América Latina* (Montevideo, Uruguay: Universidad de la Republica, Facultad de Humanidades y Ciencias, Departamento de Publicaciones, 1989).

11. Donna R. Gabaccia and Fraser M. Ottanelli, eds., *Italian Workers of the World: Labor Migration and the Formation of Multi-Ethnic States* (Urbana: University of Illinois Press, 2001).

12. On Herder's thought on the origins of nations and national cultures in the natural world, see Hugh Barr Nisbet, "Die Naturgeschichte und naturwissenschaftliche Modelle in Herders *Ideen zur Philosophie der Geschichte der Menschheit*," in Regine Otto, ed., *Nationen und Kulturen: Zum 250. Geburtstag Johann Gottfried Herders* (Würzburg: Königshausen & Neumann, 1996), 153–164.

13. See Benedict Anderson, *Imagined Communities: Reflection on the Origin and Spread of Nationalism* (London: Verso Press, 1983; rev. ed. 1991).

14. On Lamarck, see Madeline Barthelemy-Madaule, *Lamarck, the Mythical Precursor: A Study of the Relations Between Science and Ideology* (Cambridge, MA: MIT Press, 1982).

15. Maurizio Viroli, *For Love of Country: An Essay on Patriotism and Nationalism* (Oxford: Clarendon Press, 1997).

16. Francis Jennings, *The Invasion of America: Indians, Colonialism, and the Cant of Conquest* (New York: W.W. Norton, 1976), ch. 4.

17. Winthrop D. Jordan, *White Over Black: American Attitudes Toward the Negro, 1550–1812* (New York: W.W. Norton, 1977; 1st ed. 1968), 11–28; Jennings, *Invasion of America*, 56–57; Roy Harvey Pearce, *The Savages of America; A Study of the Indian and the Idea of Civilization* (Baltimore: Johns Hopkins University Press, 1965), 55.

18. Ronald Sanders, *Lost Tribes and Promised Lands: The Origins of American Racism* (New York: Harper Perennial, 1992), 356; Marilyn C. Baseler, *"Asylum for Mankind": America, 1607–1800* (Ithaca, NY: Cornell University Press, 1998), 52–55.

19. See Brendon Bradshaw and Peter Roberts, eds., *British Consciousness and Identity: The Making of Britain, 1533–1707* (New York: Cambridge University Press, 1998); Linda Colley, *Britons: Forging the Nation, 1707–1837* (New Haven: Yale University Press, 1992).

20. See Samuel Stanhope Smith, *Essay on the Cause of the Variety of Complexion and Figure in the Human Species* (Philadelphia, Robert Aitken, 1787); on Smith, see William Stanton, *The Leopard's Spots: Scientific Attitudes Toward Race in America 1815–59* (Chicago: University of Chicago Press, 1960), 3–9.

21. Thomas Jefferson, "Notes on the States of Virginia," in Merrill D. Peterson, ed., *The Portable Thomas Jefferson* (Harmondsworth, UK: Penguin Books, 1975), 186.

22. Pearce, *The Savages of America*, 232.

23. On the 1790 naturalization law, see Baseler, *"Asylum for Mankind,"* 255–260.

24. Tyler Anbinder, *Nativism and Slavery: The Know Nothings and the Politics of the 1850s* (New York: Oxford University Press, 1992); Dale T. Knobel, *Paddy and the Republic: Ethnicity and Nationality in Antebellum America* (Middletown, CT: Wesleyan University Press, 1996); Knobel, *America for the Americans: The Nativist Movement in the U.S.* (New York: Twayne, 1996).

25. Felix Cohen, "Americanizing the White Man," *American Scholar* 21 (1952): 177–191; John Canup, *Out of the Wilderness: The Emergence of an American Identity in Colonial New England* (Middletown, CT: Wesleyan University Press, 1990).

26. Candice Bredbenner, *A Nationality of Her Own: Women, Marriage, and the Law of Citizenship* (Berkeley: University of California Press, 1998), 18–19.

27. J. Hector St. John de Crèvecoeur, "What Is an American?," in his *Letters of an American Farmer* (London: Printed for T. Davies, 1782).

28. Benjamin Franklin to Thomas Percival, Oct. 14, 1773, "Marginalia in a Pamphlet by Matthew Wheelock," in Drew R. McCoy, *The Elusive Republic: Political Economy in Jeffersonian America* (New York: W.W. Norton, 1980), 58.

29. Lyman L. Johnson, *The Development of Slave and Free Labor Regimes in Late Colonial Buenos Aires, 1770–1815*, occasional paper, Latin American Studies Consortium of New England; no. 9 (Storrs: University Center for Latin American & Caribbean Studies, University of Connecticut, 1997).

30. Early race relations in Latin America are explored in James Schofield Saeger, ed., *Essays on Eighteenth-Century Race Relations in the Americas* (Bethlehem, PA: Lawrence Henry Gipson Institute, 1987); Magnus Mörner, *Race Mixture in the History of Latin America* (Boston: Little, Brown, 1967); Charles Ralph Boxer, *Race Relations in the Portuguese Empire, 1415–1825* (Oxford: Clarendon Press, 1963).

31. For English speakers unfamiliar with the history of Argentina, a good starting place is David Rock, *Argentina, 1516–1987: From Spanish Colonization to Alfonsin* (Berkeley: University of California Press, 1987).

32. Domingo Sarmiento, *Conflicto y Armonías de las Razas en América* (Buenos Aires: La Cultura Argentina, 1915), cited in Amy Elizabeth Shea, "Constructing the 'Guiding Fictions' of Nationhood: The Argentine Centennial of the Revolución de Mayo," (M.A. thesis, University of North Carolina at Charlotte, 1999), 3.

33. Domingo F. Sarmiento, *Facundo or, Civilization and Barbarism*, translated by Mary Mann (New York: Penguin Books, 1998), 28. See also Nicholas Shumway, *The Invention of Argentina* (Berkeley: University of California Press, 1991), 131–139; and Diana Sorensen Goodrich, *Facundo and the Construction of Argentine Culture* (Austin: University of Texas Press, 1996).

34. Sarmiento, *Facundo*, p. 16.

35. George Reid Andrews, *The Afro-Argentines of Buenos Aires, 1800–1900* (Madison: University of Wisconsin Press, 1980), ch. 6. See also Andrews, "The Black Legions of Buenos Aires, Argentina, 1800–1900," in Darien J. Davis, ed., *Slavery and Beyond: The African Impact on Latin America and the Caribbean* (Wilmington, DE: Scholarly Resources Books, 1995).

36. Sarmiento, *Facundo*, p.16.

37. For Argentina's two largest immigrant groups, see Samuel L. Baily, *Immigrants in the Lands of Promise: Italians in Buenos Aires and New York City, 1870–1914* (Ithaca, NY: Cornell University Press, 1999); and José Moya, *Cousins and Strangers: Spanish immigrants in Buenos Aires, 1850–1930* (Berkeley: University of California Press, 1998).

38. Juan Bautista Alberdi, *Las "Bases" de Alberdi*, edited by Jorge Mayer (Buenos Aires: Editorial Sudamericana, 1969), cited in Shea, "Constructing the 'Guiding Fictions,'" 26.

39. See Hilda Sabato, *La Política en las Calles: Entre el Voto y la Movilización. Buenos Aires, 1862–1880* (Buenos Aires: Editorial Sudamericana, 1988).

40. A good introduction is Lucy Riall, *The Italian Risorgimento: State, Society, and National Unification* (London: Longman, 1994).

41. Quoted in Francesco Leoni, *Storia della contrarivoluzione in Italia (1789–1859)* (Naples: Guida, 1974), 44.

42. On Italy's democratic nationalists, see Clara Maria Lovett, *The Democratic Movement in Italy, 1830–1876* (Cambridge, MA: Harvard University Press, 1982).

43. Spencer Di Scala, *Italy: From Revolution to Republic, 1700 to the Present* (Boulder, CO: Westview Press, 1995), 66–67.

44. Quoted in John Dickie, "Stereotypes of the Italian South 1860–1900," in Robert Lumley and Jonathan Morris, eds., *The New History of the Italian South: The Mezzogiorno Revisited* (Exeter, UK: University of Exeter Press, 1997), 122.

45. George W. Stocking, *Victorian Anthropology* (New York: Free Press, 1987). For an introduction to Italian positivism, see Emilio R. Papa, ed., *Il positivismo e la cultura italiana* (Milan: Franco Angeli, 1985).

46. Quoted in Alfredo Niceforo, *Italiani del nord e italiani del sud* (Florence: Tip. Cooperativa, 1899), 9.

47. Gabaccia, *Italy's Many Diasporas*, 52–53.

48. John Dickie, *Darkest Italy: The Nation and Stereotypes of the Mezzogiorno, 1860–1900* (New York: St. Martin's Press, 1999); Jane Schneider, *Italy's "Southern Question": Orientalism in One Country* (New York: Berg, 1998); Vito Teti, *La razza maledetta; Origini de Pregiudizio Antimeridionale* (Rome: Manifestolibri, 1993).

49. Pancaldi, *Darwin in Italia*; Giovanni Landucci, "Darwinismo e nazionalismo," in *La*

cultura italiana tra '800 e '900 e le origini del nazionalismo, Biblioteca dell'Archivio Storica Italiano 22 (1981): 103–187.

50. Italy was arguably the birthplace of modern criminology—beginning with the work of eighteenth-century philosopher Cesare Beccaria, *Dei delitti e delle pene* (Liverno: Coltellini, 1764). Lombroso's most influential works include *La donna delinquente: La prostituta e la donna normale* (Turin: L. Roux, 1894); *L'uomo delinquente: In rapporto all' antropologia, alla giurisprudenza ed alla psichiatria (Cause e Rimedi)* (Turin: Fratelli Bocca, 1897). Both Lombroso and Ferri were prominent socialists; see Enrico Ferri, *Socialismo e criminalità, appunti di Enrico Ferri* (Rome, Turin, and Florence: Fratelli Bocca, 1883).

51. Cesare Lombroso, *L'Antisemitismo e le scienze moderne* (Turin: L. Roux, 1894); Lombroso, *L'uomo bianco e l'uomo di colore: Letture sull'origine e le varietà delle razze umane,* 2nd ed. (Turin: Fratelli Bocca, 1892).

52. Cesare Lombroso, *In Calabria (1862–1897)* (Catania: N. Giannotta, 1898).

53. Cesare Lombroso, *Gli anarchici* (Turin: Fratelli Bocca, 1894); see also Daniel Pick, "The Faces of Anarchy: Lombroso and the Politics of Criminal Science in Post-Unification Italy," *History Workshop* 21 (1986): 60–86.

54. Peter D'Agostino, "Craniums, Criminals, and the 'Cursed Race': Italian Anthropology in American Racial Thought, 1861–1924," *Comparative Studies in Society and History* 44: 2 (2002): 319–343.

55. Giuseppe Sergi, *Ari ed italici: Attorno all'Italia preistorica con figure dimonstrative* (Turin: Fratelli Bocca, 1898). Quotation is from Giuliano Pancaldi, *Darwin in Italy: Science across Cultural Frontiers* (Bloomington: Indiana University Press, 1983), 166.

56. Alfredo Niceforo, *L'Italia barbara contemporanea: Studi ed appunti* (Milano and Palermo: Remo Sandron, 1898), 294.

57. Ibid., 6.

58. Quoted in Claudio Segrè, *Fourth Shore: The Italian Colonization of Libya* (Chicago: University of Chicago Press, 1974), 18.

59. Italian intellectuals had long attempted to define migration as a form of demographic imperialism. See, for example, Gerolamo Boccardo, *L'emigrazione e le colonie* (Florence: Le Monnier, 1871); see also Ronald S. Cunsoli, "Enrico Corradini and the Italian Version of Proletarian Nationalism," *Canadian Review of Studies in Nationalism* 12: 1 (1985): 47–63.

60. Donna R. Gabaccia, Dirk Hoerder, and Adam Walaszek, "Emigration and Nation-Building During the Mass Migrations from Europe," in Nancy Green and François Weil, eds., *European Emigration* (forthcoming).

61. For a general introduction to the topic, see Richard Graham, *The Idea of Race in Latin America, 1870–1940* (Austin: University of Texas Press, 1990); for Argentina, Eduardo A. Zimmermann, "Racial Ideas and Social Reform: Argentina, 1890–1916," *Hispanic American Historical Review* 72: 1 (Feb. 1992): 23–45.

62. Nancy Leys Stepan, *"The Hour of Eugenics": Latin America and the Movement for Racial Improvement, 1918–1940* (Ithaca, NY: Cornell University Press, 1991), 138–139.

63. See Oscar Terán, *José Ingenieros: Pensar la Nación* (Buenos Aires: Puntosur, 1987).

64. See Daniel Pick, *Faces of Degeneration: A European Disorder, c. 1848–c.1918* (Cambridge: Cambridge University Press, 1989).

65. Juan Bautista Alberdi, *Peregrinación de Luz del Día: o, Viaje y Aventuras de la Verdad en el Nuevo Mundo* (Buenos Aires: La Cultura Argentina, 1916), cited in Goodrich, *Facundo*, 144.

66. Augusto Bunge, *La Conquista de la Higiene Social* (Buenos Aires: 1910–1911), vol. 1, 7–19, cited in Eduardo A. Zimmermann, *Los Liberales Reformistas: La Cuestión Social en la Argentina 1890–1916* (Buenos Aires: Editorial Sudamericana, 1995), 112.

67. Mirta Lobato, "The *Patria degli italiani* and Social Conflict in Early Twentieth Century Argentina," in Gabaccia and Ottanelli, eds., *Italian Workers of the World*. More generally see Hebe Clementi, *Migración y Discriminación en la Construcción Social* (Buenos Aires: Editorial Leviatan, 1995).

68. Julia K. Blackwelder and Lyman Johnson, "Changing Criminal Patterns in Buenos Aires, 1890–1914," *Journal of Latin American Studies* 14 (1984): 369.

69. On the influence of Lombroso in the Americas, see David A. Jones, *History of Criminology* (Westport, CT: Greenwood Press, 1986), 81–125; Ricardo D. Salvatore, "Criminology, Prison Reform, and the Buenos Aires Working Class," *Journal of Interdisciplinary History* 23: 2 (Autumn 1992): 279–299; Eugenia Scarzanella, *Italiani malagente: Immigrazione, Criminalità, razzismo in Argentina, 1890–1940* (Milano: Franco Angeli, 1999); Zimmerman, *Los Liberales Reformistas*, ch. 4.

70. See Zimmerman, *Los Liberales Riformistas*, 127–130.

71. Samuel L. Baily, "The Italians and the Development of Organized Labor in Argentina, Brazil, and the United States, 1880–1914," *Journal of Social History* 3: 2 (Winter 1969–1970): 123–134; Baily, "The Italians and Organized Labor in the United States and Argentina," *International Migration Review* 1: 3 (Summer 1967): 55–66; Osvaldo Bayer, "L'influenza dell'immigrazione italiana nel movimento anarchico argentino," in B. Bezza, *Gli Italiani Fuori d'Italia*, (Milan: F. Angeli, 1983), 531–548; Donna Gabaccia and Fraser Ottanelli, "Diaspora or International Proletariat? Italian Labor, Labor Migration, and the Making of Multiethnic States, 1815–1939," *Diaspora* 6: 1 (Spring 1997): 61–87.

72. Eusebio Gómez, *La Mala Vida en Buenos Aires*, quoted in Zimmermann, *Los Liberales Reformistas*, 132; see also Patricio Gell, "Los Anarquistas en el Gabinete Antropométrico," *Entrepasados: Revista de Historia* 11: 2 (1992): 7–24.

73. José Hernández, *El Gaucho Martin Fierro: A Facsimile Reproduction of the First Edition*, translated by Frank G. Carrino, Alberto J. Carlos, and Norman Mangouni (Delmar, NY: Scholars' Facsimiles & Reprints, 1974).

74. Ibid.; Zimmermann, *Los Liberales Reformistas*, 151–156.

75. English-only readers can usefully consult Sandra McGee Deutsch, *Counterrevolution in Argentina, 1900–1932: The Argentine Patriotic League* (Lincoln: University of Nebraska Press, 1986); and Paul H. Lewis, *The Crisis of Argentine Capitalism* (Chapel Hill: University of North Carolina Press, 1990). For the long-term evolution of twentieth-century nationalism, see James P. Brennan, *Peronism and Argentina* (Wilmington, DE: Scholarly Resources Books, 1998).

76. On Anglo-Saxonism in the United States, see Reginald Horsman, *Race and Manifest Destiny: The Origins of Amerian Racial Anglo-Saxonism* (Cambridge, MA: Harvard University Press, 1981).

77. I borrow this image from Michael C. LeMay, *From Open Door to Dutch Door: An Analysis of U.S. Immigration Policy Since 1820* (New York: Praeger, 1987).

78. On the long-term legacy, see Eric Foner, *Reconstruction: America's Unfinished Revolution, 1863–1877* (New York: Harper & Row, 1988). Works of comparative history especially emphasize the function of white supremacy in creating unity among whites in conflict. See George M. Fredrickson, *White Supremacy: A Comparative Study in American and South African History* (Oxford: Oxford University Press, 1981); Anthony W. Marx, *Making Race and Nation: A Comparison of South Africa, the United States and Brazil* (Cambridge: Cambridge University Press, 1998). These studies leave unanswered the question of why, if the function of white supremacy was to increase social harmony among whites, immigration restriction of white Europeans emerged as southern and northern whites found their reconciliation.

79. A readable summary is Roger Daniels, *Not Like Us: Immigrants and Minorities in America, 1890–1924* (Chicago: Ivan R. Dee, 1997).

80. 61st Congress, 3rd session, Reports of the Immigration Commission, *Dictionary of Races or Peoples*, Senate Document no. 662 (Washington, DC: U.S. Government Printing Office, 1911).

81. *Dictionary of Races or Peoples*, 82.

82. D'Agostino, "Craniums, Criminals, and the 'Cursed Race.'"

83. *Dictionary of Races*, p. 82.

84. Ferri's work was translated in English before Lombroso's; both had considerably less influence in the United States than in Argentina. See Enrico Ferri, *The Positive School of Criminology*, translated by Ernest Untermann (Chicago: Kerr, 1906); Cesare Lombroso, *Crime: Its Causes and Remedies*, translated by Henry P. Morton (Boston: Little, Brown, 1911; repr. Montclair, NJ: Patterson Smith, 1968); Nicole Hahn Rafter, *Creating Born Criminals* (Urbana: University of Illinois Press, 1997), 114–115.

85. Robert Orsi, "The Religious Boundaries of an Inbetween People: Street *Feste* and the Problem of the Dark-Skinned 'Other' in Italian Harlem, 1920–1990," *American Quarterly* 44 (Sept. 1992); James R. Barrett and David Roediger, "In-between Peoples: Race, Nationality and the New Immigrant Working Class," *Journal of American Ethnic History* 16 (1997): 3–44.

86. Madison Grant, *The Passing of the Great Race: or, The Racial Basis of European History* (New York: C. Scribner, 1916).

87. Gary Gerstle, "Liberty, Coercion, and the Making of Americans," Journal of American History 84: 2 (Sept. 1997): 524–558.

88. The decline of scientific racism among scholars in the United States began with the work of Franz Boas, and culminated with the publication of Ashley Montagu's 1941 lecture published in 1942 as *Man's Most Dangerous Myth: The Fallacy of Race* (New York: Oxford University Press, 1974). See also Elazar Barkan, *The Retreat of Scientific Racism: Changing Concepts of Race in Britain and the United States Between the World Wars* (Cambridge: Cambridge University Press, 1992), xi; and George S. Stocking, *In Search of Human Nature: The Decline and Revival of Darwinism in American Social Thought* (New York, 1991), ch. 3.

89. Since the introduction to this volume includes a good introduction to whiteness studies of Italian-Americans, I omit specific references here.

90. Rudolph J. Vecoli, "The Making and Un-Making of the Italian Working Class," in Philip J. Cannistraro and Gerald Meyer, eds., *The Lost World of Italian-American Radicalism* (Westport, CT: Praeger Press, forthcoming); Thomas J. Sugrue, *The Origins of the Urban Crisis: Race and Inequality in Postwar Detroit* (Princeton, NJ: Princeton University Press, 1996); Thomas A. Guglielmo, *White on Arrival: Italians, Race, Color, and Power in Chicago, 1890–1945* (New York: Oxford University Press, 2003).

91. Herbert Gans, "Symbolic Ethnicity: The Future of Ethnic Groups and Cultures in America," *Ethnic and Racial Studies* 2 (Jan. 1979): 1–20; Mary C. Waters, *Ethnic Options: Choosing Identities in America* (Berkeley: University of California Press, 1990), 157–158.

92. Richard Alba, *Italian Americans: Into the Twilight of Ethnicity* (Englewood Cliffs, NJ: Prentice-Hall, 1985).

93. Jonathan D. Sarna, "From Immigrants to Ethnics: Toward a New Theory of 'Ethnicization,'" *Ethnicity* 5 (1978): 370–378; Thomas Dublin, *Becoming American, Becoming Ethnic* (Philadelphia: Temple University Press, 1996).

94. David Richards, *Italian American: The Racializing of an Ethnic Identity* (New York: New York University Press, 1999).

95. Andrews, *The Afro-Argentines of Buenos Aires*, 212–216.

96. Nancy L. Green, "*Le Melting Pot*: Made in America, Produced in France," *Journal of American History* 86: 3 (Dec. 1999): 1188–1208.

CHAPTER 4

In this essay *Negro* will be rendered in quotations as a proper noun with a capital N. When in quotations and in lowercase, I have indicated that situation with [*sic*]. I wish to acknowledge colleagues Perra S. Bell, Jesse Hiraoka, and Louise Carroll Wade, who have given me the benefit of their insights. I also thank Jennifer Guglielmo for her support.

1. Ernest J. Gaines, *The Autobiography of Miss Jane Pittman* (New York: Bantam Books, 1971), 230–231.

2. Thomas A. Guglielmo, *White on Arrival: Italians, Race, Color, and Power in Chicago, 1890–1945* (New York: Oxford University Press, 2003); Matthew Frye Jacobson, *Whiteness of a Different Color: European Immigrants and the Alchemy of Race* (Cambridge, MA: Harvard University Press, 1998); Louise Reynes Edwards-Simpson, "Sicilian Immigration to New Orleans, 1870–1910: Ethnicity, Race and Social Position in the New South" (Ph.D. diss., University of Minnesota, 1996), 15. She cites Alfred Stone's *Studies in American Race Problems* (New York: Doubleday, Page, 1908), 172–174.

3. Edwards-Simpson, "Sicilian Immigration," 15–18; David A. J. Richards, *Italian Americans: The Racializing of an Ethnic Identity* (New York: New York University Press, 1999).

4. For example, see Hodding Carter, *Southern Legacy* (Baton Rouge: Louisiana State University Press, 1950), 105–118.

5. Vincenza (aka Jean) Scarpaci, *Italian Immigrants in Louisiana's Sugar Parishes: Recruitment, Labor Conditions, and Community Relations, 1880–1910* (New York: Arno Press, 1980); John V. Baiamonte, Jr., "Immigrants in Rural America: A Study of the Italians of Tangipahoa Parish, Louisiana" (Ph.D. diss., Mississippi State University, 1972).

6. "The Immigration Season Begins," *Daily Picayune* (New Orleans), Nov. 3, 1895, 9; "The Immigration Season Started," *Daily Picayune*, Oct. 19, 1901, 9. (Hereafter cited as *D-P.*)

7. The actual numbers of Italian immigrants in Louisiana are imprecise. See Edwards-Simpson, "Sicilian Immigration," 50; Evans Casso, *Staying in Step: A Continuing Italian Renaissance. A Saga of American-Italians in the Southeast United States* (New Orleans: Quadriga Press, 1984); A.V. Margavio and Jerome Salomone, "The Passage, Settlement and Occupational Characteristics of Louisiana's Italian Immigrants," *Sociological Spectrum* 1 (1981): 350.

8. I've corrected Donna Gabaccia's percentage for 1900. She claimed 90 percent of Louisiana's Italians lived in the sugar parishes, and probably arrived at that figure using a census table that used derivative numbers per 10,000 population. See Gabaccia's *Militants and Migrants: Rural Sicilians Become American Workers* (New Brunswick, NJ: Rutgers University Press, 1988), 103.

9. Letters dated Sept. 29, 1891, and Oct. 1, 1891, St. Raphael Society Collection, Center for Migration Studies, Staten Island, New York.

10. "Ascension Letter," *Louisiana Planter and Sugar Manufacturer,* Feb. 2, 1889, 56. (Hereafter cited as *LPSM.*) J. Carlyle Sitterson, *Sugar Country: The Cane Sugar Industry in the South, 1753–1950* (Lexington: University of Kentucky Press, 1953), 323, notes that a reduced efficiency of African American workers reflected more the loss of the best workers to other, higher-paying occupations and their replacement with large numbers of women and boys. He cites *Louisiana Planter* 41 (1908): 129–130.

11. Edwards-Simpson, "Sicilian Immigration," 25–27.

12. Luigi Villari, *Negli Stati Uniti* (Societa Nazionale "Dante Alighieri," 1939), 77–79.

13. Edwards-Simpson, "Sicilian Immigration," 15–18. See also Jacobson, *Whiteness of a Different Color*; and Richards, *Italian Americans*.

14. Gabaccia, *Militants and Migrants*, 85–90.

15. Scarpaci, *Italian Immigrants*, 256–257.

16. See Scarpaci, *Italian Immigrants*, 112, for a sample of plantation payroll books showing workers listed according to race: whites, Italians (sometimes Dagos) and "colored" (sometimes "darkies"); and "The Plantation Labor problem," *LPSM*, Dec. 5, 1896, 362.

17. "Meeting of the Sugar Planters Association," *LPSM*, Feb.17, 1900, 107.

18. Gabaccia, *Militants and Migrants*, 105–106.

19. John Rodrigue, "Raising Cane: From Slavery to Free Labor in Louisiana's Sugar Parishes 1862–1880" (Ph.D. diss., Emory University, 1992), 401–405; Sitterson, *Sugar Country*, 316.

20. *LPSM*, July 18, 1903.

21. "Local Letters—Iberville," *LPSM*, Feb. 2, 1895, 68; Gabaccia, *Militants and Migrants*, 85–90.

22. *LPSM*, Nov. 16, 1901, 315; Gabaccia, *Militants and Migrants*, 106.

23. Edwards-Simpson, "Sicilian Immigration," 24–27. See also Margavio and Salomone, "The Passage," 350, 356–357.

24. Sitterson, *Sugar Country*, 316–317.

25. *Louisiana Capitolian*, Apr. 21, 1881, 2; William Ivy Hair, *Bourbonism and Agrarian Protest: Louisiana Politics 1877–1900* (Baton Rouge: Louisiana State University Press, 1969), ch. 8. Yet we do know that in 1907 blacks "attacking" Italian laborers at Tremont Lumber Company in Jackson Parish, a lumber region, was seen as "something new." *D-P*, Dec. 19, 1907, 5; and Guice A. Giambrone, "Rise and Decline of Italian Immigration in Louisiana 1880–1924" (M.A. thesis, University of Southwestern Louisiana, 1972), 31 and 52.

26. *LPSM*, Sept. 19, 1891; *LPSM*, Jan. 19, 1895; *Daily Times*, (Donaldsville: Dec. 9, 1896); *LPSM*, Aug. 24, 1907, 117; Interview with Gaetano Mistretta by author, Nov. 1965.

27. See James R. Barrett and David Roediger, "Inbetween Peoples: Race, Nationality and the 'New Immigrant' Working Class," *Journal of American Ethnic History* 16:3 (Spring 1997); David Roediger, "Gaining a Hearing for Black-White Unity: Covington Hall and the Complexities of Race, Gender and Class," in *Towards the Abolition of Whiteness: Essays on Race, Politics, and Working Class History* (London: Verso Press, 1994), 150.

28. James Fickle, "The Louisiana Texas Lumber War of 1911–1912," *Louisiana History* 16:1 (1975): 76, 73.

29. Interview with Mrs. Brocato by author, Nov. 14, 1965. See also letter from Riley Le Blanc to author, Raceland, Louisiana, 1965; and Scarpaci, *Italian Immigrants*, 148–149.

30. "Ascension," *LPSM*, Mar. 31, 1900, 195; Dr. C. M. Brady, "The Prevalence and Diagnosis of Yellow Fever in the Colored Race," *New Orleans Medical and Surgical Journal*, 58 (Jan. 1906): 550–554; and Brady, "The Circumstances and Conditions of the First Appearance of Yellow Fever in New Orleans and Country Parishes," *New Orleans Medical and Surgical Journal* 58, (Mar. 1906): 743–749; "Citizens Mass Meeting," *St. Mary Banner*, Aug. 5, 1905, 3.

31. George E. Cunningham, "The Italian, a Hindrance to White Solidarity in Louisiana, 1890–1898," *Journal of Negro History* 50 (Jan. 1965): 32. Cunningham cites the *Times-Democrat*, Aug. 10, 1896.

32. "Murder," *Plaquemines Protector* (Ponte a la Hache), Apr. 2, 1904, 2; *Kentwood Commercial*, Mar. 17, 1900.

33. "Latest News in All Louisiana," *D-P*, Dec. 19, 1908, 16 (Monroe is in north-central Louisiana). Guglielmo, *White on Arrival*, [mss.] 17, observed that "Italians could be both racially inferior 'Dagoes' and privileged whites simultaneously."

34. David John Hellwig, "The Afro American and the Immigrant, 1880–1930: A Study of Black Social Thought" (Ph.D. diss., Syracuse University, 1973), 24, 27, 30, 47; John Higham, *Strangers in the Land: Patterns of American Nativism 1860–1925* (New York: Atheneum, 1972); Arnold Shankman, "This Menacing Influx: Afro-Americans on Italian Immigration to the South, 1880–1915," *Mississippi Quarterly* 21:1 (Winter 1977–1978); Hellwig, "The Afro American," 46–47.

35. Hellwig, "The Afro American," cites *The Colored American Magazine* 12:5 (May 1907), 332 and 12:8 (Sept. 1907): 174.

36. Alfred Holt Stone, "The Economic Future of the Negro," in *Economic Studies in the American Race Problem* (New York: Doubleday, 1908); and Edwards-Simpson, "Sicilian Immigration," 83.

37. Hellwig, "The Afro American," 29–30.

38. See Sitterson, *Sugar Country*, 323, 317

39. "Peonage Cases," *D-P*, Jan. 16, 1908, 8; Luigi Villari, "Gli Italiani nel Distretto Consolare di New Orleans," *Bollettino dell' Emigrazione,* (1907): 28; Count Gerolamo Moroni, "L'Emigrazione Italiana nel distretto Consolare di Nuova Orleans," 1853; Moroni, "I peonage nel Sud degli Stati Uniti," *Bollettino dell' Emigrazione* (1910): 405–422.

40. Guglielmo, *White on Arrival*, [mss.] 81, 126, 209, 244.

41. Dino Cinel, "Sicilians in the Deep South: The Ironic Outcome of Isolation," *Studi Emigrazione* 97 (Mar. 1990): 67, 72–73; Scarpaci, *Italian Immigrants*, 204–206; Count Gerolamo Moroni, "La Louisiana," *Bollettino dell' Emigrazione* (1913): 31–53; Gabaccia, *Militants and Migrants*, 104.

42. Scarpaci, *Italian Immigrants*, 150–151, 227, 256–257; Giambrone, "Justice in Amite City," has an excellent account of the 1926 trial of six Italians in Amite, Louisiana, which resulted in all six being executed for the murder of one man. See also John Baiamonte, Jr., *Spirit of Vengeance: Nativism and Louisiana Justice, 1921–1924* (Baton Rouge: Louisiana State University Press, 1986).

43. In *Italian Americans*, Richards introduces a compelling hypothesis that southern Italian immigrants responded to racism in Italy and the United States by submerging their ethnicity within familial boundaries while adopting the outward appearance of the dominant culture as a protective shield. In a more contemporary analysis, Rudolph Vecoli maintains that the persistence of Italian ethnicity is more than a response to the politicization of race and ethnicity within official U.S. government policy. Vecoli, "Are Italians Just White Folks?" *Italian Americana* 13:2 (Summer 1995): 149–165.

44. Edwards-Simpson, "Sicilian Immigration," 38.

45. Letter dated Dec. 17, 1901, John Pharr Papers, Louisiana State University Archives.

46. Gabaccia, *Militants and Migrants*, 102–103; "Local Letters, Iberville" *LSPM,* Dec. 27, 1902, 405.

47. "Italian Ambassador Sees Settlers on Plantations," *D-P*, May 24, 1905, 4.

48. How great a role did violence and discrimination play in undermining African American economic activity? We know that black farmers near Baton Rouge in 1890 "were shot, whipped or otherwise molested and told to sell their property cheaply or be killed." Hair, *Bourbonism*, 189. See also Mark Schmitz, "The Transformation of Southern Cane Sugar Sector 1860–1930," *Agricultural History*, 53: 1 (Jan. 1979): 280. Schmitz notes

that "Nonwhites were largely excluded from farm ownership in the cane district and from participation except as hired laborers."

49. Sitterson, *Sugar Country*, 314; Rodrigue, "Raising Cane," 561.

50. Interview with Bernard Mistretta's son, Gaetano Mistretta, by author, Feb. 1966.

51. Moroni, "La Louisiana." In 1965 I corresponded with a retired priest, J. A. Vigliero, who had been sent from Italy to Louisiana in 1908. He traveled to towns in the sugar parishes, such as Centerville, Franklin, Jeanerette, New Iberia, and Morgan City, where he found "Italians running fruit and grocery stores, butcher shops, barrooms, etc." See also Zena Valenziano, *Italian Immigrants in Iberville Parish* (SI: Z. Valenziano 1988), 4–6.

52. "Labor in Louisiana," *Manufacturer's Record*, 1902: 466.

53. *D-P*, June 18, 1910.

54. *Jefferson Parish Police Jury Minutes*, Dec. 23, 1908 and Jan. 5, 1910; *St. Mary Banner* (Franklin, Louisiana) (1906, 1908).

55. "Labor in Louisiana," *Manufacturer's Record*, 466.

56. "Iberville Letter," *LPSM* 4 (June 28, 1890): 475.

57. However, some of the go-between activities of Italian merchants at times did provoke retaliation. The day after a fight had broken out in Independence, Tangipahoa Parish, between "whites" and Italians during a baseball game, the Natalbany store (eight miles distant) of Charlie Parlio was dynamited, and most Italians left town. "Riot Is Averted," *New Orleans Item*, July 23, 1908, 1 and 5, and July 24, 5.

58. Baiamonte, "Immigrants in Rural America," 68.

59. Baiamonte, "Immigrants in Rural America," 90; and A. V. Margavio and Jerome J. Salomone, *Bread and Respect: The Italians of Louisiana* (Gretna, LA: Pelican Publishing, 2002), 98–99.

60. Baiamonte, "Immigrants in Rural America," 56, 60, 70, 72, 73, 75.

61. U.S. Department of State, *Papers Relating to the Foreign Relations of the United States 1900*, report sent to C. Papini in New Orleans, July 26, 1899, 727; and Edward Haas, "Guns, Goats and Italians: The Tallulah Lynching of 1899," *North Louisiana Historical Association Journal* 13:2, 3 (1982): 52–54; U.S. Department of State, *Notes from the Italian Legation*, memo from the Italian Legation, Nov. 19, 1901.

62. *Papers Relating to....*, 727; and letter from Italian Ambassador Fava to Hay, Jan. 15, 1900, 440–446, 715.

63. *The Crisis*, Nov. 1910; letter from Secretary Hay to Count Macchi de Cellere, March 10, 1904, *Notes to Foreign Legations*, U.S. Department of State.

64. "Serious Trouble Expected: Italians Ordered to Leave Kentwood by Saturday Night," *The Florida Parishes* (Amite, LA), Feb. 29, 1908, 4.

65. Ginger Romero, *The Louisiana Strawberry Story* (Natchitoches, LA: Northwestern State University Press, 1984), 52, 80.

66. Editorial, *Weekly Pelican*, Oct. 8, 1887, 2; Philip D. Uzee, "Republican Politics in Louisiana, 1877–1910" (Ph.D. diss., Louisiana State University, 1950), 280–281. Uzee cites the *New Orleans Progress*, a black Democratic paper.

67. Sitterson, *Sugar Country*, 335; William P. Miles diary, Apr. 19 and May 6, 1892, William Porcher Miles Papers, Southern Historical Collection, University of North Carolina.

68. Cunningham, "The Italian," 29.

69. Ibid., 31.

70. Sitterson, *Sugar Country*, 340. The Democrats, acting for Foster, had stuffed the ballot boxes and "stolen" Negro votes. Uzee, "Republican Politics," 162; Edwin Davis, *Louisiana: A Narrative History* (Baton Rouge: Louisiana States University Press, 1965), 287.

71. Cunningham, "The Italian," 33–34

72. "Suffrage Plan to be Repaired," *Daily Picayune*, March 12, 1898, 11.

73. Higham, *Strangers in the Land*, 169, 173; Scarpaci, *Italian Immigrants*, 227–230; also see John Higham, "The Strange Career of *Strangers in the Land*," *American Jewish History* 76: 2 (Dec. 1986): 214, for his view of the changing interpretations of his work over time.

74. Barrett and Roediger, "Inbetween Peoples"; David Roediger, "White Ethnics in the United States," in *Towards the Abolition of Whiteness* (London: Verso Press, 1994). This scholarship with its provocative analyses prompted me to review my earlier research in order to clarify and redefine some of the generalizations I had made in published articles such as "A Tale of Selective Accommodation: Sicilians and Native Whites in Louisiana," *Journal of Ethnic Studies* 5:3 (1977): 37–50.

75. For many white Southerners, "Italian traits" of frugality often became a double-edged sword when the immigrants did without and purchased little from local native white merchants. Scarpaci, *Italian Immigrants*, 256–257; Margavio and Salomone, *Bread and Respect*, 356.

76. Baiamonte, "Immigrants in Rural America," 171–174. The Louisiana Farmers' Protective Union (LFPU) organized twenty-two local units in Tangipahoa, Livingston, Ascension, St. Helena, and St. Tammany parishes in the summer of 1937. James Morrison, the chief organizer for the LFPU, credited Italian support as vital to the success of the union, which accepted black and white strawberry farmers. African Americans could express their views at the meetings and could vote on all issues, but they could not become officers or directors. Its white membership consisted of "Italians, Hungarians, Germans, Cajuns and redneck."

77. Letter from George Piazza to author, Sept. 29, 1964. Piazza had established the Society in 1930.

78. See, for example, Roediger on "trading minorities" in "White Ethnics," 190.

79. Charles S. Johnson, *Growing Up in the Black Belt: Negro Youth in the Rural South* (New York: Schocken Books, 1970), 7, 10.

80. James Barrett, "Americanization from the Bottom Up: Immigrants and the Remaking of the Working Class in the U.S. 1880–1930," *Journal of American History*, 79:3 (December, 1992): 1001. See also Barrett and Roediger, "Inbetween Peoples," 27.

CHAPTER 5

1. *Richmond Planet*, Aug. 24, 1895 (no page number).

2. *Weekly Call*, Aug. 17, 1895, 1.

3. *L'Italia*, Aug. 10–11, 1895, 1. All translations by author.

4. Rayford W. Logan, *The Betrayal of the Negro: From Rutherford B. Hayes to Woodrow Wilson* (New York: 1965), quoted in George Fredrickson, *Racism: A Short History* (Princeton, NJ: Princeton University Press, 2002), 81.

5. See Iver Bernstein, *The New York City Draft Riots: Their Significance in American Society and Politics in the Age of the Civil War* (New York: Oxford University Press, 1990); David S. Cecelski and Timothy B. Tyson, *Democracy Betrayed: The Wilmington Race Riot of 1898 and Its Legacy* (Chapel Hill: University of North Carolina Press, 1998); William Tuttle, *Race Riot: Chicago in the Red Summer of 1919* (Urbana: University of Illinois Press, 1996).

6. Linda Gordon, *The Great Arizona Orphan Abduction* (Cambridge, MA: Harvard University Press, 2000), 12.

7. Edward W. Said, *Orientalism* (New York: Pantheon, 1978).

8. Gary Gerstle, "Liberty, Coercion, and the Making of Americans," *Journal of American History* 84 (Sept. 1997): 552–553.

9. See Mae N. Ngai, "The Architecture of Race in American Immigration Law: A Reexamination of the Immigration Act of 1924," *Journal of American History* 86 (June 1999): 69–70.

10. C. Vann Woodward, *The Strange Career of Jim Crow* (New York: Oxford University Press, 1957), 14–26; Fredrickson, *Racism*, 81–95

11. See Rogers Brubaker and Frederick Cooper, "Beyond 'Identity,'" *Theory and Society* 29 (2000): 1–47, for a critique of identity.

12. See James R. Barrett and David Roediger, "Inbetween Peoples: Race, Nationality and the 'New Immigrant' Working Class," *Journal of American Ethnic History* 16 (Spring 1997): 3–34; Thomas A. Guglielmo, *White on Arrival: Italians, Race, Color, and Power in Chicago, 1890–1945* (New York: Oxford University Press, 2003).

13. 1900 Manuscript Census, Illinois, Reel 238, No. T623, Brown-Bureau 1; On regional makeup of the Italian population, see Donna Gabaccia, *Militants and Migrants: Rural Sicilians Become American Workers* (New Brunswick, NJ: Rutgers University Press, 1988), 117. See also *Bureau County Republican* (hereafter BCR), Aug. 2, 1900, 12, and Jan. 23, 1913, 1; records of the Knights of Labor, 1888–1899, Local Assembly 8617 (Spring Valley), Illinois State University Archives, no specific date given—the minutes appear between May 4 and May 11, 1889 (hereafter, KL Records); John H. M. Laslett, *Nature's Noblemen: The Fortunes of the Independent Collier in Scotland and the American Midwest, 1855–1889* (Los Angeles: Institute of Labor and Industrial Relations, UCLA, 1983), 3; Elsie Gluck, *John Mitchell, Miner: Labor's Bargain with the Guilded Age* (New York: John Day, 1929), 17; Henry D. Lloyd, *A Strike of Millionaires Against Miners* (Chicago: Belford Clarke, 1890), 27–31; Karl W. Fivek, "From Company Town to Miners' Town: Spring Valley, Illinois, 1885–1905" (Certificate of Advanced Study, Northern Illinois University, 1976), 8.

14. KL Records; Jonathan Garlock, *Guide to the Local Assemblies of the Knights of Labor* (Westport, CT: Greenwood Press, 1982), 63; John H. M. Laslett, "'A Parting of the Ways': Immigrant Miners and the Rise of Politically Conscious Trade Unionism in Scotland and the American Midwest, 1865–1924," in Laslett, ed., *The United Mine Workers of America: A Model of Industrial Solidarity?* (University Park: Pennsylvania State University Press, 1996), 429–432. On Italian radicals in the upper Illinois valley, see Casellario Politico Centrale [CPC], Cavedagni Ersilia in Grandi, Busta 1205, Marietti, Andra, Antonio Giuseppe, Busta 113, and Michele di Gioccomo, Busta 3062, Archivio Centrale dello Stato, Rome; *Grido degli Oppressi*, Oct. 24, 1892, 4; "Movimento Operai," *Questione Sociale* (hereafter QS), Oct. 30, 1897; "Oglesby, Ill," *QS*, July 6, 1901; Paul Avrich, *Anarchist Portraits* (Princeton, NJ: Princeton University Press, 1988), 166; Gabaccia, *Militants and Migrants*, 116–117; Gianna S. Panofsky, "A View of Two Major Centers of Italian Anarchism in the United States: Spring Valley and Chicago, Illinois," in Dominic Candeloro, Fred L. Gardaphe, and Paolo A. Giordano, eds., *Italian Ethnics: Their Languages, Literature and Lives: Proceedings of the 20th Annual Conference of the American Italian Historical Association, Chicago, Illinois, November 11–13, 1987* (Staten Island, NY: American Italian Historical Association, 1990), 272–273. On French radicals, see Ronald Creagh, "Socialism in America: The French-Speaking Coal Miners in the Late Nineteenth Century," in Marianne Debouzy, ed., *In the Shadow of the Statue of Liberty: Immigrants, Workers, and Citizens in the American Republic, 1880–1920* (Urbana: University of Illinois Press, 1992), 151–153.

15. See article by "Mandamus," *BCR*, Jan. 10, 1889, for Spring Valley's coal riches and *BCR*, May 31, 1894, 3, for fears about immigrants.

16. Stanley Dalton Dodge, "Bureau and the Princeton Community" (Ph.D. diss., University of Chicago, 1925), first quote, 75; second quote, 48.

17. Federal Writers' Project (Illinois), Works Progress Administration, *Princeton Guide*, 1939, (5). Princeton, Illinois: Republican Printing Co.

18. George B. Harrington, *Past and Present of Bureau County, Illinois* (Chicago: Pioneer Publishing, 1906), 107–108; *The Biographical Record of Bureau, Marshall and Putnam Counties, Illinois* (Chicago: S. J. Clarke, 1896), 9–10.

19. Duncan McDonald Papers, Box 3, Folder 15, p. 7, State of Illinois Historical Library and Archives, Springfield; "Riotous Italians" *State Ledger*, (Topeka), Aug. 9, 1895; Fivek, "From Company Town to Miners' Town," 61–3.

20. *L'Italia*, Aug. 10–11, 1895, 1.

21. *United Mine Workers Journal* (hereafter UMWJ), Sept. 27, 1894, 1.

22. "Eight for Joliet," BCR, Nov. 21, 1895.

23. *Ottawa Daily Journal* (hereafter ODJ), May 23, 1894, 3; BCR, July 12, 1894, 4.

24. BCR, May 2, 1901, 12.

25. *Daily Republican*, Feb. 7, 1906, 4.

26. BCR, Feb. 22, 1906, 6.

27. *Chicago Tribune* (hereafter CT), Aug. 7, 1895, 6.

28. BCR, Aug. 6, 1896, 8.

29. CT, Aug. 6, 1895, 2.

30. BCR, Nov. 17, 1898, 1.

31. BCR, Sept. 19, 1895, 1.

32. See Richard Williams, *Hierarchical Structures and Social Value: The Creation of Black and Irish Identities in the United States* (New York: Cambridge University Press, 1990), 2–3.

33. *L'Italia*, Aug. 10–11, 1895, 1.

34. Ibid.

35. Gordon, *Great Arizona Orphan Abduction*, 12.

36. Quoted in Charles A. Lofgren, *The Plessy Case* (NY: Oxford Univ. Press), 1987, 28.

37. Williams, 4.

38. ODJ, Apr. 23, 1894, 3.

39. *Journal of the Knights of Labor*, Aug. 1, 1895, 1. On wage slavery, see David Roediger, *The Wages of Whiteness* (New York: Verso, 1991), 65–92; David Montgomery, *Beyond Equality: Labor and the Radical Republicans, 1862–1872* (Urbana: University of Illinois Press, 1981), 30–31; and Bruce Laurie, *Artisans into Workers: Labor in Nineteenth-Century America* (New York: Hill and Wang, 1989), 151.

40. Roediger, *Wages of Whiteness*, 68.

41. QS, Oct. 20, 1895, 5.

42. UMWJ, Nov. 1, 1894, 8.

43. *L'Italia*, Aug. 10–11, 1895, 1.

44. BCR, May 2, 1895, 9.

45. *National Labor Tribune*, Aug. 9, 1894, 5; Morton S. Baratz, *The Union and the Coal Industry* (New Haven, CT: Yale University Press, 1955), 52; Priscilla Long, *Where the Sun Never Shines: The History of America's Bloody Coal Industry* (New York: Paragon House, 1989), 154–156; Maier B. Fox, *United We Stand: The United Mine Workers of America, 1890–1990* (Washington DC: United Mine Workers of America, 1990), 102–112.

46. BCR, Aug. 8, 1895, 4; CT, Aug. 5, 1895, 1. The spelling of Rollo's name changes.

47. Criminal case 3623, *The People of the State of Illinois* v. *Peter Marietto, et. al.*, Aug.

term, 1895, Bureau County Courthouse, Circuit Clerk and Clerk Probate Court, Princeton, IL (hereafter, Case 3623); BCR, Sept. 5, 1895, 7.

48. *Daily Inter Ocean* (hereafter DIO) Aug. 20, 1895, 1, and Aug. 13, 1895, 2.

49. BCR, Aug. 8, 1895, 4, and Aug. 22, 1895, 5; DIO Aug. 13, 1895, 1. Each paper published the investigating committee's report on the riot.

50. *L'Italia*, Aug. 10–11, 1895, 1.

51. *Vorbote*, Aug. 14, 1909, 6.

52. CT, Aug. 8, 1895, 1.

53. *Illinois State Journal*, Aug. 5, 1895, 1; *New York Times*, Aug. 5, 1895, 8; BCR, Aug. 22, 1895, 5; DIO, Aug. 5, 1895, 1, and Aug. 22, 1895, 5.

54. "Eight for Joliet," BCR, Nov. 21, 1895.

55. DIO, August 5, 1895, 1; "Eight for Joliet," BCR, Nov. 21, 1895.

56. BCR, Aug. 15, 1895, 5.

57. Ibid.

58. Ibid., and BCR, Aug. 22, 1895, 5.

59. DIO, Aug. 5, 1895, 1.

60. Ibid; CT, Aug. 5, 1895, 1; *Augusta Daily Tribune*, Aug. 5, 1895, 1; BCR, Aug. 8, 1895, 1; *New York Times*, Aug. 6, 1895, 3. See also Paul Gilje, *Rioting in America* (Bloomington: Indiana University Press, 1996), 179–180; Tuttle, *Race Riot*, 64; Elliott Rudwick, *Race Riot at East St. Louis, July 2, 1917* (New York: Atheneum, 1972), 33, 49–50.

61. BCR, Aug. 8, 1895, 1.

62. DIO, Aug. 6, 1895, 1–2.

63. Ibid.

64. Ibid.

65. BCR, Aug. 8, 1895, 1.

66. DIO, Aug. 6, 1895, 1–2, and Aug. 7, 1895, 1–2.

67. DIO, Aug. 7, 1895, 2.

68. "Miscellaneous," *Langston City Herald*, Aug. 24, 1895.

69. DIO, Aug. 8, 1895, 2.

70. Ibid.

71. Ibid.; BCR, Aug. 22, 1895, 5.

72. DIO, Aug. 13, 1895, 2; BCR, Aug. 22, 1895, 5.

73. *L'Italia*, Aug. 25, 1895, 1.

74. "Eight for Joliet," BCR, Nov. 21, 1895.

75. BCR, Aug. 8, 1895, 4.

76. *Vorbote*, Aug. 14, 1895, 6.

77. DIO, Aug. 8, 1895, 2.

78. Ibid.

79. Ibid.

80. Ibid.

81. Ibid.; BCR, Aug. 15, 1895, 5; UMWJ, Aug. 15, 1895, 8.

82. "Eight for Joliet," BCR, Nov. 21, 1895.

83. Roberta Senechal, *The Sociogenesis of a Race Riot: Springfield, Illinois, in 1908* (Urbana: University of Illinois Press, 1990), 2, 193.

84. BCR, Aug. 22, 1895, 5.

85. Lawrence H. Fuchs, "The Reactions of Black Americans to Immigration," in Viginia Yans-McLaughin, ed., *Immigration Reconsidered: History, Sociology, and Politics*

(Oxford: Oxford University Press, 1990), 295–296; David J. Hellwig, "Black Attitudes Toward Irish Immigrants," *Mid-America* 59 (Jan. 1977), 39, 43, 45.

86. *L'Italia,* August 10–11, 1895, 1.

87. "The Illinois Outrage," *The Afro-American*, Aug. 10, 1895.

88. *Langston City Herald*, Sept. 21, 1895, 1.

89. "The Trouble in Illinois," *The Richmond Planet*, Aug. 17, 1895.

90. "The Leaders of the Spring Valley," *Richmond Planet*, Aug. 24, 1895.

91. UMWJ, Sept. 26, 1895, 5; Spring Valley City Council minutes, Sept. 3, 1895.

92. BCR, Oct. 3, 1895, 8.

93. Ibid.

94. BCR, Aug. 22, 1895, 1.

95. Case 3623.

96. DIO, Aug. 17, 1895, 1. BCR report of Aug. 22, says that Clark had thirty-eight warrants.

97. Case 3623; BCR, Aug. 22, 1895, 1.

98. Case 3623.

99. Ibid.

100. QS, May 30, 1903; "Spring Valley, Ill.," *Il Grido degli Opressi*, June 8, 1894. See also Creagh, "Socialism in America," 153; BCR, Aug. 2, 1894, 1; Criminal case 3634, *People of the State of Illinois* v. *Peter Lauer, et al.*, Oct. 6, 1894, Bureau County Courthouse, Circuit Clerk and Clerk Probate Court, Princeton, IL.

101. DIO, Aug. 13, 1895, 2.

102. DIO, Aug. 17, 1895, 1.

103. Case 3623.

104. Case 3623; "Eight for Joliet," BCR, Nov. 21, 1895. The case first came before the courts of Charles Blanchard and Dorrance Dibell. Judge George W. Stipp, who fought for the Union, made the final ruling. See *The Biographical Record of Bureau, Marshall and Putnam Counties,* 183.

105. Case 3623; "Eight for Joliet," BCR, Nov. 21, 1895.

106. "Eight for Joliet," BCR, Nov. 21, 1895.

107. David Roediger, *Towards the Abolition of Whiteness: Essays on Race, Politics, and Working Class History* (London: Verso Press, 1994), 184.

108. This was an unusual stance. See Roediger, *Towards the Abolition of Whiteness*, 189–190. For immigrant challenges to nationality, see Alexander Saxton, *The Indispensable Enemy: Labor and the Anti-Chinese Movement in California* (Berkeley: University of California Press, 1971), 211. For American identity and the white race, see Gail Bederman, *Manliness and Civilization: A Cultural History of Gender and Race in the United States, 1880–1917* (Chicago: University of Chicago Press, 1995), 75–76, 179. Some towns in the area barred blacks from entering. See, for example, Ronald L. Lewis, *Black Coal Miners in America: Race, Class, and Community Conflict, 1780–1980* (Lexington: University of Kentucky Press, 1987), 85. Lewis mentions Spring Valley as one of these towns; the BCR source conflicts with this. See for example, BCR, December 11, 1902, 1.

109. BCR, Aug. 22, 1895, 5.

110. "Eight for Joliet," BCR, Nov. 21, 1895.

111. Ibid.

112. BCR, Nov. 14, 1895, 1.

113. Case 3623.

114. *L'Italia*, Dec. 21–22, 1895, 1.

CHAPTER 6

1. John Scocca, http://www2.h/=/net.msu.edu/~itam/, June 22, 2000.

2. Philip Celeste, http://www2.h/=/net.msu.edu/~itam/, June 17, 2000.

3. Philip Celeste, Aug. 3, 2000; Ben Lawton, http://www2.h/=/net.msu.edu/~itam/, Aug. 7, 2000

4. David A. J. Richards, *Italian American: The Racializing of an Ethnic Identity* (New York: New York University Press, 1999), 7, 184–185.

5. David Roediger, *Towards the Abolition of Whiteness* (New York: Verso Press, 1994), 186–187; Donna Rae Gabaccia, *Militants and Migrants: Rural Sicilians Become American Workers* (New Brunswick, NJ: Rutgers University Press, 1988), 103–104, 109–110; Gary R. Mormino and George E. Pozzetta, *The Immigrant World of Ybor City: Italians and Their Latin Neighbors in Tampa, 1885–1985* (Urbana: University of Illinois Press, 1990), 57, 82–83, 120; Richards, *Italian American*, 227–228.

6. For another critique of Richards's book, see Rudolph Vecoli, "Review of Richards' *Italian American*," http://www2.h/=/net.msu.edu/~itam/, Sept. 13, 2000.

7. For a history of the Federazione Socialista Italiana, see Mario de Ciampis, "Storia del movimento socialista rivoluzionario italiano," *La Parola del Popolo, Cinquantesimo Anniversario, 1908–1958* 9 (Dec. 1958–Jan. 1959): 136–163; Elisabetta Vezzosi, "La Federazione Socialista Italiana del Nord America (1911–1921)" (Ph.D. diss. Università degli Studi di Firenze, 1980); Vezzosi, "La Federazione Socialista Italiana del Nord America tra autonomia e scioglimento nel sindacato industriale, 1911–1921," *Studi Emigrazione* 21: 73 (Mar. 1984): 81–110; Michael Topp, *Those Without a Country: The Political Culture of Italian American Syndicalism* (Minneapolis: University of Minnesota Press, 2001). Studies of the Italian American left generally include Rudolph Vecoli, "The Italian Immigrants in the United States Labor Movement from 1880 to 1929," in Bruno Bezza, ed., *Gli italiani fuori d'Italia* (Milan: Franco Angeli, 1983), 257–306; Bruno Ramirez, "Immigration, Ethnicity, and Political Militance: Patterns of Radicalism in the Italian American Left, 1880–1930," in Valeria Gennaro Lerna, ed., *From "Melting Pot" to Multiculturalism: The Evolution of Ethnic Relations in the United States and Canada* (Rome: Bulzoni Editore, 1990), 115–141.

8. James R. Barrett and David Roediger, "Inbetween Peoples: Nationality and the 'New Immigrant' Working Class," *Journal of American Ethnic History* 16: 3 (Spring 1997): 3–44; Matthew Jacobson, *Whiteness of a Different Color: European Immigrants and the Alchemy of Race* (Cambridge, MA: Harvard University Press, 1998).

9. See Ramirez, "Immigration, Ethnicity, and Political Militance"; Vezzosi, "La Federazione"; Salvatore Salerno, "No God, No Master: Italian Anarchists and the Industrial Workers of the World," in Philip Cannistraro and Gerald Meyer, eds., *The Lost World of Italian American Radicalism: Politics, Culture, History* (Westport, CT: Greenwood Press, forthcoming).

10. Carlo Tresca, unpublished autobiography, 89–90. This autobiography is housed at the Immigration History Research Center, University of Minnesota.

11. Elisabetta Vezzosi, *Il socialismo indifferente: immigrati italiani e socialist party negli Stati Uniti del primo novecento* (Roma: Edizioni Lavoro, 1991).

12. Ramirez "Immigration, Ethnicity, and Political Militance," 129–130; Salerno, "No God," 11–12 [mss.].

13. Edwin Fenton, *Immigrants and Unions, a Case Study: Italians and American Labor, 1870–1920* (New York: Arno Press, 1975), 358, quoted in Ramirez, "Immigration, Ethnicity, and Political Militancy," 134.

14. Elisabetta Vezzosi, "Class, Ethnicity, and Acculturation in *Il Proletario*: The World War One Years," in Christiane Harzig and Dirk Hoerder, eds., *The Press of Labor Migrants in Europe and North America 1880s to 1930s* (Bremen: Labor Newspaper Preservation Project, 1985), 443–458.

15. Arturo Giovannitti, "The Brigandage of Tripoli," *International Socialist Review* 12 (Mar. 1912): 574. The *International Socialist Review* was the theoretical journal of the American Socialist Party.

16. Bifolco, "Le Barbarie della Civiltà," *Il Proletario*, Jan. 5, 1912, 4.

17. Ibid.

18. Leonardo Frisina, "La civilità d'Italia," *Il Proletario*, Apr. 19, 1912.

19. Giovanni Gianchino, "Tripoli e la Sicilia," *Il Proletario*, Jan. 5, 1912, 2.

20. Thomas A. Guglielmo, "'No Color Barrier': Italians, Race, and Power in the United States," in this anthology.

21. Jacobson, *Whiteness*, 49ff.

22. Pierrette Hondagneu-Sotelo, *Gendered Transitions: Mexican Experiences of Immigration* (Berkeley: University of California Press, 1994), 193–194. See also Hondagneu-Sotelo and Michael Messner, "Gender Displays and Men's Power: The 'New Man' and the Mexican Immigrant Man," in Harry Brod and Michael Kaufman, eds., *Theorizing Masculinities* (Thousand Oaks, CA: Sage Publications, 1994), 200–218.

23. This does not mean, of course, that the experiences of Italian Americans and Mexican Americans can be equated. Although Mexican Americans are considered white in legal terms, the histories of these two populations in the United States are too markedly different to allow any simple comparisons.

24. There is a considerable body of scholarship on the Lawrence strike and the IWW's contribution to the strike. See, for example, Philip Foner, *The Industrial Workers of the World, 1905–1917* (New York: International Publishers, 1965), 306–350; Melvyn Dubofsky, *We Shall Be All: A History of the IWW* (Chicago: Quadrangle Books, 1969), 228–258; Joyce Kornbluh, ed., *Rebel Voices: An IWW Anthology* (Ann Arbor: University of Michigan Press, 1964); Meredith Tax, "The Lawrence Strike," in her *The Rising of the Women: Feminist Solidarity and Class Conflict, 1880–1917* (New York: Monthly Review Press, 1980), 241–275; and Ardis Cameron, *Radicals of the Worst Sort: Laboring Women in Lawrence, Massachusetts, 1860–1912* (Urbana: University of Illinois Press, 1993).

25. See especially Matthew Frye Jacobson, *Special Sorrows: The Diasporic Imagination of Irish, Polish, and Jewish Immigrants in the United States* (Cambridge, MA: Harvard University Press, 1995); David Roediger, *The Wages of Whiteness: Race and the Making of the American Working Class* (New York: Verso, 1991); Eric Lott, *Love and Theft: Blackface Minstrelsy and the American Working Class* (New York: Oxford University Press, 1993); Roediger, *Towards the Abolition*.

26. See, for example, Henry Pratt Fairchild, *The Melting Pot Mistake* (Boston: Little, Brown and Co, 1926); H. B. Woolston, "Rating the Nations" *American Journal of Sociology* (November 1916): 381–390; Edward Ross, *The Old World in the New: The Significance of Past and Present Immigration to the American People* (New York: Century, 1914).

27. Tax, "The Lawrence Strike," 248.

28. Fortunato Vezzoli, "Per Ettor e Giovannitti" *Il Proletario*, May 18, 1912; see also Flavio Venanzi, "Senza tregua!" *Il Proletario*, May 18, 1912.

29. Ferdinando Fasce, *Tra due sponde: Lavoro, affari e cultura tra Italia e Stati Uniti nell'eta` della grande emigrazione* (Genoa: Graphos, 1993), 22–27; Edmondo Rossoni CPC, Busta 4466, Archivio Centrale dello Stato, Rome; John J. Tinghino, *Edmondo Rossoni: From Revolutionary Syndacalism to Fascism* (New York: Peter Lang, 1991), 44–46; Arturo

Giovannitti CPC, Busta 2439, Archivio Centrale dello Stato, Rome; "Arturo Giovannitti, poeta dei diseredati, dei ribelli e del divenire sociale, non e più," *Giustizia*, January 1960, 8; Foner, *The Industrial Workers of the World*, 343.

30. See Topp, *Those Without a Country*, ch. 3, "The 1912 Lawrence Strike."

31. Quoted in Vezzosi, "La Federazione," 81. See "Il secondo gruppo di esuli a New York," *Il Proletario*, Mar. 1, 1912. For more on the childen's exodus, see Vezzosi, "La Federazione," 80–81; Adriana Dadà, "I radicali italo-americani e la società italiana," *Italia contemporanea*, 146–147 (June 1982): 132; Peppino Ortoleva, "Una voce del coro: Angelo Rocco e lo sciopero di Lawrence del 1912," *Movimento operaio e socialista*, 4: 1–2 (1981): 13, 23.

32. Edmondo Rossoni, "I veri cospiratori" *Il Proletario*, July 6, 1912, 1.

33. Tresca, unpublished autobiography, 186–188.

34. John di Gregorio, "Fakomania: A Propos of the Union Square Incident," *Il Proletario*, May 11, 1912.

35. Like many Irish arrivals before them, these Italian immigrants did not seek acceptance by Anglo-Saxon culture on its own terms. Theirs was not a singular and simple project of assimilation, of becoming "American." The intensity of their rejection of this possibility in all likelihood distinguished them from many of the Italian immigrants they led in Lawrence. Peppino Ortoleva has argued that Italian immigrant workers ultimately sought through the strike a level of acceptance into American culture they had never enjoyed. If so, they were perhaps more optimistic but certainly less prescient than FSI members; in the ensuing decade, the United States would shut its doors almost completely to Italian and other southern and eastern European immigrants. Ortoleva, 24–25.

36. Edmondo Rossoni, "Primo Maggio di Guerra," *Il Proletario*, May 1, 1912.

37. Arturo Massimo Giovannitti, *The Collected Poems of Arturo Giovannitti* (Chicago: Egidio Clemente & Sons, 1962).

38. Tresca, unpublished autobiography, 191. Tresca's use of the term "manly" rather than "masculine" merits comment here. Gail Bederman offers an insightful distinction between "manliness" and "masculinity." The former stood for the loftiest ideals of (Victorian) manhood— sexual self-restraint, powerful will, strength of character. It was, in Bederman's words, "precisely the sort of middle-class Victorian cultural formulation which grew shaky in the late nineteenth century." Gail Bederman, *Manliness and Civilization: A Cultural History of Gender and Race in the United States, 1880–1917* (Chicago: University of Chicago Press, 1995), 18. Masculinity, by contrast, was used increasingly in the first decades of the twentieth century to signify more virile characteristics—aggressiveness, physical force, and male sexuality. Though Tresca used the term "manly," the context in which he used it suggests that he meant to convey that Giovannitti was the embodiment of masculinity.

39. Arturo Giovannitti, "Il Cittadino Browning," *Il Proletario*, Dec. 22, 1911, 1.

40. Arturo M. Giovannitti, "Syndicalism—The Creed of Force," *The Independent* 76: 3387 (Oct. 30, 1913): 209.

41. Tresca, unpublished autobiography, 179.

42. For a full account, see ibid., 177–191.

43. For more on the IWW's position on violence, see, for example, Foner, *Industrial Workers of the World*, 164–166; Dubofsky, *We Shall Be All*, 160–164; Paul Brissenden, *The IWW: A Study of American Syndicalism* (New York: Russell and Russell, 1957 [1919]), 278–281.

44. Dubofsky, *We Shall Be All*, 248.

45. Tresca, unpublished autobiography, 170, 173.

46. Elizabeth Faue, "Gender and the Reconstruction of Labor History: An Introduction," *Labor History* 34: 2–3 (Spring-Summer 1993): 169; Nick Salvatore. *Eugene V. Debs: Citizen and Socialist* (Urbana: University of Illinois Press, 1982); David Montgomery, *Workers' Control in America: Studies in the History of Work, Technology, and Labor Struggles* (New York: Cambridge University Press, 1979), 9–32.

47. Hondagneu-Sotelo and Messner, "Gender Displays," 208.

48. Nicola Vecchi, "Open Letter to Her Majesty the Queen," *Il Proletario*, Dec. 7, 1912.

49. Arturo Giovannitti, "La Donna e la Forca," *Il Proletario*, June 30, 1911.

50. Cameron, *Radicals of the Worst Sort*, 117–169.

51. See Francis Shor, "'Virile Syndicalism' in Comparative Perspective: A Gender Analysis of the IWW in the United States and Australia," *Radical History Review* 56 (Fall 1999): 65–77; Shor, "The IWW and Oppositional Politics in World War I: Pushing the System Beyond the Limits," *Radical History Review* 46 (Winter 1996): 74–94; Ann Schofield, "Rebel Girls and Union Maids: The Woman Question in the Journals of the AFL and IWW, 1905–1920," *Feminist Studies* 9: 2 (Summer 1983): 335–358.

52. Cameron, *Radicals of the Worst Sort*, 126.

53. Dubofsky, *We Shall Be All*, 253.

54. "Altre notizie da Lawrence: Le donne pregano," *Il Proletario*, Mar. 1, 1912.

CHAPTER 7

1. Robert Orsi, "The Religious Boundaries of an Inbetween People: Street *Feste* and the Problem of the Dark-Skinned Other in Italian Harlem 1920–1990," *American Quarterly* 44:3 (Sept. 1992): 313–347. See also James Barrett and David Roediger, "Inbetween Peoples: Race, Nationality, and the 'New Immigrant' Working Class," *Journal of American Ethnic History* 16 (Spring 1997): 3–44.

2. Rudolph J. Vecoli, "'Free Country': The American Republic Viewed by the Italian Left, 1880–1920," in Marianne Debouzy, ed., *In the Shadow of the Statue of Liberty* (Saint Denis, France: Presses Universitaires de Vincennes, 1988).

3. The best history of the Paterson group from the inception of *La Questione Sociale* to its suppression can be found in the following works by George Carey: "The Vessel, the Deed and the Idea: The Paterson Anarchists, 1895–1908" (unpublished manuscript, n.d.); "'La Questione Sociale', an Anarchist Newspaper in Paterson, N.J. (1895–1908)," in Lydio F. Tomasi, ed., *Italian Americans: New Perspectives in Italian Immigration and Ethnicity* (New York: Center for Migration Studies, 1985); and "The Vessel, the Deed, and the Idea: Anarchists in Paterson 1895–1908," *Antipode* 10: 11(1979). For a discussion of the important role played by immigrant anarchists in the origins and development of the IWW see Salvatore Salerno, *Red November, Black November: Culture and Community in the Industrial Workers of the World* (New York: State University of New York Press, 1989), ch. 2. For a discussion of the Paterson group's relationship to the IWW, see Salerno, "No God, No Master: Italian Anarchists and the Industrial Workers of the World," in Philip V. Cannistraro and Gerald Meyer, eds., *The Lost World of Italian American Radicalism: Politics, Culture and History* (Westport, CT: Greenwood Press, forthcoming).

4. Sophie Elwood, "The Roots and Results of Radicalism Among Piemontese Silk Workers, 1848–1913" (paper submitted for Certificate of Advanced Study, Wesleyan University, Apr., 1988), 80–83.

5. Nina M. Browne, "Long After Silk: Constructing Civic Identity and History in a Deindustrialized City" (M.A. thesis, New York University, 1992), 42–54.

6. Steve Golin, *The Fragile Bridge: Paterson Silk Strike, 1913* (Philadelphia: Temple University Press, 1988).

7. Vincent Parrillo, "Smokestacks and Steeples: A Portrait of Paterson," video documentary, Paterson Visitors Center, 1992.

8. Browne, "Long After Silk."

9. "Paterson Raids Give Clues to Palmer Bomb," *The Evening Mail*, Feb. 16, 1920, 1; "Raid Business Booms in Paterson; 17 Are Sent to Ellis Island," *New York Call*, Feb. 16, 1920, 1; "Terrorists Caught in Paterson Raids," *New York Times,* Feb. 16, 1920, 1.

10. "Brief History of L'Era Nuova Group of Anarchists at Paterson, N.J., Including the Activities of Certain Leaders, Official Organs and Connections with the Francisco Ferrer Association," National Archives, Washington, D.C., Record Group 65, file 61–4185.

11. Theodore Kornweibel, Jr., *Seeing Red: Federal Campaign Against Black Militancy 1919–1925* (Bloomington: Indiana University Press, 1998). See also Ward Churchhill and Jim Vander Wall, *Agents of Repression: The FBI's Secret War Against the Black Panthers and the American Indian Movement* (Boston: South End Press, 1990); Peter Matthiessen, *In the Spirit of Crazy Horse* (New York: Viking Press, 1984); and John W. Sayer, *Ghost Dancing the Law: The Wounded Knee Trials* (Cambridge, MA: Harvard University Press, 1997).

12. William Preston, *Aliens and Dissenters: Federal Suppression of Radicals, 1903–1933* (New York: Harper Torchbooks, 1963), 99.

13. Tatsuro Nomura, "Partisan Politics in and Around the IWW: The Earliest Phase," *Journal of the Faculty of Foreign Studies* 10 (1977): 86–139; Salerno, *Red November*, 69–90.

14. "Terrorists Caught in Paterson Raids," *New York Times*, Feb. 16, 1920, 1.

15. Researchers who tried to look into the record groups in the National Archives cited in William Preston's classic book, *Aliens and Dissenters*, about the "Red Scare," and John Higham's book, *Strangers in the Land*, were unable to locate the files in these record groups. They concluded that the offending parts of the record group had been destroyed in retaliation for Preston's work, or that following the publication of *Aliens and Dissenters*, the government restricted access to the files Preston had used. Where this myth actually begins is difficult to trace. The first verifiable account of the trouble researchers ran into with these records involves Melvyn Dubofsky's attempt to gain access to the record group. He did not know that the Immigration and Naturalization Service (INS) had withdrawn the "56,000 series" of materials used by Preston and retired the files to the Federal Record Center in 1960. Although he was able to enlist Senator Robert Kennedy to help open or declassify the files, the files could not be found. In her paper about the "56,000 Series," National Archives historian Marian Smith concluded: "Whether Dubofsky requested files previously withdrawn by the INS, or files still at the Archives but withheld due to FBI restrictions, he left with the impression that the FBI somehow controlled access to INS files, and now did so because of Preston's book." Subsequent researchers also encountered difficulties and attributed them to some conspiracy on the part of the FBI. But the fact that records were missing does not necessarily mean they were destroyed. Rather, we now know that they were consolidated into A-files or C-files or simply misplaced. In 1996 the "56,000 series materials" were returned to the INS. It is in this record group that much of the material on the Paterson anarchists, as well as files on hundreds of other Italian immigrant activists, can be found. See Marian Smith, "Back from the Grave: The Life, Death, and Future of INS Historical Subject Files" (unpublished manuscript, n.d).

16. National Archives, RG 65, File 61–4185.

17. W.E.B. Du Bois, "The Souls of White Folk," reprinted in David R. Roediger, ed., *Black on White: Black Writers on What It Means to Be White* (New York: Schocken Books,

1998); Alfreda M. Duster, *Crusade for Justice: The Autobiography of Ida B. Wells* (Chicago: University of Chicago Press, 1970).

18. U.S. Senate, *Investigation Activities of the Department of Justice*, 66th Congress, 1st Session, Senate Document 153 (Washington, DC: U.S. Government Printing Office, 1919), 13.

19. Kornweibel, *Seeing Red*, 69.

20. National Archives, Washington D.C., Record Group 85, Records of the Immigration and Naturalization Service, Entry 9, Subject Correspondence File, 1906–1956, File 54235/36.

21. Little is known about Pedro Esteve (1866–1925), considered the leading Spanish anarchist in the United States. Esteve's relationship with anarchism began in Barcelona, where he participated in the Catalonian anarchist movement and worked with Barcelona's principal anarchist newspaper, *El Productor*. In the early 1890s Esteve left Barcelona for the United States. He moved between New York, where he organized seamen; Colorado, where he participated in union-forming activities with miners; and Tampa, Florida, where he organized cigarmakers. Esteve frequently shared the platform with Emma Goldman and acted as her interpreter. In addition to intermittently editing *La Questione Sociale* between 1899 and 1906, Esteve also edited *El Despertar* (Paterson, 1892–1895?, 1900), *El Esclavo* (Tampa, 1894–1898?), and *Cultura Obrera* (New York, 1911–1912, 1921–1925). In Ybor City, Florida, he ran La Poliglota, a small anarchist press. He married the Italian anarchist Maria Roda. See Paul Avrich, *Anarchist Voices: An Oral History of Anarchism in America* (Princeton, NJ: Princeton University Press, 1995), 143, 391, 393; Gary A. Mormino and George E. Pozzetta, "Spanish Anarchists in Tampa, Florida, 1886–1931," in Dirk Hoerder, ed., *"Struggle a Hard Battle": Essays on Working-Class Immigrants* (De Kalb: Northern Illinois University Press, 1986); Gary A. Mormino and George E. Pozzetta, *The Immigrant World of Ybor City*, (Chicago: University of Illinois Press, 1987) 145–174; Joan Casanovas, "Pedro Esteve (1865–1925): Un Anarquista Catala a Cavall de Dos Mons I de Dues Generacions," Papers of George E. Pozzetta, Immigration History Research Center, University of Minnesota, Minneapolis; Emma Goldman, *Living My Life* (New York: Garden City Publishing Company, 1934), 150; Carey, "The Vessel, the Deed and the Idea."

22. Carey, "The Vessel, the Deed and the Idea" (unpublished manuscript), 287–291.

23. Ludovico Caminita, "Odio di Razza," *La Questione Sociale*, May 18, 1906.

24. Avrich, *Anarchist Voices*, 483.

25. Carey, "The Vessel, the Deed and the Idea," (unpublished manuscript), 315–316.

26. James Sandos, *Rebellion in the Borderlands: Anarchism and the Plan of San Diego, 1904–1923* (Norman: University of Oklahoma Press, 1992), 53.

27. It is difficult to say when Caminita's association with the Magonistas began or the exact date that his Italian-language column appeared. At presently no archive has a full run of *Regeneración*. From what has survived, it appears that the column began in November 1911. Examples of Caminita's graphics can be found in *Regeneración* in the period between 1912 and 1916. James Sandos included a poster designed by Caminita in his book, *Rebellion in the Borderlands*, 53. Following the suppression of *La Questione Sociale*, its successor, the newspaper *L'Era Nuova*, began coverage of the Mexican Revolution. Under the title "La Rivoluzione nel Messico" one can find continued (often front-page) reports on the Mexican Revolution through 1916. For the announcement of Caminita's propaganda tour, see *Regeneración*, Nov. 11, 1911, 3.

28. "I Delitti della Razza Bianca," *La Questione Sociale*, Feb. 20, 1909, 1.

29. "Razze Superiori, Imparate!," *L'Era Nuova*, Feb. 27, 1915; "Questione di Razze?" *L'Era Nuova*, Jan. 30, 1915; "Guerra di razze," *L'Era* Nuova, Feb. 6, 1915, 2.

30. Vecoli, "'Free Country.'"

31. Vecoli, "'Free Country,'" 45–46. See also "Non Lotta di Razza," *Il Proletario*, June 4, 1909.

32. Vecoli, "'Free Country,'" 45–46.

33. Walter White, *Rope & Faggot: A Biography of Judge Lynch* (New York: Alfred A. Knopf, 1929); Richard Gambino, *Vendetta* (New York: Doubleday, Inc.,1977); Edward F. Haas, "Guns, Goats and Italians: The Tallulah Lynchings of 1899," *North Louisiana Historical Association Journal*, 13 (1982), 45–58; James E Cutler, *Lynch-Law* (Montclair, NJ: Patterson Smith, 1969), 178–180; James Allen, et al., *Without Sanctuary, Lynching Photographs in America* (New York.: Twin Palms, 2002), 167–169; Robert P. Ingalls, "Lynching and Established Violence in Tampa, 1895–1935," *Journal of Southern History* 53:4 (Nov. 1987): 613–644.

34. The case that she referred to involved the judicial execution of six Italians in Amite, Louisiana, for the alleged murder of an innkeeper. See Glem G. Hearsey, "The Six Who Were Hanged" (n.p., n.d.); and John V. Baiamonte, Jr., *Spirit of Vengeance: Nativism and Louisiana Justice, 1921–1924* (Baton Rouge: Louisiana State University Press, 1986).

CHAPTER 8

1. Philip Lamantia, "Surrealism in 1943," *VVV* no. 4 (1944): 18–20.

2. See, for example, the quotations on the back cover of Lamantia's *Bed of Sphinxes* (San Francisco: City Lights, 1997).

3. "Poetic Matters" originally appeared in *Arsenal/Surrealist Subversion* no. 3 (1976): 6–10, and "Radio Voices: A Child's Bed of Sirens" in the "Surrealism & Its Popular Accomplices" issue of *Cultural Correspondence* (1979): 25–31. (A few months later that special issue was published as a book by City Lights.) Both essays are reprinted in Ron Sakolsky, ed., *Surrealist Subversions: Rants, Writings & Images by the Surrealist Movement in the United States* (New York: Autonomedia, 2002).

4. Lamantia is mentioned but rarely discussed in most books on the Beats. Data about him on Beat-related internet sites are devoted almost entirely to his pre-1960 activity, and tend to be sadly inaccurate.

5. Exceptions include radical oral historian Paul Buhle and French critic Yves Le Pellec, whose interviews are cited throughout these notes.

6. Nancy J. Peters, "Philip Lamantia," in Ann Charters, ed., *The Beats: Literary Bohemians in Postwar America*, volume 1, *Dictionary of American Biography*, vol. 16 (Detroit: Gale Research/Bruccoli Clark, 1983), 329–336.

7. The best overall history of surrealism is Gérard Durozoi, *Histoire du Mouvement Surréaliste* (Paris: Editions Hazan, 1997), recently issued in an English translation by the University of Chicago Press.

8. On the early history of surrealist politics, see Maurice Nadeau, *The History of Surrealism* (New York: Macmillan, 1965). For the movement's current politics, see Sakolsky, *Surrealist Subversions*; and the website www.surrealism-usa.org.

9. Franklin Rosemont, ed., "Surrealism: Revolution Against Whiteness," special issue of *Race Traitor* (Summer 1998).

10. Penelope Rosemont, ed., *Surrealist Women: An International Anthology* (Austin: University of Texas Press, 1998).

11. Among them were *First Papers of Surrealism*, catalog of the 1942 exhibition (New

York: Coordinating Council of French Relief Societies, 1942); Nicolas Calas, *Confound the Wise* (New York: Arrow Editions, 1942); and four books by André Breton: *Arcane 17* (New York: Brentano's, 1945); an expanded edition of *Le Surréalisme et la Peinture* (New York: Brentano's, 1945); *Young Cherry Trees Secured Against Hares* (New York: View, 1946); and *Yves Tanguy* (New York: Pierre Matisse, 1946).

12. Peters, "Philip Lamantia," 331.

13. I have discussed this period in my introduction to *What Is Surrealism? Selected Writings of André Breton* (New York: Monad Press, 1978; new ed., New York: Pathfinder, 2000).

14. Peters, "Philip Lamantia," 331.

15. Philip Lamantia, telephone interview with the author, Jan. 12, 1992.

16. Paul Buhle, "Interview with Martocchia and Lamantia," Oct. 31, 1982, in the Oral History of the American Left collection in the Tamiment Library, New York University; transcript, 11.

17. Buhle interview, 10.

18. Peters, "Philip Lamantia," 331. On the critical, academic, and popular reception of surrealism in the United States from the 1920s on, see also my Foreword to M. E. Warlick, *Max Ernst and Alchemy: A Magician in Search of Myth* (Austin: University of Texas Press, 2001). On CIA funding of antisurrealist cultural groups, see Frances Stonor Saunders, *Who Paid the Piper? The CIA and the Cultural Cold War* (London: Granta Books, 1999).

19. See the remarks of Congressman George A. Dondero (R., Mich.) in the *Congressional Record*, Aug. 16, 1949.

20. Lamantia, telephone interview with the author, Jan. 12, 1992. It is only to fair to add that Lamantia readily admits that he did learn a lot from Rexroth.

21. Donald M. Allen, ed. *The New American Poetry* (New York: Grove Press, 1960), 440.

22. André Breton, "Away with Miserabilism!" in his *Surrealism and Painting* (New York: Harper & Row, 1972), 347–348. See also my preface to the catalog of the World Surrealist Exhibition, *Marvelous Freedom / Vigilance of Desire* (Chicago: Black Swan Press, 1976), as well as Franklin Rosemont, Penelope Rosemont, and Paul Garon, eds. *The Forecast Is Hot! Tracts & Other Collective Declarations of the Surrealist Movement in the U.S., 1966–1976*, (Chicago: Black Swan Press, 1997).

23. On surrealism and religion, see Sakolsky, *Surrealist Subversions*, 361–373.

24. Prospectus for the New American Poetry Circuit (San Francisco, 1969).

25. Lamantia, telephone interview with the author, Jan. 12, 1992.

26. Philip Lamantia, *Ekstasis* (San Francisco: Auerhahn Press, 1959), unpaginated. Further on in the same book is a shorter poem dedicated to Hoffman.

27. Lamantia, telephone interview with the author, Jan. 12, 1992.

28. David Roediger, "A Long Journey to the Hip Hop Nation," in Sakolsky, *Surrealist Subversions*, 595.

29. Tom J. Lewis, "Get Hip," *International Socialist Review* (Dec. 1910): 352. See also "The Hippest Union in the World," in Franklin Rosemont, *Joe Hill: The IWW & the Making of a Revolutionary Workingclass Counterculture* (Chicago: Charles H. Kerr, 2003), 393–396.

30. Ira Gitler, *Swing to Bop: An Oral History of the Transition in Jazz in the 1940s* (New York: Oxford University Press, 1985). For a surrealist view of "hip" as related to bebop, see Joseph Jablonski's introduction to Lord Buckley, *Hiparama of the Classics* (San Francisco: City Lights, 1980). A later version of Jablonski's text appears in Sakolsky, *Surrealist Subversions*, 597–599.

31. Robin D. G. Kelley, "The Riddle of the Zoot," in his *Race Rebels: Culture, Politics, and the Black Working Class* (New York: The Free Press Macmillan, 1994), is the most insightful and detailed account I know of the hipster "culture of opposition."

32. Ben Sidran, *Black Talk* (New York: DaCapo, 1981), 114. The immediately following quotation is from the same book, 109.

33. Peters, "Philip Lamantia," 333.

34. Other surrealists of the time who were ardent enthusiasts of bop and post-bop jazz include Robert Benayoun, Victor Brauner, Aube Elléouet (Breton's daughter), Enrique Gomez-Correa, Gérard Legrand, Roberto Matta, Gellu Naum, Stanislas Rodanski, Claude Tarnaud, and Michel Zimbacca. On surrealism and African American music, see Gérard Legrand, *Puissances du Jazz* (Paris: Arcanes, 1953); Paul Garon, *Blues and the Poetic Spirit,* new ed. (San Francisco: City Lights, 1996; 1st ed. 1975); Robin D. G. Kelley, *Freedom Dreams: The Black Radical Imagination* (Boston: Beacon Press, 2002); and "Black Music: Sounds of the History of Freedom," in Sakolsky, *Surrealist Subversions*, 611–646.

35. Aimé Césaire, *Les Armes Miraculeuses* (Paris: Gallimard, 1946).

36. Norman Mailer, *The White Negro* (San Francisco: City Lights, 1957).

37. John A. Williams, "My Man Himes: An Interview with Chester Himes," *Amistad* 1 (1970), 43.

38. Lamantia, telephone interview with the author, Jan. 12, 1992.

39. See, for example, William Everson's comments in David Meltzer, *The San Francisco Poets*, (New York: Ballantine), 1971, 98.

40. Peters, "Philip Lamantia," 332.

41. Jayne Cortez, "Mainstream Statement," in Sakolsky, *Surrealist Subversions*, 278.

42. Quoted in "Naropa's War on Poetry," in *Arsenal/Surrealist Subversion* no. 4 (1989): 185. See also Tom Clark, *The Great Naropa Poetry Wars* (Santa Barbara, CA: Cadmus Editions, 1980).

43. Kenneth Rexroth was not far off the mark when he complained that Kerouac insisted on writing about "jazz and Negroes" despite the obvious fact that these were subjects "Jack knows nothing about." See Rexroth's review of *The Subterraneans* in *San Francisco Chronicle*, Feb. 16, 1958.

44. Lamantia, "Poetic Matters," in Sakolsky, *Surrealist Subversions*, 283–290.

45. Ibid., 283.

46. Ibid., 283–284.

47. Ibid., 285–286.

48. Allen Ginsberg, "Encounters with Ezra Pound: Journal Notes," in Lawrence Ferlinghetti, ed., *City Lights Anthology* (San Francisco: City Lights, 1974), 9–21.

49. "Devolution of the Pound," in *Arsenal/Surrealist Subversion* no. 3 (Chicago: Black Swan Press, 1976), 94.

50. In the 1970s and 1980s, Philip and I often discussed a kind of "surrealist anti-canon" that, in addition to the poets already cited here, included the nineteenth-century Unitarian trance poet Jones Very and Benjamin Paul Blood (theorist of "anaesthetic revelation"); anarchist Voltairine de Cleyre; Mary Austin; Lew Sarett; Lola Ridge; and the IWW writer T-Bone Slim (Matt Valentine Huhta).

51. Lamantia, "Poetic Matters," 283. For Corso's comments on the Black Mountain group ("mental gangsters . . . hip squares"), see Lawrence Lipton, *The Holy Barbarians* (New York: Julian Messner, 1959), 132–133. Martin Duberman's *Black Mountain: An Exploration in Community* (New York: Dutton, 1972) is a highly enthusiastic study of the school, although the author does note its miserable record on race matters (one of its

founders and central figures was a racist, and the faculty included an unabashed Nazi), as well as its extreme homophobia and misogyny (Charles Olson, for example, banned women from his classes). In response to my query (circa 1989), Philip told me that, among his contemporaries, he thought Gary Snyder was "doing good work."

52. Lamantia, "Poetic Matters," 287.

53. Lamantia, "Notes Toward a Rigorous Interpretation of Surrealist Occultation," originally published in *Arsenal/Surrealist Subversion* no. 3 (1976): 10; reprinted in Sakolsky, *Surrealist Subversions*, 440.

54. Surrealist appreciations of "primitive" art are numerous. For a sampling, see *Sculptures d'Afrique, d'Amérique, d'Océanie: Collection André Breton et Paul Eluard* (Paris: Charles Ratton, 1931; reprinted New York: Hacker Art Books, 1972); André Breton, *Surrealism and Painting*; Nancy Cunard, "Surrealism, Ethnography, and Revolution," in Penelope Rosemont, *Surrealist Women*, 26–28; Vincent Bounore, *Vision d'Océanie* (Paris: Editions Dapper, 1992).

55. See Franklin Rosemont, "Surrealists on Whiteness, from 1925 to the Present," *Race Traitor* no. 9 (Summer 1998): 7–8.

56. Jayne Cortez, "Léon Damas: Human Writes Poetry," in Sakolsky, *Surrealist Subversions*, 193.

57. On Césaire, see especially Robin D. G. Kelley's introduction, "A Poetics of Anticolonialism," to the fiftieth anniversary edition of Césaire's *Discourse on Colonialism* (New York: Monthly Review Press, 2000.

58. Peters, "Philip Lamantia," 333.

59. The two examples (and five others) are included in Lamantia's *Becoming Visible* (San Francisco: City Lights, 1981), 82–83. For an account of the game, see Penelope Rosemont, "Time-Travelers' Potlatch: Notes on a Surrealist Game," in her *Surrealist Experiences: 1001 Dawns, 221 Midnights* (Chicago: Black Swan Press, 2000), 109–115. See also Gale Ahrens et al., "Time-Travelers' Potlatch," in Sakolsky, *Surrealist Subversions*, 217–221.

60. The resulting text of one of these games is included in Philip Lamantia *et al.*, "The Chairman of Absinthe," in Sakolsky, *Surrealist Subversions*, 208–209.

CHAPTER 9

Acknowledgments

Heart-felt thanks go to Jah for life, love, and hip-hop; my father for your perseverance, love, and commitment to our family, for the gift of music, and for teaching me how to forgive; my sister for your amazing courage, inspiration, guidance, and healing wisdom; my brother for your advice, encouragement, and calm, caring presence; grandma and grandpa for always being there; Kym Ragusa and Joseph Sciorra for offering such helpful feedback; and my extended family and friends for unconditional love and continued support. This piece is dedicated to my family, and The Anonymous, in memory of Yusuf Hawkins, Michael Griffith, and my mother.

1. All lyrics © 2002 Manifest. For more info, check www.manifestworld.com

2. Some of Hip Hop's notable exceptions include: Old School Writers Fuzz One (R.I.P.), Seen, Cavs, Boots 167, Billy167, John150, Cook-2, Dee, Fane, Pi-2, Kirs, K2, Risco, Rocky-1, Shark, Si-1, Sike, Tear-2, Tek, Siko, Vinny, Comet, and Sar 1 all brought an Italian American presence and visionary concepts of unity to the early New York graffiti scene; DJ Francis Grasso (R.I.P.), Kid Capri, DJ Muggs, DJ Skribble and New School emcees princess Superstar, Don Scavone, Guinea Love of Northern State, Johnny Blanco,

Lord Roc, Joe Summa, Pizon, Cali Bella, JoJo Pellegrino, Genovese, and poet Ursula Rucker do the same today. See Joseph Sciorra, "Opening Comments," unpublished paper delivered at the symposium "Eye-Talian Flava: The Italian American Presence in Hip Hop," John D. Calandra Italian American Institute, Queens College and Casa Italiana Zerilli-Marimò, New York University, October 5, 2001.

3. Not until 1999, with the emergence of Eminem, did a credible white Hip-Hop artist succeed in capturing and holding the public's attention, hence the hysteria around him and his subsequent reign at the top of the charts.

4. For an indispensable account of the early days see *Yes Yes Y'All: The Experience Music Project Oral History of Hip Hop's First Decade* (New York: Da Capo Press, 2002).

5. For more on the Italian hip-hop movement, check Joseph Sciorra's remarkable site www.italianrap.com.

6. These lyrics are an interpolation of a 1963 speech by former Ethiopian Emperor His Imperial Majesty Haile Selassie I before the United Nations.

7. *Wonders of the African World* (New York: Alfred A. Knopf, 1999), p. 25.

CHAPTER 10

Acknowledgments
I wish to acknowledge the support that my research on Leonard Covello has received at various times from the John D. Calandra Italian American Institute, the Rockefeller Foundation, the Professional Staff Congress / City University Research Foundation, and the Balch Institute.

1. In the 1930s, Italian Harlem was home to eighty thousand first- and second-generation Italians. "Harlem School Outbreaks Laid to Hoodlumism," *Herald Tribune*, Oct. 3, 1945. See also Gerald Meyer, "Italian Harlem: America's Most Italian Little Italy," in Philip Cannistraro, ed., *The Italians of New York: Five Centuries of Struggle and Achievement* (Milan: Mondaldori, 1999), 57–68.

2. Robert Freeman, "Exploring the Path of Community Change in East Harlem, 1870–1970" (Ph.D. diss., Fordham University, 1994), 358.

3. Many of the newspaper articles cited in this paper were collected by Don Dodson (the executive director of the Mayor's Committee on Unity). The page numbers are only occasionally present on the clippings. These articles can be found in Covello Collection: Box 54, Folder 7. Henceforth, Covello Collection will be indicated by CC; box by B; and folder by F.) The Covello Collection is deposited in the Historical Society of Pennsylvania in Philadelphia.

4. See Leonard Covello, *The Social Background of the Italo-American School Child: A Study of the Southern Italian Family Mores and Their Effect on the School Situation in Italy and America* (Leiden: E. J. Brill, 1969); and with Guido D'Agostino, *The Heart Is the Teacher* (New York: McGraw-Hill, 1958). On Covello, see these articles by Gerald Meyer: "Leonard Covello (1887–1982): An Italian American's Contribution to the Education of Minority-Culture Students," *Italian American Review* (Fall 1996): 36–44; "Leonard Covello: A Pioneer in Bilingual Education," *The Bilingual Review* (Jan.–Aug. 1985): 55–61; "Leonard Covello and Vito Marcantonio: A Lifelong Collaboration for Progress," *Italica* (Spring 1985): 54–66.

5. Leonard Covello, "The Italian Teachers Association: Eighteenth Annual Report—School Year, 1938–1939," in Francesco Cordasco, ed., *The Italian Community and Its Language in the United States: The Annual Reports of the Italian Teachers Association* (Totowa,

NJ: Rowman and Littlefield, 1975), 380. *The Annual Reports of the Italian Teachers Association* ceased publication as of the 1938–1939 issue. This was one consequence of the war, which also brought about a reduction in the teaching of the Italian language, Italian-language broadcasts, and Italian American organizational life. See Robert Schaffer, "Multicultural Education in New York City during World War II," *New York History* (July 1996): 314.

6. On cultural pluralism, which developed in opposition to the coercive acculturation imposed by "Americanization," see Susan Dicker, *Languages in America: A Pluralist View* (Philadelphia: Multilingual Matters, 1996), 35; Nicholas Montalto, "The Forgotten Dream: A History of the Intercultural Education Movement, 1924–1941" (Ph.D. diss., University of Minnesota, 1977).

7. Shaffer, "Multicultural Education," 301–332. The term "intercultural," which is now out of use, roughly equates with the current term "multiculturalism."

8. "Community Centered School," chapter 13, "Recreation," unpublished manuscript. CC: B 19, F 19/7.

9. "Community Mass Meeting," program of Oct. 8 meeting in Benjamin Franklin, CC: B 54, F 13.

10. Renzo Dalzin, "William Spiegel," *Benjamin Franklin Year Book,* 1942, 3. During this period, with the exception of Boys High in Brooklyn, Franklin's basketball team, was unequaled. Joseph Dorinson, interview, Oct. 31, 2002.

11. Covello, *The Heart*, 187.

12. "Notes on the Racial Incident at Franklin," unsigned but probably Covello, CC: B 54, F 7.

13. This narrative of these events has been culled almost entirely from a fact sheet developed by a group of faculty meeting on Monday, Oct. 1, and then distributed in English and Italian on Tuesday, Oct. 2. "Benjamin Franklin High School/James Otis Junior High School, Dr. Leonard Covello." CC: B 54, F 4. "Police Reassure Mothers, Guard Harlem School," *Herald Tribune*, Sept. 29, 1945.

14. "Police Reassure Mothers."

15. "Notes on the Racial Incident at Franklin."

16. "500 Boys Battle in East Harlem." Unidentified clipping, CC: B 54, F 7.

17. "Wallander Maps School Protection," *World-Telegram*, Sept. 29, 1945.

18. "Police Reassure Mothers," *Herald Tribune*, Sept. 29, 1945.

19. "Student 'Strikes' Flare into Riots in Harlem Schools: Knives Flash in Street Fights as Elders Join Pupils in Battling the Police," *New York Times*, Sept. 29, 1945, 1; "2,000 High Students Battle in Race Riot," *Daily News*, Sept. 29, 1945; "Chicago, Harlem Torn by School Race Strife," and "Harlem School Riots Bring Petition for Race Segregation," *New York Post*, Sept. 29, 1945.

20. Untitled, four-page report on initial articles about the incident organized into two columns—one with summaries of the articles and the other with Covello's version of the events. Although this piece was unsigned, its first-person voice and writing style indicate Covello's authorship. CC: B 54, F 7.

21. "2,000 High Students Battle in Race Riot."

22. "Chicago, Harlem Torn by School Race Strife" and "Harlem School Riots Bring Petition for Race Segregation," *New York Post*, Sept. 29, 1945.

23. "Agitators Blamed in School Riots as Cops Man Buildings," *Daily News*, Sept. 30, 1945), 4; "High Schools Get Police Guard as New Outbreaks Are Hinted," *Daily Mirror,* Sept. 30, 1945, 5.

24. "School Fights Bring Study," *PM*, Sept. 30, 1945, 13.

25. "Provvedimenti dopo i tumulti di Pleasant Ave.: Le scuole sarrano protete," *Il Progresso Italo-Americano*, Sept. 30, 1945.

26. "Demand Mayor Act on Harlem Anti-Negro Riot: See School Outbreak as Part of a Nationwide Racist Plot," *Sunday Worker*, Sept. 30, 1945.

27. "The Community School and Race Relations," unpublished manuscript (Nov. 19, 1945), 6. CC: B 20, F 9. Excerpts from Covello's manuscript, however, were mentioned in the text of an article titled "Social Front," published in the journal, *A Monthly Summary of Events and Trends in Race Relations* (sponsored by the Social Science Institute at Fisk University), which minimized the events at Franklin, and went on to state: "Perhaps, the most significant aspect of the affair was the positive manner in which it was approached by the administration, faculty, and student body with the cooperation of concerned community organizations." (Dec. 1945), 138–139.

28. Benjamin Franklin was housed in an architecturally distinguished, redbrick, Georgian-style edifice that spanned two blocks. The interior boasted terrazzo floors, wainscoted walls, and inset display cases, as well as an oversized auditorium and library. It had community rooms, an auditorium with balcony with a capacity of fifteen hundred, and its roof boasted the only greenhouse in any New York City high school. CC: B 20, F 20. With one façade overlooking the community (incidentally, dwarfing Our Lady of Mount Carmel Church, Italian Harlem's "cathedral"), and a second façade overlooking the East River, Benjamin Franklin represented a major civic monument, that was intended to serve not only as a school but, in accordance with Covello's philosophy, also as a community center. Today, Franklin's auditorium is dedicated to Covello, and remains (aside from a senior citizens center in East Harlem) the only memorial to Covello.

29. Chapter 16, "Adult Education." CC: B 19, F 19/11.

30. Untitled set of minutes with a handwritten notation: "Meeting—Sunday Eve—Sept. 30, 1945 at Mr. Covello's home." CC: B 54, F 4. Although not listed in the minutes as "present," Robert Shapiro, an English teacher at Franklin, is identified as being present at this meeting in Robert Peebles, "Leonard Covello: A Study of an Immigrant's Contribution to New York City" (Ph.D. diss., New York University, 1967), 281.

31. Despite his management position, Covello always maintained a warm relationship with the Communist-led Teachers Union. In 1938, for example, he was a speaker at its annual convention, and at its 1941 conference he received the union's annual award for his "outstanding contributions to education democracy." "The Student Movement Comes of Age," *New York Teacher* (Feb. 1938): 14; "Educational Conference," *New York Teacher* (Apr. 1941): 10.

32. Covello recalled in his biography that Kuper had "always made himself available . . . . [and was someone who Covello] could always count on his advice, help, and active participation in all our undertakings." Covello, *The Heart*, 194.

33. Covello, *The Heart*, 115, 163, 188. Rose was Covello's second wife. His first wife, Mary Accurso, Rose's sister, was also a teacher; she died in 1914, a year after their marriage. The Accurso family arrived in Italian Harlem from Avigliano in Basilicata (Covello's hometown) before the Covellos. Like Covello, both Mary and Rose had converted to Protestantism (22, 55, 67, 101–102).

34. Harlem House (today Fiorello LaGuardia Memorial House), which is located on East 116th Street, between Second and First Avenues, was founded as the Home Garden in 1898 by a Canadian Methodist missionary, Anna Ruddy who was a great influence on Covello. Marcantonio worked in Harlem House while attending New York University Law School and met Miriam Sanders there. See Meyer, "Italian Harlem: Portrait of a Community," 61–62.

35. Peebles, "Leonard Covello," 199; see the letterhead of East Harlem League for Unity, Dec. 4, 1945. CC: B 54, F 11. "Unity League Sees Increased Tension; Inquiry into Incident in [East] Harlem Brings Warning, with Plea for Better Safeguards," *New York Times*, Dec. 11, 1945.

36. See Gerald Meyer, *Vito Marcantonio: Radical Politician, 1902–1954* (Albany: SUNY Press, 1989); Gerald Meyer, "The American Labor Party: 1936–1956," in Immanuel Ness and John Ciment, eds., *The Encyclopedia of Third Parties in America* (Armonk NY: M. E. Sharpe, 2000), vol. 1, 682–690.

37. Benjamin Franklin's graduation ceremony, June 28, 1939. CC.

38. This assignment was taken by "RAC," Rose Accurso Covello. "Minutes—Sunday Eve—Sept. 30, 1945." CC: B 54, F 4.

39. "Minutes—Sunday Eve—Sept. 30, 1945." CC: B 54, F 4.

40. This was not an entirely impractical proposal because Michael Pinto, Marcantonio's law partner, represented the left-led Film Technicians Union.

41. "Who Gets Hurt?" / "Chi ha Sofferto da Tutto Questo?" CC: B 54, F 4. No printed copy exists in either the Marcantonio Papers, which are deposited in the Manuscript Division of the New York Public Library, or the Covello Collection; nor does any published source refer to its distribution as a leaflet.

42. Meyer, *Vito Marcantonio*, 133–134.

43. Manuscript "Community Centered School," ch. 16, "Adult Ed." CC: B 19, F 19/22.

44. Covello to Rev. Guido Steccati, Oct. 1, 1945. CC: B 54, F 13.

45. "Incident—Sept. 27–28." CC: B 54, F 4.

46. "Harlem School Tension Eases, Five Inquiries On: Students Warned against 'Bilboism': Four Hundred Police Stand Guard on Streets," *New York Herald Tribune*, Oct. 2, 1945.

47. "Benjamin Franklin High School/James Otis Junior High School, Dr. Leonard Covello." CC: B 54, F 4.

48. "Athletic Coaches Scored by Mayor," *New York Times*, Oct. 1, 1945.

49. "Guard Harlem Schools to Bar Riot," *New York Journal American*, Oct. 1, 1945, 2.

50. Ted Poston, "Calls Race Riot Story 'Bilbo-Type Smear,'" *New York Post*, Oct. 1, 1945, 4. One of the five African American teachers, Layle Lane, who taught at Franklin from its founding in 1934 until her retirement in 1953, has been described as "High school teacher, civil rights pioneer, teacher unionist, Socialist activist, [Socialist Party] political candidate, lifelong pacifist, adventurer, and humanitarian." Jack Schierenbeck, "Lost and Found: The Incredible Life and Times of (Miss) Layle Lane," *American Educator* (Winter 2000–2001): 4, 19.

51. "'One of Those Things': Cops Call School Riot," *Daily Worker*, Oct. 1, 1945, 2.

52. "Teachers Urge City Officials to Act in School Race Friction; Protect Negroes," *Daily Worker*, Oct. 1, 1945, 2.

53. "Marcantonio, [Benjamin] Davis Call for Unity Against Fascist Provocation in High School Clash," *Daily Worker*, Oct. 1, 1945, 2; "Marcantonio e Davis denunziano il pericolo di provcazioni: I disordini di Harlem atribuiti al lavoro di agenti fascisti," *L'Unità del Popolo*, Oct. 6, 1945, 1; "School Rioting Endangers Unity," *People's Voice*, Oct. 6, 1945, 2.

54. "Racial Tension in School Eases," *New York Daily Mirror*, Oct. 2, 1945.

55. John Hughes, "Faculty, Kids Act to Thwart Racial Battles," *Daily News*, Oct. 2, 1945, 8; Lola Paine and Harry Raymond, "Rout Bilboism, Is Plea to Pupils Returning

After Harlem Riot," *Daily Worker*, Oct. 3, 1945, 3;"Centinaia di Poliziotti . . .," *Il Progresso*, Oct. 2, 1945.

56. "Harlem School Tension Eases," *Herald Tribune*, Oct. 2, 1945.

57. On the manuscript, Covello crossed out "fully" before "accepted." "The Community School and Race Relations," 7.

58. "School Inquiry Sifts for Agitators," *World-Telegram*, Oct. 2, 1945. This article also reported that "students entered the building quietly. There were no signs of tension or disorder." The *Daily News* also published the positive attendance figures. "School's Muster Rises After Riot," *Daily News*, Oct. 3, 1945, 24.

59. "The Parents of Boys Who Are Absent Today" (Oct. 1, 1945). CC: B 54, F 4.

60. "Board of Education Scored: Handling of Disorders Seen Causing a Setback to Human Relations," *World-Telegram*, Oct. 3, 1945. See also "Blame Harlem Outbreak on Economic Unrest," *New York Post*, Oct. 3, 1945, 16. The following day, the *Herald Tribune* quoted Rose Russell, of the Teachers Union, that overcrowded classes "contribute to the low morale of the teachers and is one of the major causes of unrest during the last few weeks." "Teachers' Groups Call N.Y. Schools Understaffed," *Herald Tribune*, Oct. 4, 1945. Algernon Black, a leader of the Ethical Culture Society, for many decades played an active role in New York City's liberal community. See also "[Peter] Cacchione Holds Officials Evade Duty in School Riots," *Daily Worker*, Oct. 4, 1945, 4;"Students Plan Program to End Racial Strife: Alumni of Benjamin Franklin H. S. to Its Defense," *PM,* Oct. 3, 1945, 16.

61. Interview with Dominic Ammariti, 1999.

62. Untitled manuscript, dated Oct. 6, 1945, of an address broadcast over WOV, CC: B 54, F 20.

63. Covello to Parents, Oct. 5, 1945. CC: B 54, F 13.

64. Marcantonio to Friend, Oct. 3, 1945. CC: B 54, F 13.

65. Although he was not an observant Catholic and married a Protestant, Marcantonio maintained warm relations with the local Catholic clergy. See Gerald Meyer, "Italian Harlem's Biggest Funeral: A Community Pays Its Last Respects to Vito Marcantonio," *Italian American Review* (Spring 1997): 108–120.

66. Checklists of names of invitees; program of meeting with names of participants; telegram from Rev. John Mulcahy to Covello, Oct. 8, 1945. CC: B 54, F 13.

67. "One Thousand Parents again Uphold Racial Accord: Meeting at Franklin School Reaffirms Faith in Community Program," *PM*, Oct. 9, 1943, 12.

68. "One Thousand Parents," 12. For Marcantonio's response to Rankin, who was a exceptionally virulent racist, see Annette T. Rubinstein, *I Vote My Conscience: Debates, Speeches, and Writings of Vito Marcantonio* (New York: John D. Calandra Italian American Institute, 2002), 204–205.

69. A. Salimbene to Covello, Oct. 8, 1945. CC: B 54, F 13.

70. "Resolution at the Community Mass Meeting at the Benjamin Franklin High School: Monday, October 8, 1945." CC: B 54, F 13. The adjective "trivial" before "incident" was crossed out in the original draft

71. Memo from Covello to Faculty and to the students of Benjamin Franklin High School and James Otis Junior High School, Oct. 9, 1945. CC: B 54, F 13. Pledge card and parental-consent card. CC: B 54, F 13. The minutes of the September 30 meeting record that the "newspaper articles [be] used in SS [Social Science] classes as example of how bad reporting is done." In fact, they were discussed in every class. This was a critical decision, because key aspects of this fight-back depended on student initiative and involvement.

72. Covello to Faculty, Oct. 9, 1945. CC: B 54, F 13.

73. "School's Intercultural Program Seen in Need of Stronger Support: Under-Surface Race Tension Is Still a Problem Particularly at Benjamin Franklin; More Well-Trained Teachers Urged," *Herald Tribune*, Oct. 7, 1945.

74. Mr. Shapiro to all English teachers, "Slogans for Columbus Day Parade," Oct. 4, 1945. CC: B 54, F 4.

75. "Columbus Day Tributes Today," *Daily Mirror*, Oct. 12, 1945.

76. "Unity and Pleas for Aid to Italy Mark Columbus Day Fetes Here," *New York Times*, Oct. 13, 1945.

77. "Fifty-three Thousand March in Two Columbus Day Parades," *Herald Tribune*, Oct. 13, 1945.

78. "Mayoral Rivals Join Forty Thousand in Columbus Fete," *Daily Mirror* (Oct. 13, 1945), p. 6. There were no girls in Benjamin Franklin, so the "girl" personifying the Statue of Liberty was either a girlfriend or a sister of one of Franklin's students, or a very pretty boy.

79. "Un' Immensa Fiumana di Popolo Onora Cristoforo Colombo Lungo la 5th Ave.," *Il Progress Italo-Americano*, Oct. 13, 1945, 2. The efficacy of the parade as a device for healing and creating solidarity was tied to the processional mode that is a critical component of southern Italian culture. Joseph Sciorra, interview, Sept. 26, 2002.

80. Gerald Meyer, "Frank Sinatra: The Popular Front and an American Icon," *Science & Society* (Fall 2002): 320–321.

81. "Sinatra to Give Ideas on School Cultural Plan: Singer Says He's Going to 'Lay It on the Line' in Talk at Franklin High," *PM*, Oct. 23, 1945.

82. "Frank Sinatra," program for Oct. 23, 1945, assembly. Oct. 4, 1945. CC: B 54, F 16.

83. "Sinatra Tells Kids of Racism," *PM*, Oct. 24, 1945, 14. The article was accompanied by two photos.

84. "The Voice Talks to the Boys," *Daily News*, Oct. 24, 1945, 4.

85. "'He Speaks Our Language,' Say Boys Who Heard Sinatra Talk on Bias," *Daily Worker*, Oct. 27, 1945, 4. On Sinatra and "The House I Live In," see Meyer, "Frank Sinatra," 318–320.

86. Meyer, *Vito Marcantonio*, 5.

87. Alan Schaffer, *Vito Marcantonio: Radical in Congress* (Syracuse, NY: Syracuse University Press, 1966), 5.

88. Peebles, "Leonard Covello," 295.

89. Peebles, "Leonard Covello," 260–262; "Towards Building a Better Community," *East Harlem News* (March 1941). Issues of the *East Harlem News* in the possession of the author.

90. "Two New High Schools Put into Operation," *New York Times*, Feb. 3, 1942, 17; "Mayor Tells Boys of Facing Two Wars: New School Dedicated," *New York Times*, April 17, 1942, 22. Miriam Sanders played a central role in the East Harlem Council of Social Agencies, which among other things had organized the communitywide campaign to establish Benjamin Franklin in East Harlem.

91. Within the community, the Harlem Legislative Conference—a coalition of more than one hundred political, social, and religious organizations in Italian, Spanish, and Black Harlem—had widely disseminated this point of view. The ALP, which had a large presence in the community, also promulgated this outlook. Community-centered education was, of course, congruent with this outlook. The infusion of the school and the community with activities based on this political perspective created the foundation for the fightback campaign. Covello, *The Heart*, 242.

CHAPTER 11

1. Erin McGauley Hebard, "Irish Americans and Irish Dance," in Philip L. Kilbride, Jane C. Goodale, and Elizabeth R. Ameisen, eds., *Encounters with American Ethnic Cultures* (Tuscaloosa: University of Alabama Press, 1990), 116–132, esp. 128, 130.

2. Harry C. Silcox, *Philadelphia Politics from the Bottom Up: The Life of Irishman William McMullen* (Philadelphia: Balch Institute for Ethnic Studies, 1989), 109; Biagio Castagna, *Bozzetti americani e coloniali* (Salerno: Jovane, 1907), 64; Richard A. Varbero, "Philadelphia's South Italians and the Irish Church: A History of Cultural Conflict," in Silvano M. Tomasi, ed., *The Religious Experience of Italian Americans* (Staten Island, NY: American Italian Historical Association, 1975), 31–52; Gaeton Fonzi, "The Italians Are Coming! The Italians Are Coming!," *Philadelphia Magazine* 62: 12 (Dec. 1971): 98–102, 171–181; Michael Barone and Grant Ujifusa, eds., *The Almanac of American Politics: 1984* (Washington, DC: National Journal, 1983), 1003–1004; Alan Ehrenhalt, eds., *Politics in America: The 100th Congress* (Washington, DC: Congressional Quarterly, 1987), 1281.

3. Ruby Jo Reeves Kennedy, "Single or Triple Melting Pot? Intermarriage in New Haven, 1870–1950," *American Journal of Sociology* 49: 4 (Jan. 1944): 331–339; David A. Hollinger, *Postethnic America: Beyond Multiculturalisn* (New York: Basic Books, 1995), 19–50.

4. Albert James Bergesen, "Neo-Ethnicity as Defensive Political Protest," *American Sociological Review* 42: 5 (Oct. 1977): 823–825; Anna Maria Martellone, "Italo-American Ethnic Identity: A Plea against the Deconstruction of Ethnicity and in Favor of Political History," *Altreitalie* 3: 6 (Nov. 1991): 106–113.

5. Nathan Glazer and Daniel Patrick Moynihan, *Beyond the Melting Pot: The Negroes, Puerto Ricans, Jews, Italians, and Irish of New York City* (1963; Cambridge, MA: MIT Press, 1970), xxvi.

6. George Lipsitz, *The Possessive Investment in Whiteness: How White People Profit from Identity Politics* (Philadelphia: Temple University Press, 1998), esp. 15–18, 95.

7. Stefano Luconi, "The Influence of the Italo–Ethiopian Conflict and the Second World War on Italian-American Voters: The Case of Philadelphia," *Immigrants and Minorities* 16: 3 (Nov. 1997): 3–7.

8. David R. Roediger, *Colored White: Transcending the Racial Past* (Berkeley: University of California Press, 2002), 34–37, 142–144, 163, 167; Robert Orsi, "The Religious Boundaries of an Inbetween People: Street *Feste* and the Problem of the Dark-Skinned Other in Italian Harlem, 1920–1990," *American Quarterly* 44: 3 (Sept. 1992): esp. 321; George Lipsitz, *Rainbow at Midnight: Labor and Culture in the 1940s* (Urbana: University of Illinois Press, 1994), 69–83; Michael Denning, *The Cultural Front: The Laboring of American Culture in the Twentieth Century* (New York: Verso, 1996), 36; Gary Gerstle, *American Crucible: Race and Nation in the Twentieth Century* (Princeton, NJ: Princeton University Press, 2001), 201–237.

9. Richard N. Juliani, *The Social Organization of Immigration: The Italians in Philadelphia* (1971; New York: Arno Press, 1980), 185–187; Stefano Luconi, *Little Italies e New Deal: La coalizione rooseveltiana e il voto italo-americano a Filadelfia e Pittsburgh* (Milan: Angeli, 2002), 152–158; Stefano Luconi, "The Response of Italian Americans to Fascist Antisemitism," *Patterns of Prejudice* 35: 3 (July 2001): 3–23; John F. Bauman, "Public Housing in the Depression: Slum Reform in Philadelphia Neighborhoods in the 1930s," in William W. Cutler III and Howard Gillette, Jr., eds., *The Divided Metropolis: Social and Spatial Dimension of Philadelphia, 1800–1975* (Westport, CT: Greenwood Press, 1980), 241–242; Allan M. Winkler, "The Philadelphia Transit Strike of 1944," *Journal of American History* 59: 1 (June 1972): 73–89; Ronald L. Filippelli, "Philadelphia Transit Strike of

1944," in Ronald L. Filippelli, ed., *Labor Conflict in the United States: An Encyclopedia* (New York: Garland, 1990), 419–421; Allen M. Stearne, "Il contributo degli americani di origine italiana al progresso degli Stati Uniti," *Il Popolo Italiano*, Oct. 11, 1942, 5; "Bond Drive to Mark Columbus Day Here," *Philadelphia Inquirer*, Oct. 12, 1942, 2; "Un italo-americano stato ora decorato," *Il Popolo Italiano*, Oct. 31, 1942, 2.

10. Judith Goode and Jo Anne Schneider, *Reshaping Ethnic and Racial Relations in Philadelphia: Immigrants in a Divided City* (Philadelphia: Temple University Press, 1994), 34; Stephanie G. Wolf, "The Bicentennial City, 1968–1982," in Russell F. Weigley, ed., *Philadelphia: A 300–Year History* (New York: Norton, 1982), 722–723.

11. Fred Hamilton, *Rizzo: From Cop to Mayor of Philadelphia* (New York: Viking, 1973); Joseph R. Daughen and Peter Binzen, *The Cop Who Would Be King: Mayor Frank Rizzo* (Boston: Little, Brown, 1977), 92–123; S. A. Paolantonio, *Frank Rizzo: The Last Big Man in Big City America* (Philadelphia: Camino, 1993), 37–102.

12. Thomas F. Parker, ed., *Violence in the U.S.*, 2 vols. (New York: Facts on File, 1974), vol. 1, 104–111; Joseph S. Clark, Jr., and Dennis J. Clark, "Rally and Relapse, 1946–1968," in Weigley, ed. *Philadelphia*, 676; "Search for an Heir," *Time*, Oct. 27, 1967, 36; *The Bulletin Almanac: 1968* (Philadelphia: Evening Bulletin, 1968), 482; Mike Madden, "Politics in Mantua and Philadelphia Since World War II," *Penn History Review* 6: 1 (Spring 1998): 71–72.

13. Arlen Specter with Charles Robbins, *A Passion for Truth: From Finding JFK's Single Bullet to Questioning Anita Hill to Impeaching Clinton* (New York: William Morrow, 2000), 208, 212; Grace Elizabeth Hale, *Making Whiteness: The Culture of Segregation in the South, 1890–1940* (New York: Pantheon Books, 1998), 199–239; Frank Burnstein, "Letter to the Editor," *Philadelphia Inquirer*, Nov. 27, 1967, 12; "Law and Order," *Sons of Italy Times*, Nov. 27, 1967, 1; Richardson Dilworth Papers, box 48, folder "Hate Letters," Historical Society of Pennsylvania, Philadelphia.

14. William J. McKenna, "The Negro Vote in Philadelphia Elections," *Pennsylvania History* 32: 4 (Oct. 1965): 414; Conrad Weiler, *Philadelphia: Neighborhood, Authority, and the Urban Crisis* (New York: Praeger, 1974), 91–92; John P. Corr, "White Votes Defeated Bond," *Philadelphia Inquirer*, May 22, 1969, 1, 4. Philadelphia's voting statistics include no ethnic breakdown. It has, therefore, been assumed that the election returns from the precincts in which at least 80 percent of registered voters were of Italian descent are representative of the vote of the Italian American community as a whole. The ethnic concentration of the city's precincts has been calculated through a check of the Italian-sounding last names of registered voters as reported in the *Street Lists of Voters* for the years concerned in the Philadelphia City Archives. The votes are from the *Fifty-fourth* and the *Fifty-eighth Annual Report of the Registration Commission for the City of Philadelphia* (Philadelphia: Dunlap Printing Company, 1959, 1963).

15. Ivor Crow, "Prospects for Party Realignment: An Anglo-American Comparison," *Comparative Politics* 12: 4 (July 1980): 396; James H. J. Tate with Joseph McLaughlin, "In Praise of Politicians," *Evening Bulletin*, January 23, 1973, 18.

16. John F. Bauman, "Rizzo, Frank L.," in Melvin G. Holli and Peter d'A. Jones, eds., *Biographical Dictionary of American Mayors, 1820–1980: Big City Mayors*, (Westport, CT: Greenwood Press, 1981), 306; Carolyn Teich Adams, "Philadelphia: The Private City in the Post-Industrial Era," in Richard H. Beznard, ed., *Snowbelt Cities: Metropolitan Politics in the Northeast and Midwest Since World War II* (Bloomington: Indiana University Press, 1990), 215. The votes are from the *Sixty-third* and the *Sixty-sixth Annual Reports of the Registration Commission for the City of Philadelphia* (Philadelphia: Dunlap Printing Company, 1968, 1971). For the criteria adopted to elaborate the sample of the Italian American vote, see note 14.

17. Stefano Luconi, "'Mobsters at the Polls': The Mafia Stereotype of the Media and Italian-American Voters in Philadelphia in the Early 1950s," in Mary Jo Bona and Anthony Julian Tamburri, eds., *Through the Looking Glass: Italian & Italian/American Images in the Media* (Staten Island, NY: American Italian Historical Association, 1996), 38–50; Celeste A. Morello, *Before Bruno: The History of the Philadelphia Mafia*, 2 vols. (Philadelphia: Jeffries & Manz, 1999–2001); Larry Kane, *Larry Kane's Philadelphia* (Philadelphia: Temple University Press, 2000), 131; W. Thacher Longstreth with Dan Rottenberg, *Main Line Wasp: The Education of Thacher Longstreth* (New York: Norton, 1990); Anthony Lombardo, as quoted in A. Harold Datz, "Snatching Defeat from the Jaws of Victory: The 1967 Mayoralty Election in Philadelphia" (A.B. thesis, Temple University, n.d.), xviii.

18. Daughen and Binzen, *The Cop Who Would Be King*, 195–196; Kitsi Burkhart, "Residents Block Truck at Whitman Park Project in S. Phila.," *Evening Bulletin*, Apr. 19, 1971, 18; Raymond C. Brecht, "Can City Revive Whitman Park Homes Plan?," *Evening Bulletin*, May 25, 1971, 3; "Whitman Park Residents Resume Daily Picketing," *Evening Bulletin*, July 7, 1971, 5; "Woman Raps Whitman Plan for Housing," unidentified newspaper clipping, Aug. 13, 1971, "Whitman Park" file, Temple University Urban Archives, Paley Library, Philadelphia; Jim Smith, "Rizzo Tells Why He Curtailed Whitman Housing," *Philadelphia Daily News*, Apr. 22, 1975, 22.

19. Kane, *Larry Kane's Philadelphia*, 131; Joe Davidson, "24-Year Whitman Park Fight Ending?," *Evening Bulletin*, Mar. 16, 1980, 4; Paolantonio, *Frank Rizzo*, 187.

20. Sandra Featherman, "Italian American Voting in Local Elections: The Philadelphia Case," in Richard N. Juliani and Philip V. Cannistraro, eds., *Italian Americans: The Search for a Usable Past* (Staten Island, NY: American Italian Historical Association, 1989), 49–51 (to which the percentages of registration and votes refer); transcript of an interview with Thomas M. Foglietta by Walter M. Phillips, Philadelphia, June 24, 1980, 12, Walter M. Phillips Oral History Project Transcripts, box 3, Temple University Urban Archives.

21. Fred Hamilton, "Whitman Park Project: 20 Years of Controversy," *Philadelphia Daily News*, Nov. 22, 1976, 22; Hizkias Assefa and Paul Wahrhaftig, *The MOVE Crisis in Philadelphia: Extremist Groups and Conflict Resolution* (Pittsburgh: University of Pittsburgh Press, 1990), 3–94; Paolantonio, *Frank Rizzo*, 221–227.

22. Bob Frumps, "Rizzo Warns of Radicals," *Philadelphia Inquirer*, Sept. 22, 1978, 1A, 6A; Jill Porter and Stephan Rosenfeld, "Rizzo Courts Voters in Colorful Speech," *Philadelphia Daily News*, Sept. 22, 1978, 3, 20; Bob Frump, "Rizzo's Message Clear as Black and White," *Philadelphia Inquirer*, Sept. 24, 1978, 1B, 12B; Sandra Featherman, *Philadelphia Elects a Black Mayor: How Jews, Blacks and Ethnics Vote in the 1980s* (Philadelphia: American Jewish Committee, 1984), 9, 13, 21, 40 (to which the percentages in the text refer).

23. Jack Citrin, Donald Philip Green, and David Sears, "White Reactions to Black Candidates: When Does Race Matter?" *Public Opinion Quarterly* 54: 1 (Spring 1990): 94.

24. Tom Infield, "Goode Relentlessly Pursues Critical White Votes," *Philadelphia Inquirer*, Oct. 9, 1987, 1B; S. A. Paolantonio, "The Philadelphia Story," *In These Times*, Oct. 17–23, 1990, 22; Howard Schneider, "The Election in Black and White," *Philadelphia Daily News*, Nov. 20, 1987, 6, 44; Mary Ellen Balchunis, "A Study of the Old and New Campaign Politics Models: A Comparative Analysis of Wilson Goode's 1983 and 1987 Philadelphia Mayoral Campaigns" (Ph.D. diss., Temple University, 1992), 151; John F. Bauman, "W. Wilson Goode: The Black Mayor as Urban Entrepreneur," *Journal of Negro History* 77: 3 (Summer 1992): 150, 153–154. The percentages in the text refer to Sandra Featherman, *Jews, Blacks and Urban Politics in the 1980s: The Case of Philadelphia* (Philadelphia: American Jewish Committee, 1988), 3–6.

25. Sandra Featherman and Allan B. Hill, *Ethnic Voting in the 1991 Philadelphia Mayoral Election* (New York: American Jewish Committee, 1992), 3–4, 8 (to which the percentage in the text also refers); Phyllis C. Kaniss, *The Media and the Mayor's Race: The Failure of Urban Political Reporting* (Bloomington: Indiana University Press, 1995).

26. Paul Kleppner, *Chicago Divided: The Making of a Black Mayor* (DeKalb: Northern Illinois University Press, 1985); Robert Huckfeldt and Carol Weitzel Kohfeld, *Race and the Decline of Class in American Politics* (Urbana: University of Illinois Press, 1989); Carolyn T. Adams, "Race and Class in Philadelphia Mayoral Elections," in George H. Peterson, ed., *Big-City Politics, Governance, and Fiscal Constraints* (Washington, DC: Urban Institute Press, 1994), 13–36; Thomas M. Carsey, "The Contextual Effects of Race on White Voter Behavior: The 1989 New York City Mayoral Election," *Journal of Politics* 57: 1 (Feb. 1995): 221–228.

27. Bill Tonelli, *The Amazing Story of the Tonelli Family in America: 12,000 Miles in a Buick in Search of Identity, Ehnicity, Geography, Kinship, and Home* (Reading, MA: Addison-Wesley, 1994); "Arts Committee for Green," Apr. 19, 1971, press release, Americans for Democratic Action Papers, accession 38, box 14, folder 30, Temple University Urban Archives; Leonora Riccinti, "Letter to the Editor," *Evening Bulletin*, Apr. 25, 1976, 12; "Recall Petitions Ruled Invalid," *Philadelphia Inquirer*, Aug. 25, 1976, 1–2. For the 1971 Democratic primaries, see Richard A. Keiser, "The Rise of a Biracial Coalition in Philadelphia," in Rufus P. Browning, Dale Rogers Marshall, and David H. Tabb, eds., *Racial Politics in American Cities* (New York: Longman, 1990), 54–55.

28. Paul Goldenberg, "Tony Imperiale Stands Vigilant for Law and Order," *New York Times Magazine*, Sept. 29, 1968, 30–31, 117–122, 124, 126; Mark L. Levy and Michael S. Kramer, *The Ethnic Factor: How America's Minorities Decide Elections* (New York: Simon and Schuster, 1972), 174; David K. Shipler, "The White Niggers of Newark," *Harper's Magazine* 245: 1467 (Aug. 1972): 77–83.

29. Fox Butterfield, "Newark's New Minority, the Italians, Demand Equity," *New York Times*, Aug. 28, 1971, 27 (author's emphasis).

30. Michael Novak, *The Rise of Unmeltable Ethnics: Politics and Culture in the Seventies* (New York: Macmillan, 1972).

31. Jody McPhillips, "Paolino Gala Sets Ethnic Limits," *Providence Journal-Bulletin*, Aug. 15, 1996, B1, B4; Elliot Krieger, "Money, Party Backing Not Enough," *Providence Journal-Bulletin*, Sept. 11, 1996, A1, A9; Maureen Moakley and Elmer Cornwell, *Rhode Island Politics and Government* (Lincoln: University of Nebraska Press, 2001), 32–33.

32. Levy and Kramer, *The Ethnic Factor*, 174; Emmett H. Buell, Jr., and Richard A. Brisbin, Jr., *School Desegregation and Defended Neighborhoods: The Boston Controversy* (Lexington, MA: Lexington Books, 1982), 61–66; Connie Maffei and Tracy Amalfitano, as quoted in Jeanne F. Theoharis, "'We Saved the City': Black Struggles for Educational Equality in Boston, 1960–1976," *Radical History Review* no. 81 (Fall 2001): 76–77, 79.

33. Irving Lewis Allen, "Variable White Ethnic Resistance to School Desegregation: Italian-American Parents in Three Connecticut Cities," in William C. McCready, ed., *Culture, Ethnicity, and Identity: Current Issues in Research* (New York: Academic Press, 1983), 1–16; John F. Stack, Jr., "Ethnicity, Racism, and Busing in Boston: The Boston Irish and School Desegregation," *Ethnicity* 6: 1 (Mar. 1979): 21–28; Ronald P. Formisano, *Boston Against Busing: Race, Class, and Ethnicity in the 1960s and 1970s* (Chapel Hill: University of North Carolina Press, 1991); Jonathan Rieder, *Canarsie: The Jews and Italians of Brooklyn Against Liberalism* (Cambridge, MA: Harvard University Press, 1985). For animosities that pitted Italian Americans against Jews and Irish in New York City and Boston in the 1930s, see Ronald H. Bayor, *Neighbors in Conflict: The Irish, Germans, Jews, and Italians of New York City, 1929–1941* (Baltimore: Johns Hopkins University Press, 1978); John F. Stack, Jr.,

International Conflict in an American City: Boston's Irish, Italians, and Jews, 1935–1944 (Westport, CT: Greenwood Press, 1979).

34. Van Gosse and Kavita Philip, "Mumia Abu-Jamal and the Social Wage of Whiteness," *Radical History Review* no. 81 (Fall 2001): 9; Richard N. Juliani, "Community and Identity: Continuity and Change Among Italian Americans in Philadelphia," *Italian American Review* 6: 2 (Autumn–Winter 1997–1998): 46–47.

CHAPTER 12

Acknowledgments
I am grateful to Gil Fagiani, Zulma Ortiz-Fuentes, Stephanie Romeo, and Francisca Viera for their critical comments on an earlier draft of this essay. I am eternally indebted to this volume's editors, Jennifer Guglielmo and Salvatore Salerno, for their generous invitation, patience, and insightful editorial comments.

1. Micaela di Leonardo, *The Varieties of Ethnic Experience: Kinship, Class, and Gender Among California Italian-Americans* (Ithaca, NY: Cornell University Press, 1984), 194–205.

2. See David R. Roediger, *The Wages of Whiteness: Race and the Making of the American Working Class* (New York: Verso, 1993), for a cogent analysis of race and labor in this country.

3. Johnathan Rieder, *Canarsie: The Jews and Italians of Brooklyn Against Liberalism* (Cambridge, MA: Harvard University Press, 1985).

4. For additional information on PRRWO, see Basilio Serrano, "'¡Rifle, Cañón, y Escopeta!': A Chronicle of the Puerto Rican Student Union," and Iris Morales, "¡PALANTE, SIEMPRE PALANTE!: The Young Lords," in Andrés Torres and José E. Velázquez, eds., *The Puerto Rican Movement: Voices from the Diaspora* (Philadelphia: Temple University Press, 1998), 141 and 221.

5. For more information on Bologna at this time, see Luciano "Bifo" Capelli and Ermanno "Gomma" Guarneri, *Alice è il diavolo: Storia di una radio sovversiva* (Milan: ShaKe Edizioni Underground, 2002).

6. John Kifner, "Slain Man's Neighbors Rebuff Appeal by Police," *New York Times*, Oct. 26, 1977, n. p.

7. Kathy Dobie, "The Boys of Bensonhurst," *Village Voice*, Sept. 5, 1989, 34–36, 38.

8. Reports of racial tension in Bensonhurst before 1989 are found in Barbara Grizzuti Harrison, "Going Home: Brooklyn Revisited (November 1974)," in *Off Center* (New York: Playboy Paperbacks, 1981), 13–30; and Jeff Coplan, "Life and Death on the Color Line: Racial Crisis in Bensonhurst," *Village Voice,* May 24, 1983, 11–18, 42.

9. The media attempted to provide sociological glosses to the murder: John Kifner, "Bensonhurst: A Tough Code in Defense of a Closed World," *New York Times*, Sept. 3, 1989, sec. A, 1, sec. B, 4; Howard W. French, "Hatred and Social Isolation May Spur Acts of Racial Violence, Experts Say," *New York Times*, Sept. 4, 1989, sec. L, 31; and Nelson George compared Italian American and African American youth, pointing out the former's diminishing economic and cultural influence in the city and their resulting sentiment, "pessimism about their future is justified, and that pessimism breeds hate," "Brooklyn Bound," *Village Voice*, May 29, 1990, 27–28. For a more in-depth analysis of the conditions that were the social foundation for racist violence in Bensonhurst, see Judith N. DeSena, "Defending One's Neighborhood at Any Cost?: The Case of Bensonhurst," in Harral E. Landry, ed., *To See the Past More Clearly: The Enrichment of the Italian Heritage, 1890–1990,* (Austin, TX: Nortex Press, 1994), 177–190.

10. William K. Stevens, "White Philadelphian, 13, Is a Model to Those Combating Racist Incidents," *New York Times*, Nov. 24, 1986, sec. B, 14.

11. Don Terry, "6 White Men Attack Black Man with Bats and Sticks on S.I. Street," *New York Times,* June 23, 1988, sec. B, 1, 2.

12. Spike Lee's fifth film, *Jungle Fever,* was dedicated to Yusuf and, coincidentally, featured my sister Annabella as the Italian American secretary who has an affair with her African American boss.

13. For an account of the killing, the street demonstrations, and legal trials, see John DeSantis, *For the Color of his Skin: The Murder of Yusuf Hawkins and the Trial of Bensonhurst* (New York: Pharos Books, 1991), and the 1990 video documentary *Seven Days in Bensonhurst,* produced by Thomas Lennon.

14. At the time of this writing, a convicted serial rapist came forward claiming to be the sole perpetrator of the crime. On December 20, 2002, a New York State Supreme Court judge annuled all verdicts against the five convicted men.

15. For critiques of the media's portrayal of Bensonhurst, see Jerome Krase, "Bensonhurst, Brooklyn Italian American Victims and Victimizers," in Frank M. Sorrentino and Jerome Krase, eds., *The Review of Italian American Studies* (New York: Lexington Books, 2000), 233–244; and Donald Tricarico, "Read All About It!: Representations of Italian Americans in the Print Media in Response to the Bensonhurst Racial Killing," in Adalberto Aguirre, Jr. and David V. Baker, eds. *Sources: Notable Selections in Race and Ethnicity*, (Guilford, CT: McGraw-Hill/Dushkin, 2001), 291–319. Progressive political representatives of Bensonhurst wrote op eds months later: Frank J. Barbaro, "About Politics: The Mosaic's Missing Tiles," *New York Newsday*, Jan. 16, 1990, 52, 54; and Sal F. Albanese, "About Press: They Still Don't Speak for Us," *New York Newsday,* Apr. 18, 1990, 52, 54.

16. Michael Powell, "At Church, It's Quiet, but Scary," *New York Newsday*, May 21, 1990, 3.

17. Bob Dury, "Black Teen Shot Dead in B'klyn Race Attack," *New York Newsday*, Aug. 25, 1989, 5, 25. Others would note the good deeds of Italian American women in the aftermath of the killing: Daniela Gioseffi, "Breaking the Silence for Italian-American Women," *VIA: Voices in Italian Americana* 4:1 (1993), 1–14; and Maria Laurino, "Italian, with a Difference," *New York Newsday*, Sept. 5, 1991, 54, 108. Italian American women writers also were compelled to write memoirs in response to the killing: Barbara Grizzuti Harrison, "Women and Blacks and Bensonhurst," *Harper's Magazine*, Mar. 1990, 69–79, 82; Marianna De Marco Torgovnick, "On Being White, Female, and Born in Bensonhurst," in *Crossing Ocean Parkway* (Chicago: University of Chicago Press, 1994), 3–18; and Maria Laurino, "Bensonhurst," in *Were You Always an Italian?: Ancestors and Other Icons of Italian America* (New York: W. W. Norton, 2000), 121–155. Novelist Nicholas Montemarano has written a fictionalized account of the crime in *A Fine Place: A Novel* (New York: Context Books, 2002). See also Montemarano's description of writing the novel, "Truth in Fiction," *Doubletake* (Fall 2000): 107–113.

18. Stephanie Romeo, "Women of Substance," in "Letters," *New York Newsday*, Sept. 11, 1991, 87. See also "'Anger Is an Energy': From Bensonhurst to Transcendence" (unpublished paper, delivered at the conference of the American Italian Historical Association, Washington, DC, 1992).

19. Susan Brenna, "Raising Their Literary Voices," *New York Newsday*, Apr. 3, 1995, sec. B, 4–5. See also Robert Viscusi, "Breaking the Silence: Strategic Imperatives for Italian

American Culture," *VIA: Voices in Italian Americana* 1:1 (Spring 1990): 1–13, and "iawa Faces the Community" (unpublished paper delivered at the symposium "Italian American Studies Programs and Organizations: Interface with the Community," Center for Italian Studies, State University of New York at Stony Brook, Oct. 29, 1994).

20. For more on the Madonna Nera, see Lucia Chiavola Birbaum, *Black Madonnas: Feminism, Religion, and Politics in Italy* (Boston: Northeastern University Press, 1993); Salvatore Salerno, "The Black Madonna and Italian American Identity" (unpublished paper delivered for the Bush Faculty Development grant, Metro State University, Jan. 26, 1995); and the traveling exhibition "'Evviva La Madonna Nera!': Italian American Devotion to the Black Madonna," curated by Joseph Sciorra and designed by B. Amore for the John D. Calandra Italian American Institute, Queens College.

21. For more information on *rap italiano*, see my personal website, www.italianrap.com, and my article "'Hip Hop from Italy and the Diaspora: A Report from the 41st Parallel," *Altreitalie* 24 (Jan.–June 2002): 86–104, also available at http://www.fondazione-agnelli.it/altreitalie/aita24/saggio4.htm.

22. Gerald Meyer, *Vito Marcantonio: Radical Politician, 1902–1954* (Albany: State University of New York Press, 1989); Paul S. D'Ambrosio, *Ralph Fasanella's America* (Cooperstown, NY: Fenimore Art Museum, 2001); Dorothy Gallagher, *All the Right Enemies: The Life and Murder of Carlo Tresca* (New Brunswick, NJ: Rutgers University Press, 1988); Nunzio Pernicone, "Carlo Tresca's *Il Martello*," *The Italian American Review* 8:1 (Spring/Summer 2001): 7–55; Jennifer Guglielmo, "Italian American Women's Political Activism in New York City, 1890s-1940s," in Philip V. Cannistraro, ed., *The Italians of New York: Five Centuries of Struggle and Achievement* (New York: New-York Historical Society and John D. Calandra Italian American Institute, 1999), 103–113, and "Donne Sovversive: The History of Italian American Women's Radicalism," *Italian America* (Sept. 1997): 8–11; William Mello, "The Legacy of Pete Panto and the Brooklyn Rank-and-File" (unpublished paper delivered at the symposium "Italians on the New York Waterfront: A Tribute to Peter Panto" of the John D. Calandra Italian American Institute, Queens College, Oct. 13, 2001); Margaret Hooks, *Tina Modotti: Radical Photographer* (San Francisco: Pandora, 1993); Mildred Constantine, *Tina Modotti: A Fragile Life* (San Francisco: Chronicle Books, 1993).

23. Tom Collins, "'We Love the Man,'" *New York Newsday*, Apr. 3, 1992, n. p. In New York neighborhoods like Bensonhurst, the mafia holds a special attraction as a source of employment and prestige. In 1992, Federal Judge Jack Weinstein imposed severe sentences on members of the Colombo crime family, stating that "Young, impressionable males in the Italian-American community are lured into the destructive life of these mobs. . . ." Pete Bowles, "Crime Pays," *New York Newsday*, May 25, 1993, n. p.

24. George De Stefano, "Ungood Fellas," *The Nation*, Feb. 7, 2000, 31–33; Maria Laurino, "From the Fonz to 'The Sopranos,' Not Much Evolution," *The New York Times*, Dec. 24, 2000, "Arts and Leisure," 31, 40. For a different approach to Italian American hip-hop, see Manifest's essay "The Front Lines: Hip-Hop, Life, and the Death of Racism," in this volume.

25. Juliet Ucelli and Gil Fagiani, "Italian Americans and the Columbus Hype," *School Voices* (Mar. 1992): 10–11; George De Stefano, "About Columbus: We Don't Need a Macho Hero," *New York Newsday*, Oct. 9, 1992, 56, 58.

26. Stuart Hall, "New Ethnicities," in Kobena Mercer, ed., *Black Film, British Cinema*, ICA Document 7, (London: Institute of Contemporary Arts, 1988), 27–31.

CHAPTER 13

Acknowledgments
Sangu du sango meu means "blood of my blood" in Calabrian dialect. I would like to thank Jennifer Guglielmo for urging me to write this piece, for showing me that I was ready to tell my story, and for creating, through this book, a place of community in which to tell it. Thanks also to Joe Sciorra for his encouragement and honest criticism. His essay was an inspiration, and in many ways, mine is a response to his. Thank you to Katya Romeo for her help with the Calabrian dialect.

CHAPTER 14

A different version of "Figuring Race" first appeared under the title "Figuring Race: Kym Ragusa's *fuori*" in *Shades of Black and White: Conflict and Collaboration Between Two Communities*, edited by Dan Ashyk, Fred Gardaphe, and Anthony J. Tamburri (New York: American Italian Historical Association, 1999).

1. Kym Ragusa's videos include *Demarcations* (1991), *Blood of my Blood* (1995), *Passing* (1996), and *fuori/outside* (1997).

2. See Edvige Giunta, "Dialects, Accents, and Other Aberrations," *New Jersey Mosaic* (Spring 1997): 4, 7.

3. *Pane e cioccolata*, an Italian film directed in 1973 by Franco Brusati, depicts the vicissitudes of Italian workers abroad through the story of Giovanni Garofalo, a southern Italian immigrant in Switzerland. Not only does the film expose the prejudice of the Swiss against southern Italians, but it shows, through the juxtaposition of the protagonist to a northern Italian *industriale,* how southern Italians are victims of multiple forms of prejudice and economic exploitation. See Peter Bondanella, *Italian Cinema: From Neorealism to the Present* (New York: Continuum, 1991), 329–332.

4. Literally the phrase translates "in the face of the *terrone*," which means "in spite of being *terrone*," though the Italian expression has a certain untranslatable poignancy.

5. Antonio Gramsci has eloquently described the historical conditions of the oppressions of the Italian South in *The Southern Question*, trans. and intro. by Pasquale Verdicchio (West Lafayette, IN: Bordighera, 1995).

6. In 1997, the chosen topic for the American Italian Historical Association Conference was relations between Italian Americans and African Americans. Selected essays appear in Dan Ashyk, Fred L. Gardaphe, and Anthony Julian Tamburri, eds., *Shades of Black and White: Conflict and Collaboration Between Two Communities. Proceedings of the 30th Annual Conference of the American Italian Historical Association* (Staten Island, NY: American Italian Historical Association, 1999).

7. Louise DeSalvo, *Breathless: An Asthma Journal* (Boston: Beacon, 1997), 150. As a memoir, *fuori/outside* is part of a rich tradition created by Italian American and African American women writers that includes works such as Maya Angelou's *I Know Why the Caged Bird Sings* (New York: Bantam, 1971); Mary Cappello's *Night Bloom* (Boston: Beacon, 1998); Louise DeSalvo, *Vertigo* (New York: Dutton, 1996); Sandra M. Gilbert, *Wrongful Death* (New York: Norton, 1995); Audre Lorde, *The Cancer Journals* (San Francisco: Aunt Lute, 1980); and Audre Lorde, *Zami: A New Spelling of My Name* (Freedom, CA: The Crossing Press, 1994). Many of the strategies of the memoir are used by Italian American and African American women in works of poetry and fiction. See for example, Maria Mazziotti Gillan, *Where I Come From: New and Selected Poems* (Toronto: Guernica, 1995); Tina De Rosa, *Paper Fish* (New York: The Feminist Press, 1996); Jamaica

Kincaid, *The Autobiography of My Mother* (New York: Penguin, 1997); and Sapphire, *Push* (New York: Vintage, 1997). On an African American female tradition of autobiography, see Joanne Braxton, *Black Women Writing Autobiography: A Tradition Within a Tradition* (Philadelphia: Temple University Press, 1989). On Italian American women's memoirs, see Caterina Romeo, "Esplorare il passato, riscrivere il presente: Tradizione e innovazione nel memoir delle scrittrici italo americane" (Ph.D. diss., University of Rome, la Sapienza, 1999–2000); and "Forging Public Voices: Memory, Writing, Power," in Edvige Giunta, *Writing with an Accent: Contemporary Italian American Women Authors* (New York: Palgrave, 2002), 117–137. For a comparative analysis of African American and Italian American women writers, see Mary Jo Bona, "'Circles and Circles of Sorrow': Remembering Community in Selected Works of African American and Italian American Women," in *Shades of Black and White*, 303–315.

8. *Blood of my Blood*, produced before *fuori/outside*, represents a preliminary exploration of the themes of the later videos. However, this video is not available to the public. The other videos are distributed by Third World Newsreel in New York.

9. "If the legal and social history of Jim Crow often turned on the question 'Who Was Black?,'" writes David Roediger, "the legal and social history of immigration often turned on the question 'Who Was White?'" A complicated social process that equated whiteness and access to citizenship would make it possible for so-called white ethnics, such as the Italians, the Jews, or the Irish, to become "white." See Roediger, *Towards the Abolition of Whiteness: Essays on Race, Politics, and Working Class History* (London: Verso, 1994), 182.

CHAPTER 15

This essay was originally published in *Common Quest* 4:2 (Winter 2000): 8–17.

AFTERWORD

1. Jane Addams, *Twenty Years at Hull House* (New York: Macmillan, 1909), 183.

2. See Valerie Babb, *Whiteness Visible: The Meaning of Whiteness in American Literature and Culture* (New York and London: New York University Press, 1998), 138–149; and Elizabeth Lasch-Quinn, *Black Neighbors: Race and the Limits of Reform in the American Settlement House Movement* (Chapel Hill: University of North Carolina Press, 1993), esp. 22 and 14–30 passim.

3. As quoted in Matthew Pratt Guterl, *The Color of Race in America, 1900–1940* (Cambridge, MA and London: Harvard University Press, 2001), 68.

4. In addition to Thomas A. Guglielmo's essay in this volume, see his *White on Arrival* (New York and Oxford: Oxford University Press, 2003; for Wilson, see Gwendolyn Mink, *Old Labor and New Immigrants in American Political Development: Union, Party and State, 1875–1920* (Ithaca, NY: Cornell University Press, 1986), 223 and 226. See also Liette Gidlow, "Delegitimating Democracy: 'Civic Slackers,' the Cultural Turn, and the Possibilities of Politics," *Journal of American History* 89 (Dec. 2002): 939.

5. On naturalization, race, and whiteness, see Ian Haney-López, *White by Law: The Legal Construction of Race* (New York and London: New York University Press, 1996), 37–110; on the "dark white" racial category, see especially *In re Najour*, C.C.N.D.; Ga., 174 Fed. 735 (1909).

6. W.E.B. Du Bois, in Julius Lester, ed., *The Seventh Son: The Thought and Writings of W.E.B. Du Bois*, 2 vols. (New York: Vintage, 1971), vol. 2, 4.

7. W.E.B. Du Bois, *The Autobiography of W.E.B. Du Bois* (New York: International, 1975 [1968]), 122; Du Bois, *Darkwater: Voices from Within the Veil* (New York: Harcourt, Brace and Howe, 1920), 51; Du Bois, in Daniel Walden, ed., *W.E.B. Du Bois: The Crisis Writings* (Greenwich, CT: Fawcett Publications, 1972), 123–124; Claude McKay, *A Long Way from Home: An Autobiography* (San Diego: Harcourt Brace Jovanovich, 1970 [1937]), 274–275.

8. Nadia Venturini, "'Over the Years People Don't Know': Italian Americans and African Americans in Harlem in the 1930s," translated by Michael Roede, in Donna R. Gabaccia and Fraser Ottanelli, eds., *Italian Workers of the World: Labor Migration and the Formation of Multiethnic States* (Urbana and Chicago: University of Illinois Press, 2001), 209, quoting Du Bois.

9. Du Bois, as quoted in Jacalyn Harden, "Double-Crossing the Color Line: Japanese Americans in Black and White Chicago, 1945–1996" (Ph.D. diss., Northwestern University, 1999), 287.

10. Thomas Holt, "The Political Uses of Alienation: W.E.B. Du Bois on Politics, Race and Culture," *American Quarterly* 42 (June 1990): 313.

11. Robert F. Foerster, *The Italian Emigration of Our Times* (Cambridge, MA: Harvard University Press, 1919), 408, 356–400 passim; Cheryl Harris, "Whiteness as Property," *Harvard Law Review* 106 (June 1993): 1709–1791.

12. W.E.B. Du Bois, as quoted in Herbert Aptheker's fine introduction to the reprint edition of Du Bois's *The Gift of Black Folk* (Millwood, NY: Kraus, Thomson Editions, 1975 [1924]), 5.

13. Ibid, 1–29.

14. W.E.B. Du Bois, *An ABC of Color* (New York: International, 1969), 139. See also Lester, ed., *Seventh Son*, vol. 2, 82; and Nancy J. Weiss, "Long-Distance Runners of the Civil Rights Movement: The Contribution of Jews to the NAACP and the National Urban League in the Early Twentieth Century," in Jack Salzman and Cornel West, eds., *Struggles in the Promised Land: Towards a History of Black-Jewish Relations in the United States* (New York and Oxford: Oxford University Press, 1997), 143–144.

15. Patricia J. Williams, "*Metro Broadcasting, Inc.* v. *FCC*," *Harvard Law Review* 104 (1990): 525.

16. W.E.B. Du Bois, "The Negro Mind Reaches Out," in Alain Locke, ed., *The New Negro: An Interpretation* (New York: Albert and Charles Boni, 1925), 412.

17. Rudolph Vecoli, "Are Italian Americans Just White Folks?," *Italian Americana* (Summer 1995): 156 and passim.

18. I take "disillusioned" from Franklin Rosemont's "Notes on Surrealism as a Revolution Against Whiteness," *Race Traitor* 9 (Summer 1998): 29.

Contributors

Rosette Capotorto is the author of a chapbook of poetry titled *Bronx Italian.* A two-time recipient of the Edward F. Albee Writing Fellowship, she is completing a novel *Pop Beads*, based on her Bronx childhood, and is a mother, educator, and sometime community organizer. She is, and always will be, a native New Yorker.

Louise DeSalvo is the Jenny Hunter Professor of Literature and Creative Writing at Hunter College. She is the author of *Vertigo* (winner of the Gay Talese Prize for Literature, recently reissued) and of the memoirs *Breathless* and *Adultery.* Most recently, she has co-edited, with Edvige Giunta, *The Milk of Almonds: Italian American Women Writers on Food and Culture*, and published a new edition of *Melymbrosia: A Novel by Virginia Woolf.* She has just completed a memoir, *Crazy in the Kitchen*, about the cultural conflicts in her multigenerational Italian American family.

Donna R. Gabaccia is Mellon Professor of History at the University of Pittsburgh. Her books on Italian international migration include *Women, Gender and Transnational Lives* (edited with Franca Iacovetta), *Italian Workers of the World* (edited with Fraser Ottanelli), *Italy's Many Diasporas*, and *Militants and Migrants: Rural Sicilians Become American Workers.*

John Gennari is Assistant Professor of English and ALANA U.S. Ethnic Studies at the University of Vermont. His book *Canonizing Jazz: An American Art and Its Critics* is forthcoming.

Edvige Giunta is Associate Professor of English at New Jersey City University. She is the author of *Writing with an Accent: Contemporary Italian American Women Authors* (2002) and *Dire l'indicibile: Memoir di autrici italo americane* (2002). With Louise DeSalvo she co-edited the anthology *The Milk of Almonds: Italian American Women Writers on Food and Culture* (2002), and with Maria Mazziotti Gillan and Jennifer Gillan she coedited *Italian American Writers on New Jersey* (2003).

Jennifer Guglielmo is Assistant Professor of History at Smith College. She is currently completing a book on Italian women's political and cultural activism in New York City (1880–1945), and beginning another book on grassroots coalitions among working-class women in Harlem during the 1930s and 1940s.

Thomas A. Guglielmo is Assistant Professor of American Studies at the University of Notre Dame and author of *White on Arrival: Italians, Race, Color, and Power in Chicago, 1890–1945* (2003). He is presently at work on a history of the U.S. racial order during World War II.

Stefano Luconi teaches the history of North America at the University of Florence and specializes in Italian immigration to the United States. His most recent book is *Little Italies e New Deal: La coalizione rooseveltiana e il voto italo-americano a Filadelfia e Pittsburgh* (2002).

Manifest is a New York-born and bred hip-hop producer. His credits include Eminem, Mystic, Wu-Tang Clan, Jurassic 5, Dilated Peoples, and The Anonymous. A former rapper, he has been active in hip-hop culture since the late 1980s, performing alongside KRS-One, Rock Steady Crew, Biz Markie, Cutty Ranks, Black Eyed Peas, Medusa, and Faith Evans.

Caroline Waldron Merithew is Assistant Professor of History at the University of Dayton. She is currently writing a book on the hybrid culture of immigrant miners and their families, and developing a new project on immigrant widows in the United States.

Gerald Meyer is Professor of History at Hostos Community College (CUNY), and a Visiting Professor at the John D. Calandra Italian American Institute/Queens College. He is the editor, with Philip Cannistraro, of *The Lost World of Italian American Radicalism* (forthcoming).

Ronnie Mae Painter is a native New Yorker, born and raised in Astoria, Queens. She is a musician, photographer, and metal sculptor. Her photographs have been shown at Lincoln Center, and her sculpture exhibited at the MoCada Museum in Brooklyn, and most recently at Gallery One Twenty Eight in Manhattan. She is currently at work on a series of wood and metal crosses inspired by her Black/Italian/Catholic roots.

Kym Ragusa is a writer and filmmaker. Her films, including the documentaries *Passing* and *fuori/outside*, draw upon her African American and Italian American family histories to explore the politics of race and community. She is currently working on a memoir to be published by W. W. Norton & Co. in 2005.

David R. Roediger is Babcock Professor of History at the University of Illinois, Urbana–Champaign. He is author of *Colored White: Transcending the Racial Past* (2002), *Towards the Abolition of Whiteness: Essays on Race, Politics, and Working Class History* (1994), *The Wages of Whiteness: Race and the Making of the American Working Class* (1991), and *Our Own Time: A History of American Labor and the Working Day* (1989), and editor of *Black on White: Black Writers on What It Means to Be White* (1998).

Franklin Rosemont is the editor of the University of Texas Press Surrealist Revolution series, and in 1998 guest-edited a special issue of the journal *Race Traitor*, "Surrealism: Revolution Against Whiteness." His most recent collection of poetry is titled *Penelope: A Poem*.

Salvatore Salerno is the author of *Direct Action and Sabotage: Three Classic I.W.W. Pamphlets* and *Red November, Black November: Culture and Community in the Industrial Workers of the World*. He is currently writing a book on industrial unionism and transnational radicalism in an early twentieth-century Italian anarchist community in Paterson, New Jersey.

Vincenza Scarpaci holds a courtesy faculty appointment at the University of Oregon. She is the author of *A Portrait of Italians in America* (1982), among other publications. Currently she is researching the Italian agriculturalists in Walla Walla, Washington.

Joseph Sciorra is the Assistant Director of Academic and Cultural Programs at Queens College's John D. Calandra Italian American Institute. He is co-editor of a bilingual edition of verse by Sicilian American poet Vincenzo Ancona, *Malidittu la lingua/Damned Language*, and the author of *R.I.P.: Memorial Wall Art*, a collection of photographs by Martha Cooper documenting memorial graffiti. Sciorra also maintains a personal website about Italian hip-hop at www.italianrap.com.

Michael Miller Topp is Associate Professor of History at the University of Texas, El Paso. He is the author of *Those Without a Country: The Political Culture of Italian American Syndicalists* (2001) and *"That Agony Is Our Triumph": A Documentary History of the Sacco-Vanzetti Trial* (forthcoming).

Index